Allegorical Quests
from Deguileville to Spenser

# Allegorical Quests
# from Deguileville to Spenser

Marco Nievergelt

D. S. BREWER

First published 2012
D. S. Brewer, Cambridge


ISBN 978-1-84384-328-3


D. S. Brewer is an imprint of Boydell & Brewer Ltd
PO Box 9, Woodbridge, Suffolk IP12 3DF, UK
and of Boydell & Brewer Inc.
668 Mount Hope Ave, Rochester, NY 14620-2731, USA
website: www.boydellandbrewer.com


A CIP catalogue record for this book is available
from the British Library


The publisher has no responsibility for the continued existence or accuracy of URLs for external or
third-party internet websites referred to in this book, and does not guarantee that any content on
such websites is, or will remain, accurate or appropriate


Papers used by Boydell & Brewer Ltd are natural, recyclable products
made from wood grown in sustainable forests

Printed and bound in Great Britain by
CPI Group (UK) Ltd, Croydon CR0 4YY

I wish to dedicate this book to the memory of
John Julius, Marquis de Amodio (1909–2003),
without whose support the project
could not have seen the light of day.

# Table of Contents

# Acknowledgements

Medieval didactic poetry traditionally features a rather helpless male protagonist, whose aimless meanderings can only be transformed into a proper quest thanks to the providential intervention of one or often several female guides. It is largely thanks to three such guides that the ideas contained in the present book have developed a sense of purpose and direction. I first wish to thank Helen Cooper for getting me started on my own quest, giving me an initial glimpse of its ultimate destination and providing me with the necessary equipment to undertake the journey. I owe the greatest gratitude to Helen Moore for keeping an errant pilgrim on course, and for accompanying me through the successive stages of the quest itself. I have benefited enormously not only from her knowledge of the subject and the period, but have been inspired and encouraged by her rigour, generosity and unwavering interest in my work. Finally, I also wish to thank Sally Mapstone, who has repeatedly helped me to redefine the trajectory of my quest at crucial moments, preventing me from engaging battle with invincible or inexistent dragons. I would also like to express my gratitude to John Julius, Marquis de Amodio (1909–2003), for endowing the Berrow Foundation and supporting me for three years during which I was able to conduct most of my initial research at Lincoln College, Oxford.

I have benefited from the support, advice and expertise of many other colleagues and friends over the years, both in Switzerland and in Britain. I wish to thank in particular Eric G. Stanley, for his generosity, inspiration and support, and for looking after an often hungry and thirsty pilgrim. For helpful comments on various parts of the book at various stages, I would like to thank Antoinina Bevan-Zlatar, Graham Caie, Lukas Erne, Thomas Herron, Claire Jowitt, Denis Renevey, Richard Rowley, Kirsten Stirling and Juliette Vuille. I am also grateful to a number of people who have generously shared their own, often as yet unpublished or ongoing, research with me; first among those must be mentioned the 'Deguilevillians': Frédéric Duval, Josephine Houghton, Philippe Maupeu, Fabienne Pomel and Graham Robert Edwards, and all the participants of the Deguileville congress in Cerisy, 4–8 October 2006, and of course Stephanie Kamath for sharing so much material and for the effort in co-organising a further congress on the reception of Deguileville in Lausanne on 21–23 July 2011, along with all of the participants of the congress. I also wish to thank Alexandra Gajda, D. Mark Smith, Robert Fajen, Roweena Archer and Mishtooni Bose for having granted me access to otherwise as yet inaccessible or unpublished research or for having otherwise supplied me with valuable information. A number of further colleagues provided stimulating discussions over the years, along with encouragement and interest: Tamara Atkin, Sarah Baccianti, Roberto Biolzi, Kenneth Clarke, Rory Critten, Tony Edwards, Darragh Greene, Andrew Hadfield, Katherine McClune, Jean-Claude Mühlethaler, Alessandra Petrina, Eva Pibiri, Helen Swift, Christiania Whitehead, Edward Wilson and the participants of the Tudor Reading Group in Oxford. Finally, I was also fortunate enough to benefit from the comments of an impressively perceptive anonymous press reader, who also kindly agreed to disclose his identity to me after the completion of the process: Alex Davis. His comments were truly eye-opening, and helped me clarify the overall argument of the book, and I would like to express my gratitude for his important contribution. Further, Camille Marshall here in Lausanne provided vital help at the stage of proofing and formatting, and saved me from insanity. At every stage of production Caroline Palmer and Rohais Haughton have been invariably patient and helpful, and I would like to thank them both very specially. Only the book's faults and shortcomings I can finally claim as being truly my own.

I would also like to thank Barbara I. Gusick and Matthew Z. Heintzelman, editors of *Fifteenth-Century Studies*, and Andrew Hadfield and Jennifer Richards, editors of *Renaissance Studies*, for their kind permission to rework previously published materials in the book, together with the publishers represented by Caroline Palmer for Boydell and Brewer and Matt Jenkins for Wiley. An earlier version of Chapter 6 appeared in *Renaissance Studies* 24:4 (2010), while some ideas from Chapter 5 were more fully developed in an article for *Renaissance Studies* 23:1 (2009), and portions of Chapter 2 were elaborated in a piece in *Fifteenth-Century Studies* 36 (2011). Finally I am grateful to the *Société Académique Vaudoise* for their financial contribution to publication costs.

Closer to home, my parents have patiently encouraged me over the years, and will be pleased to see that what may have appeared at times like a foolish quest has eventually borne fruit. But above all else Eléonore, *squaio philosophicus*, deserves a monument for supporting me throughout with her curiosity, encouragement, charm and good humour, and for putting up with me as a person in all kinds of states over the last six years.

Paris
Valentine's Day 2012

# Abbreviations

## Primary works
(For details of editions used please refer to bibliography)

| | |
|---|---|
| *Am* | Edmund Spenser, *Amoretti* |
| *Âme* | Guillaume de Deguileville, *Le Pèlerinage de l'âme* |
| *CCH* | Edmund Spenser, *Colin Clouts Come Home Againe* |
| *CD* | Olivier de la Marche, *Le Chevalier délibéré* |
| *CG* | Stephen Bateman, *A Christall Glasse of Christian Reformation* |
| *Chemin* | Jean de Courcy, *Le Chemin de vaillance* |
| *Chevalier* | Thomas III de Saluces, *Le Livre du chevalier errant* |
| *CL* | Stephen Hawes, *The Conforte of Lovers* |
| *Ep* | Edmund Spenser, *Epithalamion* |
| *EV* | Stephen Hawes, *The Example of Vertu* |
| *FQ* | Edmund Spenser, *The Faerie Queene* |
| *HB* | Edmund Spenser, *An Hymne in Honovr of Beavtie* |
| *HHB* | Edmund Spenser, *An Hymne in Honovr of Heavenly Beavtie* |
| *HL* | Edmund Spenser, *An Hymne in Honovr of Love* |
| *Jhesucrist* | Guillaume de Deguileville, *Le Pèlerinage Jhesucrist* |
| *Livre* | René d'Anjou, *Livre du cuer d'amours espris* |
| *LR* | Edmund Spenser, *A Letter to Raleigh* |
| *Manhode* | *The Pilgrimage of the Lyfe of the Manhode* |
| *PP* | Stephen Hawes, *The Pastime of Pleasure* |
| *Vie* | Guillaume de Deguileville, *Pèlerinage de vie humaine* (generic) |
| *Vie¹* | Guillaume de Deguileville, *Pèlerinage de vie humaine* (1st version, 1331) |
| *Vie²* | Guillaume de Deguileville, *Pèlerinage de vie humaine* (2nd version, 1355) |
| *Voyage* | Jean de Cartheny, *Le Voyage du Chevalier Errant* |
| *WK* | William Goodyear, *The Wandering Knight* |

## Journals, series and monograph titles

| | |
|---|---|
| EETS | Early English Text Society |
| *ELH* | *English Literary History* |
| ERL | John King, *English Reformation Literature: The Tudor Origins of the Protestant Tradition* (Princeton, NJ: Princeton University Press, 1982) |
| OS | Original Series |
| *PMLA* | *Journal of the Modern Language Association of America* |
| *PL* | *Patrologia Latina*, ed. Jacques-Paul Migne |
| *SpS* | *Spenser Studies* |

## Others

| | |
|---|---|
| BNF | Bibliothèque Nationale Française |
| BL | British Library |
| *DNB* | *Oxford Dictionary of National Biography* |
| *OED* | *Oxford English Dictionary* |

# Introduction

Albrecht Dürer's famous engraving, *The Knight, Death and the Devil* (1513), shows the picture of a mounted soldier, sternly looking ahead and seemingly unaware of the threat posed by the two monstrous creatures approaching his horse. In the background, outside of the knight's field of vision and towering high above the group, is a city built on a distant and inaccessible rock. The two planes of the picture are suspended in a state of tension: its foreground with the suggestion of struggle, combat, movement and its static background hinting at repose, safety and deliverance. The tension results from an implied narrative that reverberates with traditional, near archetypal meanings: the figure of the *miles christianus* engaged in a struggle against the Devil and the Seven Deadly Sins, the tortuous path of the Christian pilgrim, and the promise of the heavenly kingdom as the ultimate goal of the spiritual quest.

Something about Dürer's engraving, though, betrays a more urgently topical, precise meaning, derived from its relevance within its specific historical context. The knight, conspicuously solitary on his quest, has been interpreted as the representative of a new quintessentially lay spirituality and theology. As a figure of the active life, the knight symbolises a newly emancipated Christian layman, confidently advancing on his own, individual and lonely spiritual quest. His posture makes him the embodiment of a 'virile' lay spirituality, and his imperturbable gaze expresses something like an Erasmian self-mastery.[1] The Rider's gaze points outside of the frame of the engraving, beyond the limits of the wasteland depicted towards an eschatological resolution, dimly shadowed in the city on the rock. Such Erasmian associations are often invoked with reference to Dürer's supposed source, Erasmus's *Enchiridion Militis Christiani*, a didactic treatise built around the central metaphor of the Christian warfare.[2]

Alternatively, the engraving may also be telling an altogether more sombre story, that of a knight, representative of an entire social group in crisis that has lost its way, its values and its reason of being within the ever more complex socio-political reality of the early sixteenth century. From this perspective the knight is not an

---

[1]  See Erwin Panofsky, *The Life and Art of Albrecht Dürer*, 4th edn (Princeton, NJ: Princeton University Press, 1955), pp. 151–4.

[2]  In his own diary entry from 1519 Dürer also exhorts Erasmus to take over from Luther as 'Ritter Christi' and lead the incipient Reformation. See also Andreas Wang, *Der 'Miles Christianus' im 16. und 17. Jahrhundert und seine Mittelalterliche Tradition: ein Beitrag zum Verhältnis von sprachlicher und graphischer Bildlichkeit* (Bern: Peter Lang, 1975), pp. 158–63.

exemplary figure to be emulated, but rather a distracted, foolish sinner in desperate need of a sermon. His gaze is no longer confident but blank and oblivious. He simply does not see the New Jerusalem hidden behind the infernal rocks in the foreground and is heading straight for the jaws of hell. The stylistic features of the engraving further suggest that Dürer is not merely depicting a sinful, wandering Everyman, but a 'crusty old warrior' in the attempt to stage a subtle, understated parody of the fashionable contemporary equestrian portrait. Deconstructing conventional canons of representation, Dürer questions the legitimacy of knightly self-glorification in the wake of recent abuses and denunciations, and calls for a redefinition of chivalric valour, virtue and honour.[3]

Whilst this book focuses on a single tradition, like Dürer's engraving it tells two stories: that of the quest as a metaphor for the Christian life, and that of the quest as a metonymy for the transformations undergone by the knight, also a figure of the layman, in the context of late medieval and early modern society. All of the motifs, themes and problems briefly evoked in connection with Dürer's engraving resurface in one form or another in the literary tradition of the allegorical knightly quest. All works discussed in what follows draw from the same storehouse of motifs and metaphors, and the several questing knights that we encounter in these works all embody some form of a struggle towards self-understanding and self-definition. The motif of the questing knight of course visualises a universal, seemingly trans-historical conception of the Christian life as journey and struggle, but the works studied in this book constantly tweak such traditional forms to express new meanings, shaped by specific contexts and the wider shift in sensibilities associated with the transition between what we commonly define as the 'Middle Ages' and the 'early modern' period. The continuity displayed by the literary tradition of the quest-allegory across this historical divide is striking, and raises interesting questions about the usefulness of the current practice of periodisation.

The tradition of the allegorical quest-narrative lends itself particularly well to such a reconsideration of a process of historical transformation, since quest-narratives are themselves concerned with notions of 'becoming', unpacked in the form of a journey that leads its protagonist through foreign, uncharted territory on a quest for an identity of some sort:[4] 'le chevalier à la recherche de lui-même'.[5] This exploratory nature, inherent as it were in the very structure of quest narratives,

---

[3]   E. H. Gombrich, 'The Evidence of Images', in Charles S. Singleton, ed., *Interpretation: Theory and Practice* (Baltimore, MD: Johns Hopkins University Press, 1969), pp. 98–102; Patricia Emison, 'Dürer's Rider', *Renaissance Studies* 19:4 (2005), 511–22.

[4]   Helen Cooper, 'Quest and Pilgrimage: "The adventure that God shall send me"', in her *The English Romance in Time: Transforming Motifs from Geoffrey of Monmouth to the Death of Shakespeare* (Oxford: Oxford University Press, 2004), pp. 45–105, here pp. 49–57 in particular. See also the essays in Phillipa Hardman, ed., *The Matter of Identity in Medieval Romance* (Cambridge: D. S. Brewer, 2002).

[5]   Reto Bezzola, *Le sens de l'aventure et de l'amour* (Paris: La Jeune Parque, 1947), quoted in Cooper, *The English Romance in Time*, p. 49.

makes them a wonderful vehicle for the exploration of new, tentative and often problematic identities; it is therefore perfectly fitting and revealing that Spenser, the
latest author discussed in what follows, should adopt this very tradition of allegorical
quest narratives as a vehicle to 'fashion a gentleman or noble person in vertuous and
gentle discipline' (LR 8).[6] Accordingly, the study that follows is based on the fundamental assumption that allegorical quest narratives do not constitute, as is often
assumed in more cursory treatments of this material, a static or conventional literary
genre that may be largely dismissed as an inert continuation of 'medieval' literary
models and their supposedly anachronistic ideologies:[7] I argue instead that quest
narratives function as vehicles for a variety of often daring, complex and largely
experimental reflections on the shifting sense of identity, self-understanding and
self-representation in the period 1350–1600.

Charges of anachronism concerning chivalric literature and imagination in the
early modern period are largely based on the assumption that knighthood and
chivalry possess any single and stable significance, or that they represent a clearly
defined and circumscribed set of material, social and cultural practices associated
with a particular period. Defining chivalric practice as decadent, anachronistic or
simply typical is therefore largely dependent on what one assumes chivalry to be in
the first place, and the charge of 'decadence' tells us little about the function of a
particular set of practices, imaginative patterns and motifs in a given context and
period.[8] This fallacy, frequently pointed out in revisionist studies of early modern
chivalry and knighthood, is ultimately again the product of a problem of excessively
rigid periodisation.[9] Following the lead of such recent work, the present study
considers the practices and concepts associated with chivalry and knighthood not
so much as having a stable significance or 'content', but rather as vehicles, 'forms'

[6]  Spenser's 'Letter to Raleigh', in Edmund Spenser, The Faerie Queene, ed. A. C. Hamilton
(Harlow: Pearson, 2001), pp. 714–18.
[7]  Even recent, sympathetic reassessments are often condescending about allegorical quest
narratives, which are often dismissed as such, and made to merely 'demonstrate the revolutionary
genius of Spenser's poetic intervention', Kenneth Borris, 'Allegory, Emblem and Symbol', in
Richard McCabe, ed., The Oxford Handbook of Edmund Spenser (Oxford: Oxford University
Press, 2010), pp. 437–61, here 453.
[8]  The notion of the 'decadence' of chivalric practices goes back to Johan Huizinga's seminal but
often misunderstood Waning of the Middle Ages, trans F. Hopman (London: Penguin, 1955).
Subsequent works have elaborated this idea, e.g. Raymond Lincoln Kilgour, The Decline of
Chivalry as Shown in the French Literature of the Late Middle Ages (Cambridge, MA: Harvard
University Press, 1937), which has remained influential until very recently, for instance in the
work of Arthur B. Ferguson, The Indian Summer of English Chivalry: Studies in the Decline and
Transformation of Chivalric Idealism (Durham, NC: Duke University Press, 1960), and The
Chivalric Tradition in Renaissance England (Washington, DC: Folger Shakespeare Library, 1986).
For a corrective see Maurice Keen, 'Huizinga, Kilgour and the Decline of Chivalry', Medievalia
et Humanistica 8 (1977), 1–20. For a similar argument, see also my article on 'The Chivalric
Imagination in Elizabethan England', Literature Compass 8:5 (2011), 266–79.
[9]  Jennifer R. Goodman, Chivalry and Exploration, 1298–1630 (Woodbridge: Boydell, 1998),
p. 6.

making up a highly adaptable language that can articulate widely different 'contents', meanings and discourses.[10] Accordingly, I argue that the figure of the questing knight is not so much a stable, strictly or even quintessentially medieval incarnation as is commonly assumed,[11] but rather a *Grenzgänger*, a 'crosser of borders'. The knight negotiates constant transitions between the different 'worlds' of romance, between multiple roles, sets of values and expectations, and knightly identity is therefore defined in terms of movement rather than stasis, as a manifestation of constant process of 'becoming' rather than an expression of already achieved 'being'. If there is something like a knightly identity, it is precisely postulated in terms of the uncertainty inherent in the pattern of the knightly quest and adventure. This instability does not merely apply to 'post-medieval' manifestations of chivalry, but has deeper historical roots: as originally suggested by Georges Duby, the very appearance of the figure of the knight in the twelfth-century consciousness, as exemplified for instance in the romances of Chrétien de Troyes, was itself the symptom of an earlier crisis of identity that affected an entire social group, that of the *juvenes* and *bachelers*, who already saw in the adventures of errant knights the refractions of their own struggles for social recognition, self-definition and self-understanding.[12]

On the back of these metaphorical, historical and social implications of knightly adventure, the tradition of the allegorical knightly quest in the sixteenth century need not necessarily be concerned with the physical practice of knighthood at all, and becomes a vehicle for a wide range of ideas and ideologies.[13] The emphasis is rather on the symbolic potential of knight-errantry, its capacity for becoming the vehicle for different discourses that are rooted in an imaginative amplification of the conceptions of the quest and psychomachia.[14] The 'knight' functions essentially as a representative

---

[10]  For recent reconsiderations of chivalry in the early modern period, see for instance Alex Davis, *Chivalry and Romance in the English Renaissance* (Cambridge: D. S. Brewer, 2003); Sydney Anglo, ed., *Chivalry in the Renaissance* (Woodbridge: Boydell, 1990); Richard C. McCoy, *The Rites of Knighthood: The Literature and Politics of Elizabethan Chivalry* (Berkeley: University of California Press, 1989); Alan Young, *Tudor and Jacobean Tournaments* (London: George Philip, 1987).

[11]  This misconception abounds in 'popular' treatments of the subject, a symptomatic example being Norman F. Cantor's book on John of Gaunt, which is also a dangerously sweeping and simplistic narrative of the advent of 'modernity', as its title implies: *The Last Knight: The Twilight of the Middle Ages and the Birth of the Modern Era* (New York: Free Press, 2004).

[12]  See especially Georges Duby, 'Dans la France du Nord-Ouest au XIIᵉ siècle: les "jeunes" dans la société aristocratique', *Annales. Économies, Sociétés, Civilisations* 19 (1964), 835–46. For a further elaboration of the idea, see notably Duby, *La société chevaleresque. Hommes et structures du Moyen Age 1* (Paris: Flammarion, 1988), and Jean Flori, *L'essor de la chevalerie, XIᵉ–XIIᵉ siècles* (Genève: Droz, 1986). For a concise and useful overview, see Tony Hunt, 'The Emergence of the Knight in France and England 1000–1200', *Forum for Modern Language Studies* 17:2 (1981), 93–114.

[13]  Unless otherwise qualified I use the word 'ideology' in the broadest sense to designate a 'systematic scheme of ideas'; *OED*, 'ideology', (4).

[14]  For calls to re-evaluate the importance of the chivalric imagination in shaping the course of history, with special reference to discovery and exploration, see Goodman, *Chivalry and Exploration*, pp. 1–24, and Joan Pong Linton, *The Romance of the New World: Gender and the Literary Formations of English Colonialism* (Cambridge: Cambridge University Press, 1998).

of the *vita activa* more generally and therefore easily becomes the perfect figure of the layman's entanglement with worldly contingency. Among the self-appointed legatees of such knightly identity, literal or metaphorical, we find courtiers, counsellors, governors or even the aristocracy and gentry more generally – but the group also includes figures as diverse and sometimes improbable as those of the merchant, the man of letters, the adventurer, the poet, the humanist, the protestant apocalyptic moralist or a combination of all these. In the efforts to define the emergent or shifting identities of social groups as well as more strictly individual selves, the imaginative capital of chivalry was appropriated and used as raw material to forge a new secular ethos that could nevertheless boast of its links with the most prestigious of the secular ideologies of the recent past. The knightly quest here becomes largely an allegory of self-definition, a journey towards establishing a corporate or individual identity for which the conceptual terminology is as yet non-existent.[15]

Within the large and unwieldy category of quest narratives in the period I have identified a more restricted group of works that share a number of formal features, a group that because of the numerous and complex intertextual relations between its individual texts may be said to constitute an actual literary tradition. All texts discussed here present themselves as explicitly allegorical knightly quest-narratives resonating with religious meanings, and thus combine formal features of knightly romance and spiritual allegory. The coexistence of these rather different features and associated modes can be explained with reference to the history and evolution of the tradition, which points back to its roots in Guillaume de Deguileville's *Pèlerinage de vie humaine*, a seminal late medieval allegory that has been attracting an increasing amount of attention in recent criticism, discussed here in Chapter 1. Further intertextual relations between the texts, discussed in detail in the following chapters and supported by references to the circulation and availability of specific texts at a given time and place, confirm that what we are looking at is in fact a tightly connected 'family' of texts. From this point of view, then, the present book may simply be thought of as providing a discussion of the transformations of a specific branch of the 'Deguilevillian' tradition with particular reference to the circulation, reception and influence of the texts in that family. Yet from another, enlarged perspective, the arguments presented in the following chapters also participate in a number of much wider and more fundamental debates about the emergence of early modern identities and subjectivities, the supposedly novel drive towards 'self-fash-ioning' in the sixteenth century and its problematic relationship with older, medieval and often more markedly religious or transcendentalising discourses employed to understand, conceptualise and construct the self. Before providing a detailed outline of the specific arguments of each chapter, I will therefore briefly discuss what I see as the present study's overall contribution to such debates.

---

[15]  See for instance, Michael Stroud, 'Chivalric Terminology in Late Medieval Literature', *Journal of the History of Ideas* 37:2 (1976), 323–34; Laura Caroline Stevenson, *Praise and Paradox: Merchants and Craftsmen in Elizabethan Popular Literature* (Cambridge: Cambridge University Press, 1984), pp. 1–8 and 107–30.

\*    \*    \*

Jacob Burckhardt famously observed in 1860 that in the Middle Ages 'man was conscious of himself only as member of a race, people, party, family or corporation – only through some general category', before going on to relate the birth of the modern self around 1400 to the advent of the Renaissance in Italy.[16] Although this statement has obviously been qualified or contradicted in a number of ways over the last century and a half by hosts of medievalists, early modernists and other scholars and thinkers, the notion has stuck, shaping the assumptions of entire generations of historians, literary scholars or historians of *mentalités*. Indeed, in 2011, Stephen Greenblatt still characterises the medieval world in much the same manner in the ambitiously titled *The Swerve: How the World Became Modern*:

> The household, the kinship network, the guild, the corporation – these were the building blocks of personhood. Independence and self-reliance had no cultural purchase; indeed, they could scarcely be conceived, let alone prized. Identity came with a precise, well-understood place in a chain of command and obedience.[17]

David Aers, among others, provides an important account of the process by which, almost subliminally and unnoticed, this assumption has infiltrated and profoundly shaped the thinking of even the most 'radical' critics produced by the recent dominant trend of Renaissance scholarship, the New Historicism or Cultural Materialism.[18] Much of early modern scholarship is thus shown to be affected, consciously or not, by what Aers identifies as an essentialist, simplistic and monolithic view of the Middle Ages: 'It is in relation to the medieval monolith that the allegedly new subjectivity of "Renaissance self-fashioning" is to be defined.'[19] This essentialist view goes back to the puzzlingly named 'Historical Scholarship' associated especially with the work of D. W. Robertson, which is to a large extent responsible for the still influential view of the Middle Ages as a quiet, static and monolithic historical period – a view that is, paradoxically, postulated on an implicit acceptance of Burckhardt's argument concerning the emergence of a sense of conflicted modern selfhood in direct connection with the Italian Renaissance. Although Aers's 'Whisper in the Ear of Early Modernists' dates from 1992, it seems that the whisper may not have received quite the attention it deserves, and it will

---

[16] Jacob Burckhardt, *The Civilization of the Renaissance in Italy*, trans. S. G. C. Middlemore (London: Phaidon Books, 1965), p. 81, and chapter 2 more generally.
[17] Stephen Greenblatt, *The Swerve: How the World Became Modern* (New York and London: W. W. Norton, 2011), p. 16.
[18] David Aers, 'A Whisper in the Ear of Early Modernists; or, Reflections on Literary Critics Writing the "History of the Subject"', in David Aers, ed., *Culture and History, 1350–1600: Essays on English Communities, Identities and Writing* (Hemel Hempstead: Harvester Wheatsheaf, 1992), pp. 177–202; and Lee Patterson, 'On the Margin: Postmodernism, Ironic History, and Medieval Studies', *Speculum* 65:1 (1990), 87–108.
[19] Aers, 'A Whisper', p. 191.

be useful to reiterate it here. Medievalists over the past thirty years have of course been very diligent in their attempts to provide more nuanced and often challenging studies of the conflicted and complex forms of plural 'medieval selves';[20] early modernists however have for a long time been rather reluctant to respond to Aers's challenge to provide a more balanced, nuanced and properly diachronic history of the evolution of the subject in the period 1300–1600, and have only recently begun to work in this direction.

Let me stick with Aers's useful reflections for a little longer. Aers identifies three possible reasons that may help us to explain the tenacious survival of such a simplistic, idealist understanding of the medieval period by some early modern scholars, despite their claims to be writing a 'radical' history of English culture and mentalities. First, he mentions the distorting effects of our disproportionate attachment to what have become canonical texts and figures, and points out the 'readiness to construct large-scale cultural generalisations on the basis of a few prescriptive texts',[21] texts whose canonical status is often left strangely unexamined precisely by those critics who claim to be writing a 'new' history. The second reason concerns the laboriousness associated with the production of a genuinely diachronic history, and the comparative ease afforded by the writing of an 'anecdotal history' and the adoption of inherited assumptions and master-narratives. An example of how such anecdotal history helps to perpetuate the myth of the 'Renaissance', where supposedly 'something surged up against the constraints that centuries had constructed around curiosity, desire, individuality, sustained attention to the material world, the claims of the body', can again be found in Greenblatt's recent *The Swerve*. There a Promethean Poggio Bracciolini, who 'did not like monks', re-discovers Lucretius's *De Rerum Natura*, a book that is presented as providing nothing less than 'the basis for the contemporary rational understanding of the entire world' rescuing from behind the 'high walls that hedged about the mental life of the monks', its precious 'words that were in the best possible case uncontaminated by the mental universe

---

[20] The amount of secondary literature on the subject is overwhelming, and I list here only a selection of the most influential general studies, with useful bibliographies and overviews of the debate: Alan Macfarlane, *The Origins of English Individualism : The Family, Property and Social Transition* (New York: Cambridge University Press, 1978); Caroline Walker Bynum, 'Did the Twelfth Century Discover the Individual?', *Journal of Ecclesiastical History* 31 (1980), 1–17; Michel Zink, *La subjectivité littéraire: autour du siècle de Saint Louis* (Paris: Presses Universitaires de France, 1985); Aaron Gurevich, *The Origins of European Individualism*, trans. Katharine Judelson (Oxford: Blackwell, 1995); Jean-Claude Schmitt, 'La découverte de l'individu: une fiction historiographique?', in *Le corps, les rites, les rêves, le temps: essais d'anthropologie médiévale* (Paris: Gallimard, 2001), pp. 241–62; Peter Haidu, *The Subject Medieval/Modern: Text and Governance in the Middle Ages* (Stanford, CA: Stanford University Press, 2004); Brigitte Miriam Bedos-Rezak and Dominique Iogna-Prat, eds, *L'individu au Moyen Age: individuation et individualisation avant la modernité* (Paris: Flammarion, 2005). The most useful and stimulating recent overview I find to be Barbara H. Rosenwein, 'Y avait-il un "moi" au haut Moyen Age?', *Revue historique* 633 (2005), 31–52.

[21] Aers, 'A Whisper', p. 195.

of the lowly scribe who copied them'. Alongside this unsympathetic sketch of medieval culture, *The Swerve* performs a by now customary acknowledgment that this 'cultural shift is notoriously difficult to define', but its narrative in essence remains that of the heroic Renaissance humanist who 'without realising it, became a midwife to modernity', and who – one suspects, like the humanistic Greenblatt himself – 'despised that time and regarded it as a sink of superstition and ignorance'.[22]

The third, and I believe most important, reason evoked by Aers is to do with the reluctance of many radical critics to engage with the complexities of the Christian tradition that stretches across the historical divide of the Middle Ages and the Renaissance. Indeed, some of the more extreme forms of New Historicist criticism, and this until very recently, have tended to almost systematically reduce all forms of religious discourse in early modern literature to mere politics or power struggles in disguise, going as far as arguing that in the Renaissance we witness 'a displacement of the metaphysical (divine/natural law) by the social. The contradictions of history flood the space vacated by metaphysics. Correspondingly, the metaphysically constituted subject *suddenly* becomes a decentred, contradictory subjectivity' [my italics].[23] Although I began the work for this book with no very clear expectation about what my texts were going to tell me, it is fair to say that at some level I expected this rather simple story of the disappearance of a 'metaphysically constituted subject' – very vaguely defined – to be confirmed. The result is, however, rather different, and rather more interesting.

While writing the following chapters, I have tried to heed Aers's whisper, and this study as a whole may best be seen as a contribution to the kind of slow, collaborative, incremental and laborious history of the subject that Aers exhorts us to write. The reasons for the selection of the texts have little to do with their presence or absence from the literary canon; in this sense Edmund Spenser can tell us no more or no less than Stephen Bateman for the kind of history I am trying to write. The criteria for exclusion or inclusion were strictly formal, and texts were selected because they constitute a tradition, a naturally interconnected family of texts that demands to be rehabilitated, not least because of its popularity in the fifteenth and sixteenth centuries, in contrast with its nearly total neglect by modern critics. I have tried to avoid any simplistic historical teleology, striving to let the texts speak with their own voices, and I hope that my conclusions have crystallised with something like a naturalness, an inevitability that is not, however, definitive or absolute in any way. Aware of the risk of generalisation in writing this kind of history, I provide no exhaustive statement or definitive conclusion about the emergence of the modern subject, or about Spenser's supposedly superior 'literary' achievements; the

---

[22] Greenblatt, *The Swerve*, quotations respectively from pp. 9–10, 36, 8, 28, 18, 10, 13, 18. For a critical review of Greenblatt's work, see also Colin Burrow, '*The Swerve* by Stephen Greenblatt – A Review', *The Guardian*, Review Section, 24 December 2011, p. 9.

[23] Jonathan Dollimore, *Radical Tragedy: Religion, Ideology, and Power in the Drama of Shakespeare and his Contemporaries*, 2nd edn (Hemel Hempstead: Harvester Wheatsheaf, 1989), p. xxxi.

conclusions that do emerge are tentative, but are moving in the same direction as recent work exploring the interpenetration of sacred and secular culture in the period on the one hand, or criticism that has made a deliberate effort to produce a truly diachronic history on the other.[24] Despite their formal similarities, the texts are very diverse, and the story they tell is of course multiple, contradictory, plural and tentative – certainly not univocal, linear or teleological in any way;[25] but the conclusion that emerges from a cumulative assessment of the tradition has something to do with the tenacious and paradoxical persistence of a 'metaphysical' self-understanding for the fashioning of early modern *secular* identities. Although this was by no means a foregone conclusion when I began work on these texts, in the light of the analyses presented in the following chapters, it appears that a claim like Dollimore's regarding the sudden displacement of a supposedly 'metaphysically constituted subject' by a 'decentred, contradictory subjectivity' is untenable.

My objection to Dollimore's statement, and its silent and often unconscious adoption by many later critics, is twofold. On the one hand, as Aers, Patterson and many others have repeatedly and insistently pointed out, the construction of medieval selves and identities is simply much more complex than is generally assumed, and there are very strong arguments for situating the first signs of the emergence of something like a 'shadowy private self' at the very latest at the end of the fourteenth century, possibly as early as the thirteenth and twelfth, or arguably even in the early Middle Ages.[26] On the other hand, the issue goes deeper than a

---

[24] Two symptomatic examples would be the following collections of essays: Lawrence Besserman, ed., *Sacred and Secular in Medieval and Early Modern Cultures; New Essays* (Basingstoke: Palgrave, 2006), pp. 1–15; Gordon McMullan and David Matthews, eds, *Reading the Medieval in Early Modern England* (Cambridge: Cambridge University Press, 2007), especially the essay by James Simpson, 'Diachronic History and the Shortcomings of Medieval Studies', pp. 17–30. For the increasing interest in religion *qua* religion in early modern studies, see also Ken Jackson and Arthur F. Marotti, 'The Turn to Religion in Early Modern Studies', *Criticism* 46 (2004), 167–90; and Brian Cummings, *The Literary Culture of the Reformation: Grammar and Grace* (Oxford: Oxford University Press, 2002), p. 12.

[25] Philippe Maupeu, in his study of the impact and reception of Deguileville on 'autobiographical' allegorical narratives in France until ca. 1500, similarly stresses the diversity of the material, warning about the risk of imposing simplistic literary-historical teleologies for the mere sake of univocal linearity, and accordingly presents his analysis as a sequence of interconnected but clearly separate studies of texts as I do in what follows. See Philippe Maupeu, *Pèlerins de vie humaine: autobiographie et allégorie narrative, de Guillaume de Deguileville à Octovien de Saint-Gelais* (Paris: Champion, 2009), pp. 37–41. The book's methodology, the criteria for determining the corpus, and the implicit and explicit assumptions about the importance and influence of Deguileville are largely analogous to my own, and it was extremely encouraging to find out about Maupeu's research as I was completing my own. His study provides as it were the perfect historical and methodological foundation for my own discussion of a still later 'layer' of Deguilevillian tradition in sixteenth-century England.

[26] David Aers, 'A Whisper'; and ibid., 'The Self Mourning: Reflections on *Pearl*', *Speculum* 68:1 (1993), 54–73; ibid., '"In Arthurus Day": Community, Virtue, and Individual Identity in *Sir Gawain and the Green Knight*', in his *Community, Gender and Individual Identity: English Writing*

mere backdating of the point of origin of this 'modern self', and the opposite but complementary point needs to be made more insistently: in a way, it appears not only that the Middle Ages were much more 'modern' than is generally assumed, but it conversely appears that the Renaissance was much more 'medieval' than many of the radical critics would allow for.[27] The logical absurdity of this statement suggests to me that the very terms 'medieval' and 'modern' may themselves be useless, since they reify precisely the kind of rigid historical dichotomy that impedes our understanding of a complex and non-linear cultural dynamic. What I mean by the statement is that thinking in terms of binary opposites may not be very helpful, and in fact logically untenable, since there is no such thing as a *pure* 'metaphysically constituted subject' or a *pure* 'decentred, contradictory subjectivity' – just as no cultural phenomenon is either purely 'medieval' or 'modern'. Thus it emerges that the binary opposition of the secular and the sacred on the one hand, and the medieval and the modern on the other, are in reality two different aspects of a larger, central problem due to our understanding of history and culture in terms of stable, discrete and mutually exclusive conceptualisations. In reality however such terms are by definition interdependent, being postulated against their polar opposite and therefore by necessity acknowledging the existence of that opposite, actively implicating that 'other' in the constitution of 'the self'. So, for all their diversity, the modern selves produced by the quest-allegories I discuss in the following chapters all suggest that the 'metaphysically constituted subject' that Dollimore associates with the 'Middle Ages' is, in fact, importantly, inextricably and constructively implicated in the construction of the very 'modernity' that sets itself up in antithesis to its predecessor and unacknowledged ancestor. The point has been made before, which helps to validate my own conclusions and suggest that further work is needed in this sense: as Hans Blumenberg observes concerning the vexed issue of the 'secularisation' associated with modernity:

> The worldly power that is pictured as operative in the process of secularisation is for its part, and as such, just as much a product of the original inadmissible persistence in existence of the world, which could not remain what it had been before, as was its self-described 'unworldly' counterpart. This fact removes the

---

*1360–1430* (London: Routledge, 1988), pp. 153–78, from which I borrow the expression of a 'shadowy private self', p. 177; Lee Patterson, 'On the Margin'; ibid., '"What is Me?": Hoccleve and the Trials of the Urban Self', in his *Acts of Recognition: Essays on Medieval Culture* (Notre Dame, IN: University of Notre Dame Press, 2010), pp. 84–109. For a discussion of the shifts in the ways of understanding the self in the twelfth and thirteenth centuries, see e.g. A. C. Spearing, *Readings in Medieval Poetry* (Cambridge: Cambridge University Press, 1987), p. 12 and *passim*; Caroline Walker Bynum, *Metamorphosis and Identity* (New York: Zone Books, 2001); Zink, *La subjectivité littéraire*. For an important redefinition of terms, and a study of the early articulations of a 'self' in the early Middle Ages, see Rosenwein, 'Y avait-il un "moi" au haut Moyen Age?'.

[27] A similar point is made by Haidu, *The Subject Medieval/Modern*, p. 1.

suggestion of an almost Gnostic dualism from the rivalry of powers that is presupposed in the concept of secularisation.[28]

In a recent volume discussing early modern autobiography – itself a problematic concept, intricately tied up with our notions of the self and identity – the authors observe that, '[t]he instinct to read the transient moment against a motionless backdrop of eternity seems endemic in early modern sensibilities.'[29] Elsewhere – and this complicates our very usage of the supposedly transparent term of the 'self' – it is argued that early modern diaries record 'the expression of an "I" as bequeathed by God, and thus experienced, as it were, in the third person. The commitment of "self" to the pages of a journal is always and everywhere a conversation with God, so that one speaks of "oneself" in the passive voice.'[30] Whereas the comments apply to strictly autobiographical texts unlike the ones discussed here, they identify a key problem that needs to be addressed by all studies of the self, identity or their representations in the period 1300–1600: as all early modern selves knew and remembered, the human self is never single, but at least double, since, as the medieval dictum goes, *in homine duo sunt*,[31] or as Calvinist preacher William Perkins has it, 'Every Person is a double person and under two regiments. ... In the first regiment I am a person of mine own self, under Christ ... In the temporal regiment, thou art a person in respect of another.'[32] To be more precise, the self is not so much double in the sense of an 'either-or' dichotomy, but is rather produced by a constant dialectic negotiation along a spectrum that connects its two extremes – the 'metaphysical', integrated self at one end, and the 'decentred' individual one at the other.[33]

---

[28] Hans Blumenberg, *The Legitimacy of the Modern Age*, trans. Robert M. Wallace (Cambridge, MA: MIT Press, 1983), p. 48, see also pp. 77–9. I find the original German more lucid and powerful: 'Die weltliche Instanz, die im Vorgang der Säkularisierung als handelnd vorgestellt wird, ist ihrerseits und als solche ebenso wie die sich als "unweltlich" ausgebende Gegenspielerin ein Produkt des ursprünglich unzulässigen Fortbestandes der Welt, die nicht bleiben konnte, was sie vorher gewesen war. Dadurch verliert die Rivalität der Instanzen, die in dem Begriff der Säkularisierung vorausgesetzt ist, den Zug eines fast gnostischen Dualismus', Hans Blumenberg, *Die Legitimität der Neuzeit* (Frankfurt am Main: Suhrkamp, 1966; repr. 1988), p. 59. A very similar idea is also developed by Simpson, 'Diachronic History and the Shortcomings of Medieval Studies'.

[29] Ronald Bedford, Lloyd Davis and Philippa Kelly, *Early Modern English Lives: Autobiography and Self-Representation, 1500–1660* (Aldershot: Ashgate, 2007), p. 44.

[30] Bedford, Davis and Kelly, *Early Modern English Lives*, p. 3.

[31] Saint Thomas Aquinas, *Summa Theologica* (Roma: Typographiae Forzani, 1894), II.2, q.26, art.4.

[32] William Perkins, 'A Dialogue of the State of a Christian Man', in *A Treatise Tending vnto a Declaration whether a Man Be in the Estate of Damnation or in the Estate of Grace* (London, 1590 – STC 19752), pp. 121ff, quoted and discussed in Bedford *et al.*, *Early Modern English Lives*, p. 39.

[33] In his study of the late medieval tradition of autobiographical allegory derived from Deguileville, Philippe Maupeu proposes a very similar spectrum for the conceptualisation of the self in the period 1330–1500, *Pèlerins de vie humaine*, p. 36.

This reminds us that if selves were increasingly 'fashioned' in early modern England, they were fashioned not only out of or against *social* pressures, as Greenblatt rightly insists in his *Renaissance Self-Fashioning*,[34] but that such selves were equally fashioned against or in dialogue with *metaphysical* pressures, those of that tenacious 'metaphysically constituted subject' with its 'medieval' roots, as critics, even New Historicists, have begun to realise in recent years.[35]

Our problems to do with this double nature of the self ultimately go back at least as far as Augustine, often invoked as the supposed founding father of Western interiority – an interiority quite different however from that of Dollimore's 'decentred, contradictory subjectivity'. As Charles Taylor explains in his monumental study of the evolution of the self in western culture, 'Augustine makes the step to inwardness . . . because it is a step towards God', and the inward movement towards the self is really a movement upwards, as individual identity is effaced, reabsorbed into the recollection of God's image out of which the human self is made: 'When we get to God, the image of place becomes multiple and many-sided. In an important sense the truth is *not* in me. I see the truth "in" God. Where the meeting takes place, there is a reversal.'[36] We can even say with Weintraub that:

> at the heart of Augustine's experience lay the insight that the self was not sufficient unto itself . . . A stronger power than he pulled him beyond himself, instilling a transcendent longing he could not satisfy on his own . . . In that conception the self desiring to be its true self is a being living in and out of another being (*ein Auf-Gott-Bezogensein*), and becoming a full self is a growing surrender of the self to God.[37]

Here we have, indeed, the metaphysical self that Dollimore invokes, but this metaphysical self, like its polar opposite, can never be pure or absolute or simply 'given', in the Middle Ages or any other historical period. Even to Augustine this higher self is rather a vanishing point, and the *Confessions* ultimately are the account of his own efforts to become and attain that supreme self – a self we can never quite *be* but can only approach asymptotically, until the eschatological reunion with the divine is finally effected in the City of God towards which we all travel. And for Augustine the essential figure of the human effort to attain this interior, divine self, is the figure of the pilgrimage. This concept, as I will discuss in Chapter 1, lies at the heart of Deguileville's *Pèlerinage de vie humaine*, which tells the story of the

[34] Stephen Greenblatt, *Renaissance Self-Fashioning: From More to Shakespeare* (Chicago, IL: University of Chicago Press, 1980).

[35] On the question of whether, and in what sense, Greenblatt's more recent *Hamlet in Purgatory* (Princeton, NJ: Princeton University Press, 2001) turns to religion and takes religion seriously, see the useful article by Jackson and Marotti, 'The Turn to Religion in Early Modern Studies'.

[36] Charles Taylor, *Sources of the Self: The Making of Modern Identity* (Cambridge: Cambridge University Press, 1989), pp. 132 and 135.

[37] Karl Joachim Weintraub, *The Value of the Individual: Self and Circumstance in Autobiography* (Chicago, IL: University of Chicago Press, 1978), p. 46.

formation of such a resolutely 'Augustinan self' through the account of a moral and epistemological pilgrimage. This higher self is simultaneously attained and exploded in the New Jerusalem, City of God, which is both the final vanishing point of man's pilgrimage and the ultimate signifier of man's process of allegorical discernment on the way to finding 'itself' – or God.

The drama of human existence is therefore played out somewhere in the battle-ground between the extremes of this Augustinian self and a more 'decentred' self – and the latter, according to the hugely influential Augustinian model, is largely reducible to that which *prevents* man from attaining his true, interior and divine self. Deguileville, the Cistercian monk, conceptualises the self in just such a way: 'the soul must divest itself of that false self, of that illusory personality of the egotistical will that has been bred by the fall', as Etienne Gilson observes concerning the Cistercian spirit.[38] Accordingly this Augustinian conceptualisation of the self is ingrained in the very structure of the allegorical quest tradition sparked by Deguileville, and all the later, derivative texts in the tradition inherit this conceptu-alisation, even if they often attempt – and nearly invariably fail – to adjust it to new ideological and historical environments. Within an Augustinian worldview, the more strictly individual self we commonly postulate in the modern period can never become something to be cultivated for its own ends, but may at best provide us with the effective means of overcoming 'itself'. This self, like the rest of creation, is subjected to Augustine's well known injunction to 'use' and not to 'enjoy' the created world as God's gift: 'Neither should a person enjoy himself, if you think closely about this, because he should not love himself on his own account, but only on account of the one who is to be enjoyed.'[39]

The whole issue of the 'discovery' of the modern self thus appears as funda-mentally misconceived, as, precisely, it postulates a beginning, an emergence of a new form of selfhood, whereas the Augustinian model in fact already presupposes the conflictual coexistence of these two interdependent conceptualisations of selfhood from the very start.[40] As Barbara Rosenwein has recently argued, there are signs of the existence of such a modern self already in the early Middle Ages, and what we designate as a modern self may indeed be, paradoxically, a transhistorical condition *a priori* implicit in every form of existential awareness.[41] It is therefore less a matter of fixing 'the birth' of the modern self in history, than of identifying the multiple and complex reasons why at certain moments in history – whose path

---

[38] Etienne Gilson, *La théologie mystique de Saint Bernard* (Paris: Vrin, 1934), p. 151: 'l'âme se dépouille de ce faux moi, de cette personnalité illusoire du vouloir propre que le péché a introduit en elle', cited and discussed in Maupeu, *Pèlerins de vie humaine*, p. 15, n. 2; translation mine.

[39] Saint Augustine, *On Christian Teaching*, ed. and trans. R. P. H. Green (Oxford: Oxford University Press, 1997), p. 17. See also below, Ch. 1, p. 25.

[40] A very similar, more general point about the coexistence of two different conceptions of 'subjectivity' in the Middle Ages is also made by Haidu, *The Subject Medieval/Modern*, pp. 9–10.

[41] Rosenwein, 'Y avait-il un "moi" au haut Moyen Age?', 42–3, developing the argument for transhistorical selfhood by Alain Boureau, 'Un royal individu', *Critique* 593 (1996), 845–57.

may well not be linear or teleological – this self acquires a greater importance and thus retains the attention of particular individuals or groups, becoming as it were an unavoidable or legitimate subject of study and speculation for these actors in history. And the individual, solitary self, of course, easily becomes the focus of attention during historical periods characterised by crises of the wider, corporate and collective structures of identity – political, ecclesiastical, communitarian.[42]

The resurgence of such a latent individual selfhood in moments of historical crisis therefore is as much an undesirable but unavoidable burden as an exhilarating, liberating discovery. This invites and forces us to redefine simplistic narratives of the 'discovery' of a supposedly liberating modern drive towards self-fashioning in the sixteenth century – and in this sense, the 'long later Middle Ages' constitute a major turning point in history, a moment of crisis feeding new, tentative and often anguished and retrograde articulations of identity. This unease about confronting one's individual selfhood emerges not only in the 'Renaissance' quest-narratives studied in what follows, but already appears rather strikingly in the case of Hoccleve, so often invoked in discussions of late medieval selves, self-representation and auto-biography.[43] The individual self we encounter in Hoccleve's writings is not so much something to be cultivated, as we modern readers would expect, but rather an obstacle preventing his reintegration in a more universally and socially accepted form of selfhood: 'Having fallen into a psychological depth he is unable to fathom, … Hoccleve seeks escape in a comfortingly familiar paradigm'[44] – a paradigm that however fails to have the desired effect and appears as weakened, insufficient to assuage the anxiety of a late medieval urban self like Hoccleve's. In the process, Hoccleve's 'return' to a traditional paradigm produces, paradoxically, a 'new' form of tentative self-understanding.

In the process of writing the present study, it has emerged that despite the massive changes and shifts in the period, and the proliferation of alternative, innovative secular discourses, the metaphysically constituted self *does* remain a force to be reckoned with even in the Renaissance, and is in fact one of the most powerful constitutive forces of the very modern self that supposedly replaces it. In Chapters

---

[42] This forces us to envisage that the evolution of interiority may not be linear, as argued by Aers, 'A Whisper', pp. 196–7. Such crises had already helped to produce the voice of Augustine himself, at the watershed between late classical culture and the emergent Christian tradition he himself shaped so powerfully: 'the case of Augustine is symptomatic of the cultural problem that occurs when the culture bearers themselves lose trust in the efficacy of their culture. … The thoughtful individual experiencing this shock, no longer able to find the answer for his life in the given ones of his culture, suddenly faces immense tasks in reorienting himself – including, perhaps, the task of helping to transform his culture', Weintraub, *The Value of the Individual*, p. 43.

[43] E.g. John Burrow, 'Autobiographical Poetry in the Middle Ages: The Case of Thomas Hoccleve', *Proceedings of the British Academy* 68 (1982), 389–412; Stephan Kohl, 'More than Virtues and Vices: Self-Analysis in Hoccleve's "Autobiographies"', *Fifteenth-Century Studies* 14 (1988), 115–27; Patterson, '"What is Me?"'.

[44] Patterson, '"What is Me?"', p. 91.

3–7 in particular it emerges that the various experiences of self-fashioning envisaged by the several questing heroes do not simply unfold against social pressures that attempt to circumscribe, co-opt or subvert such attempts, but unfold in a landscape that is further circumscribed by a metaphysical or transcendentalising horizon. It is not the self's failure – or success – in positioning itself within a merely social, temporal framework that is the determining moment of self-definition, as Greenblatt's model implies, but the realisation that the very terms of such Renaissance self-fashioning, pitching the individual against social, political, religious and temporal reality alone, are *in themselves* insufficient to provide effective, solid and lasting answers to the problem of identity which remains haunted by metaphysical questions – metaphysical questions which should not be subsumed within the 'religious' alone, with its institutional and political superstructures so prominent in New Historicist criticism. Attempts at self-fashioning in the social arena are as it were frustrated by the realisation of the necessarily contingent, transitory and makeshift nature of both the individual and the social self in the face of eternity, but the experience of *failure* associated with the self's encounter with the larger, metaphysical framework is, precisely, a crucial final step in the constitution of that very self. The modern self only attains its full complexity and 'modernity' when it recognises its own limits through an experience of failure, and begins to construct itself in terms of an elusive, unattainable transcendental resolution. This longing for deliverance from the very self that modernity is condemned to fashion, is a desire that can only ever be metaphysical.

*   *   *

The chapters that follow are structured chronologically, in the hope of giving a clear overview of the development of the tradition as a prelude to the detailed study and discussion of the English works. The forms and *topoi* that provide the basis for the later developments are discussed in Chapter 1, and largely consist of two core conceptions: the idea of a symbolic journey or pilgrimage, and that of a spiritual struggle or psychomachia. These two conceptions are as it were fused in the emergence of the seminal 'Pilgrimage of Life' allegory, Deguileville's *Pèlerinage de vie humaine*, where the element of combat is often latent or implicit.

In 1973 Siegfried Wenzel first postulated the existence of a literary 'genre' of the 'Pilgrimage of Life' in the Later Middle Ages, and his criteria for selection remain largely valid today. Wenzel insists on the exact *function* of the familiar pilgrimage motif in this genre: the journey motif is identified as 'the controlling structure of the poem', rather than being merely 'part of its larger structure'.[45] This allows us to distinguish the genre of the 'Pilgrimage of Life' from other literary works that merely exploit or refer to the pilgrimage motif intermittently, such as the *Roman de la rose*

---

[45]  See Siegfried Wenzel, 'The Pilgrimage of Life as a Late Medieval Genre', *Medieval Studies* 35 (1973), 370–88.

or Langland's *Piers Plowman*, as well as literature that uses the pilgrimage motif as a narrative framework rather than a controlling structure, such as Chaucer's *Canterbury Tales*.[46] The genre must also be distinguished from the numerous journeys to the otherworld and underworld, such as Dante's *Commedia*, Raoul de Houdenc's *Songe d'Enfer*, Rutebeuf's *Voie du Paradis*, the 'Saint Patrick's Purgatory' group of texts and Deguileville's own *Pèlerinage de l'âme*.[47] All of these texts in some manner presuppose the existence of a *conception* of life as pilgrimage, albeit not necessarily identified with any literary *genre*: the emergence of the latter is largely enabled by a single seminal poem, Guillaume de Deguileville's *Pèlerinage de vie humaine*. Following not only Wenzel, but also more recent work by Maupeu as well as the claims of Deguileville's near contemporaries such as Philippe de Mézières,[48] it is possible to see the *Pèlerinage* as a foundational paradigm, providing the model for all subsequent adaptations and transformations. To account for the intriguing and sometimes bewildering variety of such derivative works, however, I suggest that it may be more appropriate to think of this group of texts as a more fluid and adaptable 'tradition', rather than a genre in the strict sense.

The *Pèlerinage de vie humaine*, first composed in 1331 and part of a wider Pilgrimage trilogy, has increasingly attracted the attention of a wide range of scholars over the last thirty years, and is finally being acknowledged as a truly seminal text as well as a richly suggestive doctrinal allegory in its own right.[49] It has been described as 'the best-known doctrinally inspired encyclopaedic allegory of the late Middle Ages,'[50] and it is hard to overestimate the impact of the work and the wider tradition it sparked and fed.[51] Moreover, the influence of the whole trilogy, and of the *Vie* in particular, reaches far beyond the mere province of the literary, as it also affected wider developments in the fields of iconography, drama, lay devotion and spirituality as well as the late medieval imagination more generally. In the light of such a resurgence of interest in Deguileville, it is striking that until very recently

---

[46] Wenzel's decision to exclude *Piers Plowman* has been questioned by Dee Dyas, *Pilgrimage in Medieval English Literature, 700–1500* (Cambridge: D. S. Brewer, 2001), pp. 145–70. Dyas also discusses Chaucer's use of the notion of 'Pilgrimage of Life' in the *Canterbury Tales*, pp. 171–204.

[47] See especially, Fabienne Pomel, *Les voies de l'au-delà et l'essor de l'allégorie au Moyen Age* (Paris: Champion, 2001). For the general use of the pilgrimage motif see also Julia Bolton Holloway, *The Pilgrim and the Book: A Study of Dante, Langland and Chaucer* (New York: Peter Lang, 1987).

[48] Maupeu, *Pèlerins de vie humaine*. For Mézières see his *Songe du vieil pèlerin*, ed. George Coopland (Cambridge: Cambridge University Press, 1969), Mézières also explicitly and repeatedly acknowledges his use of Deguileville's allegory as a paradigm; see also Pomel, *Les voies*, pp. 544–5 and Maupeu, *Pèlerins de vie humaine*, pp. 339–99.

[49] For an edition of the three *pèlerinages*, see Guillaume de Deguileville, *Le pèlerinage de vie humaine*; *Le pèlerinage de l'âme*; *Le pèlerinage Jhesucrist*, ed. J. J. Stürzinger (London: Roxburghe Club, 1893; 1895; 1897).

[50] Joan H. Blythe, 'Deguileville, Guillaume de', in A. C. Hamilton, ed., *The Spenser Encyclopedia* (Toronto: University of Toronto Press, 1990), p. 211.

[51] See Ch. 1.

Wenzel's lucid and useful analysis has remained virtually without response or further discussion. While studies of individual works have appeared, no wider study of the 'Pilgrimage of Life' *as a genre* or *tradition*, has been undertaken. I will examine merely one facet of its literary posterity, namely that of the allegorical knightly quest as derived from Deguileville's paradigm, and in particular its transformations in sixteenth-century England. Thus, while I broadly accept the validity of Wenzel's analysis, the present discussion arises out of a desire for greater precision and specificity in describing the transformations undergone by the paradigm. Rather than being merely 'typical' pilgrimage of life allegories in the manner of Deguileville as they may appear at first sight,[52] the texts studied here constantly re-elaborate, alter, prune and expand Deguileville's model to accommodate the more specific and immediate concerns of each author and his environment.

The notion of psychomachia, derived largely from the Pauline conception of the Christian life as a perpetual struggle against the enemies of Faith, is inextricably tied up with the Christian allegory of life as a journey, as Dee Dyas has observed.[53] Deguileville constantly weaves this idea into his text, for instance with his ample development of the Christian armour from Ephesians, or his lengthy descriptions of the pilgrim under attack from the Seven Deadly Sins. While for Deguileville the psychomachic allegory is clearly the vehicle for a moral and doctrinal exposition, its lively narrative seems to have stimulated the imagination of late medieval readers on other planes as well. Finding Deguileville's work referred to as an improbable 'Romaunce of þe Monk', as in the case of the early fifteenth-century English prose translation,[54] suggests that Deguileville was rather too successful in his efforts to animate his doctrinal abstractions. The lively descriptions of the pilgrim's encounters and struggles along the way indeed already contain an undeniable potential for a romance-like development.[55] Chapter 2 therefore discusses the adaptation of the Pilgrimage pattern to the needs of a more knightly audience, where the implicit combat against moral or psychological abstractions is to some extent literalised and takes on a romance-like form that I term the 'quest' proper. The works studied in Chapter 2 thus attempt to absorb the formal patterns of the chivalric romance quest into the mode of religious allegory, striving to articulate something like an ideal of

---

[52] This is implicit in the discussion of Patrick Cullen, *Infernal Triad: The Flesh, the World, and the Devil in Spenser and Milton* (Princeton, NJ: Princeton University Press, 1974), pp. 3–67. See also p. 22, n. 62 below.

[53] Dyas, *Pilgrimage*, pp. 161–8.

[54] *The Pilgrimage of the Lyfe of Manhode*, 2 vols, ed. Avril Henry, EETS OS 288 and 292 (Oxford: Oxford University Press, 1985–8), vol. 1, p. 175, l. 7295. Some of the French manuscripts equally designate the poem as 'li romans du moisne', see Stürzinger, *Pèlerinage de vie humaine*, p. 423.

[55] This is the guiding principle of Rosemond Tuve's discussion of Deguileville in *Allegorical Imagery: Some Mediaeval Books and their Posterity* (Princeton, NJ: Princeton University Press, 1966), pp. 145–218. See also the references in C. S. Lewis, *The Allegory of Love: A Study in Medieval Tradition* (Oxford: Clarendon Press, 1936), pp. 264–77.

a lay chivalry within a wider religious worldview. While the allegories retain some of their universal and exemplary resonance, the hero engaged in the quest is no longer an Everyman but rather a representative of a particular social group. It is not surprising, then, to observe that all four authors discussed in Chapter 2 should happen to be knights themselves, all attempting to redefine the possibilities of following, *as knights*, in the footsteps of Deguileville's pilgrim. This new, less exclusively transcendentalising and more markedly social concern also results in an enhanced autobiographical dimension of the narratives, which further complicates their relationship to Deguileville's model.

The attempt to integrate quest and pilgrimage was not new, and had never been easy; it can be traced back to earlier romances, most obviously the *Queste del Saint Graal* from the French Vulgate cycle, or the curious bipartition of Guy of Warwick's career as knight and pilgrim,[56] and it had ultimately helped to produce the very concept of the crusade.[57] Yet this new development was characterised by the careful and systematic nature of the attempted synthesis, striving to properly subsume knighthood within a wider and deeply Christian perspective. So, it was no longer a question of scattering a few religious references throughout a largely chivalric work, or of converting formerly sinful knights to the straight and narrow path,[58] but of making the paths of the knight and pilgrim converge, or in fact, coincide. The problem with this synthesis is, quite simply, that the convergence of quest and pilgrimage also requires the integration of two ethical systems largely at odds with one another: Christianity, guilt-culture, self-abnegation on the one hand; knighthood, shame-culture and worldliness on the other. Hence, the quests provide the occasion for implicit and at times explicit theoretical debates about the actual possibility of achieving such a synthesis, but often end up exacerbating the tension instead of resolving it. The knight's wandering becomes more and more an allegory of each specific author's attempts to reconcile the respective demands of knighthood and Christianity, by balancing the entanglement in secular, temporal affairs expressed by chivalric quest narratives with the transcendentalising drive inherent in the notion

---

[56] See especially Judith Weiss, 'The Exploitation of Ideas of Pilgrimage and Sainthood in *Gui de Warewic*', in Laura Ashe, Ivana Djordjevic and Judith Weiss, eds, *The Exploitations of Medieval Romance* (Cambridge: D. S. Brewer, 2010), pp. 43–56.

[57] On the convergence of quest and pilgrimage, allegory and romance, see Cooper, 'Quest and Pilgrimage'. On the Vulgate *Queste*, see especially Pauline Matarasso, *The Redemption of Chivalry: A Study of the* Queste del Saint Graal (Genève: Droz, 1979). On the crusades and their links with the ideas of pilgrimage and chivalric quest, see Barbara N. Sargent-Baur, ed., *Journeys Toward God: Pilgrimage and Crusade* (Kalamazoo, MI: Medieval Institute Publications, 1992); Alain Labbé, Daniel W. Lacroix and Danielle Quéruel, eds, *Guerres, voyages et quêtes au Moyen Age: mélanges offerts à Jean-Claude Faucon* (Paris: Champion, 2000); Danielle Buschinger, ed., *La croisade: réalité et fictions (Actes du Colloque d'Amiens, 1987)* (Göppingen: Kümmerle Verlag, 1989); Huguette Taviani, ed., *Voyage, quête, pèlerinage dans la littérature et la civilisation médiévales* (Aix-en-Provence: CUER-MA, 1976).

[58] See Andrea Hopkins, *The Sinful Knights: A Study of Middle English Penitential Romance* (Oxford: Clarendon Press, 1990).

of pilgrimage. Secular and religious values, romance and allegory, body and soul confront one another in the attempt of finding a 'path' or synthesis that balances the mutual demands of the active and contemplative ideals.[59] Crucially, these attempts to formulate a new paradigm are derived from, but are no longer identical with, Guillaume de Deguileville's contemplative and ultimately monastic model.

Despite the diversity of the works studied in the main body of the book in Chapters 3–7, two main tendencies may be identified in the evolution of the allegorical knightly quest in sixteenth-century England. On the one hand, the figure of the knight becomes a representative of the social group that claims to have inherited the function, ethos and prestige of the medieval knight, albeit in a mutated form. On the other, the knight returns to being a figure for the Christian Everyman as in Deguileville's paradigm, but with an added emphasis on his active role and presence in the world, fittingly signified by his being not a pilgrim but a knight, essentially a representative of the *vita activa*. These two tendencies cannot be separated and may rather be seen as the two poles, the extremes of a spectrum within which the allegorical knightly quest unfolds. Thanks to the powerful evocative potential of the archetypal metaphors of the journey and psychomachia, the allegorical knightly quest lends itself perfectly to becoming a figure for the layman's attempts to find his place in a secular, yet metaphysically framed world, embracing at once the political, spiritual and personal struggles and conflicts.

The work of Stephen Hawes, discussed in Chapter 3, is a clear example of the difficulty of achieving a synthesis of multiple, discontinuous and often contradictory ethical systems. As Groom of the Chamber of Henry VII, Hawes clearly writes for the court and imagines his quests as articulating a model, even a blueprint for the education of the new sophisticated breed of the Tudor knight and courtier. His hero's quest is at once a journey towards moral excellence, the beatific vision that is the heavenly reward for such excellence, but also towards earthly love, learning, social advancement and political power, all cast in the form of an allegorical chivalric romance. The desire for such a synthesis appears as the central concern of Hawes's three principal works, *The Example of Vertu* (1503–4), *The Pastime of Pleasure* (1505–6) and *The Conforte of Lovers* (1510–11), which gives us the unique opportunity of tracing the evolution of his ideal through time, and Hawes's final disillusion with his initial project.

If the allegorical knightly quest on the one hand becomes a vehicle for articulating the ideal of a new social group claiming a lineal descent from medieval knighthood, on the other it also serves a more intensely religious purpose. The works studied in Chapters 4 and 5 tip the unsteady balance between secular and spiritual in favour of religious instruction, thus to some extent restoring the original purpose of Deguileville's paradigm. Here knighthood returns to being largely a metaphor for

---

[59] On such irreconcilable tensions, conceived as a pairing of body and soul, see Jon Whitman, 'The Body and the Struggle for the Soul of Romance: *La Queste del Saint Graal*', in Piero Boitani and Anna Torti, eds, *The Body and the Soul in Medieval Literature* (Cambridge: D. S. Brewer, 1999), pp. 31–61.

the Christian life, albeit a particularly fitting one given the Post-Reformation atmosphere of conflict. The knight's journey thus becomes a perfect image for the urgent need to redefine the 'path' of the new, reformed Christian pilgrim in the midst of the institutional, dogmatic and epistemological uncertainties produced by the Reformation.

Stephen Bateman's *Travayled Pylgrime* (1569), discussed in Chapter 4, is a translation of Olivier de la Marche's *Chevalier délibéré* (1483). Here the journey takes the form of a 'wandering' as a figure for man's post-lapsarian exile. Conceived as an irremediably fallen Protestant Everyman, the knight is unable to 'read' the allegorical signs he encounters on his quest with any degree of certainty. At the same time, the knight is prevented from slipping into despair by the certainty of his election, and his wandering is sustained by the belief in an imminent eschatological resolution. Thus, while from the individual, interior point of view the knight is truly 'errant', he sees himself as participating within a larger, historical movement that anticipates the apocalyptic revelation. Drawing on the contemporary apocalypticism of John Bale in particular, Bateman inscribes his knight's lonely individual wandering into the collective pilgrimage of the True Church of Christ towards its eventual triumph over the forces of Antichrist. The moral psychomachia inherited from Deguileville is thus doubled, supplemented by an epistemological struggle that opposes the lonely pilgrim to the deceptions and illusions of the false Church of Antichrist.

In many ways William Goodyear's *Voyage of the Wandering Knight* (1581), discussed in Chapter 5, may be seen as a reaction against the doctrinal, confessional and political controversies sparked by the likes of Bateman, Bale and Foxe. His work is more than any other an attempt to restore the universality and simplicity of Deguileville's paradigm. The work is again a translation, this time of Jean de Cartheny's *Voyage du Chevalier errant* (1552/1557). Cartheny's work in turn draws directly from Deguileville's *Pèlerinage de vie* and Thomas de Saluces's *Chevalier errant* (1394–6), but is supplemented by the Counter-Reformation agenda of its author, a Flemish Carmelite. Conceived as a catechismal manual, the work leads the reader through the successive steps of the knight's conversion and instruction in the orthodox Catholic doctrine, all the while avoiding any form of confessional polemic. Goodyear's translation shares its source's disregard for religious polemic, and equally concentrates on the universalising and unifying potential of the allegorical journey of the Christian Everyman. While Goodyear aligns the work's doctrine with that of the Elizabethan settlement, he leaves the larger structure of the work strikingly unaltered. This suggests the possibility of fruitful inter-confessional exchanges in the literature of the period, and raises wider questions about the usefulness of rigid denominational discriminations in the study of religious sensibilities in Elizabethan England. Goodyear's lack of concern with contemporary theological and doctrinal debates argues for the existence of a much more fluid, tolerant and lively form of popular devotion below the more easily documented official, institutional polemic.

In Chapter 6 we return to a more markedly secular, courtly allegory that is in many ways reminiscent of Hawes's experiments, with Lewes Lewkenor's *Resolved Gentleman* (1594), another translation of Olivier de la Marche's *Chevalier délibéré*.

The work must be read within the dynamics of late Elizabethan politics, and again exploits the motifs of quest, exile, wandering and psychomachia to represent the knight's problematic relationship with the court. As with Hawes, the quest serves as a narrative framework to devise a new model for the courtier, now explicitly identified as an Elizabethan gentleman, inheriting and transforming the ethos of La Marche's Burgundian chivalry. Yet Lewkenor's quest is fraught with difficulties from the very beginning, and never displays the kind of optimistic confidence found in Hawes's early works. So, whereas Lewkenor's new paradigm of the humanist knight is more carefully balanced than Hawes's unwieldy synthesis, his hopes for its realisation are rather more slender and less optimistic. Again the wider project is doubled by a more directly personal interest and involvement, and the quest also becomes a personal plea for political advancement, prompting an identification of the ideal gentleman and its translator, Lewkenor himself. Read in parallel with episodes from Lewkenor's life, his knight's wandering acquires a striking autobiographical dimension, which in turn conceals a wider commentary on both the political and religious climate of the 1590s.

Edmund Spenser's debts to the tradition, discussed in Chapter 7, are undeniable, yet ultimately very difficult to pin down. He may have known some, all, or none of the texts that are discussed in the present study, although the first option is most likely, and attempts to link him to most of these works have appeared in the past.[60] While interesting connections have sometimes been uncovered, often such studies imply some sort of teleological perspective determined by modern notions of canonicity and poetic value or merit. The present study as a whole, however, deliberately seeks to avoid being merely a study of Spenser's 'sources' and sees Spenser more simply as one of several other writers contributing to the continuation of the allegorical quest tradition. The texts studied in Chapters 3–6, I argue, deserve to be read on account of their own relevance as efforts of self-fashioning articulated through the medium of the allegorical knightly quest, and not only because they constitute a literary tradition that somehow clumsily foreshadows Spenser's monumental achievements.[61] I argue instead that it is precisely the tentative, experimental

---

[60] On Deguileville, see Frederick Morgan Padelford, 'Spenser and The Pilgrimage of the Life of Man', *Studies in Philology* 28:2 (1931), 211–18. On Hawes, Friedrich Zander, *Stephen Hawes' 'Passetyme of pleasure' verglichen mit Edmund Spenser's 'Faerie Queene' unter Berücksichtigung der allegorischen Dichtung in England. Ein Beitrag zur Quellenfrage der 'Faerie Queene'* (Rostock: Hinstorffs Buchdruckerei, 1905); Carol V. Kaske, 'How Spenser Really Used Stephen Hawes in the Legend of Holiness', in George M. Logan and Gordon Teskey, eds, *Unfolded Tales: Essays on Renaissance Romance* (Ithaca, NY: Cornell University Press, 1989), pp. 119–36. On Bateman, Kathrine Koller, 'The Travayled Pylgrime by Stephen Bateman and Book Two of The Faerie Queene', *Modern Language Quarterly* 3 (1942), 535–41; Anne Lake Prescott, 'Spenser's Chivalric Restoration: From Bateman's *Travayled Pylgrime* to the Redcrosse Knight', *Studies in Philology* 86:2 (1989), 166–97; Dorothy F. Atkinson, 'The Wandering Knight, the Red Cross Knight, and "Miles Dei"', *Huntington Library Quarterly* 7:2 (February 1944), 109–34.

[61] See p. 3, n. 7 above.

and often 'unsuccessful' nature of these earlier works in the tradition that made them
so powerfully relevant and interesting for a reader like Spenser.[62] Their very
hesitancy, instability and fluidity allow these earlier works to become part of the
raw materials used by Spenser to think through the potentials of his own allegory,
thereby setting out to 'fashion' an early modern secular ideal of 'vertuous and gentle
discipline', a project that is in turn self-contradictory, self-divided and ultimately
open-ended.

The final chapter of the book is less concerned to assess the impact of specific
individual works on Spenser, but rather attempts to understand *how* Spenser seems
to build the *Faerie Queene* on his awareness of the tradition as a whole, with all its
multiple and at times discordant voices. While specific works have undoubtedly
functioned as 'sources' for particular incidents and passages in the *Faerie Queene*,
and such borrowings are also discussed, I situate the influence of the tradition at a
deeper level, and argue that Spenser may fruitfully be thought of as reflecting on
the entirety of the tradition that precedes him. Aware of the internal tensions,
contradictions and frustration produced by these allegories, Spenser conceives his
own project as a meditation on the possibility of devising an exemplary, paradigmatic allegorical quest at all. Spenser may thus ultimately best be thought of as
entering into a dialogue with the works discussed in this book, thinking in their
terms, and striving indeed to 'overgo' them by attempting the ultimate balancing act
between secular and religious, historical and universal that the previous quest
narratives had failed to achieve. Yet despite his attempt to enlarge the range of
meanings offered by the form through a recourse to multiple parallel quests of his
titular heroes/virtues, ultimately Spenser is forced – after six books, twenty years
of poetic career and as many years in the service of the queen – to acknowledge
that the balancing act of idealism and pragmatism has once more failed. The sites
of the unexpected apotheosis of Spenser's allegory – Colin Clout's Mount Acidale
and the Arlo Hill of the *Mutabilitie Cantos* – ultimately reveal powerful, profound
continuities between Spenser and his predecessors, and suggest that he too finally
wrenches his quest away from temporal, historical reality to perform a final transcendentalising leap that sends us back to the tenacious paradigm of Deguileville's
universalising spiritual quest.

---

[62]  In this sense my analysis both resembles and differs from Cullen's, *Infernal Triad*, pp. 3–67,
the only other critic who provides an overall assessment of the impact of the 'pilgrimage' tradition
on Spenser. Cullen insists, rightly, on Spenser's greater sophistication in confronting epistemological issues that are also moral, but on the whole presents a rather reductive view of the
tradition, arguing for example that 'the simplistic expectations of the pilgrimage genre do not
hold for the world Spenser portrays', p. 24. Accordingly his analysis refers to the tradition in
highly general terms, postulating a uniformity and stability, even inertness that falls short of the
complexity of the form and its very diverse embodiments discussed in this study. Spenser's poem
clearly differs from the work of his predecessors, but it does so precisely because Spenser was
able to appreciate and 'think through' the complexity and internal difficulties of the earlier
tradition, not because Spenser was breathing new life into a 'simplistic' genre.

# 1

# *Homo Viator:* Guillaume de Deguileville's *Pèlerinage de vie humaine*

## Pilgrimage and Psychomachia

The conception of life as a journey is implicit in the entire tradition of the 'pilgrimage of life' allegories, and is also one of the fundamental figures of the human condition, recurring throughout widely different cultures with broadly analogous functions.[1] The wayfaring hero, figure of man, is at present in an incomplete or unfulfilled state of being, and his journey always denotes some sort of transformation, a 'becoming', a quest for an as yet elusive identity. The Christian conception of the journey, while it is largely shaped by biblical motifs, reverberates nevertheless with echoes of older narratives rooted in an archetypal pattern of departure and transformation, such as classical stories of Odysseus, Perseus, Jason, Theseus and Aeneas, or the more humble forms of the folktale and legend.[2] Among the biblical sources, the Old Testament narratives of the exile and wandering of the people of Israel in the Pentateuch are the earliest to develop the metaphor, especially the episodes of Exodus, the Darkness of Egypt and Abraham in search of God in the desert.[3] This understanding of human

---

[1]  The following account draws on a number of works, especially Dyas, *Pilgrimage*, pp. 12–26; F. C. Gardiner, *The Pilgrimage of Desire: A Study of Theme and Genre in Medieval Literature* (Leiden: Brill, 1971), pp. 1–52; Gerhart B. Ladner, 'Homo Viator: Mediaeval Ideas on Alienation and Order', *Speculum* 42:2 (1967), 233–59. For an account of the medieval practice rather than the conception of pilgrimage, see Jonathan Sumption, *Pilgrimage: An Image of Mediaeval Religion* (London: Faber and Faber, 1975), and Diana Webb, *Pilgrimage in Medieval England* (London: Hambledon and London, 2000); and ibid., *Medieval European Pilgrimage, c. 700–c. 1500* (Basingstoke: Palgrave, 2002).

[2]  For the basic pattern of the archetypal 'Journey', see Joseph Campbell's classic work, *The Hero with a Thousand Faces* (Princeton, NJ: Princeton University Press, 1972), pp. 49ff; Leonard J. Bowman, 'Itinerarium: The Shape of the Metaphor', in Leonard J. Bowman, ed., *Itinerarium: The Idea of Journey* (Salzburg: Institut für Anglistik und Amerikanistik, Universität Salzburg, 1983), pp. 3–33.

[3]  Dyas, *Pilgrimage*, pp. 12–20.

existence as 'exile' is fundamental, and these Old Testament narratives become foundational for the later developments of the Christian notion of pilgrimage as transmitted by the Epistle to Hebrews 11:13–16, where imitation of the Old Testament
figures as models for Christian faith is encouraged. The Exodus of the people of
Israel becomes an image, a paradigm of the individual Christian's journey towards
God, thus prompting early Christian monastic communities to seek voluntary exile
in the desert.[4] The exile may be collective, inflicted upon the whole people of Israel,
as well as individual, as lived out in Abraham's search for the Promised Land. The
exile-motif also shapes two further master narratives of Christianity: the fall of
Lucifer and the banishment of Adam and Eve from the Garden of Eden. All these
narratives are ultimately developments of a single central idea, namely that of
humankind's alienation from God and its subsequent wandering in a 'foreign' land
that is far removed from an original heavenly home.

The notions of exile and pilgrimage are both related to the wider idea of a journey,
but refer to different states of being associated with different moments of that
journey. Exile implies exclusion, wandering and sometimes aimlessness, while
pilgrimage is always directed towards a clearly apprehended destination, often
imagined as a return to one's homeland. In the case of biblical narrative, this return
to the heavenly home is also a re-establishment of the pre-lapsarian condition, a
process that within the Christian perspective is inextricably tied up with the
historical incarnation, crucifixion and resurrection of Christ.[5] It is the advent of
Christ that reopens the path towards humankind's spiritual homeland – 'I am the
Door' (John 10:9) – and thus allows the transition from a state of mere wandering
to one of pilgrimage. Jesus himself is often thought of as a pilgrim,[6] an exemplary
figure of self-sacrifice, descending into the material world only to point beyond it
to man's forgotten ancestral heavenly home. Consequently the Christian liturgy, as
a re-enactment of the sacrifice of Christ, is equally structured around the motif of
the eastward journey, image of the return to the lost Earthly Paradise traditionally
situated in the Orient.[7]

Once the heavenly home, ultimate destination of the human pilgrimage, has been
identified, man needs to accept his present condition of existence as impermanent
and illusory, as expressed in 1 Peter and 2 Corinthians. Man embarks on the journey

---

[4]   E.g. Sumption, *Pilgrimage*, pp. 94–7; Dyas, *Pilgrimage*, pp. 29–32.
[5]   As in Bonaventure's influential account of a mystical journey to God through Christ, the *Itinerarium Mentis in Deum*, trans. Ewert Cousins, *The Soul's Journey into God* (New York: Paulist
Press, 1978). See also Leonard J. Bowman, 'What Kind of Journey Is Bonaventure's *Itinerarium?*'
and Ewert Cousins, 'Bonaventure and Dante: The Role of Christ in the Spiritual Journey', both
in Bowman, ed., *Itinerarium*, pp. 94–112 and 113–31 respectively; and Nguyen Van Si, 'Les
symboles de l'itinéraire dans l'*Itinerarium mentis in Deum* de Bonaventure', *Antonianum* 68:2–3
(1993), 327–47.
[6]   Notably Guillaume de Deguileville's third pilgrimage, the *Pèlerinage Jhesucrist*. See also
Ladner, 'Homo Viator', 250; and Dyas, *Pilgrimage*, p. 21.
[7]   Jean Daniélou, *Bible et liturgie: la théologie biblique des sacrements et des fêtes d'après les Pères
de l'Église* (Paris: Editions du Cerf, 1951), pp. 44–8; Sumption, *Pilgrimage*, pp. 89–94.

in the hope of attaining a higher state of being, signified by the stability and permanence of his ultimate destination, the Heavenly City, symbol of definitive deliverance from earthly vicissitudes and oppression.[8] The most powerful and lasting picture of the City as man's eschatological haven is painted in the Book of Revelation,[9] where the motif of the New Jerusalem completes the fundamental pattern of the Christian journey: fall, exile, redemption through Christ, pilgrimage and reintegration. Crucially, the journey that is outlined is at once macro- and micro-cosmic, applicable to the history of humankind from the fall to the apocalypse, as well as to each individual Christian's personal quest for salvation. It is largely the second, individual journey that provides the potential for moral didactic developments, and thus allows the emergence of the 'Pilgrimage of Life' tradition in the later Middle Ages.

The idea of the Christian journey proved to be enormously influential in the writings of the early Fathers, and may be seen as a leading metaphor in the thought of such crucial figures as Origen, Gregory the Great, Augustine of Hippo and Cyprian.[10] Progressing through a foreign and inhospitable land, man is confronted with a number of hardships, obstacles and enemies preventing his progression from this world to the next, a transition visualised by Augustine's notion of the 'two cities'.[11] The journey from the physical, earthly city of Babylon to Jerusalem, City of God, requires detachment from the entanglements of the physical world, a world that needs to be 'used' as an instrument and not 'enjoyed' as an end in itself, as Augustine memorably encapsulated this formidable task in the *De Doctrina Christiana*: 'So in this mortal life we are like travellers away from our Lord [2 Cor. 5:6]: if we wish to return to the homeland where we can be happy we must use this world [cf. 1 Cor. 7:31], not enjoy it, in order to discern "the invisible attributes of God, which are understood through what has been made" [Rom. 1:20] or, in other words, to derive eternal and spiritual value from corporeal and temporal things.'[12] For Bernard of Clairvaux, inheriting Augustine's conception of the *regio dissimili-tudinis*, the pilgrimage leads through a fallen world of deformity back to a pre-lapsarian state of divine resemblance, where man's own divine archetype is restored, as is shadowed in the parable of the Prodigal Son.[13] The pilgrimage, image of an

---

[8]  Dyas, *Pilgrimage*, pp. 21–6.

[9]  Dyas, *Pilgrimage*, pp. 25–6.

[10]  See Dyas, *Pilgrimage*, pp. 27–36; Gardiner, *Pilgrimage of Desire*, pp. 11–52. More specifically on Augustine, see Paul G. Kuntz, 'Augustine: From *Homo Erro* to *Homo Viator*', in Bowman, ed., *Itinerarium*, pp. 34–53.

[11]  Saint Augustine, *The City of God*, ed. G. R. Evans, trans. Henry Bettenson (London: Penguin, 2003). For a study of the doctrine of the two cities, see Johannes Van Oort, *Jerusalem and Babylon: A Study into Augustine's* City of God *and the Sources of his Doctrine of the Two Cities* (Leiden: Brill, 1991).

[12]  Saint Augustine, *On Christian Teaching*, ed. and trans. R. P. H. Green (Oxford: Oxford University Press, 1997), p. 10.

[13]  Etienne Gilson, '*Regio dissimilitudinis* de Platon à saint Bernard de Clairvaux', *Medieval Studies* 9 (1947), 108–30; and *La théologie mystique de saint Bernard*.

ontological transformation, thus requires a twofold effort that is at once moral and epistemological, as is most evident if one turns to Deguileville's trilogy.[14]

The ascetic detachment signified by man's existential condition as a pilgrim invites moral and didactic developments. Once the pilgrim has identified his destination and begun his journey, he needs to confront the specific dangers, obstacles and enemies that attempt to divert him from following the prescribed *itinerarium* towards his final objective.[15] This moral struggle is often articulated using a second fundamental Christian metaphor, that of the psychomachia. Not only is the psychomachia closely related to the basic notion of the 'Pilgrimage of Life' in Christian thought, but the two conceptions, battle and journey, have been identified by Angus Fletcher as the two fundamental vehicles of the allegorical mode itself.[16] Deguileville's *Pèlerinage de vie humaine*, by availing itself of both of these fundamental vehicles, fuses and elaborates the two most powerful allegories for the Christian life.

The concept of the psychomachia can be defined as the representation of a spiritual conflict in the human soul through the metaphor of physical combat. The concept is first developed in Hellenistic thought, later elaborated by Philo of Alexandria, and finally finds its fullest expression in Christian thought in the writings of Saint Paul, in particular his influential description of the Christian life as spiritual warfare in Ephesians 6:11–17 or 2 Corinthians 10:3–6.[17] The idea was later developed by Tertullian and Cyprian in particular, and by the time of Augustine was firmly established and taken for granted.[18] The fullest and most influential articulation of the concept is found in Prudentius's *Psychomachia*.[19] The work adapts the models of ancient epic and heroic verse to express Christian truths, drawing from the late Roman tradition of personification, but also refers to the Old Testament, interpreting Abraham's victory over the heathen kings as an allegory of the victory of Virtue over Vice.

Prudentius's account of the clash of the seven vices against their opposing virtues rapidly became a canonical text, and its author was often considered as *the* most Christian and Catholic author.[20] The work has been described as a kind

---

[14]  For Deguileville's debt to Bernard see Pomel, *Les voies*, pp. 385–95.

[15]  Pomel, *Les voies*, pp. 73–7.

[16]  Angus Fletcher, *Allegory: The Theory of a Symbolic Mode* (Ithaca, NY: Cornell University Press, 1964), pp. 147–80.

[17]  Morton W. Bloomfield, *The Seven Deadly Sins: An Introduction to the History of a Religious Concept, with Special Reference to Medieval English Literature* (East Lansing, MI: Michigan State University Press, 1952; repr. 1967), p. 63.

[18]  Bloomfield, *The Seven Deadly Sins*, p. 64; Joanne S. Norman, *Metamorphoses of an Allegory: The Iconography of the Psychomachia in Medieval Art* (New York: Peter Lang, 1988), pp. 8, 12 and *passim*.

[19]  Prudentius, *Psychomachia*, in *Prudentius*, vol. 1, ed. and trans. H. J. Thomson (London: Heinemann, 1949), pp. 274–343. On his sources, see Ralph Hanna III, 'The Sources and the Art of Prudentius' *Psychomachia*', *Classical Philology* 72:2 (1977), 108–15.

[20]  Sinéad O'Sullivan, *Early Medieval Glosses on Prudentius' Psychomachia: The Weitz Tradition* (Leiden: Brill, 2004), p. 20. For influential early discussions of Prudentius's *Psychomachia*, now

of 'miniature bible', replicating scriptural structure on a condensed scale and generating a pseudo-biblical commentary tradition,[21] and the *Psychomachia* also became the most important source for medieval allegories dealing with the concept of a spiritual struggle.[22] Later developed by Isidore in *De pugna virtutum adversus vitia* (PL 83, 638), Hugh of St Victor, Vincent of Beauvais[23] and finally Bernard in the *De pugna spirituali* (PL 183, 757), the notion of moral and spiritual warfare rapidly becomes a ubiquitous and foundational metaphor in Christian thought.

The battle described by Prudentius opposes cosmic absolutes rather than describing a particularised individual struggle: adopting Carolyn Van Dyke's useful formulation, it can be said that Prudentius is concerned with the universal 'Reality' of the vices as opposed to their particular 'reality' as refracted in individual human experience.[24] This focus on the universalising, paradigmatic significance of spiritual conflict is revealed most clearly by the *dénouement* of Prudentius's allegory, where a dynamic description of struggle gives way to a static representation of triumph. After their victory over the opposing vices, the virtues proceed to establish a temple that has been variously interpreted as representing the human soul, the Church triumphant and the New Jerusalem. The figure of the temple includes and subsumes all these ideas and embodies the definitive triumph of Virtue itself, no longer refracted in all its secondary, particular meanings. As dynamic struggle gives way to static and permanent symbol, the New Jerusalem becomes the final, definitive referent of the allegory as well as the vanishing point and apotheosis of human experience, both individual and cosmic.[25]

qualified by more recent research, see Bloomfield, *Seven Deadly Sins*, pp. 63–6; and Lewis, *Allegory of Love*, pp. 66–73. For an overview of recent scholarship, see Jean-Louis Charlet, 'État des études sur la *Psychomachia* de Prudence', *Vita Latina* 167 (2002), 80–7. For representations of vice and virtue, see Adolf Katzenellenbogen, *Allegories of the Virtues and Vices in Medieval Art from Early Christian Times to the Thirteenth Century*, trans. Alan J. P. Crick (London: Warburg, 1939).

[21] O'Sullivan, *Glosses on Psychomachia*, p. xx and *passim*.

[22] James J. Paxson, *The Poetics of Personification* (Cambridge: Cambridge University Press, 1994), pp. 63–81.

[23] Pomel, *Les voies*, p. 371.

[24] For a re-evaluation of the poem's merits, see especially Carolynn Van Dyke, *The Fiction of Truth: Structures of Meaning in Narrative and Dramatic Allegory* (Ithaca, NY: Cornell University Press, 1985), pp. 29–63, here p. 39.

[25] For this reading, see especially Van Dyke, *Fiction of Truth*, pp. 59–63. See also Hanna, 'The Sources'; Patrice Cambronne, 'Métamorphoses de la Terre Promise: Le Temple de l'Âme dans la *Psychomachia* de Prudence', *Revue des études anciennes* 104:3–4 (2002), 445–74, where also the idea of pilgrimage is brought to bear on the *Psychomachia*. For the development of the conception and iconography of the Heavenly Jerusalem and its impact on medieval culture, see especially Ann R. Meyer, *Medieval Allegory and the Building of the New Jerusalem* (Cambridge: D. S. Brewer, 2003).

## A New Psychomachia: *Le Pèlerinage de vie humaine*

*Vie¹*, the earlier (1331) and more successful of the two versions of the poem in terms of circulation, broadly follows the *Psychomachia* tradition, but adapts the idea of a spiritual struggle to respond to contemporary developments in theology, philosophy and the related iconography of vices, sins and remedial virtues. The twelfth and thirteenth centuries had already seen a transformation of Prudentian models, giving rise to a new iconography broadly characterised by a tendency towards greater specificity and moral interiorisation.[26] This is itself a response to the heightened interest in the systematised rational analysis of moral problems initiated by twelfth-century philosophy, and articulated in the influential penitential handbooks and *summae* of the following centuries.[27] This new shift is also characterised by a marked emphasis on penance, revealing a particular concern with the instruction of the laity in response to the fourth Lateran Council of 1215. Ultimately these developments in the twelfth and thirteenth centuries reveal the desire for a more detailed, complex and psychologically accurate analysis of spiritual conflict on the plane of individual moral choices.

By beginning his poem with a vision of the ultimate destination of the pilgrim's quest, the Heavenly Jerusalem reflected in a mirror (*Vie¹* 39ff), Deguileville maintains the eschatological focus of the Prudentian tradition, but also modifies it by deploying a careful and complex analysis of moral conflict within the timeframe of individual human life,[28] with a particular emphasis on penance.[29] The protagonists of the allegory are no longer the largely interchangeable vices and virtues themselves as with Prudentius, but the soul and body of the individual Christian *in time*, confronting the personifications of the sins and vices. As for the virtues, they are merely echoed in the Pilgrim's equipment such as his staff of Good Hope or his Pauline armour, or have otherwise been largely replaced with spiritual abstractions such as Grace Dieu, the pilgrim's guide.

The new focus of attention becomes the nature of the sins and vices themselves, and the 'pilgrimage' is turned into a process of moral and epistemological enquiry shared by the reader and the protagonist alike.[30] The exact modalities of the attack of

---

[26] See Norman, *Metamorphoses*, pp. 101–39.

[27] As examples may be quoted the influential and long-lived *Moralium dogma philosophorum* (1140s), Peraldus's *Summa de vitiis et de virtutibus* (1230s and 40s) and finally the *Somme le Roi* (1279), and their numerous adaptations and translations into the vernacular. See Tuve, *Allegorical Imagery*, pp. 57–143. On the influence on Deguileville, see Joan H. Blythe, 'The Influence of Latin Manuals on Medieval Allegory: Deguileville's Presentation of Wrath', *Romania* 95 (1974), 256–83.

[28] See Norman, *Metamorphoses*, pp. 181–96.

[29] Dyas, *Pilgrimage*, p. 191; Pomel, *Les voies*, pp. 295–312. See e.g. the appearance of Penitence personified (*Vie¹* 2005ff), the bath of Penitence (*Vie¹* 11239ff), the Hedge of Penitence separating the paths of Idleness and Occupation (*Vie¹* 6483ff).

[30] Tuve, *Allegorical Imagery*, pp. 160–6; Norman, *Metamorphoses*, p. 187.

each particular sin are significant in themselves, being the external allegorical deployment of the sin's inner nature.[31] So Sloth paralyses the pilgrim's feet with snares, Envy has eyes in the shape of piercing spears and Avarice has six arms to rob the pilgrim.[32] Also the remedies against the sins are visualised in an analogous manner, such as Penitence, carrying a mallet and a rod in her two hands, and a broom in her mouth, all followed by a detailed explanation of the mechanics of sin and penance:

> Du maillet je brise et froisse
> Par contriction, et angoisse
> Le cuer d'omme, quant est remplis
> De viez pechies et endurcis.
>
> . . .
>
> Mon balai pour tout balier
> Housser, purgier et netier
>
> . . .
>
> Mon balai si est ma lengue,
> Mon fourgon et ma palengue
> Dont toute ordure je baloie,
>
> . . .
>
> Par entiere confession
>
> . . .
>
> Adonc pour li bien chastier
> De mes cinglans verges le fier,
> Paine li doins et batement
> Pour son bien et amendment. (*Vie¹* 2055–8; 2249–63; 2301–4)[33]

This 'emblematic' elaboration of the Prudentian metaphor of physical struggle is furthermore supplemented by dialogic conflict,[34] and the extended encounters with the sins and vices in each case follow a common pattern: meeting, description of appearance and attributes, debate, recapitulation and explanation. The emphasis has shifted from the struggle as such to the recognition, analysis and rejection of the sin in an epistemological perspective.[35] The *Vie* is no longer concerned with absolute timeless moral or metaphysical abstractions, but rather with the individual

---

[31] Norman, *Metamorphoses*, pp. 191–2; Tuve, *Allegorical Imagery*, pp. 160–3.

[32] *Vie¹*, respectively 7033ff, 8191ff, 9059ff.

[33] 'With a mallet I persecute and shatter, through contrition and suffering, the heart of Man, when it is filled with old and hardened sins. My broom to sweep all, to brush, purge and clean. My tongue is my broom, my poker and my shovel with which I sweep all uncleanness through complete confession. Thus to punish it appropriately with my whipping rods I inflict pain and beating onto it, for its own good and improvement.' Translations from French are mine unless otherwise noted.

[34] Pomel, *Les voies*, pp. 377–8.

[35] Hagen, *Allegorical Remembrance: A Study of* The Pilgrimage of the Life of Man *as a Medieval Treatise on Seeing and Remembering* (Athens, GA: University of Georgia Press, 1990), pp. 39–40; Norman, *Metamorphoses*, pp. 192–4; Pomel, *Les voies*, pp. 381–4.

Christian's experience of them, and the need to identify, understand and conceptualise sin in order to overcome it. The work truly becomes a vernacular handbook, a metaphorical 'map' or *itinerarium* for travellers to the New Jerusalem.

It is not however because Deguileville's allegory is eminently Christian, functional and didactic that it can be dismissed as 'naïve'; the poem does not merely present a static, exemplary model of behaviour, but rather unpacks the philosophical and theological assumptions and implications of the broadly Augustinian or Platonic epistemology it encodes.[36] The emphasis in the poem is not on 'doing' what is morally right, but of 'discriminating' between the good and the bad, and Deguileville's account, then, is clearly finalised to equip its readers – fellow pilgrims – with sufficient epistemological and moral discernment to complete their own journey. The acts of reading and allegorical interpretation are assimilated to a process of moral and epistemological 'pilgrimage', the gradual acquisition of the metaphorical baggage – tools, skills or even armour – necessary to bring the journey to a happy end.[37] This didactic dimension is crucial for the understanding of Deguileville's work, and shapes not only the aim and the structure of his allegory, but also its method.[38]

The broad structure of the allegory, divided into four books, clearly articulates this didactic progression: the first part of Book 1 may in fact be seen as an initiation into the fundamental tenets of Christian doctrine and liturgy, and thus becomes a preparation for the subsequent journey.[39] The proto-catechism contained in the first part is as it were a theoretical survey of Christian doctrine, to be followed by the pilgrim's departure and his attempt to apply this abstract knowledge in his experience of the world.[40] This is followed by the Pilgrim's arming, and at the beginning of Book 2 the encounter with a variety of psychological abstractions such as Reason, Rude Understanding and Sapience, which functions as an induction into the human faculties of understanding and interpretation. After the pilgrim's ill-advised decision to follow the path of Idleness instead of the path of Occupation, Book 2 sees the beginning of the pilgrim's adventures in the world and his encounters with the Four 'intellectual' sins of Sloth, Pride, Envy and Anger. Book 3 relates the encounters with the three remaining, base sins, Avarice, Gluttony and Lechery and culminates with the pilgrim's half-hearted conversion through his immersion in the basin of Penitence. Book 4 describes the pilgrim's vain attempts to cross the Sea of the World until Grace Dieu shows him the Ship of Religion, identified with monastic life and prefiguring the New Jerusalem.

---

[36] See especially the discussion by Sarah Kay, *The Place of Thought: The Complexity of One in Late Medieval French Didactic Poetry* (Philadelphia, PA: University of Pennsylvania Press, 2007), pp. 70–94.

[37] This use of 'Pilgrimage' as epistemological metaphor is the central idea of Augustine's *De Doctrina*.

[38] See Tuve, *Allegorical Imagery*, in particular pp. 161–6; and Pomel, *Les voies*, pp. 457–511.

[39] Avril Henry, 'The Structure of Book 1 of The Pilgrimage of the Lyfe of the Manhode', *Neuphilologische Mitteilungen* 87 (1986), 128–41.

[40] Pomel, *Les voies*, pp. 163–7.

So, although the long and tortuous pilgrimage is not a simple and straightforward journey from A to B, Deguileville nevertheless structures his allegory according to a clear, finalised and well-ordered pattern.[41] The numerous difficulties, false starts, diversions we experience on the way never threaten to blow the actual allegory off-course, but are explorations of the pilgrim's difficulties in persevering in the quest for the straight and narrow way. Beneath the lively and at times bewildering surface of his narrative, Deguileville thus presents a clearly harnessed, teleological allegory, focusing on the final destination of the journey that is also the supreme signifier of the allegory, the Heavenly Jerusalem revealed in the initial vision. Deguileville's allegory clearly does not aim to be the kind of sophisticated and 'subversive' play of signifiers concocted by Jean de Meun,[42] but rather appears as a stabilising corrective to the dangerously slippery hermeneutics and epistemology of the *Roman de la rose*, Deguileville's counter-model evoked in the very first lines of the poem: 'En veillant avoie lëu, / Considere et bien vëu / Le biau romans de la Rose'[43] (*Vie¹* 9–11). Steven Wright has described the work as a 'contrepartie édifiante' of the *Roman de la rose*,[44] while C. S. Lewis, not entirely without reason, describes its author's intention as 'purely homiletic.'[45]

The four-book structure is thus clearly intended to organise the didactic material according to a manageable and meaningful conceptual structure, but is equally designed to help the readers and listeners navigate the text. In order to prevent his audience from going astray like his pilgrim and becoming engrossed with the mere surface of the adventure, Deguileville organises the reading of his poem over a period of four consecutive days, one for each book. At the beginning and ending of each book Deguileville supplies a reminder of this narrative-didactic framework, evoking the image of the Cistercian monk of Châalis reading and preaching to a

---

[41]  Avril Henry, '*The Pilgrimage of the Lyfe of the Manhode*: The Large Design, with Special Reference to Books 2–4', *Neuphilologische Mitteilungen* 87 (1986), 229–36. For the older, now superseded view of the *Vie* as a digressive encyclopaedic work lacking structure, see for instance Marion Lofthouse, '*Le Pèlerinage de vie humaine* by Guillaume de Deguileville with special Reference to the French MS 2 of the John Rylands Library', *Bulletin of the John Rylands Library* 19 (1935), 170–215.

[42]  See especially Alastair J. Minnis, *Magister Amoris: The Roman de la Rose and Vernacular Hermeneutics* (Oxford: Oxford University Press, 2001), pp. 1–34.

[43]  'Waking I had read, pondered and well understood the beautiful Romance of the Rose.'

[44]  Steven Wright, 'Deguileville's *Pèlerinage de Vie Humaine* as "Contrepartie Edifiante" of the *Roman de la Rose*', *Philological Quarterly* 68:4 (1989), 399–422. On the complex issue of Deguileville's debt to and attitude towards the *Roman de la rose*, and his change of attitude in the second redaction of the *Pèlerinage*, see also Sylvia Huot, The Romance of the Rose *and its Medieval Readers: Interpretation, Reception and Manuscript Transmission* (Cambridge: Cambridge University Press, 1993), pp. 207–38; John V. Fleming, 'The Moral Reputation of the *Roman de la Rose* before 1400', *Romance Philology* 18 (1965), 430–5; and Pierre-Yves Badel, *Le* Roman de la Rose *au XIVᵉ siècle: étude de la réception de l'oeuvre* (Genève: Droz, 1980).

[45]  Lewis, *Allegory of Love*, p. 264. For more sympathetic readings see Tuve, *Allegorical Imagery*, pp. 145–218; Hagen, *Allegorical Remembrance*; Pomel, *Les voies*, pp. 513–36 and 543–7.

flock of laypeople (*Vie¹* 15–34; 5055–66; 9046–54; 11404–6).[46] The near ubiquity of illuminations in Deguileville manuscripts representing this fictional didactic situation is a perfect measure of the success of Deguileville's strategy.[47] Accordingly, much recent work has often stressed the representativeness of Deguileville's work, commenting on his ability to articulate and synthesise a cluster of pre-existent ideas that were of crucial importance in shaping his contemporaries' world-view and preoccupations. So Joanne S. Norman comments on Deguileville's 'unerring choice of the most familiar and most popular themes of his time',[48] while Fabienne Pomel refers to the work as 'une oeuvre intégratrice, totalisante'.[49]

## Circulation, Reception and Impact

Deguileville's *Pèlerinage de vie humaine* exists in two distinct versions, *Vie¹* from 1331 and *Vie²* from 1355, shortly followed by the writing of the two remaining *Pèlerinages, Âme* and *Jhesucrist* (1355–8).[50] *Vie²* is a reworking of the earlier version, which may itself be a sign of the popularity reached by the work during Deguileville's lifetime. *Vie²* attempts to 'correct' and amend the imperfections of the earlier version, particularly its occasionally shaky theology, and is addressed to a more learned, clerical audience.[51] *Vie²* however looses the freshness and spontaneity of *Vie¹*, along with its storytelling appeal and the related focus on the instruction of the laity. The fictional context of the collective reading spread over four consecutive days is dropped, and the new version presents itself as a more learned work penned by an *auctor* and peppered with Latin quotations and elaborate theological excurses and explanations.[52] This coincides with a shift towards a new kind of reading, private, silent and emancipated from the linearity imposed by oral recitation,[53] as the poem displays an increased awareness of its own rapidly developing canonical status as a written source of reference.[54]

The wide-ranging and lasting appeal of Deguileville's *Pèlerinages* is reflected in the number of surviving manuscripts. Over 90 items containing one or several of the *Pèlerinages* survive, among which 84 manuscripts contain either *Vie¹* or *Vie²*, or

---

[46] Maupeu, *Pèlerins de vie humaine*, pp. 49–53.

[47] See Tuve, *Allegorical Imagery*, p. 181, and figs 27 and 28 on p. 152.

[48] Norman, *Metamorphoses*, p. 186.

[49] For a discussion of these 'synthetic' qualities of the *Vie*, see Pomel, *Les voies*, pp. 518–20, 543–7; Norman, *Metamorphoses*, pp. 186–94; Tuve, *Allegorical Imagery*, 182–7 and *passim*.

[50] For the classic account of Deguileville's life and works, see Edmond Faral, *Guillaume de Deguileville, moine de Châalis*. Histoire Littéraire de la France 39 (Paris: Imprimerie Nationale, 1952).

[51] Faral, *Deguileville*, pp. 29–30; Pomel, *Les voies*, pp. 524–7.

[52] Maupeu, *Pèlerins de vie humaine*, pp. 55–8, 60–2.

[53] See Paul H. Saenger, 'Silent Reading: Its Impact on Late Medieval Script and Society', *Viator* 13 (1982), 367–414, here 405–14. On Deguileville's role, see Pomel, *Les voies*, pp. 529–30.

[54] Faral, *Deguileville*, pp. 30–47; Tuve, *Allegorical Imagery*, pp. 148–9.

fragments of either.[55] The manuscripts range from lavishly illustrated, expensive copies to more clearly utilitarian ones, suggesting circulation among readers from widely different social backgrounds. Much the same story is told by the numerous adaptations and translations of Deguileville's *Pèlerinages*, whose large number is again an index of the text's popularity. *Âme*, *Vie[1]* and *Vie[2]* were all turned into French prose during the fifteenth century and later further revised and printed. The entire trilogy was refashioned into the *Roman des Trois Pèlerinages* in the early sixteenth century. The various printed versions of Deguileville's work in France, particularly *Vie*, appear to have been very popular.[56] Among the translations it is worth signalling an early Latin translation of *Âme* done under the supervision of Jean Gallopes for John, Duke of Bedford around 1427, and a further independent Latin translation.[57] *Vie* was translated into English on at least three different occasions, as well as into German, Dutch, Catalan and Spanish.[58]

A glance at the actual reception of Deguileville's trilogy, as opposed to its sole circulation, suggests that the work was not only popular, but that it quickly acquired canonical status, turning Deguileville into something like a vernacular *auctor*. The marginalia and annotations in many manuscripts, often in Latin, indeed suggest that the *Vie* in particular was used as a reference work.[59] Some of the manuscripts of Gallopes's French prose *Âme* supplement the text with a large number of biblical

---

[55] The latest count is to be found in Géraldine Veysseyre, 'Manuscrits à voir, manuscrits à lire, manuscrits lus? Les *marginalia* du *Pèlerinage de vie humaine* comme indices de sa réception médiévale', in Stephanie Viereck Gibbs Kamath and Marco Nievergelt, eds, *The Pèlerinage Allegories of Guillaume de Deguileville: Authority, Tradition, and Influence* (forthcoming). For previous overviews, see also Josephine E. Houghton, 'The Works of Guillaume Deguileville in Late Medieval England: Transmission, Reception and Context with Special Reference to *Piers Plowman*' (PhD thesis, University of Birmingham, 2007), pp. 15–32; and the chart drawn up by Géraldine Veysseyre in Fabienne Pomel and Fréderic Duval, eds, *Guillaume de Digulleville: les pèlerinages allégoriques* (Rennes: Presses Universitaires de Rennes, 2008), pp. 425–53. The overview draws on but updates the earlier work of Michael Camille, 'The Illustrated Manuscripts of Guillaume Deguileville's Pèlerinages, 1330–1426' (PhD thesis, Cambridge University, 1985); Tuve, *Allegorical Imagery*; Lofthouse, '*Pèlerinage de vie* French MS 2'; and Eugene Clasby, ed. and trans., Guillaume de Deguileville, *The Pilgrimage of Human Life* (New York: Garland, 1992).

[56] Maupeu, *Pèlerins de vie humaine*, pp. 269–304.

[57] Frédéric Duval, 'La traduction latine du *Pèlerinage de l'âme* de Guillaume de Digulleville par Jean Galopes (1427)', forthcoming.

[58] For a recent overview of the European circulation, see Ursula Peters, 'Das *Pèlerinage* – Corpus im europäischen Mittelalter: Retextualisierungsprozessen im Spiegel der Prologe', *Zeitschrift für deutsches Altertum und deutsche Literatur* 139:2 (2010), 160–90. See also Houghton, 'Deguileville in England', pp. 41–107. See also two forthcoming volumes, Andreas Kablitz and Ursula Peters, eds, *Mittelalterliche Textualität als Retextualisierung: Das „Pèlerinage"-Corpus des Guillaume de Deguileville im europäischen Mittelalter* (Heidelberg: Winter Verlag, forthcoming 2012); Kamath and Nievergelt, *The Pèlerinage Allegories of Guillaume de Deguileville*.

[59] Géraldine Veysseyre, 'Manuscrits à voir, manuscrits à lire', and ibid., 'Lecture linéaire ou consultation ponctuelle? Structuration du texte et apparats dans les manuscrits des *Pèlerinages*', in Pomel and Duval, eds, *Pèlerinages allégoriques*, pp. 315–30.

and patristic quotations in Latin that are undoubtedly intended to guarantee the orthodoxy and authority of Deguileville's work.[60] This desire to 'consecrate' an already canonical work is even more evident in Gallopes's later Latin prose version of *Âme*. The marginal quotations from the earlier French prose version are absorbed into the main body of the text, producing a more learned work in which the use of Latin confers the stamp of orthodoxy and authority. The tendency of later manuscripts and early printed versions to organise the trilogy or *Vie* through the generous use of rubrics, chapter headings and indexes confirms that it was used as a reference work, and further enhances its authority.[61] This also underscores that all of the later *remanieurs* were concerned with fostering what in their eyes was the correct reception of Deguileville's allegories. So for instance the anonymous Clerk of Angers's prose translation of *Vie*[1] (1464–5) reveals a didactic concern with guiding the readers' understanding by adding exegetical interpretations, explanatory tags and section or chapter headings.[62] The anonymous Cistercian monk rewriting the trilogy in verse in the early sixteenth century reveals a similar preoccupation, supplemented by a desire for textual stability fostered by the emergence of print.[63] Ultimately, then, such subsequent adaptations or translations and their glosses clearly share a wish of bringing out what is most universally meaningful and widely applicable in the *Pèlerinages*, consolidating the paradigmatic significance of Deguileville's *itinerarium* of human life and afterlife.

The success of Deguileville's trilogy, and of the *Vie* in particular, is also reflected in its wider impact on late medieval culture and imagination. So *Vie*[2] has recently been interpreted as a dynamic treatise on seeing and remembering.[64] Moreover, the manuscript illuminations of both *Vie* and *Âme* seem to have followed a strictly formalised pattern since an early stage, and quickly developed into a powerful and independent iconographic tradition.[65] This 'new' iconography of Vices and Virtues

---

[60] Frédéric Duval, 'La mise en prose du Pèlerinage de l'âme de Guillaume de Digulleville par Jean Galopes', *Romania* 128 (2010), 394–427.

[61] Fabienne Pomel, 'Enjeux d'un travail de réécriture: les incipits du *Pèlerinage de vie humaine* de Guillaume de Digulleville et leurs remaniements ultérieurs', *Le Moyen Age* 109 (2003), 457–71. See also Tuve, *Allegorical Imagery*, p. 179; Pomel, *Les voies*, pp. 531–2.

[62] For an edition and a detailed study of the French prose *Vie*, see Anne-Marie Legaré, *Le 'Pelerinage de Vie humaine' en prose de la Reine Charlotte de Savoie* (Ramsen: Heribert Tenschert, 2004). See also Maupeu, *Pèlerins de vie humaine*, pp. 293–314; and Houghton, 'Deguileville in England', pp. 80–8.

[63] Houghton, 'Deguileville in England', pp. 91–107.

[64] Hagen, *Allegorical Remembrance*.

[65] On the iconography of Deguileville manuscript illuminations see especially the work of Michael Camille, 'The Illustrated Manuscripts'; 'Reading the Printed Image: Illuminations and Woodcuts of the *Pèlerinage de la vie humaine* in the Fifteenth Century', in Sandra Hindman, ed., *Printing the Written Word: The Social History of Books circa 1450–1520* (Ithaca, NY: Cornell University Press, 1991), pp. 259–91; 'The Iconoclast's Desire: Deguileville's Idolatry in France and England', in Jeremy Dimmick, James Simpson and Nicolette Zeeman, eds, *Images, Idolatry, and Iconoclasm in Late Medieval England* (Oxford: Oxford University Press, 2002), pp. 151–71. See also Norman, *Metamorphoses*, pp. 181–224; Tuve, *Allegorical Imagery*, pp. 187–94;

often circulated independently from its source text, for instance in books of hours or tapestries or emblem books.[66] Deguileville has also been invoked as a source for late medieval French and English drama, and parts of the Vie are known to have been dramatised; this may have been the case with the Âme.[67] Finally, and most importantly in the present context, the Vie in particular seems to have inspired and sustained the composition of a number of subsequent original works.[68] Early readers of the Vie seem to have identified with its paradigmatic hero as is attested by a number of marginal annotations in several manuscripts.[69] Others, while starting from such identification, felt the need to redefine and adapt the paradigm of the pilgrim's *itinerarium* to allow the integration of their own experience. Among early evidence it is worth emphasising Philippe de Mézières's repeated mentions of the Vie, and his acceptance of Deguileville's work as a twofold model: it becomes the spiritual paradigm for the trajectory of the human life and the literary paradigm for his own *Songe du vieil pèlerin*, thus already taking as it were for granted the *auctoritas* of Deguileville, which will only be fully borne out in the following century.[70] Much the same can be said of Jean de Courcy's *Chemin de vaillance* discussed in Chapter 2, where Deguileville's influence is not explicitly invoked but ubiquitous.

It is now possible to take a closer look at the fortunes of Deguileville in England, the subject of Josephine Houghton-Meyer's 2007 doctoral thesis, unpublished to date. As emerges from the conclusions of Houghton's study, whilst direct, hard evidence for an early circulation of Deguileville's work in England is lacking, circumstantial evidence suggests that all three *Pèlerinages* had reached England by the early

Rosemarie Bergmann, ed., *Die Pilgerfahrt zum himmlischen Jerusalem: ein allegorisches Gedicht des Spätmittelalters aus der Heidelberger Bilderhandschrift Cod. Pal. Lat. 1969 'Pèlerinage de vie humaine' des Guillaume de Deguileville* (Wiesbaden: Reichert, 1983).

[66] Norman, *Metamorphoses*, pp. 195–6, 225–7; Richard K. Emmerson, 'A "Large Order of the Whole": Intertextuality and Interpictoriality in the *Hours of Isabella Stuart*', *Studies in Iconography* 28 (2007), 51–110; on the impact of the iconography of the *Âme*, see *The Pilgrimage of the Soul. Vol. 1: A Critical Edition of the Middle English Dream Vision*, ed. Rosemarie Potz McGerr (New York: Garland, 1990), pp. xlv–lv; on emblem books, see Anne-Elisabeth Spica, 'L'emblématique de dévotion, une héritière indirecte des *Pèlerinages* spirituels allégoriques de Guillaume de Diguileville', in Pomel and Duval, eds, *Pèlerinages allégoriques*, pp. 53–80.

[67] This is the *Jeux de Pèlerinage humaine*, edited by Gustave Cohen, *Mystères et Moralités du Manuscrit 617 de Chantilly* (Paris: Champion, 1920), pp. 91–130. On this and the influence on English drama, see also Potz McGerr, *Pilgrimage of the Soul*, pp. lii–liii. Robert L. A. Clark and Pamela Sheingorn, 'Were Guillaume de Digulleville's *Pèlerinages* "Plays"? The Case for Arras MS 845 as Performative Anthology', *European Medieval Drama* 12 (2008), 109–47. For the *Vie's* impact on a different French morality play, see Stéphanie Le Briz-Orgeur, 'La réécriture du *Pèlerinage de vie humaine* dans la *Moralité de Bien Avisé et Mal Avisé*', in Pomel and Duval, eds, *Pèlerinages allégoriques*, pp. 365–92.

[68] For the most detailed and revealing account of Deguileville's legacy, see Maupeu, *Pèlerins de vie humaine*. See also Wenzel, 'Pilgrimage of Life'.

[69] Houghton, 'Deguileville in England', p. 33.

[70] Mézières, *Songe du vieil pèlerin*; for discussion see Pomel, *Les voies*, pp. 544–5; and Maupeu, *Pèlerins de vie humaine*, pp. 341–99.

fifteenth century. *Vie* and *Âme* were particularly successful as is attested by their fifteenth-century English translations, and although only the English *Âme* was printed by Caxton, early printed French adaptations of Deguileville's work are known to have circulated in England, and would have been easily accessible to English authors working within the tradition.

The earliest full English translation from Deguileville's allegories is the anonymous prose *Pilgrimage of the Soul*, dated to 1413 by the translator's colophon. The translator is concerned to ensure an appropriate, orthodox reception of the work, and takes care to align the text with biblical and patristic authorities. The translator also aims to make Deguileville's work accessible to a wider range of readers, insisting in particular on the universal applicability and significance of Deguileville's allegory. The didactic dimension of the work is systematically enhanced, and its comprehension facilitated by the use of prose and the division into books and chapters. The translation remains otherwise close to its source, except for the amplification of a concern with heresy, possibly motivated by an anti-Lollard agenda. The choice of Deguileville's work for such a polemical purpose would again confirm its orthodox and canonical status.[71] The text survives in ten copies, and fragments of it are contained in three further manuscripts. The manuscript context suggests that it had both spiritual and literary authority, and its annotations attest its continued circulation and popularity during the fifteenth and sixteenth centuries. The work was printed twice in 1483 by Caxton, who attributes it to Lydgate.[72]

The prose translation of *Vie*[1] as *The Pilgrimage of the Lyfe of the Manhode*, dated to the first quarter of the fifteenth century, shares many of these features. The anonymous work is again a close rendering of the original, and is provided in many manuscripts with rubrications, chapter numbers and headings. As in *Soul* the translator often simplifies the presentation of the material without altering the content itself. The style of the translation is humble and straightforward, avoiding any unnecessarily ornate developments, and is clearly the fruit of a 'utilitarian', didactic appreciation of the source. It survives in six manuscripts, five of which are heavily annotated in various hands.[73]

Lydgate's verse translation of *Vie*[2] was made in 1426 for Lord Salisbury with the purpose of making Deguileville's work accessible to a wider audience unacquainted with French.[74] While it is entirely different in style it nevertheless shares the didactic

---

[71] See Potz McGerr, *Pilgrimage of the Soul*, pp. xxi–c; Houghton, 'Deguileville in England', pp. 108–28.

[72] *The Pylgremage of the Sowle* (1483 – STC 6473).

[73] Henry, *Manhode*, vol. 1, pp. xxvii–l; Houghton, 'Deguileville in England', pp. 128–39.

[74] John Lydgate, trans., Guillaume Deguileville, *The Pilgrimage of the Life of Man*, 3 vols, ed. F. J. Furnivall and Katharine B. Locock, EETS OS 78, 83 and 92 (London: Kegan Paul, Trench, Trübner & co., 1899–1904), ll. 135–8. The controversy over Lydgate's authorship may be considered settled after the discovery by Rowena Archer of an inventory of Alice Chaucer's books, containing a mention of 'the pilgrimage translated by domine John Lydgate out of frensh', in Oxford, MS Bodleian Library Ewelme A 47 (3); see Rowena Archer, 'Alice Chaucer, Duchess

intent of the other translations, which in Lydgate's case takes the form of typically verbose amplification of his source. What is added is rarely new and in most cases simply expands or dilutes elements from the source. Lydgate explicitly invites the readers' identification with the pilgrim of Deguileville's *Vie*[2] and encourages the application of Deguileville's spiritual paradigm to individual situations.[75] The translation confirms that Lydgate too, in his case by developing the exegetical role of the narrator, is concerned with ensuring the correct reception of a text he considers highly orthodox, authoritative and canonical.[76]

The *Vie* appears to have been translated a third time into English, by John Skelton, as he claims in *The Garland of Laurel* (ll. 1219–22), but no copy of this translation is known to survive.[77] The patroness of the translation is usually assumed to have been Margaret Beaufort, Henry VII's mother,[78] and the date of composition can be conjecturally situated between 1496 and 1501.[79] The existence of Skelton's translation does not only confirm the lasting appeal of the *Vie* in England, but equally suggests that Deguileville enjoyed particular favour at the court of Henry VII. Henry's Royal Library in fact also contained a copy of Vérard's 1499 edition of the Clerk of Angers's prose version illuminated by hand,[80] and a copy of the printed edition of Gallopes's prose *Âme*.[81] A further early printed work in English by William Hendred is sometimes listed as a translation of Deguileville, but is in fact a totally separate work. The work was published twice, as *Peregrinatio*

of Suffolk (d. 1475) and Her Books', talk given at the Maison Française d'Oxford on Tuesday 16 January 2007. See also Karen K. Jambeck, 'The Library of Alice Chaucer, Duchess of Suffolk', *Profane Arts* 6:2 (1998), 106–35. For the earlier debate, see Kathryn Walls, 'Did Lydgate Translate the *Pèlerinage de Vie Humaine?', Notes and Queries* 24 (1977), 103–5; and Richard Firth Green, 'Lydgate and Deguileville Once More', *Notes and Queries* 25 (1978), 105–6.

[75] *The Pilgrimage of the Life of Man*, 11. 45–6, 80.

[76] See Lisa H. Cooper, '"Markys … off the Workman": Heresy, Hagiography, and the Heavens in *The Pilgrimage of the Life of Man*', in Lisa H. Cooper and Andrea Denny-Brown, eds, *Lydgate Matters: Poetry and Material Culture in the Fifteenth Century* (Basingstoke: Macmillan, 2007), pp. 89–111.

[77] John Skelton, *The Complete English Poems*, ed. John Scattergood (Harmondsworth: Penguin, 1983), p. 347.

[78] See for instance, Susan Powell, 'Lady Margaret Beaufort and her Books', *The Library*, 6th series, 20:3 (1998), 197–240, here 231.

[79] Houghton, 'Deguileville in England', p. 166.

[80] This is San Marino, Huntington Library, 103394, reproduced in facsimile in Alfred W. Pollard, *Le Pelerinaige de Vie Humaine: Reproduced in Facsimile from the Printed Book in the Library of the Earl of Ellesmere with a Bibliographical Note by Alfred W. Pollard* (Manchester: Roxburghe Club, 1912).

[81] London, British Library, IB 41186. The edition contains the signature of the royal librarian Quentin Poulet, after Vérard's colophon. The work must have entered the Library between 1499 and 1506. See Houghton, 'Deguileville in England', pp. 43–5; and Janet Backhouse, 'The Royal Library from Edward IV to Henry VII', in Lotte Hellinga and J. B. Trapp, eds, *The Cambridge History of the Book in Britain*, vol. 3 (Cambridge: Cambridge University Press, 1999), pp. 267–73.

*humani generis* and *The Booke of the Pylgrymage of Man*.[82] Hendred presents the work as a translation of a French original, the 'Pelerynage de LHomme', also 'Peregrinatio humani generis' in Latin, transmitted via an intermediary English verse translation, which has understandably led bibliographers to assume that this was in fact a translation of Deguileville's work. The work is much shorter, and elaborates the broad analogy between the pilgrimage of life and the liturgical year, making the various Church holidays the stations of man's journey through time. I have not been able to identify any potential French source, and the relation of the work to the supposed English verse exemplar remains equally obscure and deserves further enquiry.[83] There is no connection to Guillaume Dubellay's *Peregrinatio Humana*, a condensed Latin adaptation of *Vie* printed in 1509.[84]

Translations of shorter extracts from Deguileville's works were also made. This is the case of Chaucer's 'ABC to the Virgin' from the *Vie*, and Hoccleve's translation of the 'Lament to the Virgin' from *Âme*, also recurring in the *Jhesucrist* from where Hoccleve may indeed have taken it, as argued by Houghton.[85] Chaucer's 'ABC' is the earliest surviving proof of English interest in Deguileville,[86] and may have substantially shaped the subsequent reception of his works. The dedication to Blanche of Lancaster reproduced in Speght's printed edition from 1602 is now generally rejected as apocryphal, although the argument for an early date has been convincingly revived recently.[87] It survives in nine manuscripts divorced from the original context of the *Vie*, was later integrated by the anonymous author of *Manhode*, and must therefore have circulated widely. Lydgate had equally planned to integrate Chaucer's prayer into his translation, but although the surviving manuscripts leave space for the poem to be added, the blanks were never actually filled. More remarkable than the translation itself, though, are its implications for Chaucer's knowledge of Deguileville's *Pèlerinages*. In fact Chaucer's use of imagery and motifs in his translation suggests that he knew the whole of the *Vie* and the *Âme*, as Helen Phillips has shown, and may have known *Jhesucrist* as well, as

[82]  Respectively, London: Pynson, 1508 – STC 19917.5; London: R. Faques, 1520 – STC 19918. See also A. E. B. Coldiron, 'Translation's Challenge to Critical Categories: Verses from French in the Early English Renaissance', *The Yale Journal of Criticism* 16:2 (2003), 324–5, n. 32; Powell, 'Lady Margaret Beaufort and her Books', 231.

[83]  Copy consulted: Oxford University, Queen's College, Sel.d.81(2).

[84]  Guillaume Dubellay's *Peregrinatio Humana* (Paris: Gilles de Gourmont, 1509), discussed in George Hugo Tucker, *Homo Viator: Itineraries of Exile, Displacement and Writing in Renaissance Europe* (Genève: Droz, 2003), pp. 100–109 and *passim*.

[85]  Houghton, 'Deguileville in England', pp. 167–91.

[86]  Geoffrey Chaucer, 'The ABC', in Larry Benson, ed., *The Riverside Chaucer*, 3rd edn (Oxford: Oxford University Press, 1988), pp. 637–40.

[87]  For Speght's edition, see *The Vvorkes of our Ancient and Lerned English Poet, Geffrey Chaucer, Newly Printed*. (London, 1602 – STC 5080–1). For the dedication to Blanche of Lancaster, see for instance Derek Pearsall, *The Life of Geoffrey Chaucer: A Critical Biography* (Oxford: Blackwell, 1994), p. 84. For an argument in favour of an early date, see Kathryn L. Lynch, 'Dating Chaucer', *Chaucer Review* 42:1 (2007), 1–22.

Houghton has argued.[88] Furthermore, an influence of Deguileville's *Pèlerinages* on Chaucer's other works has been repeatedly postulated, for instance for the *Book of the Duchess, House of Fame, The Parliament of Fowls*, as well as *The Canterbury Tales* with its pilgrimage framework, and would deserve further attention.[89]

The case of Hoccleve's lament is remarkably similar to Chaucer's 'ABC', as it too was conceived as a translation of a freestanding lyric, but was later interpolated into an independent, complete translation of the *Âme*.[90] The complaint survives in a single copy as an independent translation, but was integrated into the Middle English *Pilgrimage of the Soul*, and reprinted in Caxton's two editions in 1483. Hoccleve states that the translation was made for Joan FitzAlan, Countess of Hereford,[91] which again suggests that Deguileville's work enjoyed wide favour and circulation among the English aristocracy. Furthermore, Houghton's study of the translation has revealed that Hoccleve was relying on his acquaintance with at least two of Deguileville's three *Pèlerinages*,[92] and Stephanie Kamath's recent study has brought into the foreground the poet's self-representation in terms of an allegorical vocabulary heavily influenced by Deguileville and the *Rose* elsewhere in his *oeuvre*.[93]

It is worth briefly remarking on a few further connections linking Deguileville's work to England. Both Jean Gallopes's French prose version of the *Âme* (1422–7) and its later translation into Latin (1427) were produced at the behest of John, Duke of Bedford. The two surviving manuscripts of the Latin version are known to have circulated in England, although the exact date of their arrival from France remains unknown. One of the manuscripts contains annotations in English in a fifteenth-century hand.[94] The case for Deguileville's popularity with English readers

---

[88]  Helen Phillips, 'Chaucer's French Translations', *Nottingham Medieval Studies* 37 (1993), 65–82; ibid., 'Chaucer and Deguileville: The *ABC* in Context', *Medium Ævum* 62 (1993), 1–19; Houghton, 'Deguileville in England', p. 172.

[89]  For instance, V. A. Kolve, *Chaucer and the Imagery of Narrative: The First Five Canterbury Tales* (Stanford, CA: Stanford University Press, 1984), pp. 9, 12, 18, 58, 230 and *passim*; William Calin, *The French Tradition and the Literature of Medieval England* (Toronto: University of Toronto Press, 1994), pp. 302, 184–97; Kathryn L. Lynch, *Chaucer's Philosophical Visions* (Cambridge: D. S. Brewer, 2000), p. 33; Piero Boitani, '"His desir wol fle withouten wynges": Mary and Love in Fourteenth-Century Poetry', in Joerg O. Fichte, ed., *Chaucer's Frame Tales: The Physical and the Metaphysical* (Cambridge: D. S. Brewer; Tübingen: Günter Narr, 1987), pp. 83–128; David R. Pichaske, *The Movement of the Canterbury Tales: Chaucer's Literary Pilgrimage* (Norwood, PA: Norwood Editions, 1977); Rosemond Tuve, 'Guillaume's Pilgrim and the House of Fame', *Modern Language Notes* 45:8 (1930), 518–22; Charles Muscatine, 'The Parliament of Fowls: Explanatory Notes', in Benson, ed., *The Riverside Chaucer*, p. 994; Dyas, *Pilgrimage*, pp. 171–204; Stephanie Viereck Gibbs Kamath, *Authorship and First-Person Allegory in Late Medieval England and France* (Cambridge: D. S. Brewer, 2012), Chapter 2.

[90]  Houghton, 'Deguileville in England', pp. 177–91.

[91]  Thomas Hoccleve, 'Conpleynte paramont', in *'My Compleinte' and Other Poems*, ed. Roger Ellis (Exeter: University of Exeter Press, 2001), p. 60.

[92]  Houghton, 'Deguileville in England', p. 190.

[93]  Kamath, *Authorship and First-Person Allegory*, Chapter 3.

[94]  Houghton, 'Deguileville in England', pp. 42–60.

is thus further strengthened by the production of the French and Latin prose *Âme*, and the subsequent circulation in England of the Latin version.[95]

The French prose version of *Vie* by the Anonymous of Angers may also have ties to England. It was produced for the second wife of René d'Anjou, Jeanne de Laval, whose step-daughter Marguerite had married Henry VI in 1444. Anne-Marie Legaré has suggested that Jeanne de Laval may have been inspired to commission a French prose version after becoming acquainted through Marguerite with the English *Manhode* in prose, while Michael Camille supposes that it was rather Marguerite who initiated or fostered the interest of the English court in Deguileville.[96] While the two possible connections need not exclude one another and may be complementary, neither of them can be proven, but again highlight the pointed interest in Deguileville in fifteenth-century England.

The *Pèlerinages* certainly inspired or influenced further poetic works in England, apart from the ones mentioned above or studied in the following chapters. In this respect it is worth mentioning *Piers Plowman*, a work that shares a number of important structural and conceptual features with Deguileville's allegories. While a connection to the *Pèlerinages* cannot be demonstrated conclusively, the cumulative evidence weighs decidedly in favour of direct influence.[97] I have recently argued elsewhere that there is good reason to believe that the *Gawain*-Poet may also have been acquainted with Deguileville's allegory, and further work needs to be done on this connection.[98]

To conclude, then, it can safely be said that Deguileville's works circulated widely in England between the late fourteenth and late sixteenth centuries, across a wide spectrum of social groups ranging from the aristocracy to the literate laity, as is suggested by the stylistic variety of the different adaptations and the information concerning its reception. Many major English poets, such as Chaucer, Langland, Lydgate, Hoccleve and Skelton, engaged in active responses to Deguileville's work, which underscores both the literary authority and religious orthodoxy of the *Pèlerinages*. Most striking is the pervasive sense of paradigmatic significance that readers attach to *Vie* and *Âme* in particular, respectively understood as sketches of man's journey through life and the afterlife, and thus ensuring their lasting success and appeal well into the seventeenth century.[99]

---

[95] See Duval, 'La traduction latine du *Pèlerinage de l'âme*' and 'La mise en prose du *Pèlerinage de l'âme*'.

[96] Legaré, *Le 'Pelerinage de Vie humaine' en prose*, p. 176–7; Camille, 'The Illustrated Manuscripts', p. 89, n. 49; Houghton, 'Deguileville in England', pp. 62–3.

[97] John Burrow, *Langland's Fictions* (Oxford: Oxford University Press, 1993), pp. 114–18 and *passim*; George Kane, *Chaucer and Langland: Historical and Textual Approaches* (London: The Athlone Press, 1989), p. 135; Houghton, 'Deguileville in England', pp. 8–13.

[98] Marco Nievergelt, 'Paradigm, Intertext, or Residual Allegory: Guillaume de Deguileville and the *Gawain*-Poet', *Medium Ævum* 80:1 (2011), 18–40.

[99] As witnessed for instance by William Baspoole's 'Laudian' rewriting of *Manhode* by William Baspoole, *The Pilgrime*, ed. Kathryn Walls and Marguerite Stobo (Tempe, AZ: Renaissance English Text Society, 2008).

## Paradigm?

If the *Pèlerinage de vie humaine* really was a paradigm for the Christian life on earth, why did it ever need to be rewritten, adapted and altered? Whilst a study of the reception and circulation of the text largely confirms the *Vie*'s status as a spiritual handbook and paradigm, a number of elements already present in the source also suggest different interpretations. *Vie* purports to outline the pattern of individual redemption for a Christian Everyman by tracing the metaphorical *itinerarium* to reach the celestial city, but this paradigmatic pattern is occasionally disrupted by more specific, narrow and local references. In particular, the question of the identity of the pilgrim raises a number of problems. The pilgrim is represented as a suitably naïve young Everyman for most of his journey, and is clearly identified as a layman during the sacramental excursus in Book 1. He is given the sheathed sword and bound-up keys appropriate to the layman (*Vie¹* 1279–302) and excluded from ordination. Yet at a later stage in the narrative the pilgrim, after his repeated unsuccessful attempts to cross the 'Sea of the World', finally boards the 'Ship of Religion', which is an unmistakeable allegory of monastic life as the poet takes care to detail (*Vie¹* 12433–972).

This introduces the possibility that rather than being an account of a paradigmatic pilgrimage of a Christian Everyman, the *Vie* may be read as a strictly monastic allegory, preaching conversion to religious life and *contemptus mundi*, or even a sort of 'autobiographical allegory' recounting the experiences of Guillaume de Deguileville himself in the slightly de-personalised form imposed by the allegorical mode.[100] Furthermore, Deguileville's choice of the pilgrimage allegory can be explained with reference to the tradition of representing monasticism as a form of *peregrinatio in stabilitate* since the early days of the desert fathers.[101] Yet the poet goes at least some way towards resolving this inner contradiction by specifying that the monastic *via* is not an obliged passage but merely an alternative to the longer and harder path along the 'hedge of penitence', and the monastic *via* becomes a sort of shortcut to the Holy City, as Grace Dieu states:

> Et se vouloies abregier
> Ton chemin et bien acourcier
> D'aler en la belle cite
> Ou d'aler tu es excite,
> Encor bien je t'i merroie
> Sans point aler a la longue haie. (*Vie¹* 12411–6; see also 13013–14)[102]

---

[100] Debate over the nature and extent of the autobiographical dimension of the *Vie* is ongoing; see variously Faral, *Deguileville*, pp. 9–10; Hagen, *Allegorical Remembrance*, pp. 114–15; Pomel, *Les voies*, pp. 415–20 and *passim*; Henry, *Manhode*, 'Introduction', pp. xxvii, xxx–xxxi; and Maupeu, *Pèlerins de vie humaine*, esp. pp. 197–215.

[101] Dyas, *Pilgrimage*, pp. 205–15.

[102] 'And if you want to shorten your path and be faster to travel to the beautiful city where you desire to go, even so I will conduct you, without having to go along the lengthy hedge.' For discussion, see also Pomel, *Les voies*, pp. 310–12.

Furthermore, the specific monastic connotations of the Ship do not efface its broader meaning as an allegory of the Church. Deguileville here is in fact trying to have his cake and eat it: he tries to integrate self-referential elements into a larger pattern of universal, impersonal allegory, and thus attempts to subsume individual experience within a universal paradigm. This tension between historically situated, individual experience and a more universal, transhistorical paradigm is fundamental for the later development of the tradition discussed in the following chapters.

Whereas autobiographical references in *Vie¹* are at best oblique, in *Vie²* Deguileville clearly projects himself in the role of the pilgrim and vents his frustration over internal conflicts in his own monastery of Châalis, which clearly disrupts the peaceful allegorical resolution that in *Vie¹* coincided with the pilgrim's entry into the monastery, prefiguration of the depersonalised state attained in the Heavenly City.[103] The problem for Deguileville here seems to lie in the realisation that individual experience is rarely reducible to a single, universal paradigm. In *Vie¹* the creation of a single, universal narrative of the 'Pilgrimage of Life' had invited the reduction of all individual experience to the bare bones of the conceptual paradigm. From this perspective, writing allegory itself becomes a means of reaffirming the schematic order of transcendence and reintegrating individual experience within this ontological framework.[104] Yet the very concept of a 'spiritual paradigm' allows for no expansion, alteration or variation of the model provided; 'autobiographical' self-referentiality is perceived as reaching outside of the confines of the paradigm into the vicissitudes of *saeculum*, and is therefore understood as fragmentation, loss of meaning and descent into chaos.[105] The mere existence of *Vie²* is itself the best index of the impossibility of this task, as it suggests the failure of *Vie¹* to provide a viable paradigm in the face of the inexhaustible variety and unpredictability of human experience. Accordingly with the move from the first to the second redaction of *Vie*, the mood shifts from desire of integration to existential anxiety, and Fabienne Pomel has therefore described Deguileville's attempt to create a definitive, totalising, universal allegory of human experience as obsessive.[106] The poet is also increasingly concerned with human fallibility and the emotional experience of time and death, preoccupations that constantly threaten to disrupt and explode the paradigmatic, transhistorical and spiritual significance of his work.[107] The more Deguileville attempts to revisit his model in the hope of integrating his discordant personal experience, the more he becomes self-referential and the more the paradigm itself begins to disintegrate. Most interestingly, then, *Vie²* may be seen as documenting Deguileville's reader-response to his own *Vie¹*, and as revealing his failure to fit his own individual experience of the 'pilgrimage of life' within the paradigm he himself had provided.

---

[103] Pomel, *Les voies*, pp. 194–205.

[104] Pomel, *Les voies*, pp. 457–88.

[105] Ladner, 'Homo Viator', pp. 251–9.

[106] Pomel, *Les voies*, pp. 513–36. Pomel also speaks of 'étouffement du syntagmatique par le paradigmatique', p. 523, and 'amplification allégorique comme cancer narratif', p. 521.

[107] Maupeu, *Pèlerins de vie humaine*, pp. 215–66.

Later allegorical quests derived from the *Vie* similarly interrogate the very possibility of providing a paradigmatic account of the 'pilgrimage of life', although they invariably modulate the identity of the protagonist in more knightly terms. In doing so, these later allegories of course borrow from the genre of knightly romance to provide a more precise, specific model of identity for their knightly protagonist. They also develop, however, the tendencies towards autobiography already latent in Deguileville, and also exploit the numerous chivalric tropes that render the didactic allegory of the *Vie* so lively and appealing. Indeed, Deguileville already flirts with romance conventions, which earned his work the subtitle of 'li romans du moisne' in some manuscripts,[108] carried over into the English prose *Manhode* as 'þe romaunce of the monk' (7295). So the description of the pilgrim's Pauline armour (*Vie¹* 3813–4492) is certainly didactic, but plays with the familiar epic-heroic *topos* of the hero's arming.[109] Also, beyond the moral didacticism invested in the arming scene, its technical precision and specificity would certainly appeal to a knightly audience, as would the nearly ubiquitous representation of the Kingdom of Heaven as an aristocratic court, or the description of Grace Dieu as 'fille de l'empereur / Qui sur tous autres est seigneur' (*Vie¹* 297–8),[110] thus supplementing chivalric tropes with courtly ones, playing on notions of erotic subjection and service. Elsewhere, while the pilgrim travels on foot for most of his allegorical journey, on lines 8691–724 he is suddenly represented as riding on the back of the allegorical horse that signifies renown, which would no doubt resonate with the chivalric shame-culture of the poem's aristocratic readers.

Most striking for its use of chivalric *topoi*, though, is Deguileville's representation of the final destination of the journey, the New Jerusalem, as a fortress of faith. In his initial vision the dreamer describes the city guarded by 'Cherubin [qui] portier estoit / Qui un fourbi glaive tenoit, / Bien esmoulu a deux taillans.' He metes out death, precondition for entering the city and joining Christ, 'Le prince neis de la cite' and the martyrs, 'ses chavaliers, ses champions, ses soudoiers' (*Vie¹* 63–78).[111] Deguileville here borrows chivalric language to express the concept of Christian martyrdom, an idea that is again elaborated in the final stage of the poem when the dreamer reaches the Ship of Religion, pre-figuration of the Holy City. By analogy with the New Jerusalem, the convent is a 'chastiau' (*Vie¹* 12,541), also guarded by an armed porter 'Poaur de Dieu', armed with a 'grant macue' (*Vie¹* 12,580–9). The knightly metaphor is further expanded, and the Porter's blow is described in terms of a knighting ceremony: 'Bien doit ains soufrir colee / Chevalier qui entre en estour'

---

[108] *Vie¹*, p. 423.

[109] For an overview, see Derek Brewer, 'The Arming of the Warrior in European Literature and Chaucer', in Edward Vasta and Zacharias P. Thundy, eds, *Chaucerian Problems and Perspectives* (Notre Dame, IN: University of Notre Dame Press, 1979), pp. 221–43.

[110] 'Daughter of the Emperor, who is Lord over all others.'

[111] Respectively, 'The Cherub, who was the porter, held a shining blade, well sharpened with a double edge'; 'the very prince of the city'; 'his knights, his champions, his soldiers'.

(ll. 12,614–15).[112] The pilgrim joins the company of Christ's knights and soldiers by being metaphorically initiated into their order, as chivalric and monastic metaphors are fused to signify his willingness to submit to a sacrificial *imitatio Christi*.

These descriptions, while they are rather short, nevertheless frame the entire pilgrimage, and thus succeed in lending to it a chivalric aura, casting it as an allegorical knightly quest for the spiritual citadel of the New Jerusalem. Deguileville himself may already be drawing on a number of widely known interrelated traditions: the conception of the *miles christianus*,[113] the identification of Christ as Knight, previous vice-virtue iconography and literature,[114] or even works like the prose 'Vulgate' *Lancelot*, and its *Queste del Saint Graal*, incidentally a work with interesting Cistercian connections.[115] While the use of knightly elements in these passages is largely metaphorical, their presence nevertheless invites an elaboration of the military and knightly undertones that nourish Deguileville's allegory. If Deguileville allegorises knighthood, later works in turn literalise his Pauline allegories; and if Deguileville uses knighthood as a metaphor for monasticism, others like Ramon Llull use priestly metaphors to endow knighthood itself with an almost sacramental mystique.[116] With a metaphor as slippery and as evocative as that of the Pauline *miles christianus*, the temptation to 'literalise' it seems to have been too strong, and runs through all subsequent knightly adaptations of the *Vie* studied in the following chapters. In all these works, the identity of the 'knight' is fluctuating and unstable: he is suspended between being an inclusive Everyman, a more specifically defined representative of a social group, and a more properly 'errant', conflicted self in search of both corporate and individual identity during a time of crisis.

---

[112] Respectively: a 'castle', 'Fear of God', and 'a great mace'; 'A Knight who desires to enter into battle must needs receive his *colée*.' The image appears to have influenced the conclusion of *Sir Gawain and the Green Knight*, where Gawain's 'beheading' is presented as a mock-knighting ceremony; see Nievergelt, 'Paradigm, Intertext, or Residual Allegory'.

[113] See Wang, *Miles Christianus*.

[114] Michael Evans, 'An Illustrated Fragment of Peraldus's *Summa* of Vice: Harleian MS 3244', *Journal of the Warburg and Courtauld Institutes* 45 (1982), 14–68, particularly 17–20 for the early development of allegorical knighthood.

[115] Richard Barber, 'Chivalry, Cistercianism and the Grail', in Carol Dover, ed., *A Companion to the Lancelot-Grail Cycle* (Cambridge: D. S. Brewer, 2003), pp. 3–12.

[116] Llull for instance exploits the analogy of knightly armour and priestly vestments to exalt the status of chivalry; see the English version printed by Caxton, *The Book of the Ordre of Chivalry*, ed. A. T. P. Byles, EETS OS 168 (London: Oxford University Press, 1926), pp. 76ff.

# 2

# *Chivalric Transformations in Fifteenth-Century France*

The four works discussed in this chapter are derived from the model of Deguileville's *Vie*. Structural and thematic parallels in all four works unmistakeably point either directly to Deguileville, or possibly to other derivative texts in his tradition.[1] In the case of René d'Anjou's *Livre du cuer d'amour espris* (1457–77) and Olivier de La Marche's *Chevalier délibéré* (1483) this can be confirmed with reference to the presence of Deguileville manuscripts in the environment in which the poets wrote. Jean de Courcy's *Chemin de vaillance* (1424) is more obviously derivative, and the debt to Deguileville is immediately apparent, whilst Thomas de Saluces's *Livre du chevalier errant* (1494–6) entertains a more complex but no less intense relationship with *Vie*. The four works may be said to constitute a sub-genre by themselves but are also crucially important for the later development of the tradition in sixteenth-century England. So de Courcy's *Chemin* survives in a single manuscript prepared for King Edward IV of England, which was in the Royal Library and appears to have been used, I argue, by Stephen Hawes. Thomas's *Chevalier*, on the other hand, was a model for Jean de Cartheny, author of the *Voyage du chevalier errant* (1552–7), which was in turn translated by William Goodyear in 1581 and will be discussed in Chapter 5. Olivier de La Marche's *Chevalier délibéré* was translated on two occasions, by Stephen Bateman as *The Travayled Pylgrime* (1569) and Lewes Lewkenor as *The Resolved Gentleman* (1594), discussed in Chapters 4 and 6 respectively. Only René d'Anjou's allegory cannot be proven to have had any direct or indirect impact on the later English developments, although it has been suggested that it may have influenced the Middle Scots *King Hart*.[2] The poem was nevertheless included since it marks an important stage in the evolution of the tradition.

---

[1]  Such as the work of Christine de Pizan, deeply influenced by Deguileville; see Maupeu, *Pèlerins de vie humaine*, pp. 401–74. Maupeu also discusses the works of Jean de Courcy, Thomas de Saluces and Olivier de La Marche on pp. 475–529 more fully than is possible in the present context, and I accordingly refer to his account for a complementary discussion.

[2]  William Calin, 'The French Presence in Medieval Scotland: Le roi René and *King Hart*', *Florilegium* 24 (2007), 11–20.

All four works studied here share an impulse to modulate Deguileville's funda-mental paradigm in more chivalric terms, replacing Deguileville's pilgrim with a questing knight. It is no coincidence that all four texts discussed in this section come from the pens of knights, and that their allegories therefore acquire more pronounced 'autobiographical' traits.[3] The writing of a more strictly knightly adap-tation of the 'pilgrimage of life' model brings with it a number of problems. The knight, unlike Deguileville's ascetic and ultimately monastic pilgrim, cannot rely on a single system of values to guide his wanderings. He is engaged in a continuous negotiation between different, contrasting and often contradictory demands of the knightly ideal on the one hand, and Christian moral strictures on the other.[4] This balance between moral integrity and calculated worldliness is felt to be an ideal more demanding than that of a radical *contemptus mundi*: 'plus est legiere chose tous les biens du monde laissier a un seul coup que elles retenir et elles neant amer', as Thomas de Saluces muses towards the end of his hero's quest.[5] As a consequence the pilgrimage of human life, while it remains focused on a vanishing point beyond earthly existence, becomes increasingly embroiled with the contingencies of individual life on earth rather than attempting their reduction to a universal, eschatologically focused paradigm of purely moral struggle. Social, historical and political realities infiltrate and at times all but undermine Deguileville's transhistorical spiritual allegory, and create the possibilities for a more complex self-representation suspended between the exemplary and the more strictly 'autobiographical'.

The works discussed in this chapter may be characterised in many ways as experimental, since they attempt to negotiate a middle way between Deguileville's bipartition of the human pilgrimage into the mutually exclusive ways of Occu-pation and Idleness, salvation and perdition. Between the two extremes of the broad and the narrow way are revealed an infinity of intermediate solutions, where the significance of the knight's adventures is not always reducible to a simple, clear-cut moral dichotomy. This opens the door to the unlimited possibilities of a truly labyrinthine knightly *errance*, suspended between the potentially endless string of episodic adventures characteristic of the romance-quest, and the teleology of the Christian pilgrimage allegory dictated by the inflexible formal and moral strictures of Deguileville's ascetic ideal.[6] Whereas it would be reductive to see the four works as sketching something like a linear, single evolution of the tradition, it is fair to say that they move towards an increasing awareness of the complexity of achieving a synthesis of chivalric ethos and Christian morals. Also, over time the quest alle-

---

[3]  See especially the discussion by Maupeu, *Pèlerins de vie humaine*, pp. 475–529.

[4]  See also Maurice Keen, *Chivalry* (New Haven, CT: Yale University Press, 1984), pp. 32–81, and Jean Flori, *La chevalerie* (Paris: Gisserot, 1998), pp. 82–91.

[5]  'it is much easier to abandon all worldly goods rather than keeping them without loving them excessively', Tommaso III di Saluzzo (Thomas de Saluces), *Il Libro del Cavaliere Errante (BnF ms. fr. 12559)*, ed. Marco Piccat and Laura Ramello (Boves: Araba Fenice, 2008), ll. 10803–4 prose, p. 543.

[6]  See also Maupeu, *Pèlerins de vie humaine*, pp. 485–98.

gories seem to become less confident in the possibility of inscribing individual experience within the larger, exemplary paradigm of the human pilgrimage provided by Deguileville, and thus begin to explore individual identity in terms of a failure, impossibility or refusal to reduce human existential experience to strictly moral categories and the narrative paradigm of an exemplary teleological pilgrimage. By the end of the century the sense of the arbitrariness of this *errance* will be taken to such extremes as to turn the quest itself into a perpetual and aimless wandering. Gerhart Ladner aptly characterises these two contrasting, even opposite possibilities afforded by the allegory of the journey: 'Homo Viator ... is a wayfarer, a wanderer between two worlds, but in more than one sense. ... [A] stranger and wayfarer who may travel as pilgrim from and to an eternal order or may defy order as an alienated rebel or may assume the guise of a fool or be a victim of delusion.'[7] Whereas this dichotomy may hold true in the context of a strictly Augustinian understanding of the self, in the late medieval French allegories discussed in this chapter the 'self' seems to crystallise less out of a mutually exclusive choice between either of these two narratives, visualised in Deguileville's *bivium*, but rather out of an unstable and tentative exploration of the spectrum between and beyond such a dichotomy. It is in the contested no man's land between these two extremes of pilgrimage and wandering that something like individual identity begins to emerge, the result of a continuous tension and dialogue between opposite but also necessarily complementary, interdependent metaphors for the human existential condition.

## Jean de Courcy: *Le Chemin de vaillance* (1424)

The *Chemin de vaillance* was written by Jean de Courcy, a Norman knight of uncertain identity, and probably completed in 1424 when the poet had reached the advanced age of sixty-six.[8] It survives in a single splendid manuscript prepared for King Edward IV of England,[9] and remains unedited except for brief selections published by Saverio Panunzio in his partial edition of the work.[10] On the whole, the text, undoubtedly because of its monumental length of over 40,000 lines –

[7]   Ladner, 'Homo Viator', 233.

[8]   See B. Doris Dubuc, 'Le *Chemin de vaillance*: mise à point sur la date de composition et la vie de l'auteur', in Peter Rolfe Monks and D. D. R. Owen, eds, *Medieval Codicology, Iconography, Literature and Translation: Studies for Keith Val Sinclair* (Leiden: Brill, 1994), pp. 276–83.

[9]   London, BL MS Royal 14 E.II, fols 1–293; Flemish, dated to around 1473–83. See H. L. D. Ward, *Catalogue of Romances in the Department of Manuscripts in the British Museum*, 3 vols (London: British Museum, 1961–2), p. 922. See also BL MS catalogue entry at: http://www.bl.uk/catalogues/manuscripts/HITS0001.ASP?VPath=html/39208.htm&Search=14+E+II&Highlight=F [accessed 12 February 2012].

[10]  Jean de Courcy, *Le Chemin de vaillance di Jean de Courcy e l'allegoria*, ed. Saverio Panunzio (Bari: Adriatica, 1979).

prohibitive even by medieval standards – has attracted very little critical attention.[11] The poem is sometimes mentioned in works with a wider scope, but rarely discussed in any detail.[12]

Despite the text's great length and its occasional encyclopaedic ramblings, the narrative is mostly harnessed by a fairly clear and simple structural scheme. The knight's adventures, framed by the dream-*topos* inherited from Deguileville, are divided into three distinct narrative moments: his instruction in courtly manners, his deviation into an anti-courtly world of sensuality that introduces the confrontation with the sins and vices, and his return to the courtly precepts that eventually culminate in a mystical apotheosis.[13] The narrative is framed by the *Acteur*'s dream where he encounters dame Nature, 'chambrière de Dieu', who advises him to reject Sloth and Cowardice and pursue dame *Vaillance*, and directs him to her secluded abode. Nature's instruction touches on the five senses, the three platonic souls, and then moves on to praise *Vaillance*'s former champions such as the Nine Worthies and others. Thereupon Nature vanishes and leaves the *Acteur* to begin his journey alone. He immediately encounters Desire, Nature's attendant armed with a dart used to guide noble hearts towards Prowess. Arriving in the presence of Prowess and Hardiness, the *Acteur* again has to sit through an extended lesson in 'doctrine'. The concept of 'doctrine' for de Courcy is, symptomatically, a rather eclectic amalgamation of knowledge, and touches on issues as disparate as religious instruction, the seven liberal arts, largesse, courtly manners, clothing, good company, military training, tournaments, siege, construction of military devices.[14] As a conclusion to the first phase of the narrative he is led to Reason, who resides in a tower and equips him with the conventional allegorical armour vaguely reminiscent of Ephesians 6:11–17.

Arriving at the Bridge of Frailty, he is seduced by the Flesh, the World and the Devil while Prowess and Hardiness are asleep on the grass. He is increasingly intrigued by the numerous delights described by his new fellows until in the Palace of the World he sees a series of *tableaux* representing the Seven Ages of Man. In the

---

[11]   Apart from Maupeu, *Pèlerins de vie humaine*, pp. 475–529, Panunzio and Dubuc, to my knowledge, the only other article focussing on the work is Arthur Piaget, 'Le Chemin de Vaillance de Jean de Courcy et l'hiatus final des polysyllabes aux XIVᵉ et XVᵉ siècles', *Romania* 27 (1898), 582–607. There is also a partial edition I have been unable to consult, by Blanche Doris Dubuc, 'Étude critique et édition partielle du *Chemin de vaillance* de Jean de Courcy d'après le manuscrit BM Royal 14 E. II' (PhD thesis, University of Connecticut, 1981).

[12]   Wenzel, 'Pilgrimage of Life'; Armand Strubel, '*Grant senefiance a*': allégorie et littérature au Moyen Age (Paris: Champion, 2002), pp. 223–4; Pierre-Yves Badel, 'Le poème allégorique', in Daniel Poirion, ed., *La littérature française aux XIVᵉ et XVᵉ siècles*, Grundriss der Romanischen Literaturen des Mittelalters, vol. 8:1 (Heidelberg: Carl Winter, 1988), p. 143.

[13]   Panunzio, ed., *Le chemin*, pp. 16–18. For a more detailed summary, see ibid., pp. 351–69, where the rubric-headings are listed; and Piaget, '*Le Chemin*', 584–90; and Maupeu, *Pèlerins de vie humaine*, pp. 486–90, 623–5.

[14]   See for instance, fols 14vff in the manuscript. In Panunzio, ed., *Chemin*, ll. 1870ff, pp. 157ff.

inner Temple of the Palace he sees a representation of Fortune flanked by Poverty and Wealth, while in the World's own chamber he finds the images of Joy, Sadness, Work and Rest. After a brief history of the Seven Ages of Humanity, the World pursues the seduction of the *Acteur* who, following the advice of Youth, decides to remain in the Palace. Nature, disappointed with his behaviour, again sends the winged Desire in order to redirect him to the right path. The *Acteur* repents, and exhorted by Reason to retrieve his armour, continues his journey accompanied by Prudence who sets Youth to flight and leads him to Divine Wisdom with her daughters the Seven Virtues. He now has to enter the Forest of Temptation where the Seven Sins reside; he is made prisoner by Pride, freed by Humility and experiences many other similar adventures with the six remaining sins.

As he finally escapes from the claws of Lechery, the *Acteur* can enter the third section of his journey by boarding the heavily allegorised Ship of Law, and starts sailing on the River of Contemplation. Arriving finally in the Haven of Salvation, the *Acteur*, helped by Faith, ascends the seven steps representing the Sacraments leading to the Garden of *Vaillance*. There he finds the seven Fountains of Mercy, seven lights representing the Gifts of the Holy Spirit and the eight trees of the Beatitudes.[15] After some further instruction he has a vision of Paradise, the Angels and God himself. Finally, he sees dame *Vaillance*, who in a distinctively apocalyptic setting is finally identified with the Woman Clothed with the Sun from Revelation 12:1–2. Astonished and amazed, the dreamer finally awakens and concludes his poem.

The most striking characteristic of the *Chemin de vaillance* is its optimism concerning the agreement of the chivalric ethos with the moral strictures inherent in Deguileville's ultimately ascetic and transcendentalising allegory. Jean de Courcy rather simply transplants Deguileville's work into a more specifically knightly context without seeing any incompatibility, and as a consequence the formal and conceptual structures of the two works are largely analogous. Both are divided into four books, and start with a phase of theoretical instruction that introduces the protagonist's journey, whilst the quest itself mainly consists of a series of encounters with moral and psychological abstractions, and is concluded by the boarding of an allegorical ship that leads to an apocalyptic consummation. The main difference consists in the nature of the instruction received by the two protagonists, and in the structure and evolution of their didactic journey. Whereas Deguileville starts with a clearly religious instruction built around the seven sacraments, de Courcy's *Acteur* is only introduced to the sacraments in the third and final phase of his voyage. The initial phase of the *Acteur's* instruction by Nature, Prowess and Reason consists of a fairly heterogeneous mixture of different matters, ranging from highly

---

[15]  For a brief survey of such traditional groups and their ongoing influence in art and literature in the later Middle Ages and in the early Renaissance, see Tuve, 'Allegory of Vices and Virtues', in her *Allegorical Imagery*, pp. 57–143, and Samuel C. Chew, 'The Spiritual Foes of Man' and 'The Spiritual Guardians of Man', in his *The Pilgrimage of Life* (New Haven, CT: Yale University Press, 1962), pp. 70–143.

specialised technical knowledge in the ways of warfare to religious advice by the way of table manners. The main emphasis of this initial section is knightly and courtly, and it has been rightly compared to both a courtesy book and a miniature treatise of chivalry.[16]

The implication of this structural progression is that the courtly and chivalric instruction supplied in Part I is in some ways a preparation for the mystical apotheosis of Part III, and that the descent into mundane self-indulgence in Part II is merely a detour from an otherwise straight road leading from courtesy to spiritual illumination. The reader is thus invited to see the knight's spiritual apotheosis in the third part of the narrative as resulting directly from the instruction received in the first part. This works wonderfully in Deguileville as it relies on systematic doctrinal and sacramental instruction absorbed in Book 1, but de Courcy has to rely on a much more tenuous and nebulous link between the two sections, the first distinctively courtly, the third strictly mystical. The reader finds himself wondering in what ways exactly the instruction in courtly manners and skills is in any way conducive to mystical vision, but the poem gives no explanation or even hints as to the precise nature of the connection. It is true that Reason equips the knight with the traditional allegorical armour of the *miles christianus*, but this appears as a largely conventional move and the instruction is dominated by largely pragmatic, even technical knowledge. Crucially, none of the courtly and knightly skills the *Acteur* acquires in the initial phase are ever evoked again in the final section, either in themselves or even only to provide a transposed, 'allegorised' rein- terpretation of his chivalric adventures and values.

As a symptom of this newly attempted synthesis of secular and transcendental longings, de Courcy removes the motif of the parting of the ways, or *bivium*, from the allegory, as if to signal his rejection of the mutual exclusivity of Deguileville's ways of Occupation and Idleness, respectively collocated in terms of holy contem- plative existence and sinful courtly life by Deguileville. But removing the dichotomy of the two ways is not in itself sufficient to perform an actual integration of temperate, civilised worldliness in the form of courtly-chivalric education on the one hand, with mystical vision postulated on the very rejection of earthly aspirations on the other. This is manifested most clearly in the poet's insufficient differentiation between his descriptions of overindulgence in worldly pleasures, and his celebration of aristocratic manners ultimately conducive to *Vaillance*. So the descriptions of the ease and appeal of sinful living, amply described by the three arch-tempters the World, the Flesh and the Devil in Part II of the poem, draw heavily on contem- porary aristocratic practices and lifestyle. This sits oddly with the *Acteur*'s systematic training in the same kind of aristocratic sophistication as part of his apprenticeship to *Vaillance* in an earlier section. Indeed, Prowess's exhortation to dress nobly and

---

[16]  Abbé de la Rue, *Essais historiques sur les bardes, les jongleurs et les trouvères normands et anglo- normands* (Caen: F. Poisson, 1834), quoted in Piaget, 'Le Chemin', 583; Panunzio, ed., *Chemin*, p. 16.

elegantly, whilst it is meant to agree naturally with *Vaillance*, is almost identical with the Flesh's alluring description of sumptuous and by implication sinful dress.[17]

The poet makes some efforts to suffuse the *Acteur*'s largely pragmatic chivalric and courtly training with religious echoes, but the religious overtones of such 'knightly doctrine' are largely conventional and lack a convincing internal logic. For instance the discussion of the crucial role of divine Grace (*Chemin* 3346ff) interrupts the text in an entirely arbitrary manner and in no way seems to develop organically from the preceding sections where technical advice on how to resist a siege is given. His understanding of the problem of divine Grace and favour, for instance, is simplistic and contractual: 'aies toujours Dieu en memoire / et il te donnera victoire', which has none of the theological authority of Deguileville.[18] De Courcy also takes for granted that the pursuit of temporal aspirations associated with *Vaillance* – honour, renown, prowess – will inevitably and as it were automatically direct the *Acteur* towards a transcendentalising apotheosis. Thus temporal and transcendentalising aspirations seem simply juxtaposed or collapsed rather than properly fused in the *Acteur*'s quest for *Vaillance*: the subjects of dame *Vaillance* 'mainent ilz bonne vie / en l'honneur de Dieu et du monde',[19] but the poet says nothing more about the exact manner in which honour 'in the world' is in any way agreeable to God, or vice-versa.

Despite his commitment to finding an integration of the two ways of the *vita activa* and *contemplativa*, de Courcy often relapses into the Deguilevillian dichotomy of secular and spiritual. If the motif of the *bivium* itself disappears from the narrative, the actual bipartition remains ingrained in the conceptual structure of the allegory: the *Acteur*, eventually, is still forced to choose between his subjection to *Vaillance* or the World, which amounts to a rejection of worldliness in the manner of Deguileville and thus extinguishes all the possibilities for a real potential mediation or synthesis. It is revealing that the author is ultimately forced to split the figure of *Vaillance* into two, thus also fracturing and exploding the central objective of the quest and supreme referent of the allegory. So Reason reveals to the *Acteur* how there are in fact two ladies bearing the same name, one is the 'corporale *Vaillance*' ensuring fame and honour on earth, while the other is the superior 'Vaillance de l'ame', pointing towards the celestial kingdom. De Courcy clearly hesitates and contradicts himself in illustrating their relationship: celestial *Vaillance* appears as the ultimate objective of the quest, but the natural hierarchy is suddenly reversed, and celestial *Vaillance* is demoted to a mere agent, an instrument for achieving earthly *Vaillance*: 'la parfaitte vaillance, / que, par sa sainte pourveance, / te doinst boire de la fontaine / de ceste

---

[17]  Fol. 18r and fol. 50v in the MS, respectively ll. 2204–53 and 6463–510, pp. 175–7 and 240–2 in Panunzio, ed., *Chemin*.

[18]  'always remember God, and he will grant you victory', MS fol. 27v; in Panunzio, ed., *Chemin*, ll. 3463–4, p. 222.

[19]  'lead a good life to honour God and the world', MS fol. 16r; in Panunzio, ed., *Chemin*, ll. 1943–34, p. 162.

Vaillance mondaine, / tant que par bonne renommee / soit elle ta dame nommee'.[20] In his attempt to have it both ways, de Courcy repeatedly blurs the ontological and causal relationship between the two forms of *Vaillance*, and by collapsing two radically discontinuous concepts under the same name, he ends up exposing his own process of forgery. The homonymy of the two *Vaillances* is nothing more than a verbal *tour de force* that dissimulates what is in reality a forced marriage, a synthesis the poem desires but ultimately fails to produce.[21]

De Courcy, then, is in many ways a truly conventional poet, for whom the inherent validity of the poetic and spiritual models he inherits guarantees their applicability to a new context. The material he chooses is certainly traditional, and his allegorical practice is equally established, but his use of such traditional elements remains simplistic, mechanical and unquestioning, since he does not insert the inherited models into a new circuit of ideas.[22] Ultimately de Courcy does not refashion Deguileville's paradigm but merely overlays it with a second, parallel but largely incompatible, narrative postulated on a very different system of values. This desire of doing justice to both the secular and the transcendentalising momentum of the quest, forces the author to swing back and forth between these extremes, revealing the impossibility of achieving a stable balance or a genuine integration. This double narrative in itself reveals de Courcy's idealistic, but rather unsophisticated and even naïve belief in the seamless compatibility of the chivalric and ascetic ethos. The *Chemin de vaillance* then is ultimately more interesting for what it *tries* to achieve than what it really *does* achieve. From a different perspective, it is also an illuminating indicator of the tenacity of Deguileville's spiritual paradigm and its resistance to secular rewriting, a resistance that in different and more complex ways conditions the evolution of the entire later tradition of the allegorical quest narratives.

## Thomas de Saluces: *Le Livre du chevalier errant* (1394–6)

The *Livre du chevalier errant* was written by Thomas III, Marquis de Saluces, between 1394 and 1396 in the captivity of his arch-enemy the Prince of Achaia, and was supplemented by additional passages around 1403–5.[23] The text survives in two manuscripts, one in MS Paris, BNF fr. 12559, another in MS Torino,

---

[20] 'the supreme *Vaillance*, by her holy care, bids you drink from the fountain of earthly *Vaillance*, so that through good renown, she be known as your lady', Panunzio, ed., *Chemin*, ll. 29327–33, pp. 303–4.

[21] Maupeu, *Pèlerins de vie humaine*, pp. 486–90.

[22] Panunzio, 'Introduction', in *Chemin*, pp. 31–4.

[23] Robert Fajen, *Die Lanze und die Feder: Untersuchungen zum Livre du Chevalier Errant von Thomas III., Markgraf von Saluzzo* (Wiesbaden: Reichert, 2003), p. 24. For an older but still valid study, see N. Iorga, *Thomas III, marquis de Saluces: étude historique et littéraire; avec une introduction sur la politique de ses prédécesseurs et un appendice de textes* (Saint-Denis: Bouillant, 1893).

Biblioteca Nazionale L.V.6; a third manuscript, possibly the source of the other two, was lost in the eighteenth century.[24] The text long remained untouched, but has recently started to attract the critical attention it deserves. An edition of the text was produced by M. J. Ward in 1984 but remained unpublished, and a new critical edition has finally appeared in 2008, after a rather free translation into modern French by Daniel Chaubet in 2001.[25] There is some excellent critical work on the text by Bouchet, Fajen, Ruhe and Trachsler,[26] and the newly available edition will hopefully spark further discussion of this interesting and complex work. All recent criticism agrees in attributing to Thomas a previously unnoticed literary talent as well as intellectual sophistication and depth.

The *Chevalier*, like the *Chemin*, attempts a synthesis of moral didacticism and chivalric celebration, but starts from different premises and comes to radically different conclusions. The respective titles are already symptomatic of the two poets' approaches: whereas 'chemin' implies the existence of a route that simply needs to be followed, the 'errant' knight is constantly trying to locate or recover an elusive path. More precisely, in Thomas's case, the knight is actively involved in 'making' his own path as he goes along, unable to rely entirely on an inherited narrative and conceptual structure. Unlike de Courcy, who simply attempts to accommodate a knight-figure in the place of Deguileville's ascetic Everyman, Thomas seeks to redefine the terms of the allegorical journey, fashioning a new, chivalric pilgrimage of life.[27]

The chevalier's quest, then, is not chivalric in the strict sense: there is little romance-like action, and the quest itself is rather speculative and philosophical, since it consists of an implicit debate on the nature of the quest itself and its

---

[24] For a discussion of the manuscripts, see Fajen, *Die Lanze*, pp. 25–38.

[25] Marvin James Ward, 'A Critical Edition of Thomas III, Marquis of Saluzzo's *Le Livre du Chevalier Errant*' (PhD thesis, University of North Carolina at Chapel Hill, 1984); Tommaso III di Saluzzo, *Il Libro del Cavaliere Errante*, ed. Piccat and Ramello; *Le chevalier errant*, ed. and trans. Daniel Chaubet (Moncalieri: Centro interuniversitario di ricerche per il viaggio in Italia, 2001). The volume also contains a useful 'postface' by Florence Bouchet.

[26] Florence Bouchet, 'De la lecture à l'écriture, quelques modes de transfert dans le *Chevalier errant* de Thomas de Saluces', *Bien dire et bien aprandre* 13 (1995), 217–35; 'Le *Chevalier errant* de Thomas de Saluces: lectures de la description et description de la lecture vers la fin du Moyen Age', *Bien dire et bien aprandre* 11 (1993), 81–104; and 'Voyage et quête de soi: le *Livre du Chevalier errant* de Thomas de Saluces', in Labbé *et al.*, eds, *Guerres, voyages et quêtes*, pp. 31–42; 'Postface', pp. 389–98, in *Le chevalier errant*, ed. Chaubet; Fajen, *Die Lanze*; Marco Piccat, 'Tommaso III, il Marchese errante: l'autobiografia cavalleresca di un Saluzzo', Renato Bordone, 'Une tres noble jouste', both in *Il Libro del Cavaliere Errante*, ed. Piccat and Ramello, respectively pp. 5–25 and 27–35; Ernstpeter Ruhe, 'Der *Chevalier errant* auf enzyklopädischer Fahrt', in Friedrich Wolfzettel, ed., *Artusrittertum im späten Mittelalter: Ethos und Ideologie* (Giessen: Schmitz, 1984), pp. 159–76; Richard Trachsler, *Disjointures – conjointures: étude sur l'interférence des matières narratives dans la littérature française du Moyen Age* (Tübingen: Francke, 2000), pp. 311–64 and *passim*. See also Badel, *Roman de la Rose au XIV^e siècle*, pp. 315–30.

[27] Consequently, Thomas de Saluces's debt to Deguileville is less obvious, and may rely only on indirect influence mediated by the works of Thomas's friend Philippe de Mézières; see Maupeu, *Pèlerins de vie humaine*, p. 476, n. 4; Iorga, *Thomas III*, p. 64.

objective. The journey is accordingly divided into three distinct phases that represent three different ideological approaches that offer themselves to the hero, under the aegis of Love, Fortune and Knowledge respectively.[28] Roughly disposed according to an ascending hierarchy,[29] the movement through the three narrative moments marks the progression of the knight's own understanding – and is meant to stimulate the same in the reader, for whose benefit the narrator explains the logic of the tripartition in the introduction, thus enabling a critical distance from the narrated events.[30] The knight's 'errance', then, consists of a metaphorical journey through three different systems that offer themselves as possible models for the explanation of reality, defined as *Wirklichkeitsmodelle* by Ruhe.[31]

The story begins in a familiar *locus amoenus*, where the hero encounters his initial guide, Lady Knowledge. She invites him to travel towards Orient, in order to be dubbed there by a noble king, which will then enable him to seek many adventures on his subsequent journeys. Following the knighting ceremony he sets out on his quest in the company of Faith, Hope, and Labour (*Travail*). He is promptly led astray and after a series of minor initial adventures arrives at a clearing in a forest where lovers are at play and there meets his beloved. She is instantly abducted by a villain knight, *Breus sans pitié*, familiar from the prose Tristan, and so the chevalier's quest for the lady begins. The knight, soon imprisoned in pagan lands, engages in a twofold letter exchange with his beloved on the one hand and with the God of Love on the other, beseeching the latter's help. Thanks to King Arthur's intercession he is finally liberated, and travels with his lady to the court of the God of Love where they meet a host of familiar romance characters. There the idyllic peace is soon perturbed by the arrival of a cuckold, who demands satisfaction for his wife's abduction by one of Love's retainers. The situation quickly escalates and the feud soon develops into a tournament, that itself rapidly degenerates into open war, and the protagonist's lady again disappears. Disappointed with the God of Love's powerlessness to put an end to the strife, the knight eventually leaves his court and continues his quest alone.[32]

The knight now enters the second phase of the narrative, and arrives at the Court of Fortune. The mood of the narrative is correspondingly transformed, shifting from romance to exemplary history. The tyrannical arbitrariness of Fortune's rule looms

---

[28] The three sections have been broadly assimilated with the *vita voluptuosa, activa* and *contemplativa*, see Ruhe, 'Der *Chevalier errant*', p. 164. This interpretation needs to be qualified, particularly in the case of the final section, since the final objective is clearly not a renunciation of the world.

[29] Bouchet, 'Postface', p. 397.

[30] *Il Libro del Cavaliere Errante*, ed. Piccat and Ramello, fol. 1r, ll. 1–31 verse, p. 49.

[31] Ruhe, 'Der *Chevalier errant*', pp. 159ff; 'Wirklichkeitsmodell' describes not reality as such but an ideologically mediated view of existence, or even the reliance on different discourses to construct that reality.

[32] *Il Libro del Cavaliere Errante*, ed. Piccat and Ramello, fols 1–106r, ll. 1 verse–3925 prose, pp. 49–332. For the most detailed summary of the story, see Badel, *Roman de la Rose au XIV* *siècle*, pp. 315–30.

over her entire court and is expressed in the random treatment of her courtiers. She inhabits a citadel built upon a steep rock, where her tributaries are disposed hierarchically according to their worldly prominence, but periodically removed from their seats and thrown outside the gates of the citadel where they are beaten and mistreated by the common people. Most of these figures in her court are contemporary or historical characters,[33] and trigger a number of embedded historical narratives that give rise to a series of moralised interpretations by Fortune, who then launches into an excursus about the seven ages of the world. Leaving the palace of Fortune, the knight witnesses a number of recent historical events, including among others the capture of Thomas de Saluces himself by the Prince of Achaia.[34]

After spending some time with a hermit who teaches the knight about the five senses, the four humours and the three platonic souls, the knight finally arrives at the abode of Knowledge, mother of his companions Faith and Hope. The object of the knight's quest is now no longer his beloved, but Lady Knowledge herself, signalling an ontological shift of the objective of the quest. This third and last phase of the quest consists largely of a moralised re-reading of the knight's previous adventures supervised by Knowledge.[35] She exposes his foolish choice of the path of damnation, and his infatuation with the mundane illusions of Love and War. This re-reading of the knight's adventures through the eyes of Knowledge is the prologue to more general and universal didactic developments, making use of the familiar ingredients of the Seven Deadly Sins and Virtues, the Pains of Hell, the *ars moriendi*. Knowledge devotes particular attention to the moral responsibilities of the knightly class, and her instruction as a whole is specifically designed to encourage a regeneration of the aristocratic *ordo* of society.[36]

Thomas's distinctive poetic voice and thought is revealed through his clever use of traditional ideas, stories and motifs, employed to generate questions, tensions and contradictions within his own text. There is something almost 'post-modern' in Thomas's skilful juxtaposition of pre-existent narrative fragments to construct his own, obliquely autobiographical narrative, constantly reflecting on its own fictional status. In the first part of the narrative, Thomas draws heavily on romance tradition: he places romance figures into his own narrative, and often makes them relate familiar episodes from the tradition of knightly romance.[37] These numerous embedded narratives virtually paralyse the protagonist's quest by deliberately fragmenting both narrative linearity and the identity of the questing knight. Rather than constructing his identity through knightly adventures, the *chevalier errant* becomes a passive listener, prevented from actively pursuing his quest and merely

---

[33]  Ruhe, 'Der *Chevalier errant*', p. 165, Fajen, *Die Lanze*, pp. 97–8.

[34]  *Il Libro del Cavaliere Errante*, ed. Piccat and Ramello, fols 106r–170v, ll. 3925 prose–8285 prose, pp. 332–477.

[35]  See especially Bouchet, 'De la lecture à l'écriture' and 'Le *Chevalier errant*'.

[36]  *Il Libro del Cavaliere Errante*, ed. Piccat and Ramello, fols 170v–208v, ll. 8285 prose–end, pp. 477–553.

[37]  For further discussion, see Ruhe, 'Der *Chevalier errant*', p. 165.

participating in indirect, fictional adventures.[38] This ultimately reveals the existence of a gap separating the reality he inhabits from the literary ideal, and exposes the internal contradictions and unsustainability of the *Wirklichkeitsmodell* espoused by Love's followers.[39]

Despite this implicit denunciation of the courtly world, Thomas is in the difficult position of being unable to reject a courtly-aristocratic ideal *en bloc*. His own position as a member of the ruling class, as well as his natural inclination, do not allow him to completely turn his back on the mundanity inherent in the aristocratic lifestyle and take refuge in a strictly clerkly *contemptus mundi*. Fittingly, at an earlier stage of the quest, the knight only briefly toys with the idea of retiring to a hermitage, 'une grant maison qui ressembloit religion', until the irresistible knightly urge to ride out on the quest manifests itself anew.[40] Furthermore, despite his own reservations concerning the literary ideal of love and chivalry, Thomas undoubtedly delights in the retelling and adaptation of particular episodes from the romance tradition.[41] So the description of the elaborate preparations for the sumptuous tournament opposing the Lovers and Cuckolds is undeniably enthusiastic – even if its splendour is to be shattered by the degeneration of the tournament into chaotic and brutal war. The evocation of the aesthetic pleasures of the aristocratic way of life, coupled with the awareness of their falsity, perfectly emblematises Thomas's dilemma.

The disillusion with the ideal of love is the prelude to a new phase of the narrative, introducing the knight to an entirely novel *Wirklichkeitsmodell*. The model proposed by Fortune counterbalances Love's simplistic optimism with an almost unconditional pessimism and fatalism. The insight to be gained at Fortune's court is again textually mediated, this time through embedded historiographical and exemplary narratives delivered by historical or contemporary characters. Rather predictably, the insight revolves around the unreliability of worldly gifts and earthly bliss,[42] but Thomas's knight once more hesitates to accept Fortune's point of view as final. If Fortune's perspective is a useful antidote to Love's naïve optimism, it nevertheless goes to the opposite extreme, categorically denying the possibility of order and meaning in human history and society. The fatalistic notion of Fortune's fickleness and the ensuing *contemptus mundi* are not however compatible with the

---

[38] Fajen, *Die Lanze*, pp. 4–5, 191 and *passim*. A total of up to thirty other traditional stories are worked into the fabric of the *Chevalier errant*, ranging from romances to historiography and devotional literature, three genres that respectively dominate the three main phases of the text.

[39] E.g. *Il Libro del Cavaliere Errante*, ed. Piccat and Ramello, fols 52v–54v, ll. 1145–311 prose, pp. 197–201. For a more extended discussion, see Fajen, *Die Lanze*, p. 89.

[40] *Il Libro del Cavaliere Errante*, ed. Piccat and Ramello, fol. 4r, ll. 290–336 verse, pp. 56–7, citation ll. 291–2. For more ample discussion, see Maupeu, *Pèlerins de vie humaine*, pp. 501–3.

[41] Ruhe, 'Der *Chevalier errant*', p. 165.

[42] On Fortune, see for instance the classic studies by Howard Rollin Patch, *The Goddess Fortune in Mediaeval Literature* (London: Cass, 1967); and Chew, 'The World of Fortune', in his *The Pilgrimage of Life*, pp. 35–69.

poet's own calling as an aristocrat and temporal ruler, and therefore need to be redefined. Despite the tyranny of Fortune, and the social abuses of the aristocracy he repeatedly denounces, Thomas does believe in the possibility of regenerating the social order, and the writing of the whole *Livre du chevalier errant* is ultimately an exhortation of the entire knightly class to embrace moral responsibility, and act as guarantors of a social order that replicates the structure of a divinely ordained cosmos.[43] This conflicted but tenacious optimism sustains Thomas's belief in the possibility of a transcending synthesis of the two opposing models he has explored. Neither the naïvety of Love nor the cynical pragmatism of Fortune is a viable solution for Thomas's learned and sceptical knight in search of a model of behaviour integrating secular demands with the moral and ethical principles of Christianity, and his knight accordingly sets out to discover a further, synthetic *Wirklichkeitsmodell*.

The final stage of the knight's instruction, under supervision of knowledge, starts with a retrospective re-reading of the knight's earlier adventures – adventures that were themselves textually mediated rather than experienced at first hand. On the one hand, the worldviews defended by Love and Fortune respectively are definitively dismantled, and on the other, an allegorising re-reading of earlier adventures becomes the basis for establishing a composite and more balanced ideal of chivalry within a spiritual perspective. So the knight's initial journey towards the Orient to be knighted is allegorised as a pilgrimage to Jerusalem, and the noble king who dubs him is identified with Christ himself. The symbolism of the knighting ritual is amply explored with reference to its quasi-sacramental status.[44] This interpretation is crucial, as it forms the basis for Thomas's entire redefinition of the chivalric ideal by attempting to disentangle the traditional conception of chivalry as a religiously inspired and socially useful ideal from its courtly and self-glorifying developments. Thomas strives to regenerate the *order* of chivalry, understood as an active agent in the perpetuation of a divinely sanctioned cosmic *order* it is also part of.[45]

Knowledge thus sketches a new picture of the chivalric ideal, clearly earthly, but set within a wider, transcendental and eschatological framework. Only the awareness of the ultimately spiritual and metaphysical object of the quest can truly regenerate earthly chivalry: 'dessevre ton esperit de ton corps par penseez et par desiriers, et is hors de ce monde morant. Va en la terre des vivanz ou nulz ne muert ne envieillist,

---

[43]  Fajen, *Die Lanze*, pp. 162–6.

[44]  Two influential treatises that develop this aspect are *The Book of the Ordre of Chivalry*, ed. A. T. P. Byles; and the *Ordène de Chevalerie*, ed. Keith Busby, with *Le Roman des Eles de Raoul de Hodenc* (Utrecht: John Benjamins, 1983).

[45]  This conception of cosmic 'order', and the position of knighthood within it, is the central preoccupation of Ramon Llull's *Book of the Ordre of Chivalry*, where the division into seven chapters is explicitly said to reflect the order of the seven planetary spheres. See Alfred T. Byles's translation of the original Catalan opening in his introduction to the English version by Caxton, p. xxxi, n. 1. In Caxton and several other translations the analogy is lost as the Book is divided into eight chapters.

c'est en Paradis.'[46] The detachment predicated by Knowledge is however not absolute or definitive: the knight is not an Everyman turned Cistercian monk like Deguileville's ascetic pilgrim who can ultimately find refuge in his *contemptus mundi*, but a social agent engaged in upholding and regenerating a divinely inspired and metaphysically framed structure of social order. But the predominantly secular, chivalric focus of the entire work derives its proper significance and legitimacy only from being set within this eschatological frame – just as the *errance* that takes up the bulk of the narrative only acquires meaning retrospectively, in the light of the pilgrimage-paradigm that is glimpsed towards the end of the poem.

Thomas's ideological programme, clarified only at the end of his knight's quest, is ambitious and fragile, and cannot escape the internal contradictions created by the encounter of two fundamentally opposite ethical systems. His awkward treatment of the issue of worldly honour and renown is symptomatic of the instability of his synthesis. Thomas can neither reject honour entirely, nor accommodate the concept comfortably within the Christian framework, and the problematic overlap between the notions and the terms of Honour, Renown and Vainglory is never clarified. Renown, that in de Courcy so easily and simplistically coalesces with spiritual apotheosis under the label of a double *Vaillance*, is for Thomas a much more problematic issue. Initially 'honneur' is invoked positively by Lady Knowledge to prompt the hero to seek knightly initiation,[47] but later, reconsidering the early stages in the knight's adventures, 'honour' is identified as a fickle and false gift of Fortune,[48] and Knowledge herself brands the quest for renown, now identified as one of the manifestations of 'vainegloire', as the Devil's work.[49] The problem is fundamental, and is not limited to the rather abstract notion of 'honour', but affects the very status of the *vita activa* itself, as is reflected in Thomas's treatment of worldly goods at large, what he calls the 'petiz biens'. These are first accepted conditionally, interpreted as the gifts of God destined to comfort human pilgrims on the long and difficult 'voyes' towards salvation and thereby intended to foster fallen man's longing for the greater, transcendent goods of the spirit;[50] this idea however is almost

---

[46] 'separate your spirit from your body, both in your thought and your desires, and leave behind this dying world. Go into the true Land of the Living where no one dies or grows old; that is called Paradise' ; *Il Libro del Cavaliere Errante*, ed. Piccat and Ramello, fols 201v–202r, ll. 10636–8 prose, p. 539.

[47] *Il Libro del Cavaliere Errante*, ed. Piccat and Ramello, fol. 2r, ll. 81, 83 verse, p. 51.

[48] *Il Libro del Cavaliere Errante*, ed. Piccat and Ramello, fol. 185v, l. 9378 prose, p. 506.

[49] 'tempte le deable par vainegloire en trois manieres . . . quant il desire et quiert et pourchace loz et renommee, et en celle entencion fait ces biens, non mie pour Dieu proprement, mais pour le monde'; 'The Devil tempts us through vainglory in three manners: when he desires and longs for and strives after praise and renown, and with that precise intention performs good deeds, not for the sake of God as such, but for the sake of the world', *Il Libro del Cavaliere Errante*, ed. Piccat and Ramello, fol. 185v, ll. 9402–11 prose, p. 507.

[50] 'sont ainsi comme jouelez aux enffanz que il donne pour nous soulacier et pour nostre amour attraire a soy pour ce que il scet bien que nous sommes flevez et tendrez et ne pouons tenir les apres voyes de povreté, d'angoisse ne de martire'; 'Thus they are like toys for children, which he

instantly retracted in the same passage, as worldly goods are now, quite simply, denounced as the work of the Devil to confound unwary pilgrims: 'ce sont les engins du Deable par quoy il deçoit les amez en mil manieres et prent et lieve et tient'.[51] The uncertainty about the status of these worldly goods is ultimately metonymic for the instability of Thomas's fundamentally divided, ambivalent appreciation of secular life itself, more specifically in its aristocratic-chivalric manifestation. His final synthesis of temperate worldliness and piety, then, is a tightrope exercise that is as fragile as it is sophisticated; recognising the difficulty of achieving such a compromise he laconically concludes that 'plus est legiere chose tous les biens du monde laissier a un seul coup que elles retenir et elles neant amer'.[52]

## René I d'Anjou: *Le Livre du cuer d'amour espris* (1457–77)[53]

The *Livre du cuer d'amour espris* was written between 1457 and 1477, and survives in six manuscripts, the most splendid and representative one being MS Vienna, Oesterreichische Nationalbibliothek, *Codex Vindobonensis* 2597,[54] prepared for René's own personal use. Whilst the work has long attracted the attention of historians because of the author's prominence as a political figure and that of art historians because of the particularly striking miniatures in the manuscript, the history of the strictly literary appreciation of the work is relatively short.[55] Initiated by Daniel Poirion,[56] the modern critical re-examination of the text has in particular sought to emphasise the complexity and ambiguity of René's work, concentrating on such issues as the intricate relationship between author, narrator and *Acteur*,[57]

gives us as relief and solace, and to nourish our love for him, since he knows we are weak and frail and cannot long endure the hard ways of poverty, suffering and martyrdom' ; *Il Libro del Cavaliere Errante*, ed. Piccat and Ramello, fol. 203v, ll. 10762–5 prose, p. 542.

[51] 'The Devil's instruments, through which he deceives souls in thousands of ways and captures, entraps and holds them', *Il Libro del Cavaliere Errante*, ed. Piccat and Ramello, fol. 203v, ll. 10778–9 prose, p. 542. For the whole, complex section, see ll. 10758–804 prose, pp. 542–3; for similarly negative comments on worldly goods, see also fol. 185v, ll. 9378–99 prose, pp. 506–7.

[52] See above, p. 46 n. 4.

[53] A more detailed study of the *Livre du cuer* and the *Chevalier délibéré* can be found in Marco Nievergelt, 'The Quest for Chivalry in the Waning Middle Ages: The Wanderings of René d'Anjou and Olivier de la Marche', *Fifteenth-Century Studies* 36 (2011), 137–67.

[54] For a discussion of the manuscripts and their dating, see René d'Anjou, *The Book of the Love-Smitten Heart*, ed. and trans. Stephanie Viereck Gibbs and Kathryn Karczewska (London: Routledge, 2001), p. xxi. I will refer to this edition throughout as *Livre*.

[55] For a full bibliography, see Gibbs and Karczewska, eds, *Livre*, pp. lv–lviii; and *Le livre du cœur d'amour épris*, ed. Florence Bouchet (Paris: Le Livre de Poche, 2003), pp. 57–63.

[56] Daniel Poirion, 'L'allégorie dans le *Livre du cuer d'amours espris* de René d'Anjou', *Travaux de linguistique et de littérature* 9:2 (1971), 51–64.

[57] Susanne Rinne, 'René d'Anjou and his *Livre du cuer d'amours espris*: The Roles of Author, Narrator, and Protagonist', *Fifteenth-Century Studies* 12 (1987), 145–60.

the autobiographical dimension modulating the allegory,[58] or the dominant melancholic temperament.[59] A number of discussions have also emphasised the work's self-conscious status as a literary artefact,[60] and its related monumentalist poetics.[61]

The *Livre* distances itself somewhat from the traditional pattern of the allegorical 'Pilgrimage of Life', particularly because of its conception of the journey as an amorous quest. There is no explicit mention of the influence of Deguileville, yet the echoes of the *Vie* in particular are numerous, and René's knowledge and interest in the *Pèlerinage* trilogy is unquestionable. In 1437 he had commissioned the production of a manuscript containing all three *Pèlerinages* as a gift for his chamberlain,[62] and his second wife Jeanne de Laval commissioned the anonymous clerk of Angers's prose version of *Vie*.[63] In the *Livre du cuer*, Deguileville's traditional moral abstractions, such as embodiments of vices and virtues, mingle and sometimes strangely coalesce with psychological and amorous ones inspired by the *Roman de la rose*.[64] As a consequence the object of the quest is ambiguously suspended between the *Acteur*'s literal beloved, and the allegorical personification of Mercy, carrying implications of a higher, transcendentalising quest.

The story is set within a twofold frame: first, it is presented as a letter sent to Jean de Bourbon as a request for advice in matters of love, and second, it appears as an account of the usual allegorical dream-vision. The slumbering dreamer initially

[58] Joël Blanchard, 'L'effet autobiographique dans la tradition: le *Livre du cuer d'amours espris* de René d'Anjou', in Keith Busby and Erik Kooper, eds, *Courtly Literature: Culture and Context* (Amsterdam: Benjamins, 1990), pp. 11–21.

[59] Michel Zink, 'La tristesse du coeur dans *Le Livre du cuer d'amour espris* de René d'Anjou', in Didier Coste and Michel Zéraffa, eds, *Le Récit Amoureux* (Seyssel: Champ Vallon, 1984), pp. 22–38.

[60] Sally Tartline Carden, 'Forment pensifz ou lit me mis: le songe dans *Le Livre du cuer d'amours espris*', *Lettres Romanes* 49 (1995), 21–36.

[61] Daniel Poirion, 'Les tombeaux allégoriques et la poétique de l'inscription dans *Le Livre du cuer d'amour espris* de René d'Anjou', *Comptes rendus des séances de l'Académie des Inscriptions et Belles-Lettres* (1990), 321–34.

[62] This is MS Philadelphia, Rosenbach Museum and Library MS 241/2, described in James R. Tanis and Jennifer A. Thompson, eds, *Leaves of Gold: Manuscript Illumination from Philadelphia Collections* (Philadelphia, PA: Philadelphia Museum of Art, 2001), p. 207, no. 71; see also Houghton, 'Deguileville in England', pp. 28–9, 38; and Bergmann, *Die Pilgerfahrt zum himmlischen Jerusalem*, p. 34.

[63] See above, Ch. 1, pp. 34, 40. For a detailed survey of the House of Anjou's pointed interest in Deguileville, see Anne-Marie Legaré, 'La réception du *Pèlerinage de Vie humaine* de Guillaume de Digulleville dans le milieu angevin d'après les sources et les manuscrits conservés', in Sophie Cassagnes-Brouquet, Amaury Chanou, Daniel Pichot and Lionel Rousselot, eds, *Religion et mentalités au Moyen Age: mélanges en l'honneur d'Hervé Martin* (Rennes: Presses Universitaires de Rennes, 2003), pp. 543–52.

[64] Daniel Poirion, 'Le miroir magique', in Marie-Thérèse Gousset, Daniel Poirion and Franz Unterkircher, eds, *Le coeur d'amour épris: reproduction intégrale en fac-similé des miniatures du Codex Vindobonensis 2597 de la Bibliothèque nationale de Vienne* (Paris: Philippe Lebaud, 1981), p. 61.

observes how the God of Love extracts the heart from the dreamer's breast and hands it to Desire. The Heart is then endowed with human form, equipped with an allegorical, vaguely Pauline armour, and accompanied by Desire he sets out on a quest for the lady Sweet Mercy, imprisoned by Discord in a fortress and chained by Fear and Shame. On the edge of the forest they reflectively contemplate a jasper column bearing an inscription exhorting amorous loyalty, a meditation interrupted by the arrival of lady Hope who anticipates part of the coming adventures and directs the questers. In the forest they arrive at a hermitage inhabited by the dwarf Jealousy, who hides and imprisons the helpless youth Fair Welcome and tricks the two companions into taking the wrong path. Night falls and they eventually arrive in a clearing, where they drink from an ominous fountain, which triggers a storm that lasts all night and causes the Heart to have premonitory nightmares. The next morning they wake up to find an inscription identifying the fountain as the Fountain of Fortune. The companions depart and soon arrive in the Valley of Deep Reflection, reaching the abode of Melancholy and attempting to cross the frail bridge over the River of Tears, where the Heart is unhorsed by the black knight Worry and miraculously rescued by lady Hope. Lady Hope then instructs them about the identity and purpose of Worry, and directs them towards the subsequent steps to be taken on the quest.

Following Worry to the castle on the Mount of Dejection, they defy and overcome its Lord, Anger, who then asks to be spared and forgiven, thereupon promptly betraying the two anew and imprisoning the Heart in the castle. Desire fortunately escapes and solicits the help of the God of Love through his Barons Humble Request, Honour and Renown. The Heart is rescued and the castle destroyed, and they can continue their quest in the company of Largesse, another of Love's Barons. They continue their journey through an allegorical landscape, crossing the Plain of Sorrowful Reflection and passing the Abode of Grievous Sighing, and after a series of minor adventures finally arrive on the seashore. There they board a ship attended by the two maids Trust and Understanding and set out to reach the palace of the God of Love to request his advice and assistance in the quest for Mercy. They momentarily find comfort for the night on the island of Friendship and Company, and sail on the following morning, finally reaching the island of the God's palace. There they find the glittering Castle of Pleasure, the Church or Hospital of Love made out of precious stone and silver, and Love's Cemetery. Lady Courtesy, in a religious habit, takes them on a tour of the monuments, showing them countless epitaphs and arms of famous deceased lovers. Among the tombs the author mentions only the most splendid ones dedicated to Love's greatest poets: Ovid, Machaut, Boccaccio, Jean de Meun, Petrarch and Chartier and then goes on to describe the vulgar pit outside the precincts of the cemetery, where all the bodies of faithless lovers are thrown and thus condemned to anonymity. They go on to contemplate a number of amorous relics and finally Pity gives them advice on the steps to follow and is sent to Mercy as a messenger. They finally arrive at the splendid and crystalline castle of the God of Love, where they see a number of marvels, monuments, tapestries and further relics. Having formally sworn allegiance to the God, they finally set out to liberate Mercy after a brief detour through the God of Love's splendid garden. After the successful rescue of Mercy, however, the Heart is basely ambushed by Gossip and Refusal upon leaving the castle and Mercy returned to captivity. The dreamer René finally awakes, decides to commit his dream to writing and concludes by resuming the epistolary frame that introduced his entire quest.

René's debt to the literary past is extensive, self-conscious and deliberately high-lighted within his own narrative, making the question of literary influence itself one of the large themes of his narrative. Particularly interesting is the role of his two central models, invoked explicitly in the text, the *Queste del Saint Graal* and the *Roman de la rose*.[65] René thus ostensibly sets out to harmonise spiritual chivalry and erotic allegory – but it has not always been sufficiently emphasised that René consistently and systematically undercuts the seemingly exalted and idealising notion of love that this produces.[66] The motto adopted by the God of Love is symp-tomatic: 'a cuers volages' (*Livre* § 235); while this alludes to the Winged Heart, symbol of the hero's quest sustained by the 'wings' of desire and introducing suggestions of angelic ascent, this also resonates with the alternative meaning of 'volages' as 'unsteady, inconstant'.[67] The expression is with all likelihood directly taken from Raison's speech in the *Roman de la rose*, condemning the folly of fickle and inconstant lovers: 'Le *cuer* que tu as trop *volage* / te fist entrer en tel folage' [my italics].[68] René's oblique suggestion of the convergence of 'volage' with 'folage' is certainly not devoid of a moralising hint[69] as can be confirmed by one brief look at René's *Mortifiement de vaine plaisance*, written little earlier than the *Livre* and often seen as forming a 'diptych' with the latter.[70] The fissures opened in the idealising picture of love in the *Livre* acquire their proper moral and ideological significance only when referred to René's more markedly religious concerns voiced in the *Mortifiement*.

---

[65]   The *Queste* is mentioned in Stanza 3. The influence of the *Roman* is so pervasive and apparent that it hardly needs proof. Nevertheless, it is also made part of the narrative: while paying homage and swearing allegiance to the God of Love, the Heart himself has to promise to read the *Roman* (*Livre* § 263), which thus becomes the canonical text of the God of Love's 'religion'.

[66]   Joël Blanchard rightly maintains that more generally the peculiar nature of René's text has not been sufficiently emphasised by earlier criticism, 'L'effet autobiographique', p. 11.

[67]   Gibbs and Karczewska, eds, *Livre*, 'Introduction', p. xxxix.

[68]   Guillaume de Lorris and Jean de Meun, *Le roman de la rose*, 3 vols, ed. Félix Lecoy (Paris: Champion, 1973–5), ll. 3044–5. It is, to say the least, striking that the long passage in question is reproduced almost verbatim in Thomas's *Livre du chevalier errant*, see Badel, *Roman de la Rose au XIV^e siècle*, pp. 320–1.

[69]   As suggested by Poirion, 'Le miroir magique', pp. 51–7.

[70]   Equally focused on the central figure of the 'heart', the *Mortifiement* together with the *Livre* can even be thought of as forming a 'diptych', see Poirion, 'L'allégorie dans le *Livre*', 63–4, and 'Le miroir magique', pp. 38–52. For an edition, see René d'Anjou, *Le mortifiement de vaine plaisance de René d'Anjou: étude du texte et des manuscrits à peintures*, ed. Frédéric Lyna (Paris: Rousseau; Bruxelles: Weckesser, 1926).

If René thus exposes the God of Love's ideal as potentially immoral, he complicates things by making his amorous quest in turn resonate with spiritual overtones. The spiritual echoes that reverberate through the God of Love's court, though, are built on unstable ground, and the attentive reader cannot avoid interrogating their credibility and authenticity. A diffused sense of spiritual splendour magically hangs over the God's island, which 'mieux *sembloit* etre chose espirituelle que terrienne' [my italics] (*Livre* § 139, ll. 85–6),[71] without being further qualified. The exact same description is later applied to the castle itself (*Livre* § 234), and again the reader is somewhat frustrated by the lack of symbolic detail and depth. René, rather than elaborating any detailed spiritual associations triggered by the place, is content to generate a vague impression of transcendence. Preferring to concentrate on the aesthetic 'effect', René indulges in an overload of sensual enjoyment of 'figures' as objects perceived in their contingency, rather than detailing their allegorical significance.[72] Spiritual allegory in the manner of Deguileville has given way to an aestheticising, impressionistic allegory. This 'impressionism' ultimately distracts both the Heart and reader from the successful exegesis of the quest-allegory, and instead enchants him with a sensual experience. René's re-elaboration of the New Jerusalem-motif emblematises this shift: the Holy City, arch-referent of Deguileville's allegory, has vanished from the poem, displaced by the alluring but deceptive vision of the God of Love's castle, a counterfeit Jerusalem. Only distant and unconvincing echoes of the crystalline symbolism of the New Jerusalem survive, drowned out by an overwhelming sense of aesthetic marvel experienced in the presence of sensually rendered brilliancy.[73]

René systematically deconstructs his own dream and the ideals it articulates by exposing their fictional artificiality. Above the gates of the Castle of the God of Love, representing the apotheosis of René's marvellous-mystical vision with its echoes of the New Jerusalem, the Heart finds a magic mirror upheld by two statues (*Livre* § 236). The statues, made of amber, are 'aornees d'or d'alquimye fait de la quinte essence' (*Livre* § 236),[74] and hold a mirror with a diamond surface. Their

---

[71] '*seemed* more a spiritual matter than an earthly one'. All translations are from the Gibbs and Karczewska edition of the *Livre*.

[72] See Blanchard, 'L'effet autobiographique', pp. 13–14 in particular. The same desire to cumulate sensual impressions and effects is reflected in René's sumptuous and extravagant lifestyle, characterised by his tendency to accumulate and collect art, literature, wild animals and exotic mirabilia. He is, in fact a 'collector of sensations'; see Poirion, 'L'allégorie dans le *Livre*', 59–64; and Zink, 'La tristesse du coeur', p. 28; and Gibbs and Karczewska, eds, *Livre*, 'Introduction', pp. xiv–xv.

[73] On the prevalence of an aesthetic of light in René's artistic taste in general, see Poirion, 'Le miroir magique', p. 27. More specifically on his fusion/confusion of an aesthetic and mystical appreciation of light, ibid., p. 77. See also A. Lecoy de La Marche, *Le Roi René: sa vie, son administration, ses travaux artistiques et littéraires. D'après les documents inédits des archives de France et d'Italie*, 2 vols (Paris: Firmin-Didot, 1875) on René's taste for brilliancy reflected in his passion for precious stones, metals and jewellery, vol. 2, pp. 114–26, as well as stained glass, vol. 2, p. 13.

[74] 'adorned with gold through alchemy of quintessence made'.

names, though, soon raise doubts about the actual status of the mirror: they are identified as Fantasy and Imagination. This invites a rather negative interpretation, implying that we are not confronted with Macrobian *somnium* but rather with hallucinatory *phantasma*.[75] This also deconstructs the genuinely revelatory, visionary potential of allegory as expressed in Deguileville, where the symbol of the mirror enables the pilgrim's initial vision of the Heavenly City.[76] Also the description of the statues makes the authenticity of their reflective operation doubtful; rather than being simply golden, they are 'aornees', that is, 'adorned' or 'covered' in alchemical and therefore man-made, fabricated gold. René, certainly familiar with alchemical experiments,[77] may have known only too well that despite the many successful attempts at 'gilding' metals, a proper transmutation was something altogether different. The two statues, Fantasy and Imagination, are furthermore identified as the architects of the God of Love's castle (*Livre* § 236), which further destabilises the shaky foundations of René's ethereal ideal. The dream of an ideal mystical-amorous chivalry is definitively unmasked as a self-deceptive, unsubstantial projection of utopian fancy.

Despite his own, all too self-conscious awareness of the falsity of his amorous and chivalric dream, René cannot entirely give up the hope of realising it, as is proven by the mere existence of the *Livre*. If René has, unlike Jean de Courcy and Thomas de Saluces, really given up hopes of achieving a synthesis, he cannot resist the temptation to indulge in the 'mal savoureux' (*Livre* § 2) conjured by this evocation of an ostensible past golden age of love and chivalry. Thrown into deep rapture, the Heart meditatively contemplates some thirty lovers' epitaphs followed by six poets' tombs without ever tiring of the melancholic delight procured by this repetitive experience. For him the lovers' epitaphs, speaking from beyond the grave, are monuments glorifying a hopelessly lost ideal of integrity, balancing the knightly Grail, the New Jerusalem and the pursuit of erotic Love. Yet this bygone, fabricated world forever eludes René, as ultimately the many epitaphs merely signify the absence and inexistence of the ideal itself.[78] The writing on the epitaphs, and that of the poets it

---

[75] The agency of 'phantasie' clearly suggests an association with the macrobian *phantasma*, or oneiric apparition devoid of meaning. See also Poirion, 'Le miroir magique', p. 33. René cultivates the ambiguity of a visionary vs. hallucinatory dream throughout; see also Carden, 'Forment pensifz ou lit me mis', 24. On Macrobian notions in medieval dream-literature, see A. C. Spearing, *Medieval Dream Poetry* (Cambridge: Cambridge University Press, 1976), pp. 8–11, 18, 25 and *passim*. For Macrobius's own categories, see Macrobius, *Commentary on the Dream of Scipio*, trans. William Harris Stahl (New York: Columbia University Press, 1952), pp. 87–90. On issues of imagination and fantasy in the late Middle Ages and Early Renaissance see also William Rossky, 'Imagination in the English Renaissance: Psychology and Poetic', *Studies in the Renaissance* 5 (1958), 49–73.

[76] See Ch. 1, p. 28.

[77] Along with the many scholars and artists René entertained at his court, astrologers and alchemists were a constant presence, see Poirion, 'Le miroir magique', p. 54. Also on the numerous goldsmiths employed by René, see de La Marche, *Le Roi René*, vol. 2, pp. 114–26.

[78] Poirion, 'Les tombeaux allégoriques', 326.

commemorates, becomes both testament and sole residue of a former age moved by a noble but unsubstantial, fanciful ideal. It is of course deeply significant that the Heart should see among the many epitaphs also René's own; like his illustrious predecessors and contemporaries, he inscribes his own identity within this fictional monument, and commits his legacy to posterity in the form of statuary writing. In this context the *Livre* itself stands as an epitaph to this unsubstantial past, its imagined dreams, ideals and literature, at once solidly sculpted in marble and thinly refracted in the ethereal magic mirror, framed by a delirious dream. After the dissipation of the dream, René's writing of the *Livre* remains the only consolation and compensation for the quest's failure, a relic as it were, and invites a redefinition of the quest's object as an escapist, fetishised literary fantasy in the form of a book.[79] The physical book, and its monumentalised literary content becomes the quest's new object, an epitaph, a 'tomb of allegory'[80] that is unable to signify anything beyond its material contingency, a surrogate for the absence of its original object that is revealed as an unsubstantial projection of individual fancy.

The *Livre*, as well as René's own increasingly more lavish lifestyle in the later years of his reign, reveals him as seeking refuge and consolation in a baroque and self-deluding overload of aesthetic 'impressionism', compensating for his political failures in real life. René, nominally king of Jerusalem, unable to recover his lost oriental kingdom with its entire ballast of cultural, legendary, symbolic and apocalyptic associations, placates his frustration through the controlled fabrication of his own counterfeit paradise.[81] Powerless to reach either the earthly or the celestial kingdom of Jerusalem in his lifetime, René undertakes a literary quest for the ethereal celestial palace of the God of Love, a surrogate fantasy that in turn inspires the edification of his own, private Jerusalem at the courts of Angers and Aix,[82] as well as its post-mortem extension, an elaborate tomb whose building René carefully supervised from 1445 onwards.[83]

---

[79]  Carden, 'Forment pensifz ou lit me mis', 34–5.

[80]  Armand Strubel, 'Le *Livre du cuer d'amours espris*, un "tombeau" de l'allégorie', in Brigitte Pérez-Jean and Patricia Eichek-Lojkine, eds, *L'allégorie de l'Antiquité à la Renaissance* (Paris: Champion, 2004), pp. 401–14.

[81]  'Déçu dans ses ambitions politiques et militaires, il trouva une sorte de compensation morale à ses échecs en exerçant un mécénat averti', Christian de Mérindol, *Le Roi René (1409–1480): décoration de ses chapelles et demeures* (Paris: Editions de la Réunion des musées nationaux, 1981), p. 5.

[82]  René in fact compares the God's celestial castle to his own palace at Samur in the *Livre*, § 234. For a detailed account of René's passionate and meticulous interest in the construction and decoration of his various courts and palaces, see de La Marche, *Le Roi René*, vol. 2, 'Architecture', pp. 3–67. For his passion for gardening, determining his desire of shaping an equally paradisiacal 'oasis de son propre choix', see ibid., p. 51. This enthusiasm for pleasure grounds is again reflected in the long description of the God of Love's clearly mock-Edenic garden in the *Livre*, § 275.

[83]  For René's tomb, see in particular de La Marche, *Le Roi René*, vol. 2, pp. 20ff, and Poirion, 'Les tombeaux allégoriques', 327.

## Olivier de La Marche: *Le Chevalier délibéré* (1483)[84]

The *Chevalier délibére* was written in 1483 by Olivier de La Marche, knight, diplomat and crucial figure at the Burgundian court at the time of Philip the Good, Charles the Bold and Mary of Burgundy.[85] Among all the works discussed in this chapter, the *Chevalier délibéré* proved to be the most successful and influential. It survives in sixteen manuscripts, and its first printed edition published by Vérard in 1488[86] was followed by ten further editions before the end of the sixteenth century.[87] The work was equally translated and adapted on several occasions, producing two distinct Spanish versions published in several editions, two independent translations into English, discussed here in Chapters 4 and 6, and one into Dutch.[88] A modern critical edition with facing translation appeared in 1999 and provides the basis for the following discussion.[89] Despite the considerable amount of criticism focusing on de La Marche as courtier, poet and historiographer, the *Chevalier délibéré* has remained a rather elusive text. Its peculiarities have not been systematically discussed and placed in the literary and political context of the age. While a lot of interesting research has focused on the afterlife of the text and its many translations, transformations and mutations,[90] the highly unusual and idiosyncratic nature of de La

---

[84]  Again, for a fuller discussion along the present lines, see Nievergelt, 'The Quest for Chivalry in the Waning Middle Ages'.

[85]  After Charles's death de La Marche entered the Habsburg household of Maximilian I, husband of Mary, and became preceptor to their son Philip the Fair. The classic study of Olivier de La Marche's life is Henri Stein, *Olivier de la Marche: historien, poète et diplomate bourguignon* (Bruxelles: F. Hayez; Paris: A. Picard, 1888).

[86]  Published in facsimile as *Le Chevalier Délibéré by Olivier de La Marche, printed at Paris in 1488* (Washington, DC: Library of Congress, 1946).

[87]  The exact number of editions is uncertain, see Carleton W. Carroll, 'Transformations d'un texte: les premières éditions du *Chevalier Délibéré*', *Le Moyen Français* 44–5 (1999), 75–85.

[88]  See Emile Picot and Henri Stein, *Recueil de pièces historiques imprimées sous le règne de Louis XI reproduites en fac-similé avec des commentaires historiques et bibliographiques* (Paris: Société des Bibliophiles François, 1923), pp. 322–45. The exact number of Spanish editions of Acuña's translation is uncertain, see Susie Speakman Sutch and Anne Lake Prescott, 'Translation as Transformation: Olivier de La Marche's *Le Chevalier délibéré* and its Hapsburg and Elizabethan Permutations', *Comparative Literature Studies* 25 (1988), 282 n. 3, 286 n. 10.

[89]  Olivier de La Marche, *Le chevalier délibéré (The Resolute Knight)*, ed. and trans. Carleton W. Carroll and C. Hawley Wilson (Tempe, AZ: Arizona Centre for Medieval and Renaissance Studies, 1999).

[90]  Carlos Claveria, *Le Chevalier Délibéré de Olivier de la Marche y sus versiones españolas del siglo XVI* (Zaragoza: Institucion 'Fernando el Catolico', 1950); Klaus Heitmann, 'Die Spanischen Uebersetzer von Olivier de la Marches *Chevalier Délibéré*: Hernando de Acuña und Jeronimo de Urrea', in Karl-Hermann Körner and Klaus Rühl, eds, *Studia Iberica: Festschrift für Hans Flasche* (Bern: Franke, 1973), pp. 229–46; Sutch and Prescott, 'Translation as Transformation'; Prescott, 'Spenser's Chivalric Restoration'; Hernando de Acuña, trans., *El caballero determinado*, ed. Nieves Baranda and Victor Infantes (Toledo: Antonjo Pareja, 2000); Susie Speakman Sutch,

Marche's original work has not been brought out sufficiently. In order to understand the precise implications of its later English transformations, an initial study of the *Chevalier délibéré* itself, within its own cultural context, is essential.

De La Marche's poem is certainly not just 'yet another pilgrimage-allegory', but nevertheless relies on the reader's acquaintance with that particular medieval genre. De La Marche appears to have been directly influenced by earlier texts in the tradition: Deguileville's *Pèlerinages* trilogy was present in at least two different manuscript copies in the library of the dukes of Burgundy, and the *Livre du cuer* also appears to have influenced the Burgundian poet, as recently argued by Jacques Paviot.[91] As is the case with René d'Anjou, de La Marche deliberately alters, even subverts the 'typical' quest of the *homo viator* in several respects. First, his quest is not framed by a dream vision and is narrated in the first person,[92] which invites a reading of the allegory as an account of a direct personal experience of the world; the poem is neither a spiritual dream-vision as with Deguileville, nor a projection of self-indulgent, fanciful dream as with René. Second, the *Acteur*'s quest is entirely devoid of a clearly declared final objective, which adds to the realistic urgency of personal experience a sense of aimlessness and fatality. While with Deguileville the destination of the quest is revealed in the initial vision of the New Jerusalem, and with Thomas de Saluces the object is redefined *en cours de route*, de La Marche's *Acteur* embarks on his quest almost by default, without any specific objective: 'Je partis hors de ma maison / par une

---

'La réception du *Chevalier délibéré* d'Olivier de la Marche aux XV^e et XVI^e siècles', *Le Moyen Français* 57–8 (2006), 335–50.

[91] For de La Marche's knowledge of the *Livre du cœur*, see Jacques Paviot, 'Le chevalier délibéré d'Olivier de la Marche dans la littérature morale (XV^e–XVI^e s.)', *Publications du Centre Européen d'Etudes Bourguignonnes* 43 (2003), 161–70. Concerning the influence of Deguileville, Paviot acknowledges the presence of the trilogy in the ducal library, but argues against de La Marche's knowledge of the work, a claim that remains unsubstantiated. To support the argument for a connection, one may begin by invoking the usual practice of encouraging the Burgundian *rhétoriqueurs* and panegyrists to avail themselves of the materials in the ducal library, as submitted by Georges Doutrepont, *La littérature française à la cour des ducs de Bourgogne: Philippe le Hardi, Jean sans Peur, Philippe le Bon, Charles le Téméraire* (Paris: Champion, 1909), and expanded by Catherine Emerson, *Olivier de La Marche and the Rhetoric of 15th-Century Historiography* (Woodbridge: Boydell, 2004), pp. 119–20. On the manuscripts of the trilogy in the Dukes's possession, today Brussels Bibl. Royale MS 10197–8, listed in an inventory from 1404, and Brussels, Bibl. Royale MS 10176–8, listed in the inventory of 1467, see Georges Dogaer and Marguerite Debae, *La librairie de Philippe le Bon* (Brussels: Bibliothèque Albert I^er, 1967), pp. 44–5, items nos 55 and 56. Beyond the general, thematic parallels between the two works, one may also point to direct echoes in the text, such as the encounter and altercation between Idleness and Occupation, found in *Vie*[1] 6521–890, and arguably echoed in the *CD* in § 139. Another example may be found in the imagery used by de La Marche to describe 'how to attain the City of God And to scale the holy heavens' (*CD* § 311), which develops Deguileville's distinctive iconography of the Holy City – often reproduced in miniatures – 'besieged' by the virtuous souls who literally scale its ramparts with the help of ladders and ropes (*Vie*[1] 125ff).

[92] Like Thomas de Saluces's *Livre du chevalier errant*, which shares de La Marche's auto-biographical tendencies. See Maupeu, *Pèlerins de vie humaine*, pp. 475–529.

soubdaine achaison' (CD § 1),[93] and continues to wander disoriented for much of his quest: 'Sans sçavoir en quel lieu j'aloye' (CD § 24).[94]

Contrary to his initial lack of purpose and 'deliberation' the *Acteur* exhibits occasional bursts of spiritual insight and desire, and he later expresses his intention of 'Querre Dieu, le monde fuir / Servir l'asme et le corps pugnir' (CD § 35),[95] or is flattered by Understanding remarking that 'Je scay que tu as propose … de livrer ton corps au martyre' (CD § 37).[96] Yet while these remarks are echoes of the traditional understanding of a spiritual quest, they sit oddly with the hero's subsequent adventures, as the religious dimension is largely confined to Understanding's verbal instruction (CD § 280ff) and is not reflected in any way in the adventures encountered by the *Acteur*. What characterises the *Acteur's* journey is rather its inconclusiveness, its lack of a sense of orientation and true spiritual progression. The *Acteur*, in the autumn of his life, departs from his home accompanied only by Thought. Following the example of past, deceased heroes, he is exhorted to prepare himself for the imminent final battle against Accident and Debility, messengers of *Atropos*, or Death. Armed with an allegorical but secular armour he first struggles against Hutin, son of Gluttony, and then advances on his way to encounter the hermit Understanding. The hermit insists on the futility of earthly struggles and exhorts the *Acteur* to renounce the world and prepare for his final battle against the messengers of death. After a brief excursus allegorising liturgical vestments the *Acteur* is led to Understanding's treasure chamber that contains a host of 'relics', reminders of human mortality taken from biblical, classical or pseudo-historical and romance *exempla*: Cain and Abel's ploughshare, Samson's pillar, Antipater's box containing the poison for Alexander, Mordret's sword and many other objects. All the while the *Acteur* is exhorted to learn from his melancholic experience of the 'plaisir douloureux' and 'soulaz angoisseux' (CD § 73). After his departure from the hermit the *Acteur* is soon defeated by Age, becoming his prisoner but soon being released. He continues his journey through a dismal and sterile landscape, but is soon seduced by the verdant beauties of the path of Delusion, leading him to the Palace of Love. After an initial temptation by Desire he is nevertheless protected by Remembrance, and returns to the difficult yet barren path of Good Advice. The increasing accumulation of reminders of mortality finally prompts him to find refuge in the pleasures of recollection. Arriving at the manor of Fresh Memory he is introduced to Study, the only consolation to be found in old age, and is again reminded of the supreme power of his ultimate enemy, Death. With Memory he enters through a door a wide plain filled with funerary monuments, and is again exhorted to study and understand the scene. After a protracted catalogue of deceased heroes, past and present, legendary and historical, he departs accompanied

[93] 'On the spur of the moment I went outside my house.' All translations are from the Carrol and Wilson edition of the CD.

[94] 'Not knowing whither I was going.'

[95] 'Seeking God and fleeing the world, / Tending my soul and mortifying my flesh'.

[96] 'I know that you have purposed … To deliver your body to martyrdom.'

by Memory to reach the site of his final battle. They first arrive on the site of a tournament, presided over by the judge *Atropos*, and witness the defeat and death of both Philip the Good and Charles the Bold at the hands of Debility and Accident respectively. More discouraged than ever, the *Acteur* continues his journey and finally finds himself bedridden, attended by Understanding whose final teaching focuses again on the invincibility of *Atropos*.

What is immediately apparent from the preceding summary is the lack of any discernible real progression on the quest, as the protagonist returns time and again to confront the same existential questions without ever advancing towards an answer. The quest – if it is at all possible to speak of one – ends with a simple reassessment of the seemingly irreducible problem of human mortality that was evoked at the very beginning of the *Acteur*'s journey. The scattered but fragmentary allusions to the traditional scheme of the pilgrim's spiritual progression do not manage to redeem the quest's obvious aimlessness and rather highlight the absence of a true transformation and the journey's futile circularity. Thus the *Acteur*'s noble martyrdom soon acquires a rather different connotation when he fatalistically remarks: 'Sy ay ma visière baisee / com cil qui ne veut vivre plus' (CD § 267).[97] The knight's stoic 'deliberation'[98] to embrace martyrdom for an unspecified or absent cause becomes the tragic emblem of his incapacity to find a higher purpose to animate his wanderings despite Understanding's efforts. Similarly, while it is perfectly significant for the 'right' path of Good Advice to be narrow, difficult and hard, it is more profoundly ambiguous to represent it as barren and sterile (CD § 121–6).[99] While this alludes to the physical barrenness of Age, it nevertheless reverberates with an undertone of spiritual barrenness and suggests the *Acteur*'s incapacity to reap any spiritual fruit from his stoic labour. The path of Good Advice itself is represented in an increasingly more negative light, and even becomes strangely reminiscent of its complete antithesis, the infernal wilderness or *selva oscura*: 'la sont les ténèbres appertes' (CD § 123).[100]

The highest concentration of religious notions and ideas can be found at the very end of the journey, where the final encounter is felt to be imminent and instils a renewed desire for an eschatological resolution in both *Acteur* and poet. But here too the ventures into the domain of transcendence remain inconclusive, and do not manage to dispel the *Acteur*'s obsessively reiterated despair. Whilst we are tradi-

---

[97] 'I lowered my visor / like someone who no longer cares to live.'

[98] For a different, more positive interpretation of such stoicism, largely at odds with the one presented here, see René Ménage, 'Le voyage délibéré du chevalier de la Marche', in Taviani, *Voyage*, pp. 209–20.

[99] For instance at CD § 121–2: 'The road was shaking there / And full of deep muddy holes; / The air was a cold and reeking mist / Yielding a noxious and stinking scent. / Only Misery's fruit grows there; / The land shows hardly any profit: / The rent for all its worth / Pays off only in despondency. // The trees there are all sterile / and bear neither flower nor fruit. / Leaves are withered and worthless, / The grasses there are useless / In what healing art teaches. / In brief, it is such a decayed land / That there is no known food there, / Except for pears of anguish.'

[100] 'there shadows are manifest'.

tionally led to expect a transforming illumination projecting the entire quest into a different degree of reality, this metaphysical leap never really takes place. The figure of the New Jerusalem effectively disappears from the narrative and conceptual structure of the poem, and is only indirectly, verbally echoed in Understanding's instruction (CD § 311). Similarly de La Marche's timid evocation of spring at the end of the poem, distantly echoing the possibility of a renewal and rebirth (CD § 338), springs rather from a conventional afterthought than an actual belief in the possibility of resolution and resurrection. Furthermore, coming as it does after Thought's opening statement in the poem that 'n'as pas telle esperance / Qu'ont les arbres pour raverdir, Car jamais ne peulx revenir' (CD § 4),[101] the metaphor of returning spring at the end of the poem appears as self-defeating. Further, even if it is both allegorically sound and orthodox to conjecture the intervention of baptism as a 'champion' to fight in one's stead in the final battle against *Atropos* (CD § 296), this rather ingenious notion is quickly dropped as the mood again sinks into pessimistic self-commiseration a mere three stanzas later: 'car nulz ne combatra pour toi' (CD § 299).[102]

The representation of this final battle best reflects the peculiarity of the poet's concern, even obsession with the question of human transience. Physical death in Deguileville's traditional paradigm of the 'Pilgrimage of Life' had simply denoted the passage to the final stage of the journey, opening the door to its apotheosis in the New Jerusalem, and marking the end of the pilgrimage of life and the beginning of the pilgrimage of the soul. In traditional iconography too, representations of Death are ultimately designed to serve a positive spiritual purpose, denoting the liberation of the spirit from the shackles of individuality.[103] Not so in de La Marche: here death is imagined more as an interruption of the *Acteur's* journey than a part of its evolution. The *Acteur's* obsessive and stubborn determination to resist the onslaught of Accident and Debility despite Understanding's teaching (e.g. CD § 268), clearly signifies his refusal to accept the unavoidability of the experience of death. This stubbornness also denotes an incapacity – or refusal – to project the imagination beyond the experience of death into the afterlife. The focus of the human pilgrimage has shifted from the eschatological haven situated beyond mortality, to the human experience of death as such.[104] This ultimately results in an exacerbation of the power of death as a physical, human experience no longer truly related to a Christian eschatological framework.[105] Absorbing the *Acteur's* attention for the

---

[101] 'Nor do you have any hope / That you can wax green and young again / As do the trees.'

[102] 'For no one will fight in your stead.'

[103] See Chew, 'Death as a Release from Life', in his *The Pilgrimage of Life*, pp. 250–2.

[104] This change is in some respects foreshadowed by Deguileville's own shift of perspective between *Vie¹* and *Vie²*, see Ch. 1, p. 42.

[105] 'Cette attention nouvelle pour la dépouille de l'homme ne se relie pas à sa transformation après sa resurrection finale: elle immobilise les sens sur un objet qui, par lui-même, n'a aucune signification Chrétienne', Alberto Tenenti, *La vie et le mort à travers l'art du XV^{ème} siècle* (Paris: Armand Colin, 1952), p. 14.

entire duration of the 'pilgrimage', *Atropos* inhibits the visualisation of the spiritual, eschatological dimension of human existence concealed behind the imposing, totalising presence of Death personified. The experience of human mortality becomes the central concern of the *Chevalier délibéré*, replacing the New Jerusalem as the supreme agent and ultimate referent of the allegorical journey of life.

De La Marche conflates and confuses two radically different conceptions of the symbolic journey of human life, that of the temporal progression that leads man towards certain death, and that of a soteriological path that can result in either salvation or damnation. But while the two 'paths' have always been related in the Christian conception of life as journey, they have never been blurred to such a degree. In fact the temporal dimension of man's pilgrimage is traditionally only of secondary importance and constitutes a backdrop for the representation and contextualisation of man's spiritual destiny, the essential concern of all pilgrimage symbolism. In Deguileville the messengers of Death are Old Age and Infirmity (*Vie*[1] 13,043ff), and significantly their presentation is clearly separated from the psychomachia that precedes it, providing a temporal frame for the spiritual battle that is the main concern of the text. The calm, dignified acceptance of mortality exhorted in Deguileville is in complete opposition to de La Marche's obsessive anguish: 'Mort, .i. festu je ne te dout! / A mon createur mon cuer tout / Ai mis et toute ma pensee. / Fier, quant tu veuz' (*Vie*[1] 12,157–60).[106] De La Marche subverts the hierarchy between temporal and soteriological journey, replacing spiritual evolution with physical decay as the main concern of the allegorical voyage. This radical, fatalistic pessimism also distances de La Marche from the only source he openly acknowledges, Amé de Montgesoie's *Pas de la mort* (*CD* § 5).[107] The *Pas de la mort* makes use of the same motif of the tournament to represent man's struggle against Debility and Accident, but there the continuous reiteration of human mortality eventually has a redemptive, spiritually beneficial effect, whereas in de La Marche it simply heightens the sense of individual despair and powerlessness.

The highly idiosyncratic conception of mortality found in the *Chevalier délibéré* ultimately implies a latent, possibly unconscious but radical agnosticism on the poet's part,[108] replacing the Boethian confidence in the providential agency of a divine ruler with stoic, at times desperate resignation in the face of the unconditional tyranny of a senseless and definitive destroyer. It is tempting to speculate about the possible reasons for such an exasperating obsession with death on the part of de La Marche, and the *Chevalier délibéré* itself provides useful clues. The climax of the narrative is the allegorical tournament that sees the defeat and death of Philip the

---

[106] 'Death, I do not fear you in the least! I have set my heart and thought entirely on my creator. Strike whenever you please!'

[107] The work is coupled with the *Chevalier délibéré* in two manuscripts, MS Paris BNF, Rotschild 2797 and MS Oxford Bodleian Library, Douce 168. For an edition of the *Pas de la mort*, see Thomas Walton, 'Les poèmes d'Amé de Montgesoie', *Medium Ævum* 2:1 (1933), 1–33.

[108] 'Donner un sens humain à la mort et savoir l'exprimer en image c'est bouleverser le schema Chrétien', Tenenti, *La vie et la mort*, p. 38.

Good, Charles the Bold and Mary of Burgundy, de La Marche's former patrons. It can be safely conjectured that their death profoundly affected such a devoted subject as de La Marche, for whom it must have been very difficult indeed to conceive of any form of meaningful existence outside of the orbit of the Burgundian court.[109] Far from being a conventional complaint for the death of its patrons, the *Chevalier délibéré* turns their deaths into an emblem of a larger and more fundamental change. The decline of Burgundy, the last great flowering of medieval chivalric culture, epitomises for de La Marche the end of an era and the decline of the ethos to which he had heretofore dedicated his entire existence.[110]

The poet's obsession is therefore not one with strictly personal mortality, but with the disappearance of a world order – or *Wirklichkeitsmodell* – that had determined the shape and direction of his own 'journey' of life up to the present moment. Writing the *Chevalier délibéré* already in the 'autumn' of his life (CD § 1), de La Marche has entirely lost this frame of reference and is now forced to wander aimlessly among a sterile, nebulous and no longer clearly intelligible allegorical and ideological landscape. De La Marche's obsession with mortality is thus also symptomatic of a wider climate of *fin de siècle* in the later fifteenth century, determined by the widespread sense of a crumbling social and cosmic order.[111] Such a breakdown of the medieval cosmos inevitably entails for de La Marche the emergence of fundamental doubts about the wider, eschatological frame of reference that imposes meaning and order onto man's pilgrimage of life. These doubts ultimately lead to the writing of a latently but fundamentally agnostic work,[112] where the pattern of Deguileville's paradigmatic *Vie* is not merely altered, but broken and lost. The philosophical implications of the *Chevalier délibéré* are astonishingly anachronistic, as it is one of the earliest literary works in which the

---

[109] In fact upon the death of the heirless Charles the Bold in 1477 the Duchy of Burgundy reverted to the French crown, leaving only the Low Countries to his daughter Mary who soon married Maximilian I, see Richard Vaughan, *Valois Burgundy* (London: Allen Lane, 1975), pp. 256–7. 'This symbolic and practical loss to the dynasty also damaged the personal fortunes of ducal supporters, like Olivier de La Marche, whose patrimonies lay there', Graeme Small, *George Chastelain and the Shaping of Valois Burgundy: Political and Historical Culture at Court in the Fifteenth Century* (London: Royal Historical Society, 1997), p. 207.

[110] It is perfectly fitting that therefore de La Marche in the *Mémoires* should represent Charles's death as the triumph of un-chivalric, barbaric and brutal forces. His death through a 'coup de masse' is 'the antithesis of the noble ideal of courtly combat', Emerson, *Olivier de La Marche and the Rhetoric of 15th-Century Historiography*, p. 219.

[111] This anxiety about the breakdown of social and cosmic order is reflected in numerous contemporary texts, as for instance in Robert Gaguin's *Débat du laboureur, du prestre et du gendarme* (ca. 1480) where the debate of the representatives of the three 'orders' of society is a reaction to the crisis of this traditional model of tripartite social structure. See Robert Gaguin, *Roberti Gaguini Epistole et Orationes*, ed. Louis Thuasne (Paris: E. Bouillon, 1903; repr. Geneva: Slatkine, 1977).

[112] 'Alienation in this sense is indeed essentially a failure to love God and a refusal to adhere to the order which he had given', Ladner, 'Homo Viator', 235.

individual subject manages to express such a typically 'modern' sense of imprisonment and existentialist anguish in such a dramatically vivid manner.

The four works studied in this chapter establish the genre of the allegorical knightly quest derived from Deguileville's *Vie*, and trace a rough line of evolution. Whilst Jean de Courcy almost unquestioningly believes in the usefulness and appropriateness of a chivalric ideal that is both secular and religious, and Thomas III realises the necessity of refining and partially negating the terms of this convergence, René seems to represent their fusion as a noble but hopelessly idealistic and artificial dream. De La Marche equally sees the fusion of chivalric ethos and Christian values as impossible under contemporary circumstances, but goes one step further by actually deconstructing Deguileville's pattern and thus exacerbating the sense of errance and helplessness. De La Marche questions the possibility of undertaking any quest at all, and *Chevalier Délibéré* seems to mark the 'end', or a crisis of the tradition. Intriguingly, however, this very poem will play a fundamental role in shaping later English efforts to revive the tradition (Chapters 4 and 6), within a very different context and for rather different purposes.

# 3

# Stephen Hawes: The Secularised Quest

Stephen Hawes's three major works all derive from the fundamental pattern of Deguileville's *Vie*, but substantially alter the terms of the allegorical journey's significance.[1] Even if it is impossible to establish Hawes's debt to Deguileville definitively, circumstances weigh heavily in favour of Hawes's direct knowledge of the *Vie* in particular, and possibly the *Âme*. It was demonstrated in Chapter 1 that Deguileville's works enjoyed a marked popularity within Henry VII's court: Vérard's 1499 print of the prose *Vie*, illuminated by hand, must have entered the Royal Library in the same year or soon after that, and the Royal Library also held a copy of Jean Gallopes's prose reworking of *Âme* that must have been acquired between 1499 and 1506. Hawes's fellow poet and rival John Skelton claims to have translated the *Vie* himself, presumably during the period of about 1496–1501.[2] Hawes, as groom of the chamber of Henry VII, was certainly in a privileged position to obtain access to the works in the Royal Library, which also held a chivalric miscellany prepared for Edward IV containing, among other items, the sole surviving copy of Jean de Courcy's *Chemin de vaillance* studied in Chapter 2.[3] The volume, a lavish Flemish production, also contains copies of Christine de Pizan's *Epistre Othéa la déesse à* hector,[4] and a French translation of Raymond Llull's *Livre de l'ordre de chevalerie*. All of these works may have evoked Hawes's interest, particularly within the context of the dominant neo-chivalric Burgundian

---

[1]    In chronological order these are *The Example of Vertu* (1503–4) in Stephen Hawes, *The Minor Poems*, ed. Florence W. Gluck and Alice B. Morgan, EETS OS 271 (London: Oxford University Press, 1974); *The Pastime of Pleasure* (1505–6), ed. W. E. Mead, EETS OS 173 (London: Oxford University Press, 1928); *The Conforte of Lovers* (1510–11) also in *Minor Poems*.
[2]    See Ch. 1, p. 37.
[3]    See Ch. 2, p. 47, n. 9. See also Anne Sutton and Livia Visser-Fuchs, *Richard III's Books: Ideals and Reality in the Life and Library of a Medieval Prince* (Stroud: Sutton, 1997), p. 113; Henri Omont, 'Les manuscrits français des rois d'Angleterre au château de Richmond', in *Etudes romanes dédiées à Gaston Paris* (Paris: E. Bouillon, 1891), pp. 1–13.
[4]    For an edition of an English translation of this influential work, see Stephen Scrope, trans., *The Epistle of Othea*, ed. Curt F. Bühler, EETS OS 264 (London: Oxford University Press, 1970).

fashion at Henry's court.[5] The knightly re-elaboration of Deguileville's model found in the *Chemin de vaillance* in particular seems to have shaped Hawes's imagination, as discussed below. The Royal Library also contained a copy of a 1493 vellum print of Olivier de La Marche's *Chevalier délibéré*, although the work does not appear to have had a major impact on Hawes, except possibly for the woodcut programme, a connection which would deserve further study.[6]

Hawes clearly draws on both the *Vie* and the *Chemin*, but also modifies their pattern to serve his own, specific ends. If Deguileville writes a paradigmatic allegory of Everyman's pilgrimage and de Courcy narrows down that paradigm to fit the figure of a supposedly typical Christian knight, Hawes becomes even more narrowly specific. The quests themselves, while they clearly reverberate with more ample and traditional meanings associated with the psychomachia and the 'Pilgrimage of Life' tradition, are obviously taking place within the more confined cosmos of the early Tudor court and its ideals. Hawes's allegories clearly reflect typically early Tudor conceptions of the monarchy, the commonwealth, citizenship, and more specifically of knightly duty, service and obedience.[7] The transtemporal, spiritual and moral abstractions inherited from Deguileville thus progressively give way to ever more specific, local and courtly personifications that ultimately redirect the quest away from a spiritual, eschatological concern towards more clearly earthly, social and pragmatic ends. Hawes does not merely yoke together, like de Courcy's in the *Chemin*, two ideologically contrasting traditions, typified by chivalric romance and spiritual allegory, but equally attempts to integrate into his exemplary heroes' quests elements of an incipient humanism,[8] Tudor ideals of service and obedience, a secular love interest, and personal concerns with political advancement within the meritocratic early Tudor court. The structure of Deguileville's paradigm can accommodate such meanings only with great difficulty,

[5]   Gordon Kipling, *The Triumph of Honour: Burgundian Origins of the Elizabethan Renaissance* (The Hague: Leiden University Press, 1977). For Hawes's reverence for French culture and poetry more generally, see Deanne Williams, *The French Fetish from Chaucer to Shakespeare* (Cambridge: Cambridge University Press, 2004), pp. 114–80.

[6]   For the copy of the *Chevalier délibéré* in the Royal Library, today London BL IA 40645, see Sutch, 'Réception du *Chevalier délibéré*', pp. 343–4, and Pollard, 'Introduction', in his *Le Pelerinaige de Vie Humaine*, p. 23. For the particularly close relationship between text and image in Hawes, see A. S. G. Edwards, 'Poet and Printer in Sixteenth-Century England: Stephen Hawes and Wynkyn de Worde', *Gutenberg Jahrbuch* (1980), 82–8.

[7]   For the classic account, see S. J. Gunn, *Early Tudor Government, 1485–1558* (Basingstoke: Macmillan, 1995). On the impact of those ideas on the contemporary understanding of chivalric ideal, see S. J. Gunn, 'Chivalry and the Politics of the Early Tudor Court', in Sydney Anglo, ed., *Chivalry in the Renaissance* (Woodbridge: Boydell, 1990), pp. 107–8 in particular; and Ferguson, 'Chivalry and the Commonwealth', in his *Indian Summer*, pp. 104–41. See also the older study by G. R. Elton, *The Tudor Revolution in Government: Administrative Changes in the Reign of Henry VIII* (Cambridge: Cambridge University Press, 1953).

[8]   On which see especially Daniel Wakelin, 'Stephen Hawes and Courtly Education', in Mike Pincombe and Cathy Shrank, eds, *The Oxford Handbook of Tudor Literature, 1485–1603* (Oxford: Oxford University Press, 2009), pp. 53–68.

and Hawes often seems torn between his desire to preserve the pilgrimage paradigm and the realisation that his own quests are of a radically different nature.

The production of three distinct works that nevertheless all rely on the fundamental pattern of the allegorical pilgrimage suggests a process of continuing revision that is symptomatic of Hawes's dissatisfaction with his own ideological synthesis. Hawes moves from a relatively clumsy early attempt in the *The Example of Vertu* (1503–4), to a more elaborate synthesis with the *Pastime of Pleasure* (1505–6), and finally towards utter disillusion expressed in *The Conforte of Louers* (1510–11). The joint study of the three works allows a better glimpse of Hawes's mind at work, changing over time and struggling towards an integration of the multiple ideological strands that go into the making of his 'new' knight's quest. Hawes's tentative, experimental approach also helps to explain the often sketchy and 'unfinished' impression conveyed by many of his works. It is precisely because of their unaccomplished, patchwork-like nature and lack of clear focus that Hawes's works are so revealing, and may be seen as representing an ideologically transitional phase in English culture.

## The Politics of Virtue

Hawes's interest in the worldly and social dimension of his heroes' quests, rather than the strictly paradigmatic moral dimension of existence, results in the writing of a more intensely personal, at times even autobiographical allegory.[9] This is most clearly reflected in a passage from the *Example*, where the hero Youth, later to be dubbed Vertu, is told by lady Wisdom: 'Now I amytte you into your rome / In the whiche ye shall your selfe apply / Of myn owne chaumbre ye shall be grome' (*EV* 400–2). Since the post of groom of the chamber is exactly the office held by Hawes at the time, the passage works both as an oblique praise of the king's wisdom and as a manifesto of Hawes's own virtue.[10] The poem furthermore situates this scene inside an allegorical palace that certainly exploits the familiar iconography of Deguileville's celestial city, but overlays these eschatological echoes with more specific and local reference to the physical space of Henry VII's court. The poem as it were localises the court of wisdom in a citadel reminiscent of Richmond Palace, newly built by Henry in 1501, the symbolic as well as literal centrepiece of the early Tudor court culture, and a conspicuous landmark with its flamboyant turrets familiar from contemporary representations and descriptions:[11]

[9]   See Jane Griffiths, 'The Object of Allegory: Truth and Prophecy in Stephen Hawes' *Conforte of Lovers*', in Mary Carr, K. P. Clarke and Marco Nievergelt, eds, *On Allegory: Some Medieval Aspects and Approaches* (Newcastle upon Tyne: Cambridge Scholars Publishing, 2008), pp. 133–55.

[10]   On the 'politics of intimacy' developing as a consequence of the rise of the privy chamber, see David Starkey, 'Intimacy and Innovation: The Rise of the Privy Chamber, 1485–1547', in David Starkey, ed., *The English Court: From the Wars of the Roses to the Civil War* (London: Longman, 1987), pp. 71–118.

[11]   For further details on Richmond Palace, see Simon Thurley, *The Royal Palaces of Tudor England: Architecture and Court Life, 1460–1547* (New Haven, CT: Yale University Press, 1993), pp. 25–38.

Come on fayre youth and go with me
Vnto that place that is delectable
Bylded with towres of curyosyte

. . .

To se the merueyles that there be wrought

. . .

To se the towres I was agast
Set in a valey so strongly fortefyed
So gentyll compassed and well edefyed
The towres were hyghe of adamond stones
With fanes wauerynge in the wynde
Of ryght fyne golde made for the noonys (*EV* 197–213)

If John Bale, Hawes's first biographer, can be at all trusted, Hawes seems to have been chosen for office on the sole recommendation of his 'virtue'.[12] Indeed, a preoccupation with the education of a virtuous knight and courtier is a *Leitmotiv* in Hawes's work, and there is no reason to doubt the sincerity of his commitment to this ideal. Hawes devises in his works a programme for the education of the knight as a member of an aristocratic elite whose moral standards are crucial in shaping the wider reality of the new commonwealth.[13] His interest in moral standards of virtue is therefore not determined by a purely soteriological concern with the destiny of the individual soul, but by his awareness that individual virtuous behaviour can contribute to a broader social equilibrium while also ensuring personal advancement within the court.[14] Hawes is therefore a socially conscious, pragmatic and programmatic allegorist attempting to integrate social and spiritual realities rather than contrasting them, as was the case with the monastic Deguileville. This attempt is also reflected in the optimistic assumption of a mutual agreement of worldly honour with spiritual grace, one of the fundamental assumptions shaping Hawes's thought. This originally Burgundian notion, also familiar from the *Chemin*, found its way to England during the reigns of Edward IV and Henry VII, and sustains Caxton's famous prologue to Malory's *Morte Darthur*: 'But al is wryton for our doctryne and for to beware that we falle not to vyce ne synne, but t'exersyse and

---

[12]   And further, 'all his life and utterance were dedicated to demonstrating that he was, as it were, an example of virtue', see John Bale's *Scriptorium Illustrium Maioris Brytanniae* (Basel, 1557), p. 632, quoted and translated in A. S. G. Edwards, *Stephen Hawes* (Boston, MA: Twayne Publishers, 1983), p. 1.

[13]   In this Hawes already anticipates, for instance, Sir Thomas Elyot, and his *Boke Named the Governour*, ed. Donald W. Rude (New York: Garland, 1992), or Edmund Dudley's *Tree of Commonwealth*, ed. D. M. Brodie (Cambridge: Cambridge University Press, 1948). On the relationship between learning, virtue and good government, see also Kipling, *The Triumph of Honour*, pp. 11–30.

[14]   For the centrality of virtue in the context of early Tudor political thought and discourse, see also John L. Watts, '"A Newe Ffundacion of is Crowne": Monarchy in the Age of Henry VII', in Benjamin Thompson, ed., *The Reign of Henry VII: Proceedings of the 1993 Harlaxton Symposium*, Harlaxton Medieval Studies V (Stamford: Paul Watkins, 1995), pp. 42–6 in particular.

folowe *vertu*, by whyche we may come and atteyne to good fame and renomme in thys lyf, and after thys shorte and transytorye lyf to come unto everlastyng blysse in heven' [my italics].[15] The idea features prominently in the pageants devised to celebrate Prince Arthur's wedding to Katherine of Aragon in 1501, the source for what were to become mainstays of early Tudor political and dynastic propaganda.[16]

The *Example of Vertu*, Hawes's earliest surviving work, was printed on three occasions in 1509, 1520 and 1530, and among all of his works is the one where the influence of the 'Pilgrimage of Life' tradition is most obvious and direct.[17] The hero's journey begins with the encounter with lady Discretion, continues with a journey over the Sea of Vainglory to an island where he witnesses a long debate between four allegorical ladies: Wisdom, Nature, Fortune and Hardiness. After this long expository section the quest itself begins and Youth sets out to seek his beloved lady Cleanness, daughter of the King of Love, avoiding the temptations of Pride and Sensuality. Arriving at the king's castle he is equipped with an allegorical armour and prepares to confront a three-headed monster, embodiment of the World, the Flesh and the Devil.[18] Youth vanquishes the monster and marries his beloved in a heavily allegorised ceremony. The poem ends abruptly and surprisingly with the hero's death and his ascent to heaven.

Much in this story, except for the amorous dimension,[19] is reminiscent of the traditional conception of the pilgrimage of human life: Hawes for instance adopts the *topos* of the dream-vision set in the traditional *locus amoenus*, and devises a quest that at least appears like a spiritual allegory and culminates with a mystical vision. His hero, Youth, while endowed with occasional autobiographical traits, remains mostly an Everyman, and his journey therefore still appears as largely paradigmatic as is the case in Deguileville. Despite this apparent fidelity to tradition, Hawes attempts to endow his hero's journey with a multiple significance, and conceives it as a progress on several planes. It is at once a journey towards moral excellence, the beatific vision that is the transcendental reward for this excellence, but also towards earthly love, social advancement and political power. The underlying idea is that the

---

[15] Sir Thomas Malory, *Le Morte Darthur*, ed. Stephen H. A. Shepherd (New York: Norton, 2004), p. 817.

[16] See for instance Burr Wallen, 'Burgundian Gloire vs. Vaine Gloire: Patterns of Neochivalric Psychomachia', in Gregory T. Clark *et al.*, eds, *A Tribute to Robert A. Koch: Studies in the Northern Renaissance* (Princeton, NJ: Princeton University Press, 1994), pp. 156–61 in particular; Kipling, *The Triumph of Honour*, pp. 77–9; Sydney Anglo, *Spectacle, Pageantry, and Early Tudor Policy*, 2nd edn (Oxford: Clarendon Press, 1997), pp. 52–97. For an edition of the most representative account of the celebration, see *The Receyt of the Ladie Kateryne*, ed. Gordon Kipling, EETS OS 296 (Oxford: Oxford University Press, 1990).

[17] See Hawes, *Minor Poems*, p. xv.

[18] The infernal triad is conspicuously absent from Deguileville's *Vie*, but underscores Hawes's dependence on *Chemin de vaillance*, the only other quest-allegory to employ the infernal triad in such manner.

[19] The love interest is reminiscent in particular of Lydgate's *Reason and Sensuality*, an incomplete translation of the *Echecs amoureux*, as was observed by Lewis, *Allegory of Love*, pp. 271–8.

hero's journey is both literal and allegorical, courtly and spiritual, and that secular referents do not exclude but rather invite the extrapolation of higher, transcendental overtones. Hawes here, much like de Courcy, assumes an unproblematic convergence of spiritual or moral pilgrimage and courtly chivalric quest.

Hawes thus displays an interest in positive secular values from the very beginning of the *Example*. Once Youth is projected into the 'medowe amorous' (*EV* 48) of the dream-world, he encounters the traditional female allegorical personification that is to be his guide. Yet Hawes's choice of 'dyscrecyon' (*EV* 71) as an initial and by implication fundamental virtue is already highly unusual and surprising when compared with traditional female guides, such as Boethius's Philosophy, Alain de Lille's Nature and Deguileville's Grace Dieu. 'Dyscrecyon' appears as an eminently outward, 'social' virtue, unrelated to the substance of man's inner spiritual nature. Correspondingly, Discretion stresses the importance of public, social skills required of Youth, as well as the traditional moral qualities: 'consydre the grete derysyon / Whiche is in youth that may not se / No thynge appropred to his prosperyte' (*EV* 124–6). The emphasis here is not on youthful folly as such, or on its implications of sinfulness, but rather on the social stigma attached to such behaviour. Discretion's warning against the doubleness of the 'flaterynge tonge' (*EV* 106–12) further develops these preoccupations with the immediate social environment rather than supposedly timeless moral standards.

The personification of Sapience, also referred to as Wisdom, dominates the next phase of Youth's instruction. Her teaching, like Discretion's, focuses mostly on social skills and manners (*EV* 379–92), and their impact on Youth's reputation (*EV* 421–34). She seeks to ensure 'that thou condempned be not by ryghtwysnes' (*EV* 387), and warns him of the 'grete shame' (*EV* 422) awaiting the awkward courtier. Her teaching occasionally develops an almost Machiavellian ring, as when she exhorts Youth to embrace intrigue and dissimulation: 'Proue thy frende in a mater fayned / Or thou haue nede than shalt thou se / Whyther he be iustly with the reteyned' (*EV* 442–4). At the same time, Youth is exhorted to display his best behaviour in public: 'Wherefore be thou to her obedyent / . . . / And ryotous company do thou not haunt / For that wyll payre and yll thy name / Wherefore of vertuous myrth let be thy game' (*EV* 500–4). For Hawes – obviously thinking of precise social situations that he would have experienced in the context of the endless intrigues and factionalism of Henry's court[20] – the pursuit of virtuous behaviour is thus no longer encouraged with reference to the moral condition of the hero as such, but becomes instrumental to the acquisition of good reputation and the ensuing advancement within the court.

---

[20] For a discussion of these tensions within the court and their impact upon Hawes's poetry, see Alistair Fox, *Politics and Literature in the Reigns of Henry VII and Henry VIII* (Oxford: Blackwell, 1989), pp. 56–72; and Colin Burrow, 'The Experience of Exclusion: Literature and Politics in the Reigns of Henry VII and Henry VIII', in David Wallace, ed., *The Cambridge History of Medieval English Literature* (Cambridge: Cambridge University Press, 1999), pp. 793–820, here 795–7 in particular.

This redefinition of the function of virtue, however, is harnessed by a consolidated royal control on the distribution of 'honour', a notion that was in turn being radically redefined as shown by Mervyn James.[21] Honour is no longer administered collectively by a vaguely defined, corporate chivalric order, but centralised and monopolised by a monarch who progressively expands his influence to embrace political, economic, moral and religious authority alike. In a slow movement away from the model of medieval kingship, the crown had consolidated its administrative machinery in order to cope with the increasingly complex socio-economic realities of the period,[22] and this radically affected the role of the aristocracy. For Hawes and his immediate environment the knight is thus no longer a relatively independent individual or feudal military agent, bound by a loosely and collectively defined 'order' of knighthood and code of honour; instead he is perceived as an agent of a wider body politic with a rigid political and administrative structure, to whose needs and requirements he must conform.[23] Obedience and loyalty to the crown therefore become fundamental elements of Hawes's programme of education of the 'new' Tudor knight.[24] The ideal knight 'sholde be true / To his souerayn' (*EV* 834–5), reiterating Discretion's earlier exhortation to 'Be to thy kynge euer true subgete, . . . And be obedyent at euery season Vnto his grace without rebellyon' (*EV* 92–7). Even more interesting, particularly in the context of the secular-spiritual ambivalence of Hawes's ideal, is his analogy between obedience to the king and faith in the Saviour, expressed in nearly identical terms: 'So a crysten man sholde be true euer / To Ihesu Cryst that was his redemer' (*EV* 839–40), just as the knight 'sholde be true / To his souerayn' (*EV* 834–5). This assimilation of obedience to a temporal ruler with religious orthodoxy anticipates the convergence of spiritual and temporal authority in the later developments of Tudor theories of kingship, culminating with Henry VIII's claim to become head of both Church and State.[25]

---

[21] Mervyn James, 'English Politics and the Concept of Honour 1485–1642', in his *Society, Politics and Culture: Studies in Early Modern England* (Cambridge: Cambridge University Press, 1986), pp. 308–415.

[22] See Watts, '"A Newe Ffundacion of is Crowne"'.

[23] See Gunn, 'Chivalry and Politics', pp. 107–28, 108 in particular; and Ferguson, *Chivalric Tradition*, pp. 31–40.

[24] This emphasis on the nobility's obedience to the ruler also reflects Henry VII's policy of increased control over the elites of the country, in order to preserve the stability of the centralised government from the threat of factionalism and the so-called 'bastard feudalism' derived from the unchecked practice of retaining. See Margaret Condon, 'Ruling Elites in the Reign of Henry VII', in John Guy, ed., *The Tudor Monarchy* (London: Arnold, 1997), pp. 283–307; Gunn, *Early Tudor Government*, pp. 42–8 and 54–6 in particular; John Guy, *Tudor England* (Oxford: Oxford University Press, 1988), pp. 64–70.

[25] The first open manifestation of this convergence can again be traced to the wedding celebrations between Prince Arthur and Katherine. In the pageants 'Henry VII and his eldest son Arthur, Prince of Wales, were likened respectively to God the Father and Christ the Son . . . The spectacle had the immediate effect of approximating Tudor England to the kingdom of heaven', in John N. King, *Tudor Royal Iconography: Literature and Art in an Age of Religious Crisis*

Hawes's reinterpretation of the chivalric ideal in the *Example* is characteristic of the period for other reasons too, for instance in its shift away from the traditional emphasis on individual heroism and hardiness, in favour of a more moderate, strategically minded praise of political prudence[26] – and Prudence accordingly is the first and chief of the six subdivisions of Sapience. Sapience herself – who later reiterates that she is a member of the king's council (*EV* 869) – propounds an ideal of government that reflects the Tudor ideals of the 'New Monarchy', mixing sharp economic awareness with more traditional ideals of kingship:'A realme is vpholden by thynges thre / The fyrst and chyef it is the swerd /... / The seconde is lawe that euer serueth / ... / The thyrde be marchauntes that do multyply / In this realme welth and prosperyte' (*EV* 610–25). Accordingly it has been argued that Hawes, despite his commitment to a seemingly 'chivalric' educational programme, in reality promotes pragmatic, non-chivalric, mercantile or even 'middle-class' values,[27] and indeed such priorities seem particularly fitting for the reign of Henry VII, who was himself a pragmatic, careful and cunning ruler masking his *Realpolitik* with a generous cultivation of a romanticising chivalric aesthetic.[28] Hawes is clearly aware of the economic implications behind the idealising *façade* of courtly pageantry and formalism, and thus indeed seems to be the poet who most perceptively, albeit prosaically, articulates the concerns of his king.[29]

## New Quests, Old Problems

This initial, static debate section dominated by Discretion, Sapience and Prudence, contains the most distinctive expression of Hawes's originality, articulating an educational programme for the ideal Tudor knight and courtier. Social awareness has

(Princeton, NJ: Princeton University Press, 1989), p. 36. See also Anglo, *Spectacle, Pageantry*, pp. 78–83; and Starkey, 'Representation through Intimacy: A Study of the Symbolism of Monarchy and Court Office in Early Modern England', in John Guy, ed., *Tudor Monarchy*, pp. 42–78. See also Richard C. McCoy, *Alterations of State: Sacred Kingship in the English Reformation* (New York: Columbia University Press, 2002), pp. 15–22.

[26] Hawes shares his obsession with prudence with his contemporary Bernard André, the leading literary figure of the English court in the period; see Ferguson, *Indian Summer*, p. 168, and Gunn, 'Chivalry and Politics', p. 124.

[27] See Stroud, 'Chivalric Terminology'.

[28] See Anglo, *Spectacle, Pageantry*, pp. 98–108; Ferguson, *Chivalric Tradition*, pp. 45–54; and *Indian Summer*, pp. 26–32 and 158–62. On Henry VII see the classic study by Stanley B. Chrimes, *Henry VII* (New Haven, CT: Yale University Press, 1999).

[29] Or, to view matters more cynically in the light of early Tudor propaganda, it can be said with Kipling that 'Henry indulged lavishly in literature, the visual arts, and the drama, but his indulgences were characteristically of the institutional rather than the philanthropic variety'; Gordon Kipling, 'Henry VII and the Origins of Tudor Patronage', in Guy Fichte Lytle and Stephen Orgel, eds, *Patronage in the Renaissance* (Princeton, NJ: Princeton University Press, 1981), p. 164. For Hawes's relation to Henry more generally, see Robert J. Meyer-Lee, *Poets and Power from Chaucer to Wyatt* (Cambridge: Cambridge University Press, 2007), pp. 179–90.

replaced doctrinal and sacramental instruction, and the allegorical journey of life no longer leads man away from human, temporal reality towards a higher transcendental one, but becomes a quest for integration within Henry VII's court. In the light of such conspicuously social, worldly and ultimately courtly preoccupations it is rather difficult to see exactly how this same lady Discretion can also take over the role of Deguileville's Grace Dieu and 'brynge thy soule to blesse eterne / By wyse example and morall doctryne' (*EV* 82–3). Hawes clearly wishes us to see that his hero has embarked on a multivalent journey towards moral virtue and spiritual deliverance, but also towards social adroitness, earthly love (*EV* 99–105), obedience to the monarch as a key to social order (*EV* 92–8), as well as an awareness of human transience and mortality (*EV* 113–19). This multiplication of meanings certainly suggests that Hawes is here trying to articulate a 'new', synthetic ideal that transcends the opposition between secular and religious ethos, but in its very appearance as a sequence of separate, itemised meanings, this is also a powerful reminder of the difficulty of achieving such an integration. Not only does Hawes attempt to yoke together largely independent literary traditions, but in doing so he equally attempts to collapse the different ideological substructures sustaining these multiple literary forms, modes and genres.[30] The mixture of allegory, romance, early humanism with devotional, didactic, chivalric and political material – not to speak of the juxtaposition of spiritual-ascetic, courtly-amorous and political allegory – ultimately produces a puzzling forced marriage of contradictory ideologies.[31]

The beginning of the quest proper, then, puts Hawes's programme of social education and control under great pressure, and exposes his dependence on traditional imaginative patterns despite his commitment to literary and social innovation. Hawes loses his distinctive voice in this second part. After an interesting albeit tentative sketch of the new ideal of the knight-courtier-citizen, he falls back into a more conventional psychomachia enacting the universal virtue-vice dichotomy. Hawes can rely on the longstanding, sanctified authority of these traditions, but is forced to sacrifice the originality of his own educational project and of his poetic voice. A number of features typical for the genre reappear: Discretion and Youth 'came vnto a ryght grete wyldernes' (*EV* 1129), 'walked in grete derkenes' (*EV* 1131), encounter wild beasts (*EV* 1143), and finally meet 'sensualyte' and 'pryde enduyd with couetyse' (*EV* 1163–204).

Whilst these features are meaningful within the context of the traditional understanding of the spiritual quest, in the light of Hawes's more original treatment of the quest in the first half of the *Example*, they appear as extraneous and inappro-

---

[30]  See for instance the introduction to *Minor Poems*, pp. xxxix–xli; and Edwards, *Stephen Hawes*, pp. 103–8.

[31]  Skelton, more critically aware of this risk, famously reflects on the impossibility of writing allegory in a world of fluctuating signifiers and meanings as a consequence of the advent of humanism. See Helen Cooney, 'Skelton's *Bowge of Court* and the Crisis of Allegory in Late-Medieval England', in Helen Cooney, ed., *Nation, Court and Culture: New Essays on Fifteenth-Century English Poetry* (Dublin: Four Courts Press, 2001), pp. 153–67.

priate. In particular, the explicit condemnation of any sort of involvement with the 'lady of rychesse' (*EV* 1170) seems absurd in the light of Hawes's earlier perceptive comments about the importance of economic realities and their impact on royal policy. If the whore of Babylon is 'quene of *welth* and worldely glory' [my italics] (*EV* 1171), it is problematic to praise economic undertaking in the following terms 'For without marchauntes can not be / No realme vpholden in *welth* & pleasure' [my italics] (*EV* 628–9). The radical rejection of involvement in secular, economic affairs implied by Youth's behaviour during these new encounters sits oddly with the secularising tendencies of the first part and seems to go against Hawes's original wish of directing Youth's quest towards a greater involvement with mundane affairs.

Accordingly the role of Sapience is equally transformed in this later section. So her praise of prudence and circumspection in human affairs abruptly gives way to more traditional moral teaching, and lady Sapience suddenly shifts gears in her argument by asserting that because of her knowledge in the seven arts 'no man without me can go to heuen'[32] (*EV* 718), and proceeds: 'I sapience am endewed with grace / And the lode sterre of heuenly doctryne / ... / Who that lyst to me for to enclyne / He shall knowe thynges that be dyuyne / And at his ende beholde the deyte' (*EV* 771–6). While Hawes thus enacts an intriguing recuperation of secular, political and courtly values to serve spiritual ends, it is very difficult for the reader to identify exactly how the spiritual superstructure of Hawes's ideal develops out of its strictly secular roots. So, when Sapience exhorts Youth to: 'Eschew also the synne of pryde / The moder and the feruent rote / Of all the synnes at every tyde' (*EV* 456–8), she reactivates an intransigent moral stance that tends to dismiss precisely those secular and aristocratic values that Hawes is also trying to promote and celebrate as being directly conducive to a celestial apotheosis.

This abrupt transformation of the role of Sapience reveals an ideological discontinuity that in turn betrays Hawes's own uncomfortable position with regard to the innovative, hybrid ideal he is struggling to articulate. This explodes and undercuts all possibilities for re-negotiating a positive appreciation of aristocratic court-culture within a more nuanced, 'mixed' ideal that would subsume the active and contemplative ideals. In this sense, Hawes appears truly as the direct heir of Jean de Courcy, desirous to convey what he perceives to be the profound, intimate agreement of the secular, courtly and chivalric values on the one hand with the Christian ones on the other, but unable to do this without implicitly conceding their incompatibility revealed by the conceptual split between 'Vaillance de l'âme' and the 'corporale Vaillance'.[33]

The full extent of the instability of Hawes's synthesis in the *Example* appears at the end of the poem, where his hero experiences an amorous apotheosis that tries to be both secular and literal on the one hand, and spiritual and eschatological on the other. Although it is entirely absent from Deguileville's original paradigm, and thoroughly allegorised in the *Chemin*, human erotic love is the principal motive

---

[32] Hawes elaborates and amplifies this idea of the seven arts as a key to the kingdom of heaven in the *Pastime of Pleasure*, see below.

[33] See Ch. 2, pp. 51–2.

impelling Youth's journey after the end of the debate scene. Sapience, back in her pragmatic self, advises marriage 'For to eschewe all yll censualyte' (*EV* 1057), and thus seems to have a clearly literal and not allegorical marriage in mind, but it soon turns out that the Lady 'Clennes' (*EV* 1162) is in fact an allegorical personification of chastity. A similar ambivalence also pervades the description of the God of Love:[34] 'his nakednes doth sygnyfy / That true loue no thynge ellys desyreth / But the very persone and eke body' (*EV* 1324–6), but inexplicably 'His naked legge betokeneth charyte' (*EV* 1341).

This confused juxtaposition of human and divine love is expanded in the first apotheosis of the poem, Youth's marriage to Cleanness. The celebration takes place in a strongly religious and allegorised setting, with St Peter himself officiating and in the presence of other saints and the allegorical personifications of Prayer, Charity, Penitence and Humility (*EV* 1708–9), all reminiscent of the apotheosis of Deguileville's pilgrim in a Cistercian monastery. The consummation is presented as a feast 'to fede the soule with dyuyne comfort' (*EV* 1858) – yet Hawes again allows the intrusion of secular preoccupations that unsettle the picture: 'Dame fayth in stablenes so true / Ledynge with her the fayre dame pease / That welth and ryches doth well encrease' (*EV* 1784–6). Moreover, his inclusion of the blatantly pragmatic 'dame restytucyon' (*EV* 1790) alongside the theological virtues cannot avoid striking a discordant note. The apparent spiritual connotations of the apotheosis and the quest that leads up to it are suddenly dissipated by the realisation that this is after all a literal marriage, and its fruits are not sempiternal but ephemeral: 'By this tyme was I .lx. yere olde / And desyred for to lyue in peace' (*EV* 1864). Since the amorous idyll, the ostensible object of the quest, is ultimately illusory and short-lived, the quest leading up to it appears as Sisyphean in retrospect. This also forces Hawes to look for a second apotheosis in the poem, to complete the transcendentalising leap that the marriage of Vertu to Lady Cleanness fails to perform. Immediately after the marriage Vertu thus longs for the 'gardeyn gloryous / Vnto whiche now fayne wolde I go' (*EV* 1875–6), 'this lande [that] is heuen that to vs longeth' (*EV* 1883). But this final celestial epilogue, including a vision of hell and heaven, comes to stand as a sort of eschatological afterthought, entirely unrelated to the substance of the hero's quest that culminated in literal, earthly marriage. Carried off by an angel, Vertu almost seems to find heaven in spite of himself.

## Tudor Knight

Hawes wrote the *Pastime of Pleasure* in 1505–6,[35] two or three years after the *Example*, and although he makes a considerable effort to provide a more unified and organised ideological programme, the poem remains fundamentally an extended treatment of very similar ideas cast in an almost identical form – and

---

[34] See also Lewis, *Allegory of Love*, pp. 285–6.
[35] Edwards, *Stephen Hawes*, pp. 26ff.

many of the earlier problems also return. It is Hawes's longest and most important work and has therefore attracted slightly more critical attention;[36] it was also a reasonably successful work in its time, going through four editions in the sixteenth century, in 1509, 1517, 1554 and 1555.[37] The poem's broad narrative structure is directly taken from the *Example*: again the text is divided into two major sections roughly equal in length, and a process of verbal instruction precedes the hero's actual quest. The hero Grande Amoure's schooling in the seven liberal arts at the Tower of Doctrine is simply an expansion and elaboration of Vertu's edifying conversation with Sapience and Discretion in the *Example*. The actual quest occupies the second part of the narrative, and again the hero fights a series of allegorical monsters. Crucially, though, whereas the *Example* employs strictly spiritual abstractions, such as the three-headed monster of the World, Flesh and Devil, these are replaced with courtly and psychological-amorous ones in the manner of the *Roman de la rose* in the *Pastime*.[38] The quest here once more culminates with the hero's marriage to his lady, La Bell Pucell, and the ceremony is again intermittently literal and allegorical.

In the *Pastime* Hawes further elaborates his ideal of a 'new' knighthood sketched in the *Example*, and develops in particular the convergence of traditional chivalry and clerkly learning. So the long instruction in the liberal arts at the Tower of Doctrine becomes a preparation for a seemingly traditional, more strictly chivalric instruction at the Tower of Chivalry (*PP* 2935–3486).[39] The transition is carried out clumsily, but the basic idea sustaining it is certainly valid and convincing: 'It is euer the grounde of sapyence / Before that thou accomplysshe outwardly / For to reuolue vnderstandynge and prepence / All in thy selfe' (*PP* 1100–3). If this wish for a synthesis of knighthood and learning springs from an early humanist impulse, it still takes the form of a quintessentially medieval, academic curriculum comprising the *trivium* and *quadrivium*.[40] Hawes however further transforms the political signif-

[36] See especially John N. King, 'Allegorical Pattern in Stephen Hawes's *The Pastime of Pleasure*', *Studies in the Literary Imagination* 11:1 (1978), 57–67; Rita Copeland, 'Lydgate, Hawes, and the Science of Rhetoric in the Late Middle Ages', *Modern Language Quarterly* 53:1 (1992), 57–82.

[37] *The Pastime of Pleasure*, ed. W. E. Mead, 'Introduction', pp. xxix–xli.

[38] Again here Hawes seems to pick up an idea introduced by the 1501 pageants for Prince Arthur's wedding, where the erotic abstractions in the manner of the *Roman de la rose* for the first time in England become vehicles for political ideas; see Ferguson, *Chivalric Tradition*, pp. 49–50.

[39] Despite his innovations, Hawes remains massively indebted to traditional conceptions of chivalry, such as the ones found in Llull's *Book of the Ordre of Chivalry* or in *The Epistle of Othea*. Both works circulated in translation and in French, and were contained in MS Royal 14 E.ii, discussed above, Ch. 2, p. 47, n. 8. Rather than proposing a revolutionary alternative model, Hawes sees himself as reforming and reviving chivalry.

[40] The general assimilation of knighthood and wisdom, goes back at least as far as the *Epistre Othéa*, where the narrator exhorts the joining of Minerva and Pallas, respectively representing knighthood and wisdom, see for instance Stephen Scrope (trans.; ca. 1440–50), *The Epistle of Othea*, ed. Bühler, Chapter 14. Hawes may well have that precise juxtaposition in mind while he is writing the battle scenes in the *PP*, where Amoure switches between invocations of Pallas as

icance and usefulness of the chivalric ideal by integrating it more firmly within the social ideal of the commonwealth: 'Knyghthode he sayd was fyrst establysshed / The comyn welthe in right to defende' (*PP* 3361–2). While this notion too is to some extent traditional and appears for instance in Raymond Llull's *Book of the Ordre of Chivalry*,[41] it is here elaborated to fit early Tudor ideals of service and obedience, attempting to curb and stifle the military aristocracy's tenacious desire for independence:[42] 'For knyghthode is not in the feates of warre / As for to fyght in quarrel ryght or wronge' (*PP* 3368–9). In such a movement away from a more 'personal' and potentially dissident cultivation of chivalric aggression towards an ideal of service to the crown and public weal, the knightly class is invested with a new, civil and administrative mission.[43]

The knight is even conceived as an agent of social control and repression, ensuring social stability through the exercise of force:[44] 'Agaynst all suche rebelles contraryous / Them to subdue with power vyctoryous' (*PP* 3366–7). The knight becomes engaged in a sort of 'inward' war aimed at guaranteeing the stability of the 'New Monarchy' and equally new Tudor dynasty, but the allegorical ground where this *bellum intestinum* is fought is no longer the moral arena of the individual soul but rather the public and corporate 'body' of the new commonwealth. At times the martial ethos of knighthood is transformed beyond recognition: 'For euermore the spyryte of pacyence / doth ouercome the angry vyolence' (*PP* 4702–3). Consequently, Prudence again plays an important part in Hawes's project in a manner that foreshadows the familiar ideal of the shrewd, tactical Renaissance courtier. And again the 'wisdom' praised by the poem is eminently tactical and pragmatic rather than bellicose: 'Thus by your wysdome ye shall them so wynne / Vnto your frendes that dyde you so hate' (*PP* 4697–8).

Hawes thus expands many of the ideas he had already sketched in the earlier *Example*, and insists particularly on the knightly caste's transformed relationship with the monarchy. In the *Pastime* in fact the monarch is explicitly identified as the prime mover of the quest, both impelling Grande Amoure the hero to set out on his adventures and inspiring Hawes the poet to write his allegory (*PP* 1–56). No longer triggered by a vision of the New Jerusalem as in Deguileville's case, Hawes's quest is inspired by the figure of the king, himself engaged in an allegorical journey introduced by the very first lines of the work: 'Ryght myghty prynce & redoubted

goddess of wisdom and Mars as god of war, e.g. ll. 4970, 5085, 5163. The *Othea* not only circulated widely, but was equally included in MS Royal 14 E.ii, for which see previous note.

[41]   See the English version printed by Caxton, ed. Byles, Ch. 2, pp. 14–23. A French translation of the text is, again, included in MS Royal 14 E.ii.

[42]   Gunn, 'Chivalry and Politics', and Ferguson, *Chivalric Tradition*, pp. 31–6.

[43]   For the disruptive and subversive potential of aristocratic honour-culture and the centralising attempts of the monarchy to 'contain' and control such tendencies see also James, 'English Politics and the Concept of Honour 1485–1642'. On the monarchy's tendency to demilitarise the nobility and control them through the systematic creation of administrative offices tying them directly to the crown itself, see Gunn, *Early Tudor Government*, pp. 38–48.

[44]   See Gunn, *Early Tudor Government*, pp. 54–6.

souerayne / Saylinge forthe well in the shyppe of grace / Ouer the waves of this lyfe vncertayne / Ryght towarde heuen to haue dwellynge place' (*PP* 1–4). The passage clearly elaborates the image of the allegorical navigation found in Deguileville, but fuses it with the equally familiar *topos* of the Ship of State.[45] This allows Hawes to conflate the political and the spiritual, thus celebrating the supposedly providential advent of the Tudor dynasty: 'Grace steereth well, the grace of God is grete, / whiche you hathe brought to your ryall se' (*PP* 8–9). Adapting Deguileville's narrative of individual, moral transformation to fit the needs of political ideology, it is now the king's journey on the Ship of State that becomes the main term of reference and paradigm for the journey of the individual 'citizen' of the commonwealth:

> Before the lawe in a tumblynge barge
> The people sayled without parfytnes
> Throughe the worlde all aboute at large
> They hadde none ordre nor no stedfastnes
> Tyll rethorycyans founde Iustyce doubtless
> Ordenynge kynges of ryghte hye dygnyte
> Of all comyns to haue the souerainte
>
> The barge to stere with lawe and Iustyce
> Ouer the waves of this lyfe transytorye (*PP* 876–84)

Such a conception of the allegorical 'journey' as a collective, political adventure radically transforms inherited notions of knighthood and knight-errantry to fit the Tudor ideals of commonwealth, service and obedience. The knight is no longer engaged in an individual romance-like errance through a sequence of unexpected encounters, marvels and wonders, but embarks on a Ship of State that is already being steered by the 'ordenynge' operation of the monarch and his 'rethorycyans', including of course Hawes himself.[46]

The rigidity of this programme is not due, as in the case of Deguileville, to the inflexibility of religious and sacramental didacticism mobilised by the allegory; it is rather a function of the specific pressures and demands that suddenly confront the ambitious youth in the socio-political context of early Tudor England. Grande Amoure's quest ultimately becomes a new paradigm for the pilgrimage of life in those specific historical conditions, and functions as a blueprint for the education of the young knight and citizen and his service to the commonwealth. The idea of a 'template' for the education of the aspiring courtier is most clearly revealed in

---

[45] Famously used also by Barclay and Skelton, the motif is widespread and ultimately goes back to Plato. Arthur Koelbing provides an extensive list of specifically English medieval precedents, *Zur Charakteristik John Skelton's* (Stuttgart: Strecker und Schröder, 1904), p. 76.

[46] The connection between 'rhetoric' and the issue of a new 'social order' is far from being arbitrary in Hawes's thought. Rhetoric, by ordering language, performs a process analogous to the social engineering so dear to Hawes, and thus becomes a means of social order and control. See especially Copeland, 'Lydgate, Hawes, and the Science of Rhetoric'.

Hawes's use of an allegorical tapestry in the *Pastime*. On first arriving at the Tower of Doctrine, Grande Amoure discovers a rich arras picturing all of his coming adventures, which thus constitutes a sort of graphic 'abstract' of his subsequent quest (*PP* 414–76). The individual knight has no other choice than conforming to the pattern that is woven into the arras, thus becoming bound by its predetermined narrative. The knight is thus inextricably implicated in and subjected to the larger, corporate ideal of the commonwealth, but his presence inside the arras also visualises his admission to a privileged courtly space and its discourses or 'narratives'. The tapestry thus functions as a sort of matrix for knightly education, revealing the inflexible and to some extent coercive nature of Hawes's programme.

Other features in Hawes's poetry confirm his interest in the possibilities of a systematic, mechanical reproduction of his exemplary programme of education. Seth Lerer has perceptively discussed borrowings from the technical language of printing and book production in Hawes's work. The metaphorical use of such expressions implies the adoption of a rather innovative understanding of the process of reading and cognition.[47] Just as ideas and impressions may be 'printed' in the mind by analogy with the printing press, the reader is exhorted to 'prynte in his thought' (*PP* 3407) the significance of Hawes's own work.[48] The reader, assimilated with the quest's hero, is thus imagined as a blank page subjected to a process of 'imprinting'. Hawes's work itself, endlessly reproduced through an indefinite or even infinite number of 'impressions', therefore becomes a tool in the process of systematic replication of the archetypal Tudor knight, conceived as an agent of the monarchy's control over the commonwealth.[49]

Hawes's slightly sinister fascination with this kind of mechanical social engineering also shapes his conception of the Tower of Chivalry. Again the passage is introduced by the printing metaphor, 'As any man can prynte in his thought' (*PP* 3001), and prepares for a further elaboration of the mechanical imagery. On the roof of the tower is placed an elaborate 'jousting machine' composed of four automata representing mounted knights: 'And vnder each horse there was full pryuely / A grete whele made by craftly geometry / With many cogges vnto whiche were tyed / Dyuerse cordes that in the horses holowe / To euery Ioynte full wonderly applyed' (*PP* 3009–13). The mechanical regularity of the jousting automata becomes an emblem of the

---

[47] Seth Lerer, 'The Rhetoric of Fame: Stephen Hawes's Aureate Diction', *SpS* 5 (1984), 169–84, here 170.

[48] Hawes often seems to conceive the writing of poetry itself as a visual rather than verbal process, for which see Edwards, *Stephen Hawes*, pp. 24–5 and 106, and Gluck and Morgan, 'Introduction', *Minor Poems*, pp. xxxi–xxxv.

[49] This reading could be elaborated with reference to the particular interest taken by Hawes in the woodcut programme illustrating his work, which he seems to have devised in close collaboration with Wynkyn de Worde, who printed all of Hawes's surviving poems. See Edwards, 'Poet and Printer in Sixteenth-Century England'. This particular care for images may have been inspired by the similarly important function of woodcuts in Jean Lambert's print of the *Chevalier délibéré*, present in the Royal Library. See above, p. 75, n. 6.

exemplary mastery of the knightly skills and its related 'new' ethos, embodying a mechanical and de-humanised ideal of efficiency and orderly obedience that Hawes's programme imposes onto the knightly class.[50] Again the eternal repetition of an entirely mechanical and ever identical 'type' of movement appears as an imaginative amplification of the manipulative possibilities opened by the printing process.

## *Bivium*

Despite the innovative understanding of knighthood, society, commonwealth and monarchy implied by this programme of education, the hero's quest is nevertheless set within a more traditional eschatological framework that is at odds with these innovations – and the problematic ambivalence of spiritual and secular significance encountered in the *Example* comes back to haunt the allegory of the *Pastime*. Hawes initially makes a clear effort to secularise the quest more thoroughly: he abandons the frame of the dream vision, which already suggests that the quest is taking place in 'this' world, rather than a parallel world populated by timeless moral abstractions. Moreover, Hawes also tries to differentiate much more clearly between the paths of social advancement and ascetic contemplation, which are at least initially conceived as incompatible. Amoure is forced to choose between two mutually exclusive ways: 'the streyght waye of contemplacyon' (*PP* 85) and 'the waye of worldly dygnyte' (*PP* 93). Also the ending of the quest seems to confirm that the pilgrimage allegory has been 'secularised': the elaborate and heavily allegorical ceremony staged in the *Example* has been replaced by a more sober affair in the *Pastime*, described in matter-of-fact terms: 'And lex ecclesie dyde me to her wedde / After wiche weddynge there was a grete fest / Nothynge we lacked but had of the best' (*PP* 5324–6).

Whilst all of this tips the balance in favour of a more clearly secular emphasis, Hawes once more gives in to the temptation of harmonising secular and religious ideals. Although Grande Amoure chooses 'the waye of worldly dygnyte', he soon finds that this worldly path nevertheless reverberates with clearly spiritual overtones and leads to the tower of 'doctryne' (*PP* 135).[51] Even the quintessentially secular lady Fame directs the hero on a quest clearly reminiscent of an Augustinian pilgrimage towards the heavenly home, and the hero's journey to reach his beloved, La Bell Pucell, resonates with echoes of Deguileville's navigation over the Sea of the

---

[50] See also Christiania Whitehead, *Castles of the Mind: A Study of Medieval Architectural Allegory* (Cardiff: University of Wales Press, 2003), pp. 224–5. For later, Elizabethan uses of automata and mechanical devices as part of a process of social control and 'engineering', see especially Jessica Wolfe, *Humanism, Machinery, and Renaissance Literature* (Cambridge: Cambridge University Press, 2004), pp. 56–87.

[51] 'Doctrine' resonates with a religious echo, but etymologically merely evokes 'teaching' from Lat. *docere*, and its use here is therefore more confusing, vague and problematic. Again the *Chemin* seems to provide the model for this rather loose but inclusive conception of 'doctrine', see Ch. 2, p. 48.

World: 'a grate see there is / Beyonde whiche see there is a goodly lande . . . in whiche dwelleth by grete auctoryte / Of la bell pucell whiche is so fayre and bryght' (*PP* 267–75). Similarly, the mansion where Pucell receives her knight 'seemed more lyke a place celestyne / Than an erthely mansyon whiche shall away' (*PP* 5212–13). Such elaborations appear as increasingly conventional and inappropriate in a more firmly secularised setting. Similarly the hero's instruction in the seven liberal arts, which seems initially designed to prepare him for political service, suddenly appears to have a rather different, spiritual purpose. So Logic puzzlingly declares that 'My scyence is all the yll to eschewe' (*PP* 622) and promises her diligent pupil that 'In heuen aboue he shall haue dwellynge place' (*PP* 626). Rhetoric dwells in a chamber that 'More lyker was . . . / Vnto a place which is celestyall' (*PP* 663–4), and Music summarises the influence of the seven sciences onto the human soul: 'That they are waye and perfyte doctryne / To the Ioye aboue whiche is celestyne' (*PP* 1553–4).

This spiritualisation of the seven liberal arts causes several problems. First, it clashes with Amoure's initial choice to pursue the path of worldly glory rather than that of contemplation. Second, the spiritual overtones found in this section again seem largely extraneous and conventional, bearing little or no logical relation to the allegorical ladies and their respective arts. Third, neither the moral nor the more technical aspects of the education in the liberal arts, which are intended as a preparation for the subsequent quest, are ever applied or even invoked in the second, active part of the hero's journey. In fact the actual quest, this time opposing the hero to rather slippery psychological and amorous abstractions rather than the traditional moral or spiritual foes, seems to be entirely unrelated to the hero's earlier 'spiritualised' academic curriculum. Fourth, the actual objective of the quest is not moral virtue and doctrine, as this long instruction would suggest, but worldly and amorous success culminating in a literal marriage and Amoure's accumulation of wealth (*PP* 5369–75). This last incongruence has even led one critic to see the *Pastime* as 'a quest for the three lures of the world – glory, lust and . . . gold', providing 'a worldly parody of Pilgrim's elaborate education and preparation in Deguileville'.[52] Yet clearly Hawes is doing something more daring, albeit clumsily, and once more cannot resist the temptation to try and harmonise secular aspirations and a spiritual, eschatological interest. Despite the initial dichotomy of the mutually exclusive paths of 'contemplacyon' and 'worldly dygnyte' (*PP* 85 and 93), the two ways are eventually blurred, resulting in the hybrid 'waye of vertue, welthe and stablenes' (*PP* 1119).

In the final section, after Amoure's marriage, Hawes once more frames the otherwise innovative quest with a detour through familiar and established materials, here the allegorical personifications first popularised by Petrarch's *Trionfi*: Death, Fame, Time, Eternity.[53] Hawes integrates other traditional sequences, such as the Seven Deadly Sins (*PP* 5411–94), the Nine Worthies (*PP* 5495–606) with the

---

[52] Cullen, *Infernal Triad*, p. 11.
[53] Hawes is probably indebted to an iconographic source rather than Petrarch's actual work or one of its many adaptations, see King, 'Allegorical Pattern in Stephen Hawes's *The Pastime of Pleasure*'.

clear purpose of articulating a conclusive *memento mori* and framing individual existence within a higher, transcendental perspective. Yet the ideologies mobilised by such established and sanctified materials ultimately predicate a detachment from mundane existence that can only clash with Hawes's previous focus on social rather than spiritual reality. After a largely tentative and innovative exploration of new possibilities, ideological as well as poetic, Hawes thus seems to feel the urge to take refuge once more in the reliability and security of long established late medieval traditions. Again Hawes seems divided in his intent: on the one hand, he is attempting to highlight the intimate agreement of secular advancement and spiritual progression, while on the other the promises of worldly reward are necessarily shattered by the onslaught of death and the perspective of eternity.[54] The poet almost seems to retract his previous ideological experiments, thus reducing his hero's quest to a futile striving for a form of secular stability that can only ever be illusory.[55] Although Hawes sets out to establish the convergence of secular and eschatological aspirations, in reality he ends up revealing their radically incompatible natures, and his affiliation remains strangely divided. On the one hand, he directs his effort towards the consolidation of an institutional and political machinery that he associates with temporal permanence in its possibilities for endless perpetuation and replication. On the other, almost as an afterthought, he cannot help recognising the limitations of this project in the ontologically expanded perspective of eternity that he inherits from Deguileville's allegorical pilgrimage tradition.

### 'the resynge of a knyght'

The *Conforte of Lovers* is Hawes's latest surviving work, and marks a new phase of his poetic activity. The *Conforte* may still be considered a kind of allegorical quest, and is imagined as a knightly 'Iornaye' (*CL* 376) complete with the familiar arming scene. Most of the allegorical action has disappeared, however, leaving us with what is in fact a transposed, largely speculative and interior quest. In his last surviving poem Hawes looks back on the possibility of actually undertaking the quest himself, and retracing the exemplary steps he had devised for his fictional heroes in the *Example* and the *Pastime*. In many ways the *Conforte* then is a more mature and self-consciously reflective work, where the poet confronts both the ideal he had previously devised and the external reality that determines the possibilities of its application in the real world. Hawes distances himself from his earlier ideal, and complains about the external, social conditions that make its pursuit and application impossible. Hawes's exclusion from the courtly circles after the death of Henry VII[56] is therefore interpreted by the poet as a sign of the failure of the court to appreciate,

---

[54] On the complex relationship of the final scene to the earlier action, see King 'Allegorical Pattern in Stephen Hawes's *The Pastime of Pleasure*'.

[55] See also Whitehead, *Castles of the Mind*, pp. 227–9.

[56] Edwards, *Stephen Hawes*, p. 8.

promote and live up to the ideal he had previously devised. Moreover, excluded from a position of influence, both literary and political, Hawes sees himself forced to alter the terms of his ideal quest and equally needs to address his work to an entirely new audience. In particular, the desire to construct the entire work around the figure of the king, first introduced with the *Example* and more clearly developed in the *Pastime*, has entirely disappeared from the *Conforte*. With it Hawes's entire vision of the intricate relationships linking the monarch, the knightly class and the commonwealth has equally vanished, and the poet transposes the ultimate focus of his work to an entirely different degree of reality. No longer writing for the king, he ostensibly writes for an indefinite 'readership' (CL 17–21), but in fact ultimately addresses only the supreme authority of God (CL 39, 55 and *passim*).

Hawes does not so much abandon the quest-pattern, but rather redirects it towards an object that is more markedly abstract and transcendent rather than literal and political. Thus the journey no longer leads the hero through a courtly world, but away from it into a world of timeless abstractions, perceived now as an ontologically superior reality in opposition to the transitory, temporal world of the court. He returns, in what is undoubtedly a conscious move, to the *topos* of the dream vision, whose liberating and even escapist connotations he consciously under-scores: 'And in this slepe me thought I dyde repayre / My selfe alone in to a garden fayre' (CL 62–3). Because of the external pressures, intrigues and general hostility of the court, Hawes is forced to relocate his quest in this dream-world, rather than being able to undertake it freely in a recognisably social and historical space.[57] Much of the space is taken up by Hawes's explicit complaint for his loss of favour: he complains 'of myn enmyes subtylnesse / whiche awayte to take me by theyr doublenesse' (CL 207–8), that 'Aboue .xx. woulues dyde me touse and rent' (CL 163), and cryptically alludes to the reshuffling of positions at court and his own exclusion: 'Some had wende the hous for to swepe' (CL 176). In particular, Hawes bewails the estrangement from his beloved, Pucell, at the hands of conspirators within the court, blaming the workings of 'fals reporte' (CL 198). Pucell clearly is an allegorical vehicle for a variety of ideas rather than a real person. Attempts to identify her with young Mary Tudor[58] have been received with caution, since the supposition that Hawes may indeed have been involved with her sentimentally is both highly improbable and based on a misreading of literary conventions.[59] Pucell certainly signifies patronage, by Mary or more generally, but also denotes a more ample, idealised reality. She may represent, in fact, Hawes's composite ideal as it was sketched in the *Example* and *Pastime*: a conflation of moral virtue, wisdom, chivalric accomplishment, honour, social prominence and spiritual apotheosis. Her forceful separation from her suitor at the hands of conspirators thus comes to signify the impossibility of realising that composite ideal under the present conditions.

Hawes largely blames his own exclusion from the court on the hostility to his

---

[57]  For the court's hostility towards Hawes, see Fox, *Politics and Literature*, p. 64ff.

[58]  Fox, *Politics and Literature*, pp. 56–72.

[59]  James Simpson, *Reform and Cultural Revolution* (Oxford: Oxford University Press, 2002), p. 182.

poetry (CL 135ff, 183ff), itself a sign of the court's lack of wisdom and under-standing:[60] 'Some had wened for to haue made an ende / Of my bokes before they hadde begynnynge / But all vayne they dyde so comprehende / Whan they of them lacke vnderstandynge' (CL 183–6). Advocate of an obscure and cryptically allegorical style, Hawes clearly sees the main virtue of poetry as lying in its capacity for conveying revelatory, prophetic or 'fatall' (e.g. EV 901; PP 807) truths.[61] Disappointed by the realisation of the court's inability to perceive the 'perfyte veryte / of sentence' (PP 957–8) of his 'cloudy fygures' (CL 1, similar expressions also in EV 902, PP 34, 705, 870, 981), he cultivates the deliberate obscurity of his allegories as a means of protection to exclude hostile courtiers and flatterers.[62] The poet has given up hopes of attaining recognition of his poetic and prophetic genius within the circle of the court, and appeals instead to the infallible judgment of God to relieve him from his present misery: 'In god aboue the lorde of myghtes moost / I put my trust for to with-stande theyr euyll / whiche dayly wrought by the myght of the deuyll' (CL 411–13).

Hawes strengthens the vatic and prophetic dimension of his poetry his by asso-ciating it directly with the power of the Holy Ghost, and by identifying divine inspir-ation with the ability to write and decrypt 'cloudy' allegory. Indeed poetic genius and divine revelation are described in almost identical terms. The Holy Ghost reveals how:

> Frome the fader and the sone my power procedynge
> And of my selfe I god do ryght ofte inspyre
> Dyuers creatures with spyrytuall knowynge
> Inuysyble by dyuyne flambynge fyre
>
> . . .
>
> In a fayre cloude with clere rayes radyaunt
>
> . . .
>
> I do enspyre oft causynge grete prophecy
> Whiche is mysconstrued whan some do enclyne
> Thynkynge by theyr wytte to perceyve it lightly. (CL 456–9, 475, 485–7)

Similarly,

> gentyll poetes vnder cloudy fygures
> Do touche a trouth and cloke it subtylly
> Harde is to construe poetycall scryptures
> They are so fayned & made sentencyously. (CL 1–4)[63]

---

[60] It has long been assumed that this exclusion may also be linked to the literary rivalry with Skelton, which seems to be confirmed by an allusion to *Philip Sparrow* at l. 890. See note to ll. 890–6 in *Minor Poems*.

[61] On Hawes's allegorical obscurity see especially Griffiths, 'The Object of Allegory'. See also Edwards, *Stephen Hawes*, pp. 35–41.

[62] Hawes's new, self-protective use of allegory is comparable to Skelton's later strategy in *Speke Parrot*, see Burrow, 'The Experience of Exclusion', pp. 799–800.

[63] Hawes largely identifies poetic genius, by definition allegorical, with rhetoric. For his complex and idiosyncratic understanding of rhetoric, see PP 653–1407. See also Copeland, 'Lydgate, Hawes, and the Science of Rhetoric'.

The prophetic truth of poetry is misunderstood by the ignorant courtiers, and triggers the exclusion of the divinely inspired, illuminated poet from the society of men: 'God hath appered vnto many a one / Inspyrynge them with grete wytte refulgent / who lyst to rede many dayes agone / Many one wryteth trouthe yet conforte hath he none' (CL 555–8).

Hawes here assumes the stance of the prophetic, vatic poet,[64] whose obscure verses cannot be decyphered by the ignorant gaze of the hostile courtiers. Not only does Hawes therefore claim the privilege of a direct prophetic revelation, but also foresees his enemies' fall at the hands of the Almighty as a punishment for their blind ignorance of the truth contained in his poetry: 'Vpon my backe synners hath fabrysed / They haue prolonged theyr grete inyquyte / From daye to daye it is not mynysshed / Wherefore for vengeaunce by grete extremyte / It cryeth aboue now vnto the deyte' (CL 568–72). Hawes still expresses the advent of justice and retribution in his usual chivalric terms, as 'the resynge of a knyght' (CL 547), but the general apocalyptic tone of this 'coming' and the cataclysmic prophecies that accompany it (CL 540–60) suggest that Hawes is not thinking of a historical, literal return of his ideal knight in this world, but of a truly apocalyptic epilogue in the next.[65]

By pointing towards such an act of divine vengeance and retribution Hawes relocates his hero's reward, and therefore the objective and culmination of the quest, beyond the limits of earthly existence, thus returning to the apocalyptic, eschatological focus found in Deguileville. After his disillusion with the possibilities of a public recognition and secular advancement proportionate to one's moral integrity and poetic genius, he falls back into a traditional appreciation of moral virtue, not as social marker or instrument for advancement towards temporal honour, but exclusively as a measure of man's eschatological destiny. This trust in a just retribution in a future, eschatological time is also reflected in Pucell's advice to persevere on the path of virtue despite outward adversity: 'Gladde I am yf prudence be your guyde / Grace cometh often after gouernaunce' (CL 870–1), 'But be ye pacyent and ye shall be sure / Suche thynges as they ordayne vnto your gref / Wyll lyght on them to theyr owne myschefe' (CL 887–9). The quest therefore remains open-ended, unfinished, but also points towards a prophetically foreseen but ineluctable conclusion, an apotheosis relocated to a truly 'apocalyptic' future that coincides with the passage to a different degree of existence. By removing this consummation beyond the boundaries of earthly existence, Hawes locates divine justice and the reward for virtuous behaviour outside of the current socio-political context, and invokes as final judgement the authority of God himself:

> To god I sayd, / thou mayst my mater spede,
> And me rewarde / accordynge to my mede,

---

[64] See Lois Ebin, *Illuminator, Makar, Vates: Visions of Poetry in the Fifteenth Century* (Lincoln, NE: University of Nebraska Press, 1988), pp. 133–62.

[65] For an alternative, less 'transcendentalising' and more political reading of the *Conforte*, see Meyer-Lee, *Poets and Power from Chaucer to Wyatt*, pp. 187–90.

Thou knowest the trouthe / I am to the true,
whan that thou lyst / thou mayst them all subdue. (CL 39–42)

The implicit opposition between divine justice and human, political arbitrariness produces an image of the court and the monarchy as alienated from moral virtue and spiritual understanding. Ultimately, by exposing the court's inability to match the moral standards he attempted to promote with his earlier work, Hawes denies the validity of the current regime's claims to monopolise worldly honour and spiritual grace alike. Moreover, by clearly separating and in fact opposing spiritual grace and secular honour, he resists the monarchy's attempts to collapse and monopolise these two concepts according to Tudor monarchical theory.

In this sense the *Conforte* signals a clear departure from the fundamental assumption inherent in both the *Example* and the *Pastime*, namely the possibility of combining a mundane and a mystical quest, based on the supposedly natural agreement of worldly glory with spiritual grace. As a result of his disappointment with the arbitrary criteria dictating the handling of human and political affairs, Hawes now conceives the two paths as mutually exclusive, in fact opposed to one another. Like his earlier heroes, Vertu and Amoure, Hawes explores new potentialities of public and 'political' identity only in order to abandon them in the end, and return to an epilogue that reasserts the primacy of the individual spiritual destiny over – or against – one's role within the political machinery of the new monarchy. Hawes has ultimately resolved the ideological discontinuity that pervades his entire work and life in favour of the old, traditional schemes that predicate a detachment from an excessive involvement with secular affairs. This shift is the first of many literary attempts to evade the pressures of the socio-political climate in the Early Tudor period,[66] but is remarkable for effecting this movement through the return to a radically contemplative and partly solipsistic ideal of *contemptus mundi* that ultimately points back to Deguileville's *Vie*.

Hawes's *oeuvre*, for all its eclecticism, follows a rather clear line of evolution. In the *Example* the poet somewhat naïvely reproduces the belief in a natural affinity of the worldly and spiritual quests, found in works like De Courcy's *Chemin de vaillance*. Like the *Chemin*, though, the *Example* is already plagued by the difficulty of bringing literal, social advancement into agreement with spiritual progress. Like De Courcy, who is forced to conceptually split *Vaillance* in half, Hawes often merely juxtaposes and alternates between the two quests rather than integrating them. In the *Pastime* Hawes refines his programmatic quest to satisfy the needs of the early Tudor court, writing a more markedly secular allegory. He cannot, however, resist

---

[66] On how Hawes anticipates and differs from later poets and their relation to Henry VIII, see Greg Walker, *Writing under Tyranny: English Literature and the Henrician Reformation* (Oxford: Oxford University Press, 2005), pp. 430–2. On political pressures in the period more generally see Fox, *Politics and Literature*, pp. 3ff; and Burrow, 'The Experience of Exclusion'; Simpson, *Reform and Cultural Revolution*, pp. 243–54.

the temptation of forcing an additional transcendental framework onto his secular quest, and thus once more disrupts and undercuts the mundane dimension rather than accommodating it within a wider perspective. The attempt for a balanced integration of *vita activa* and spiritual and moral rectitude is abandoned altogether in the *Conforte*. After the failure of the court to conform to Hawes's project, the poet takes refuge in an entirely solipsistic form of prophetic writing. Looking forward to an apocalyptic consummation beyond socio-political contingencies, any attempt to integrate social and spiritual realities is definitively relinquished, and Hawes returns to the pattern of an individual, trans-temporal and strictly spiritual quest.

# 4

## Stephen Bateman: The Apocalyptic Quest

Stephen Bateman (1542–84) is mainly known for his monumental *Batman uppon Bartholome, his Booke* De proprietatibus rerum, *Newly Corrected, Enlarged and Amended* (1582 – STC 1538), a work that is only the final culmination of the encyclopaedic and eclectic interests that directed his activities as an author, clergyman and limner. Apprenticed to a scholar rather than university educated, his thought and work are characterised by a peculiar, sometimes idiosyncratic independent-mindedness and eclecticism.[1] Minister of St Mary Aldermansbury in the late 1560s, he entered the service of Matthew Parker sometime in 1569 or '70, becoming instituted to the rectory of St Mary, Newington Butts in January 1570, and holding in plurality a living at Merstham, Surrey, from February 1571.[2]

Bateman's choice of translating de La Marche's *Chevalier délibéré* must be seen in connection with his antiquarian interests, which must have played a crucial part in his association with Parker.[3] Bateman's *Travayled Pylgrime* (1569 – STC 1585), for all its debt to Burgundian culture, may in fact be considered as a 'chivalric' work only in a metaphorical and antiquarian sense. Bateman concentrates on the allegorical potential of his source, consolidating in particular the psychomachic dimension of the knightly quest, and elaborating the Pauline notion of spiritual battle. The notion of the archetypal Christian pilgrimage, although in its transformed or rather 'reformed'

---

[1]   The peculiarity of Bateman's thought, particularly with regard to his iconographical practice, was first brought out by Chew, *The Pilgrimage of Life*, pp. 90–3, 125, 209–10 and *passim*; and E. J. Brockhurst, 'The Life and Works of Stephen Batman, 15??–1584', (MA dissertation, University of London, 1947), p. 132.

[2]   For further biographical detail see Rivkah Zim, 'Batman , Stephan (*c*.1542–1584)', *DNB*, available at: http://www.oxforddnb.com/view/article/1704 [accessed 12 February 2012]; Brockhurst, 'The Life and Works of Stephen Batman'.

[3]   For evidence of Bateman's antiquarian activities in collaboration with Parker, see M. B. Parkes, 'Stephen Batman's Manuscripts', in Masahiko Kanno *et al.*, eds, *Medieval Heritage: Essays in Honour of Tadahiro Ikegami* (Tokyo: Yushodo Press, 1997), pp. 125–56; Kate McLoughlin, 'Magdalene College MS Pepys 2498 and Stephen Batman's Reading Practices', *Transactions of the Cambridge Bibliographical Society* 10:4 (1994), 525–34; Jennifer Summit, 'Monuments and Ruins: Spenser and the Problem of the English Library', *ELH* 70:1 (2003), 1–34.

sense, thus again becomes the central concern of the work. The precise cultural and political context of the early Elizabethan reign helps to put Bateman's work into clear perspective, while a second, larger context is provided by the Reformation, which also facilitated a transposed revival of the *topos* of the *miles christianus* more generally in the period.[4] As a result of the Reformation controversy, the metaphorical significance of the spiritual battle itself had subtly shifted: given the increasing isolation of the individual conscience consequent upon the breakdown of a clearly identifiable ecclesiastical authority, and the consolidation of more private, interior forms of religious experience, the new enemies of the Christian soldier were not so much the traditional deadly sins, vices and temptations, but the powers of illusion and deception that threaten to mislead the individual Christian scrutinising his faith. As John King has pointed out, while the medieval Everyman could rely on good works without having to engage in a process of epistemological enquiry, the emphasis in the reformed tradition was precisely on the 'passive', inward process of intellectual discrimination.[5] Following the Pauline rhetoric favoured by the Reformation, as reflected for instance in Luther's hymn *Ein' feste Burg*, the emphasis shifted towards static figures stressing the defensiveness and relative passivity of the oppressed Christian, assailed by diabolical doubts and illusions as well as ordinary temptations.[6] The response to this epistemological problem took the form fideism, resulting in still further retreat from the vicissitudes of the outward world into the castle of faith.[7]

## History and Eschatology

In the context of this increasing internalisation of spiritual conflict, Bateman's choice of the quintessentially dynamic, active metaphor of the knightly quest may seem

---

[4] Erasmus's *Enchiridion*, with its wide impact and circulation, played a fundamental role in this revival. See Wang, *Miles Christianus*, pp. 158–63. For the *Enchiridion's* fortunes in England, and its translation by Tyndale, see Erasmus, *Enchiridion Militis Christiani: An English Version*, ed. Anne M. O'Donnell, EETS OS 282 (Oxford: Oxford University Press, 1981).

[5] John N. King, *English Reformation Literature: The Tudor Origins of the Protestant Tradition* (Princeton, NJ: Princeton University Press, 1982), p. 156 (hence *ERL*). A similar shift also takes place in drama, see ibid., pp. 272–3, and 312–15. As an example see *Lusty Juventus*, reprinted in *Four Tudor Interludes*, ed. J. A. B. Somerset (London: The Athlone Press, 1974), an Edwardian popular play by R. Wever epitomising this shift. See also its discussion in David Bevington, *From Mankind to Marlowe: Growth of Structure in the Popular Drama of Tudor England* (Cambridge, MA: Harvard University Press, 1962), pp. 143–6 and *passim*.

[6] For the following argument, see King, *ERL*, pp. 155–7. For the use of figures borrowed from Revelation and applied to personal spiritual struggles and dilemmas, see also Richard Bauckham, *Tudor Apocalypse: Sixteenth-Century Apocalypticism, Millenarianism and the English Reformation, from John Bale to John Foxe and Thomas Brightman* (Appleford: Sutton Courtenay Press, 1978), p. 134.

[7] On the origins of Luther's introspective fideism, understood as the starting point of a typically modern interiorisation of the religious experience, closely related to the act of private reading, see Brian Cummings, *The Literary Culture of the Reformation*, pp. 57–101.

misplaced. Yet rather than being strictly isolated in a process of spiritual intro-spection, Bateman's pilgrim is equally engaged in wider, political quest that is quite literally militant. The individual adventures of Bateman's pilgrim are thus framed by the broader, collective quest of the English 'church militant', struggling for recog-nition and supremacy in the political and historical arena.[8] Even individual, interior spiritual conflict was inevitably framed by political issues, given the foundational impact of England's break from Rome, which came to be seen as historical crystalli-sation of a timeless spiritual struggle, reproducing the patterns of the eschatological battle from the Book of Revelation.[9] In turn, then, national and political history came to be seen through the lens of spiritual conflict, exile and pilgrimage – metaphors whose relevance had previously been restricted to the figuration of personal religious experience.

The kind of militant antipapal rhetoric that developed in the wake of the break from Rome plays a fundamental role in Bateman's thought and writing, as becomes apparent with an even cursory glance at his *Christall Glasse of Christian Reformation* (1569 – STC 1581). In the *Christall Glasse*, Bateman draws from traditional medieval vice-virtue iconography to mount an attack on the Church of Rome, thus combining traditional moral didacticism with confessional controversy.[10] The title of the work is itself symptomatic of Bateman's fusion of political and spiritual-epistemological concerns: the process of 'Reformation' is imagined as the cleansing of man's faculty of spiritual discernment, and finds its political application in the exposition of the Church of Rome's false, hypocritical claims for authority, and the latter's identification with the temporal incarnation of the Church of Antichrist. Thus the trope of spiritual warfare becomes in Bateman's hands a metaphor for the Reformation controversy itself: it signifies both militant, armed resistance to Rome as well as the efforts of the individual pilgrim to resist the sophistries of Roman religion in the imminence of the Second Coming: 'so arme your selues with the armour of God, considering that Sathan is moste busiest and full of rage in this

---

[8]   See especially work by Diarmaid MacCulloch, *The Later Reformation in England, 1547–1603*, 2nd edn (Basingstoke: Palgrave, 2001); *Tudor Church Militant: Edward VI and the Protestant Reformation* (London: Allen Lane, 1999); *The Reign of Henry VIII: Politics, Policy and Piety* (Basingstoke: Macmillan, 1995).

[9]   A number of studies examine the impact of the apocalyptic climate in the period; see espec-ially C. A. Patrides and Joseph Wittreich, eds, *The Apocalypse in English Renaissance Thought and Literature* (Manchester: Manchester University Press, 1984); Katharine R. Firth, *The Apoc-alyptic Tradition in Britain, 1530–1645* (Oxford: Oxford University Press, 1979); Bauckham, *Tudor Apocalypse*; Alexandra Walsham, *Providence in Early Modern England* (Oxford: Oxford University Press, 1999).

[10]   For this widespread practice of adapting medieval vice-virtue literature to polemical, anti-Catholic purposes in the period, see Patrick Collinson, *From Iconoclasm to Iconophobia: The Cultural Impact of the Second English Reformation* (Reading: University of Reading, 1986); and Chew, *The Pilgrimage of Life*, pp. 90–3. For a discussion of the iconographic and iconoclastic implications of Bateman's *Christall Glasse*, see also James Kearney, 'Enshrining Idolatry in *The Faerie Queene*', *English Literary Renaissance* 32 (2002), 3–30, here 9 and 20.

oure tyme, as Saincte John in hys reuelation dothe manifestly expresse' (CG A.iiir). The Christian Soldier in the *Christall Glasse* is therefore no longer merely an image of the archetypal Christian Everyman, but becomes the emblem of a specifically Protestant form of faith, a 'stedfast beleuer . . . of the veritie . . . being armed with constant zeale' (CG M.iiiir), engaged in a battle against the papal Antichrist.

Before looking at Bateman's own apocalyptic imagination and its role in the *Travayled Pylgrime*, it will be useful to retrace the main steps of the evolution of apocalyptic Protestant historicism in England up to his time. In his seminal *Image of Bothe Churches*, written in exile between 1541 and 1547 (first edition 1545 – STC 1296.5), John Bale develops a reading of the contemporary religious controversy according to patterns derived from the Book of Revelation. Expanding Luther's reading of Revelation as a prophecy of the Reformation, drawing heavily from the medieval continental apocalyptic tradition derived from Joachim da Fiore as well as the native genius of Wycliff, he developed an oppositional interpretative scheme contrasting the Churches of Christ and Antichrist.[11] Identification of the latter with the papacy and the Church of Rome invited a reading of the recent religious turmoil in England, and in particular the break from Rome, as the initial stages in the final eschatological battle between the forces of good and evil, truth and falsity, that were to herald the end of times. While Bale interpreted current events as partial, fragmentary 'refractions' of truths encoded in the final biblical book rather than literal, prophetic fulfilments of its visions, he paved the way for later speculations on the nature of the exact relation between history and the Apocalypse of Saint John.[12]

John Foxe elaborated Bale's model to provide a much more precise chronology and prophetic prognostication of the Last Days. Building on the numerical patterns contained in the Book of Revelation, he developed a detailed historicist exegesis of the Apocalypse with reference to contemporary events in England and Europe, culminating with a full-scale commentary on Revelation published posthumously under the title of *Eicasmi, seu meditationes in sacram apocalypsim* in 1587 (STC 11237). Whilst it is only in this final work that the periodisation of Church history is fully worked out according to apocalyptic patterns, his earlier work and the multiple editions of his *Acts and Monuments* (1563, 1570, 1576, 1583) document the progressive consolidation of his method.[13] Contemporary events were scrutinised in the search for clues concerning the exact scenario of the Last Days, and became elements in an all-encompassing scheme of prophetic prognostication.

---

[11]  See Firth, *Apocalyptic Tradition*, pp. 39ff, 80; and MacCulloch, *Reformation: Europe's House Divided, 1490–1700* (London: Allen Lane, 2003), pp. 553–4; Bauckham, *Tudor Apocalypse*, pp. 48–9.

[12]  See for instance King, *ERL*, in particular pp. 56–75; Firth, *Apocalyptic Tradition*, pp. 32–68; Bauckham, *Tudor Apocalypse*, in particular pp. 21–37.

[13]  *The Unabridged Acts and Monuments Online* or *TAMO* (HRI Online Publications, Sheffield, 2011). Available at: http://www.johnfoxe.org [accessed 12 February 2012].

About to face its imminent exhaustion, human history in Foxe's work was thus thoroughly unfolded and explained.[14]

Foxe's influence proved to be a lasting one throughout the entire reign of Elizabeth. Despite the return to Reformed religion, the rhetoric of oppression based on the theology of the Cross developed by the Henrician and Marian exiles remained a central factor in the construction of Protestant identity.[15] Even under Elizabeth, at least up until the *annus mirabilis* of 1588, English Protestants continued to think of themselves as persecuted and exiled members of the True Church in a world ruled by a papal Antichrist. If there was anything like an Elizabethan apocalyptic 'optimism' before the late 1580s, this was in no way a manifestation of hopes for the establishment of a millenarian messianic kingdom on earth, as has sometimes been claimed, but simply a timid sense of relief resulting from the conviction that the worst had already passed, and that final divine retribution was at hand.[16]

## Translation as 'Re-formation'

Bateman's apocalyptic-historicist perspective functions as a powerful filter for his source-text, Olivier de La Marche's *Chevalier délibéré*. Bateman nowhere acknowledges his debt to that source, and his translation, via the intermediary of Acuña's Spanish version, is correspondingly free and even idiosyncratic. Acuña already alters the text by reducing de La Marche's lengthy elegy of the house of Burgundy and supplementing it with a panegyric of his own Habsburg patrons, and Bateman tacitly eliminates both Valois and Habsburgs replacing them with the Tudors, thus setting his pilgrim's quest solidly within the context of sixteenth-century English dynastic history.[17]

Bateman's translation may be thought of as a 'reformation' of his source text to fit the new religious context, and all obvious indicators of Catholicism are excised from

---

[14] On Foxe, see for instance, Tom Betteridge, 'From Prophetic to Apocalyptic: John Foxe and the Writing of History', in David Loades, ed., *John Foxe and the English Reformation* (Aldershot: Scolar Press, 2005), pp. 210–32; and Firth, *Apocalyptic Tradition*, pp. 69–110; Bauckham, *Tudor Apocalypse*, pp. 68–90 and 113–24; King, *English Reformation Literature*, pp. 434–44.

[15] See Bauckham, *Tudor Apocalypse*, pp. 113–24 in particular; for the continuing influence of such a theology of the Cross throughout the earlier part of Elizabeth's reign, see ibid., pp. 125–44; and Firth, *Apocalyptic Tradition*, p. 85.

[16] For the older, now rejected notion of the 'Elect Nation', see William Haller, *Foxe's Book of Martyrs and the Elect Nation* (London: Jonathan Cape, 1963). For more recent reassessments, see Bernard Capp, 'The Political Dimension of Apocalyptic Thought', in Patrides and Wittreich, eds, *The Apocalypse in English Renaissance Thought and Literature*, pp. 95–6 especially; and Bauckham, *Tudor Apocalypse*, pp. 113–61. Walsham, *Providence in Early Modern England*, plays down the millenarian fervour even further, and defines the dominating apocalyptic climate up until 1640–50 as 'sombrely providential rather than euphorically millenarian', pp. 170, 307.

[17] See Prescott, 'Spenser's Chivalric Restoration'; and Sutch and Prescott, 'Translation as Transformation'. For an edition, see Hernando de Acuña, *El caballero determinado*, ed. Baranda and Infantes.

the source. De La Marche's lush allegorisation of the mass has given way to a much sterner and leaner affair, Understanding's sermon on personified virtues (*TP* D.iir–iiiv). An exhortation to seek 'the worthie state of wedlocke' (*TP* F.iir.) replaces de La Marche's advice to avoid the 'val de mariage' (*CD* § 95), as if to underscore a reorientation from the medieval contemplative model to the reformed ideal of the *vita activa*. The countless relics of human mortality accumulated in the 'cloistre de souvenance' (*CD* § 50–72) have been replaced by the purely verbal, abstract sermon administered by Understanding (*TP* D.iiv–E.ir.).[18] All of Olivier de La Marche's autobiographical references disappear, and make space for a more universally mean-ingful work, a spiritual handbook for the (now reformed) Christian pilgrim, designed to prepare him to confront both the traditional psychomachic enemies as well as the new ills characteristic of his time:

> I haue painted foorth the fonde deuise of man, and the straunge Combats that he is daylie forced vnto, by meanes of this oure feeble nature: showing also howe euery degree shoulde, or at the least wayes ought, to frame themselues, and so aduisedly to watch that we be found vigilant watchmen, aspecting the great & second coming of our lord Iesus Christ, that at what houre the theefe breake in vpon vs, wee be readie armed to withstand the same. (*TP* A.iiv–iiir)

Bateman thus systematically rewrites the allegory to fit reformed religious sensi-bilities, 'considering that Sathan is moste busiest and full of rage in this oure tyme, as Saincte John in hys reuelation dothe manifestly expresse' (*CG* A.iiir), but he also 'redeems' his source from its latent agnosticism discussed in Chapter 2, restoring a more orthodox pattern of the Christian pilgrimage of life by replacing it within its traditional eschatological framework: 'exhorting euery faythfull Christian, to haue such regarde to this their Pilgrimage here on earth, that in the lyfe to come, they may enjoy the happie gaine of endlesse felicitie' (*TP* A.3r).

To restore the paradigmatic significance of the Christian pilgrimage Bateman also adds an entirely new 'prologue' to his account of the journey. In fact his quest, rather than starting abruptly and for no particular reason like de La Marche's,[19] is prefaced by a concise account of Adam and Eve's creation and fall, providing a conceptual framework for the subsequent journey: 'For their offence they were exilde out of that pleasaunt place' (*TP* B.iir). Everyman's pilgrimage is thus clearly seen as an Adamic journey leading through a fallen world, a land of exile and alienation descended from Augustine's *regio dissimilitudinis*, back towards a restoration of man's original divine likeness.[20] Whilst this does not in itself dispel the bleak mood of the wandering, the significance of such bleakness is radically transformed by being turned into a theological point. So the pilgrim's horse, Will, is unruly (*TP* B.iiiiv), and collapses altogether before the end of the journey (*TP* N.iv and N.iiiv), as if to epitomise the insufficiency and

---

[18] On Bateman's preference of *sermo* over *visio*, see also Sutch and Prescott, 'Translation as Transformation', 304.

[19] See Ch. 2, pp. 67–8.

[20] Gilson, '*Regio dissimilitudinis* de Platon à saint Bernard de Clairvaux'.

unreliability of the 'infected' human will. But whereas in the *Chevalier délibéré* this powerlessness of the will only signifies fatalism and despair in the face of the invincible tyranny of *Atropos*, Bateman reads this helplessness theologically, as a testimony to the insufficiency of the post-lapsarian individual will when measured against the overwhelming power of divine Grace. His pilgrim's helplessness implicitly signifies for Bateman the presence of a wider, albeit as yet inscrutable, providentially orchestrated plan, and thus confirms man's dependence on divine Grace: 'Yelde thou thy selfe with all thy griefes, to the eternall king, / And call for grace while thou hast space, to *Ioue* he will thee bring' (*TP* G.iiiv). For Bateman such a confession of impotence ultimately also functions as a testimony of faith, and a prayer for deliverance.[21]

The impression of labyrinthine errance inherited from the source is equally perceived through the filter of the new theology, and now becomes a figure of the increased epistemological uncertainty preventing the pilgrim's linear advance on his journey. This fits with the altered perception of the pilgrimage motif in Reformation England, as sketched by Barbara Lewalski. Already implicit in Bateman's choice of his source is an understanding of the Christian pilgrimage as a tortuous, discontinuous journey characterised by many setbacks and frustrations rather than a smooth, steady and clearly structured progression through predetermined stages of spiritual development.[22] The pilgrim's progression through fits and starts visualises the new Protestant emphasis on man's post-lapsarian corruption of reason and understanding as well as depravity of the senses, leading to an endemic loss of discernment and orientation on his journey. Despite his choice of Understanding as the pilgrim's guide, Bateman displays a radical, Calvinist scepticism concerning the reliability of human reason, as he articulates it in the epistle to the reader in his later work, *The Doome Warning all Men to the Judgemente* (1581 – STC 1582): 'I vvarne thee that thou vse not mans reason in searching out Gods vvorkes, for the maruellous vvorkes of the Lord are great and incomprehensible' (¶. iiiv). By subtly deconstructing and fragmenting the older model of the pilgrimage of life as an orderly progression, Bateman anticipates later developments to be found for instance in the Protestant emblem books, sonnet cycles such as that of Henry Lok's *Sundry Christian Passions* and the seventeenth-century religious lyric.[23]

Bateman's pilgrimage of life is thus equally an epistemological quest – his guide

---

[21] As has been observed by Dewey D. Wallace Jr, *Puritans and Predestination: Grace in English Protestant Theology, 1525–1695* (Chapel Hill, NC: University of North Carolina Press, 1982) pp. 7–11, the acceptance of the doctrine of Predestination and the ensuing guarantee of Sanctification for the elect became a source of comfort and assurance for Reformed Christians.

[22] This idea of a systematic progression was of course developed by Catholic Counter-Reformation, for instance by Ignatius de Loyola, who reiterated and refined the idea of systematically organised, ritualised path towards spiritual illumination, finally crystallising in a manual for individual prayer and meditation, the *Spiritual Exercises*. Incidentally, it is worth mentioning also the importance of chivalric, crusading and pilgrimage symbolism in Ignatius's conversion experience and his thought as a whole. See also discussion in Ch. 5, pp. 122–4.

[23] See Barbara K. Lewalski, *Protestant Poetics and the Seventeenth-Century Religious Lyric* (Princeton, NJ: Princeton University Press, 1979), pp. 87–9, 191–3, 239–41 in particular.

is after all 'Understanding' – striving to restore man's spiritual discernment and leading him out of his exile in the *regio dissimilitudinis*. This ontological leap can only be achieved through the Second Coming of Christ, but is nevertheless fore-shadowed by the Reformation, preparing for an apocalypse of the spirit that is both micro- and macrocosmic. This notion is the central focus of Bateman's *Christall Glasse*, also appearing in 1569 like the *Travayled Pylgrime*. The symbol of the mirror, often used to represent the human imagination,[24] here implies that the Reformation itself consists of a process of epistemological cleansing, and results in a better capacity for discernment between the authentic allegories of the spirit and the coun-terfeit 'papist' allegories, or the 'craftie illusions of Sathan, by coloured imaginations' (*TP*, gloss on C.iir):[25]

> Herein is plainly shewed unto all, the estate of euery degree by order of picture and signification, to the intent, that thereby euery christian Reader may the better see the disordred abuses which daily raueth amongst us … that thereby euery Christian may the better beware the deceiuable suggestions of Sathan. (CG A.iiv)

As Bateman again repeats in the epistle to his *Golden Booke of the Leaden Goddes* (1577 – STC 1583), a work 'wherein is described the vayne imaginations of Heathen Pagans, and counterfaict Christians' (title page), only the reformed Christians live 'in the cleare light of the gospel' and can thank the Reformation for 'the openinge of our eyes and understandings' (epistle). Whilst man in his present earthly condition is bound to an indirect apprehension of such ultimate realities, as if through reflection 'in a glass, darkly', the 'Christall Glasse' of the Reformation is conceived as a purification of this indirect mode of signification and comes to function as a prelude to the final eschatological revelation, where divine realities are contemplated directly, 'face to face' (1 Corinthians 13:12):[26]

> This christall glasse wherein we may learne godly reformation, whose brightnes shineth not to the beholders therof in this world, a light to euery christian man, but in the world to come a most precious and euerlasting brightnes in endles felicitie. (CG A.iiir)

Images of crystalline light and vision abound also in the *Travayled Pylgrime*, and invariably point to such a future apotheosis, where epistemological uncertainty is finally transcended and a state of ultimate, apocalyptic clarity is achieved. In a

---

[24] Rossky, 'Imagination in the English Renaissance'.

[25] For a possible identification of the mirror of Age in the *Travayled Pylgrime* with the mirror of the *Christall Glasse of Reformation*, see Sutch and Prescott 'Translation as Transformation', 296.

[26] In this Calvinist understanding of figurative language, even the highest kind of image, the biblical one, simultaneously reveals and conceals its divine original; as a consequence the potential *unio mystica*, both ontological and epistemological, is endlessly deferred, inaccessible in the present, post-lapsarian condition and possible only in a future, post-apocalyptic state of existence. See Ernest B. Gilman, *Iconoclasm and Poetry in the English Reformation: Down Went Dagon* (Chicago, IL: Chicago University Press, 1986), p. 39.

passage newly added by Bateman, absent from both de La Marche's original or Acuña's translation, the purification of the pilgrim's sight is related: 'And *Infancie* that pretie ladde brought water for mine eies, / Whereby I might perceyue and see the cleere light from the darke' (*TP* C.iiiv). Crystalline clarity is consistently associated with transcendence in the poem; so '*Ioue* that Judge most true, / Which sittes aloft in splendent throne, of chrystall light most cleare' (*TP* D.ir), and elsewhere the Gods collectively sit 'in Chrystall throne' (*TP* D.iiiiv). Elizabeth, the illuminated godly ruler is herself endowed with 'Christall eyen' (*TP* M.iiir), as if to signify her clear and direct apprehension of transcendent truth.

Yet despite the cleansing operation performed by the Reformation, man remains bound by figures and the mediating operation of the allegorical imagination. Bateman has a truly ambivalent attitude towards figurative language, characteristic of the Protestant reluctance to indulge in allegorical readings, sustained by the aversion to the medieval method of fourfold biblical exegesis.[27] The allegorical image, suspended between the symbolic mediation of transcendent truth and the confounding operation of satanic illusion, becomes instrument of both godly revelation and papist dissimulation.[28] Finally, Bateman's scepticism and hesitancy concerning the reliability of the medieval allegorical mode he inherits and adopts, spreads a veil of epistemological uncertainty over his entire *oeuvre*, and he longs for a liberation from the world of signifying forms and figures altogether: 'Marke well therefore quoth *Memorie* although these sightes thee please, / The sights not seene with *Ioue* aboue, both breede more ioy and ease' (*TP* M.iv).

This has weighty implications for the 'readability' of Bateman's allegory and his view of the world at large, as it implies a radically sceptical understanding of the human imagination[29] that in many ways anticipates later debates reflected in particular in Spenser's *Faerie Queene*.[30] Despite the epistemological 'reformation', deliverance from

---

[27] See Tyndale's classic attack in his *Obedience of a Christian Man; facsimile of the 1528 Edition* (London: Scolar Press, 1970), fols cxxixff. George L. Scheper, 'Reformation Attitudes toward Allegory and the Song of Songs' *PMLA* 89:3 (1974), 551–62, has put such comments into perspective, pointing to the wide gap between such theoretical refutations and actual practice of Protestant exegetes, revealing an ambivalent and complex attitude towards the allegorical mode that has been confirmed by more recent research, for instance the discussion of the problematic Protestant insistence on the 'literal' sense in Cummings, *The Literary Culture of the Reformation*, pp. 15–53 in particular; on Tyndale and allegory, see also Simpson, *Reform and Cultural Revolution*, pp. 458–9, and Lewalski, *Protestant Poetics*, pp. 116–18.

[28] See Gilman, *Iconoclasm and Poetry*, p. 45 and *passim*. On the status of 'Imagination' and 'Phantasy' in Renaissance psychology, see also Rossky, 'Imagination in the English Renaissance'.

[29] It can hardly be a coincidence that Bateman would explain madness as the result of an uncontrolled imagination, see *Batman vppon Bartholome*, Bk. VII, Ch. 6.

[30] See John N. King, *Spenser's Poetry and the Reformation Tradition* (Princeton, NJ: Princeton University Press, 1990), Ch. 2, 'Spenserian Iconoclasm', pp. 65–79 in particular; and Gilman, *Iconoclasm and Poetry*, Ch. 3, 'Spenser's Painted Forgery', pp. 61–83; Isabel MacCaffrey, *Spenser's Allegory: The Anatomy of the Imagination* (Princeton, NJ: Princeton University Press, 1976); see also Gary Waller, *English Poetry of the Sixteenth Century*, 2nd edn (London: Longman, 1993), pp. 90–100.

doubt and opacity can be brought about only by direct divine intervention, and the individual himself remains entirely powerless to effect this shift through the strength of his own understanding. It is only beyond the threshold of death, in an indefinite apocalyptic future, that the fullness of meaning Bateman is longing for becomes attainable: 'The life I meane which lasteth still, in the supernal throne, / Where Gods elect in rest doth dwell' (*TP* E.iir). And only Christ himself on his Second Coming can accomplish a final fusion of object and reflection, signifier and signified, creature and creator, man and God: 'Then after death you soone shal see, / The christall glasse of light to shine. / Which glasse is Christ our Sauiour' (*CG* X.iiiir).

## A Tudor Apocalypse

This epistemological process of individual, 'microcosmic' Reformation is balanced by a political and historical process. Bateman inherits the tradition of historico-apocalyptic exegesis from his predecessors, and combines it with his own antiquarian activities undertaken on the account of his patron Matthew Parker.[31] For Parker, Bale and Foxe such antiquarian interests were systematically designed to trace an unbroken tradition linking the contemporary English Church to the early Apostolic Church in order to justify the break from Rome and the ensuing Elizabethan religious settlement.[32] In the *Travayled Pylgrime*, Bateman thus integrates the apocalyptic and fatalistic anxiety he finds in de La Marche's *Chevalier délibéré* within a more elaborate, organic inter-pretation of time and history pointing to a still wider eschatological framework. The pilgrim's wandering takes him through a world that is rich in cryptic signs that herald the imminent end of time, and so Bateman transforms de La Marche's sterile wasteland into a locus of marvels, natural wonders and curiosities:

> I sodeine was beset, with sights both huge and straunge,
> The aire full dimme began to shine, a show of state to chaunge:
> The earth began to tremble eke, it made me quake for feare,
> Infections forth also gan flie, which did much empeare,
> With miseries replenished with carefull paine and griefe. (*TP* G.iiv)

Such apocalyptic features elaborate de La Marche's more conventional pictures of

---

[31] See Parkes, 'Stephen Bateman's Manuscripts'; and McLoughlin, 'Magdalene College MS Pepys 2498'. On Parker, his life, theology and antiquarian interests, see V. J. K. Brook, *A Life of Archbishop Parker* (Oxford: Clarendon Press, 1962); and R. I. Page, *Matthew Parker and his Books* (Kalamazoo, MI: Medieval Institute Publications, 1993).

[32] See for instance, Felicity Heal, 'Appropriating History: Catholic and Protestant Polemics and the National Past', *Huntington Library Quarterly* 68:1/2 (2005), 109–34; Benedict Scott Robinson, '"Darke speech": Matthew Parker and the Reforming of History', *Sixteenth-Century Journal* 29:4 (1998), 1061–84; Norman L. Jones, 'Matthew Parker, John Bale, and the Magdeburg Centuriators', *Sixteenth-Century Journal* 12:3 (1981), 35–49. Among Parker's manuscripts survives a tran-scription of a full commentary on the Apocalypse in Bateman's hand, today Cambridge, Trinity College, MS B.2.7(50), see Parkes, 'Stephen Bateman's Manuscripts', pp. 132, 142 and *passim*.

desolation, and also point forward to the marvels described in Bateman's later *Doome*, where all such signs are read explicitly as clues for the imminence of the end:

> upon sight and search of so manye prodigious birthes, Starres of vnaccustomed appearance, enuenomed aires, from the which proceede pestilence, plague, war, hunger, frensie, ielousie and heresie, [I] haue no lesse occasion, than worthy Authors in former time, to make or set forth this *Cronicle of the Doome*, or warning to Gods Iudgement (*The Doome* ¶.iiv)

Correspondingly, the dreaded encounter with Atropos, culmination of the quest in the *Travayled Pylgrime*, no longer signifies human mortality as such, but also evokes the final eschatological battle. Bateman cleverly transforms the motif of the heraldic trumpet inherited from his source, charging it with echoes of the apocalyptic trumpets that were such a mainstay of contemporary apocalyptic imagination in England:[33]

> Sith that the howre draweth nie, be ready at the sounde
> Of trumpet shrill, with blast most cleere, thine enmies to confounde;
> The loftie sound of trumpet blowne, oft warneth to prepare,
> With speare and shield now all is knowne, of these my words beware. (*TP* B.iiiv)[34]

This sense of analogy between individual spiritual quest and the progression of history is made explicit in the *Travayled Pylgrime*, where the Pilgrim's progress towards Age is in fact parallel to the world's advance towards its own decrepitude and the Last Days. So travelling through the Desert of Age, he suddenly expands the idea of personal decrepitude into a reflection on collective, national and cosmic destiny in the imminence of doomsday:

> To thinke thereon it doth me feare, with tremblings low I quake
> For that I know the count is great, that I to *Ioue* must make.
> Full sore I languish in my heart, for to see the worlde nowe,
> Without regard of life to come (*TP* G.iiir)

It is the awareness of the world's advancing age that pushes Bateman to exhort the entire nation to regenerate its behaviour and obediently subject itself to the monarch, thereby preparing for Christ's Second Coming as righteous judge:[35] 'And

---

[33] The seven trumpets from Rev. 8 play a prominent role in both Bale's and Foxe's exegetical schemes, see Firth, *Apocalyptic Tradition*, pp. 44–6 and 93–5; Robert Crowley equally published a work entitled *The Voyce of the Laste Trumpet Blowen bi the Seue[n]th Angel* (1549 – STC 6094) again heavily influenced by Bale, while much later Anthony Marten's *A Second Sound, or, Warning of the Trumpet unto Judgment* (1589 – STC 17941) was to develop a twofold, heraldic and apocalyptic symbolism of the trumpet blast reminiscent of the one found here.

[34] For other similar examples, see e.g. *TP* F.iiiiv, I.ir, I.iiiv.

[35] This tendency is also reflected in the later development of popular religious literature and public preaching, as observed by Walsham, *Providence in Early Modern England*, p. 155: 'What cannot have escaped notice is the extent to which the language of corporate repentance and temporal deliverance overlaps with the language of individual redemption and eternal salvation … Puritan preachers subsumed self into society and macrocosm into microcosm.'

that we may while time we haue, by dutie seeke to please, / Hir royall grace our supreme head, Gods wrath thereby to pease' (*TP* M.iiir).

The parallels between the physical decline of the pilgrim's body and the decrepit cosmos are further developed by Bateman's vivid representations of physical decay and dysfunction. Just as the human bodily functions degenerate (*TP* M.iiir–M.iiiv), so the world itself becomes dysfunctional, producing abnormalities, natural wonders and disasters as clear signs of its advanced age.[36] Such signs will become the main focus of Bateman's attention in a later work, *The Doome*, which constitutes yet another attempt to uncover and interpret evidence for a steady historical progression towards the end, conceived as a collective human journey towards salvation:

> *The Doome Warning all Men to the Iudgemente*:
> Wherein are contayned for the most parte all the straunge Prodigies hapned in the Worlde, with diuers secrete figures of Reuelations tending to mannes stayed conuersion towardes GOD. (title page)

Bateman's attempt at 'phenomenological'-historical prophecy thus completes and complements Bale's and Foxe's previous efforts to locate the Apocalypse within the political and religious history of the Churches of Christ and Antichrist.

As Bateman postulates an analogy between national, collective history and individual spiritual struggle, he can easily move between prophetic-historicist and moral-allegorical readings of the Book of Revelation,[37] allowing him to think in both archetypal and historically specific terms. This also enables Bateman to move from the description of types or even archetypes to the discussion of specific historical incidents, persons and situations as manifestations of such types. Thus while he begins his work on a paradigmatic note with the mention of Pharao, understood as the archetypal persecutor of the exiled elect in Egypt, this 'type' later crystallises into the historical figure of Mary. Similarly, the reigns of Henry VIII and his son Edward VI are respectively compared to those of Salomon and David, Josaphat and Josias (*TP* I.iir). Thanks to Bateman's complex understanding of typology and exegesis, present historical circumstances acquire a multiple valence both as prophetic repetitions of episodes from the Old Testament or the early history of the Church and as macrocosmic embodiments of a trans-temporal, inward spiritual struggle. Conversely, each individual Christian recapitulates in himself the spiritual

---

[36]   For this widespread belief, interpreting natural disasters, portents and marvels as providential, divine messages and warnings related to the end of the world, see especially Walsham, *Providence in Early Modern England*, and Bauckham, *Tudor Apocalypse*, pp. 151–2, and MacCulloch, *Reformation*, pp. 554–5.

[37]   These two 'schools' of apocalyptic exegesis respectively lead back to Rupert of Deutz and Nicholas of Lyra, see Firth, *Apocalyptic Tradition*, p. 6 and *passim*; Irena D. Backus, *Reformation Readings of the Apocalypse: Geneva, Zurich, and Wittenberg* (Oxford: Oxford University Press, 2000). On the exegesis of Revelation in the medieval period more generally, see Marjorie Reeves, *The Influence of Prophecy in the Later Middle Ages: A Study in Joachimism* (Oxford: Clarendon Press, 1969).

essence of the peregrinations of Old Testament narratives.[38] This builds on the ideas originally articulated by the earlier, mid-century gospelling tradition,[39] but also anticipates later transformations that led to an identification of England with Israel or even the millenarian kingdom – which again highlights the uniqueness and originality of Bateman's thought.[40]

The centrepiece of Bateman's redefinition of the human pilgrimage as a collective journey through history is the substitution of an eulogy for the Tudor dynasty for de La Marche's lament for the downfall of his Valois patrons. De La Marche represented his patrons' clash with Atropos as a cruel and entirely destructive affair perceived as the work of sheer arbitrariness. Acuña already substantially alters this section of the text, reducing the downfall of the Valois dynasty to a mere prelude to the rise of his own Habsburg patrons.[41] For Bateman too, while the invincibility of Atropos remains undisputed, his power is nevertheless framed within a wider eschatological perspective as was already seen. As a consequence Atropos's agency within human history is only relative, and death loses some of its spectral power, being clearly subjected like his emissaries Dolor and Debilitie to the authority of God: 'Their stryuing sure is all in vaine, till God doth give him leaue' (*TP* M.iiiv). The experience of death, both on a personal and a collective plane, is now accepted rather than abhorred: 'All things created must changed be by mortall law no doute' (*TP* I.iir), 'Thus with my selfe I did agree, with Age to be content' (*TP* G.iiiiv). Bateman's meditation on death is not bred by uncontrolled panic in the face of the meaninglessness and invincibility of Death, but much like the Protestant adaptations of the traditional *ars moriendi*, is intended to promote acceptance and understanding of mortality as part of a wider and as yet only partially discernible scheme of providential meaning.[42]

This confidence in divine providence, concealed behind an apparently random mutability, equally applies to Bateman's conception of collective, national history.[43]

---

[38] Lewalski, *Protestant Poetics*, pp. 129–32.

[39] See for instance King, *ERL*, pp. 161ff.

[40] Bauckham suggests that Bateman, together with James Sanford, may have belonged to an obscure circle of Brocardists with a particular and premature interest in millenarian ideas; see *Tudor Apocalypse*, p. 219. This conjecture is based mostly on a discussion of Bateman's later work, and is therefore only tangential to a study of the *Travayled Pylgrime*, that at the most can be said to contain remote and undeveloped hints of a millenarian imagination that is yet to emerge. Lewalski equally links the increasing tendency to identify England with Old Testament Israel with the emergence of millenarianism at the end of the century, see *Protestant Poetics*, p. 130. See also Walsham, *Providence in Early Modern England*, pp. 281–325.

[41] See Sutch and Prescott, 'Translation as Transformation'.

[42] David W. Atkinson, 'The English *ars moriendi*: Its Protestant Transformation', *Renaissance and Reformation* 6:1 (1982), 1–10.

[43] The same absolute trust in divine providence, albeit at times obscured for the untrained human eye, survives in Bateman's *Doome*: 'most manifest is it therefore that whatsoeuer hath bene, is, or shal be to procede, either Celestial or Terrestrial, can not be without the fore-ordinance and prouidence of God' (¶.iir).

Such a teleological and providential conception of human history allows the exegesis of England's otherwise seemingly arbitrary recent dynastic past. The deaths, reversals of fortune and general vicissitudes affecting the Tudor dynasty now come to be seen as significant elements in an ongoing chain of events unmistakeably pointing towards an imminent apocalyptic culmination. Despite the seeming arbitrariness of premature deaths such as that of Edward VI and other unexpected setbacks in this halting advance towards a Reformation of the Church, such hardships and persecutions are patiently endured as providential signs confirming the election of the oppressed.[44] All the reigns of the successive Tudor monarchs become fragments of a wider, composite but as yet elusive picture representing the entire national and cosmic history. Bateman is here again applying to collective history a pattern that has its origins in a typically Protestant form of individual spiritual introspection.[45] As a consequence of the new awareness of the infinite variations of the personal experience of conversion and progression along the *ordo salutis*, increasing attention was being devoted to scrutinising the peculiarities of one's individual spiritual destiny.[46] All seemingly trivial and contingent experiences of one's life came to be conceived as signs and tokens allowing the slow and progressive reconstruction of God's original providential plan concerning individual salvation. And here too the final picture is progressively revealed like that of a jigsaw puzzle, advancing with every successive step towards its completion.[47] Bateman moves imperceptibly between his attention to the individual spiritual destiny of his Protestant Everyman on one hand, and the historical fate of the True Church and the English nation.

Henry VIII, the first king engaged in a struggle with Atropos in Bateman, is the initiator of the Reformation itself through his break with Rome: 'The same is he which first of all, gaue Antichrist the foyle. / Which brake the neck of Papistrie' (*TP* I.ir). Henry himself is represented as blowing the trumpet of the gospel, and is thus cast as apocalyptic herald of the coming Reformation: 'And first to sounde the Trumpet blast, of Gods true worde alowde' (*TP* I.ir). Bateman here doubles the apocalyptic connotations of the trumpet, familiar from Bale among others,[48] with an allusion to the traditional iconography of Fame: 'The same is *Henry* sure the eygth, whose fame is fixt in skie: / Whose trumpe victoriously doth sound, whose conquest can not die' (*TP* I.ir). This stresses the 'perdurable' nature of Henry's conquests, foreshadowing the advent of the eschatological Israel. This more opti-

---

[44] The self-declared Protestant elect in fact tended increasingly to postulate an inversely proportional relationship between prosperity and certainty of election, so that afflictions were often read paradoxically as marks of divine favour, see Walsham, *Providence in Early Modern England*, pp. 16–17.

[45] For such analogies between individual and collective 'pilgrimage', see Lewalski, *Protestant Poetics*, p. 67.

[46] Wallace, *Puritans and Predestination*, pp. 7–8.

[47] Walsham, *Providence in Early Modern England*, pp. 15–17

[48] Firth, *Apocalyptic Tradition*, p. 46.

mistic eschatological perspective radically transforms the meaning of death along with the significance of the Pilgrim's as well as the nation's pilgrimage. The pilgrim, along with the reader, is exhorted to 'thinke . . . still on Death and on thine ende, / And thou shalt keepe thy life so straight, that thou shalt not offende' (*TP* I.iir). Bateman's Protestant Everyman, as well as the entire body of the nation and Church, is invited to stoically follow in Henry's footsteps along the newly rediscovered path towards salvation, obscured by centuries of tyranny by the papal Antichrist.[49] Framed within the wider apocalyptic scheme that underlies the double journey of the king and nation, in a manner reminiscent of Foxe's martyrology, the deaths of all individual pilgrims come to be seen as sacrificial offerings instrumental in the edification of the eschatological Jerusalem.

Bateman's characterisation of Edward VI's reign makes use of many iconographic commonplaces established by the mid-century gospelling movement.[50] Edward is typologically cast as Josiah 'that founde Gods booke in broken walles, and made it preachte to bee' (*TP* I.iiiv), and he is seen as a continuator of the legacy of his father and predecessor, completing his work of purgation by abolishing any residual forms of pagan idolatry and confirming the break with 'Antichrist the Pope' (*TP* I.iiiir). Despite the capriciousness of Fortune and the king's premature death, Edward is represented as having accomplished his providential mission in history: he has completed the rebuilding of the Temple, steered the country clear of a relapse into old superstitions and political instability by systematically preaching and 'plainly' expounding the gospel (*TP* I.iiiv), and ultimately has completed his own, personal spiritual journey to follow his father's footsteps. No sense of despair or even arbitrariness is ever entertained, and Bateman instead further interweaves the destinies of the nation, the king and his subjects: while Edward's death is seen as resulting from the vicissitudes of Fortune, on a different plane it is equally understood providentially in direct relation to the merits and demerits of the people he governs: 'Unworthy sure quoth *Memory*, the lande was of his grace' (*TP* K.ir). This implies a view of the monarch as a servant to the people, as God's gift to the morally regenerated and reformed; conversely, the withdrawal of the divine gift is a reaction to the people's unworthiness and inconstancy.[51] Such an interpretation fits well with Bateman's generally exhortatory intent, and also anticipates his later tendency to postulate a direct causal link between the moral standard of the nation and the

---

[49] The idea of the individual pilgrimage inscribed within the wider journey of the Monarch and the entire commonwealth is already familiar from Hawes's *Pastime*, see Ch. 3, pp. 86–9. The work had in fact been reprinted twice under Mary by John Wayland in 1554 and 1555, and may have influenced Bateman directly, as is suggested by Brockhurst, 'The Life and Works of Stephen Batman', p. 84. Foxe similarly uses the image of the navigation to conflate the journeys of the Ark of the Church and the Ship of State in the 1570 edition of his *Acts and Monuments*, sig. ☞[hand]4v, see Susan Felch, 'Shaping the Reader in the *Acts and Monuments*', in Loades, ed., *John Foxe and the English Reformation*, p. 62

[50] See King, *ERL*, pp. 161–206.

[51] This is again a development of a common idea introduced by the gospelling movement of the previous generation of polemicists, such as Robert Crowley; see King, *ERL*, p. 182.

exact modality of the apocalyptic resolution, as in the *Doome*, written 'to giue vnto my country the like occasion to beware of some more monstruous plague to folow, … vnlesse some speedie amendment be found in time acceptable vnto God' (¶.iiv).

The characterisation of Mary's reign is directly linked to his interpretation of Edward's death as a punishment for the country's sins and its failure to conform to the moral standards propounded and exemplified by him. The return to Catholicism under Mary is understood as God's scourge, but conversely acts as a confirmation of the reformers' status as the oppressed elect, as is underscored by Bateman's evocation of Foxe's *Acts and Monuments* (*TP* L.iir). While Mary's reign is thus seen as a momentary resurgence of the plague of the papal Antichrist, in the wider scheme of a teleologically conceived history, it nevertheless appears as an interlude. Bateman cleverly represents Memory herself as having trouble with the recollection of Mary's reign: 'Truly quoth she, thou well hast spoke, I had hir quite forgot, / Sith small desert of memorie, she left behinde God wot' (*TP* L.iir). In the wider scheme of things her accession becomes a momentary diversion from a tortuous but inexorably advancing path leading from the Reformation to the final Revelation.

## A Reformed Garden?

With the description of Elizabeth's reign, Bateman moves into the present, a feature that fundamentally differentiates his undertaking from that of de La Marche, who, writing about an extinguished dynasty, had in fact neither a present to celebrate nor a future to look forward to. Correspondingly, a shift in mood equally takes place. If the preceding allegorical action was still situated in the conceptual *locus* of the barren Desert of Age, we now enter a much more positively connoted, lush garden, initially perceived from afar as 'a pleasaunt fielde', then slowly assimilated to the plains at the foot of mount Parnassus and the garden of Hesperides (*TP* L.iiiv–iiiir). The transition from the sterile wasteland of Age to this fertile garden thus comes to represent the historical progression from the oppression under 'Marie, a bitter floure God knowes, sprong of so swete a tree' (*TP* L.iir), to the re-flowering of the Reformation and the Tudor family tree under Elizabeth. This shift is equally figured as a passage from night to day, introducing a solar symbolism that sustains Elizabeth's subsequent royal progress in a solar chariot:[52]

> When clowdie night so darke and grim, was paste then we arose,
> Euen when *Auroras* comely hew, gan mornings cheere disclose,
> When *Cinthias* hornes were hid, when *Phaebus* tooke his race:
> In glittring Chariot through the skies, fro Esterne throne apace (*TP* L.iiiv)

---

[52]  Fittingly, the woodcut introducing Elizabeth's pageant represents her, like Phoebus and unlike the other Tudor monarchs who are shown sitting on horseback, sitting in 'A Charet set with costly stone, and plumed on euery side' (M.iiiv; woodcut on M.iiiv).

This passage from night to day and from desert to garden becomes a prelude to Bateman's praise of Elizabeth. However the blessings of this new reign and the resurgence of the reforming cause are never felt to be in any way definitive. So the queen's subjects are imagined as rejoicing in this reversal of fortune, but the divine gift they are awarded is clearly made conditional upon their own behaviour and obedience: 'God graunt therfore we thankfull be, and duties to hir show: / That lande or nation which doe loue their Prince with hart and will, God doth and will them euer blesse, in Citie, towne and hill' (*TP* L.iiiv). Elizabeth's reign is idealised to some degree, yet Bateman avoids the suggestion that its achievements are in any way permanent, and thus leaves the door open for the possibility of new persecutions, seen as a direct consequence of the lax moral standards of the queen's subjects, as had been the case with Edward. Thus the evocation of the queen's mortality is not only designed to have a humbling effect on the royal person herself, but is equally and even predominantly intended to warn her subjects that they are still within the domain of earthly mutability subject to Atropos.[53] And again for Bateman the quest of the monarch, passing through further hardships, tests and temptations, becomes the paradigm for the entire commonwealth's journey: 'With those hir Nobles of hir lande, on prograce now they ride, / Through worldly pleasures trapped way, forth on apace they glide / ... / And constant faith in Jesus Christ, Liefetenaunt hirs shall bee, / Which seekes by meanes the life to come, as all full well may see' (*TP* M.iiiv).

Far from being a simple Edenic garden, which would signify the completion and conclusion of pilgrim's and the nation's homeward journey, Bateman's garden is a complex, unstable and often contradictory allegorical space. So, on the one hand, the garden is clearly positively connoted as a symbol of the return of divine favour to the country, whereas on the other it is perceived as a potentially misleading, alluring space distracting both pilgrim and commonwealth from continuing the journey. The pilgrim, instructed by Memory, in fact experiences the garden as a diversion from his spiritual quest, as an attack upon his senses: 'And musing on it as I rode, as many mindes are bent, / To chaunged fancies newe and straunge, graue studie to preuent / ... / Now sure deere dame sayde I, this fielde bewraps my senses so / That I am rauisht with the sight, the further that I go' (*TP* L.iiiir). Such remarks imply an exhortation to avoid a premature identification of the favourable conditions of the present reign with something like a celestial kingdom: despite the return of true religion to Britain, human history is still in movement and has not reached its apotheosis and endpoint.

---

[53] See also David Davis, '"The vayle of Eternall Memorie": Contesting Representations of Queen Elizabeth in English Woodcuts', *Word and Image* 27:1 (2011), 65–76, here 71. The evocation of the queen's mortality may seem odd in the light of what has been called the 'cult' of Elizabeth, but in fact fits with the more anxious mood of the early reign when the iconography of the celestial and immortal Elizabeth, which in any case was far from being univocally celebratory, had not yet developed. See for instance, John N. King, 'Queen Elizabeth I: Representations of the Virgin Queen', *Renaissance Quarterly* 43:1 (1990), 30–74. See also Ch. 6, p. 149, n. 24.

This idea is further borne out in Memory's surprisingly relativistic remarks that follow; not only is the garden transitory and mutable, but to some it may not appear to be a garden at all: 'this field she sayd which thou doest see, so faire, so fresh and greene, Unto an other seemeth bare, as time hath euer beene' (*TP* L.iiiir). This consideration has the twofold function of including the perspective of a Catholic minority and thus moderating the idealistic fervour of Protestant triumphalism:

> To such this pleasaunt fielde of *Time*, which thou doest thinke so gay,
> A toylesse plat they holde it sure, deuoyde of comfort thay.
> Some other thinke, as they likewise, of *Balams* flocke I meane,
> Which are dispoylde in this same time, of all their comfort cleane: (*TP* L.iiiiv)

Most importantly, the desire not to gloss over but expose such internal divisions lurking beneath the seemingly ideal curtain of the garden, gives further weight to Bateman's exhortation *not* to identify the present reign with an ideal, possibly millenarian prophetic kingdom, and to look instead beyond the visible horizon for a definitive apocalyptic consummation. Bateman's representation of Elizabeth's reign as a pageant and progress thus combines Protestant triumphalism with a wider, cosmic-apocalyptic relativism. All of this fits with the dominant mood of the early Elizabethan period, a mood marked by a sense of precariousness and instability rather than the unabashedly self-confident triumphalism that was to characterise the later decades of the reign.[54] Death infiltrates the seemingly Edenic garden in other, more subtle but disturbing ways. Inheriting de La Marche's endless catalogue of deceased heroes, Bateman turns it to new uses, making the funerary monuments themselves the distinctive 'vegetation' of his garden (*TP* M.ir), and thus oddly coalescing a cemetery and a sensual pleasure garden. The function of this funerary garden remains cryptic, but in the light of the pervasive influence of Foxe's *Acts and Monuments* on Bateman, the monuments of former heroes may be assimilated to those of the martyrs for true religion.[55]

---

[54]  For a characterisation of the hopes and fears for the future under Elizabeth, see Bauckham, *Tudor Apocalypse*, pp. 125–44. For an account of the reign emphasising the halting and difficult advance of the reforming cause and the widespread uncertainty concerning religious matters, see Eamon Duffy, *The Stripping of the Altars: Traditional Religion in England 1400–1580* (New Haven, CT: Yale University Press, 1992), pp. 565–93, and Christopher Haigh, *English Reformations: Religion, Politics, and Society under the Tudors* (Oxford: Clarendon Press, 1993), pp. 235–50. The northern rising in 1569, the year of publication of both the *Travayled Pylgrime* and the *Christall Glasse*, again made the possibility of a reversal of fortunes seem very real (Duffy, p. 583). See also Simon Adams, 'Eliza Enthroned? The Court and its Politics', in his *Leicester and the Court: Essays on Elizabethan Politics* (Manchester: Manchester University Press, 2002), pp. 24–45, here 32–3. And Christopher Haigh, ed., *The Reign of Elisabeth I* (Basingstoke: Macmillan, 1984), p. 24.

[55]  The inclusion of Elizabeth among the protagonists of the pageant/tournament opposing the Tudor Monarchs to Atropos also implies her assimilation to the series of martyrs for the Protestant cause, in a manner reminiscent of her treatment in Foxe's *Actes and Monuments*; see the 1563 Edition, Book 5, pp. 1789–1802 (corrected pagination), see *The Unabridged Acts and Monuments Online* or *TAMO*. Available at: http://www.johnfoxe.org [accessed 12 February 2012].

The pilgrim's enjoyment of the pleasure garden, representing the religious and political re-flowering of Elizabeth's reign, is thus tempered by Memory's warning that this is still an earthly garden, and therefore a *locus* of mortality and transience. Memory thus redirects the pilgrim's attention away from the garden, which in de La Marche's allegory signified absolute and definitive mortality, towards the promise of eschatological resolution beyond death: 'Marke well therefore quoth *Memorie* although these sightes thee please, / The sights not seene with *Ioue* aboue, both breede more ioye and ease' (*TP* M.iv). De La Marche's melancholic monumentalism has given way to a Foxean, apocalyptic transcendentalism. While this exhortation to look beyond the horizon of earthly existence still functions as a traditional *memento mori*, on the other it discourages a naïvely optimistic political and dynastic triumphalism: 'All things created must chaunged be by mortall law no doute, / Therefore in vaine thou valiant king, art thou so highe and stoute' (*TP* I.iir), as Thanatos had observed earlier in the poem. Such reminders move the focus of the work away from an obsessive reiteration of the human, personal experience of death found in the *Chevalier délibéré*, and subjects the vicissitudes of individual existence, even that of the Tudor dynasty, to a wider design of national and cosmic destiny. The experience of death is no longer abhorred but accepted as being part of a larger scenario of apocalyptic deliverance from a 'Laberinth of endlesse woes' (*TP* H.iiir), and is eagerly anticipated rather than dreaded: 'Wherewith that I would make an ende, of this my trauayled time, / The soner then to ende this race of cankered yre and crime' (*TP* N.iiiv).

This shift in the understanding of mortality has radical implications on a number of planes. First, it clearly re-establishes the original transcendental focus of the 'Pilgrimage of Life' genre that had been lost in de La Marche: 'exhorting euery faythfull Christian, to haue such regarde to this their Pilgrimage here on earth, that in the lyfe to come, they may enjoy the happie gaine of endlesse felicitie' (*TP* A.iiir). Second, such a perspective implies a negative view of earthly, temporal existence as such, and is the expression of a truly apocalyptic rather than merely prophetic expectation.[56] As a result of Bateman's construction of an analogical correspondence between personal, national and cosmic spiritual history, this striving for a transcendental resolution undermines Bateman's own hesitant political eulogy of the Tudor Dynasty.[57] Despite all its historicist and political developments, the allegory finally points clearly beyond the present religious, political and epistemological contingencies, and longs for a definitive resolution and release – only imperfectly foreshadowed by the historical phenomenon of the Reformation. For Bateman, then, the

---

[56] For the distinction, applied to John Foxe's move from an optimistically 'prophetic' mood to a more markedly transcendentalising, apocalyptic and politically 'pessimistic' perspective, see Tom Betteridge, 'From Prophetic to Apocalyptic: John Foxe and the Writing of History'. See also Marjorie Reeves, 'The Development of Apocalyptic Thought: Medieval Attitudes', in Patrides and Wittreich, eds, *The Apocalypse in English Renaissance Thought and Literature*, p. 40.

[57] Prescott speaks of Bateman's 'hint of dissatisfaction with history and politics themselves', 'Spenser's Chivalric Restoration', p. 192.

study of human history is undertaken merely in the interest of what lies beyond it, and acquires validity only insofar as it points towards the final 'Revelation' and triumph of the True Church on the day of the Second Coming, which is also the vanishing point of a teleological history of the world. Unlike de La Marche, Bateman reintroduces the eschatological Jerusalem as the ultimate focus and arch-referent of the journey, even if the presence of the eschatological City is only implicit but all the more powerful. The very absence of any actual textual or iconographic embodiment of the Holy City from Bateman's poem, but not from his imagination, only further enhances the 'travayled' pilgrim's longing for such a metaphysical consummation.

Also on the microcosmic, personal plane, man is felt to be in a state of perpetual impotence and expectancy. The mirror of allegory, allowing the indirect, specular contemplation of divine mysteries, remains constantly cloudy despite the 'Christall Glasse's' 'Reformation', and Bateman longs for the final, eschatological intercession of Christ, himself a pure and spotless mirror, and sole agent of apocalyptic and epistemological deliverance.[58] Thus, aware of the radical deficiency of man's reason and discernment in his fallen, Adamic state, the pilgrim as well as the True Church are ultimately wholly powerless to bring the journey to completion, and are entirely dependent on the direct and final intervention of Christ. This makes the *Travayled Pylgrime* a text that until its very end is pervaded by an epistemological anxiety, an anxiety that is nevertheless channelled into a confident and patient prayer for deliverance from the limitations of earthly existence, and thus points to the resolution of that inescapable epistemological paradox beyond the limits of the visible world, to be attained only in the thoroughly reformed ontology of the Apocalypse and the Second Coming of Christ:

> Then after death you soone shall see,
> The christall glasse of light to shine.
> Which glasse is Christ our Sauiour. (CG X.iiiir)

---

[58]  The title of the *Christall Glasse* itself, with its idiosyncratic orthography, may be read as a pun on the name of 'Christ'. The assimilation of Christ to a mirror can be related to Deguileville's *Vie*, where the upper pommel of the pilgrim staff is described as Christ the spotless mirror, reflecting the image of the New Jerusalem to be reached at the end of the pilgrimage (*Vie¹* 3691–708).

# 5

# *William Goodyear: Everyman's Quest*

William Goodyear's *Wandering Knight* (1581 – STC 4700)[1] is a translation of Jean de Cartheny's *Voyage du chevalier errant* (1557), which in turn shows signs of the influence of both Deguileville's *Vie* and Thomas de Saluces's *Livre du chevalier errant*. The *Voyage* first appeared in print in 1557,[2] although the author's dedication to Mary of Hungary, Regent of the Netherlands, carries the date of December 1552. Cartheny revised his work for his second edition from 1572, and added a new dedication.[3] The work seems to have enjoyed a fair degree of popularity, and the second edition was reprinted several times, in 1587 (three editions), 1594, 1595 and 1620. The work was also translated into English (1581 and ten reprints), German (1602),[4] Dutch (1649), Welsh (1585)[5] and Latin (1606), the latter two being in manuscript alone.[6] Although biographical information about the author is scant,

---

[1]   William Goodyear, *The Wandering Knight*, ed. Dorothy Atkinson Evans (Seattle, WA: University of Washington Press, 1951).

[2]   Jehan de Cartheny, *Le voyage du chevalier errant* (Anvers: J. Bellère, 1557). Digitisation available online at http://gallica.bnf.fr/ark:/12148/bpt6k54605b [accessed 12 February 2012].

[3]   The changes made in this second edition are summarised by Nancy Oddo, 'Rémanence littéraire et propagande catholique: les pieux enjeux du *Voyage du Chevalier errant* de Jean de Cartheny (1557)', in Emmanuel Bury and Francine Mora, eds, *Du roman courtois au roman baroque* (Paris: Les Belles Lettres, 2004) pp. 309–21; see also *The Wandering Knight*, ed. Evans, pp. xii–xxiv.

[4]   Guilliaume van Gemert, *Die Werke des Aegidius Albertinus (1560–1620): ein Beitrag zur Erforschung des deutschsprachigen Schrifttums der katholischen Reformbewegung in Bayern um 1600 und seiner Quellen* (Amsterdam: Holland University Press, 1979), pp. 273ff.

[5]   On the Welsh translation of the *Voyage*, mediated by the English version, see D. Mark Smith, ed., *Treigl Y Marchog Crwydrad* (Caerdydd: Gwasg Prifysgol Cymru, 2002); and 'Y Marchog Crwydrad a'r Alegori yn yr Oesoedd Canol', *Dwned* 6 (Hydref 2000), 129–42; 'Cyfieithu'r Marchog Crwydrad: Testun Llenyddol/Crefyddol', *Llên Cymru* 24 (Gorffennaf 2001), 61–78. I also wish to thank Dr D. Mark Smith personally for giving me access to an English summary of his findings on the Welsh version, in the form of a transcript of his paper 'English and Welsh Texts of *The Voyage of the Wandering Knight*', originally presented at the sixth Lomers Annual Conference at the University of London, 17 June 2005.

[6]   For a complete list of the surviving texts of the *Voyage*, see Evans, *The Wandering Knight*, pp. xxi–xxiv.

internal evidence and Cartheny's dedication allow the reconstruction of the environment in which he was writing. Born in 1520 in Valenciennes, he entered the Carmelite Order, received his Doctorate in Theology in 1554 and soon became Regent of the convent in Brussels.[7] His reputation for great learning was only tainted by what seems to have been a youthful infatuation with evangelical ideals, which he was made to abjure publicly in 1539.

## A Catholic Everyman

The *Voyage du chevalier errant* is clearly an elaboration of the traditional medieval *topos* of the *homo viator*, and thus again combines elements of chivalric romance with the allegory of the Christian pilgrimage of life. The influence of Deguileville's *Vie* has been pointed out repeatedly, and can be traced both in the overall plan of the work, and in specific passages in the text.[8] Cartheny may well have had access to a copy of *Vie*[1] in the Library of his dedicatee, Mary of Hungary (today MS Paris BNF fr. 12462).[9] Another major influence on Cartheny, providing him with the model for a fusion of knightly romance with Christian allegory, seems to have been Thomas III's *Livre du chevalier errant*, discussed here in Chapter 2.[10] Despite the impossibility of pinpointing any direct verbal borrowings, the thematic and structural parallels are numerous and significant, and one of the manuscripts of Thomas's work, today MS Paris BNF fr. 12559, was equally in the possession of Cartheny's dedicatee between 1530 and 1558.[11] Yet while Thomas, given his knightly status, ultimately explores the possibilities for balancing literal and allegorical knighthood, Cartheny writes his allegory of the Christian knight from a more strictly contemplative perspective reminiscent of Deguileville. Significantly, though, while Cartheny clearly shares Deguileville's monastic background, he adapts the medieval monastic ideal to his immediate purpose, the instruction of the laity in post-Reformation continental Europe. Nancy Oddo defines this conspicuously

---

[7]   The most complete account of Cartheny's life is given by Evans, *The Wandering Knight*, pp. xii–xxiv. Among the sources used by Evans, see in particular Arthur Dinaux and Aimé Leroy, *Archives historiques et littéraires du Nord de la France et du midi de la Belgique*, vol. 4 (Valanciennes, 1834), pp. 279–85; and Gabriel Wessels, ed., *Bibliotheca Carmelitana: notis criticis et dissertationibus illustrata* (Rome: In aedibus Collegii S. Alberti, 1927), cols 808–9. See also *Dictionnaire de biographie française*, vol. 7, ed. M. Prévost and Roman D'Amat (Paris: Letouzay et Ané, 1956), p. 1282.

[8]   Oddo, 'Rémanence littéraire', p. 309; Evans, *The Wandering Knight*, pp. xxix–xxxvi, and notes for specific passages; James Blanton Wharey, *A Study of the Sources of Bunyan's Allegories, with special reference to Deguileville's Pilgrimage of Man* (Baltimore, MD: J. H. Furst, 1904), pp. 69–77.

[9]   Marguerite Debae, *La bibliothèque de Marie d'Autriche. Essai de reconstitution d'après l'inventaire de 1523–24* (Louvain: Peters, 1995), nr. 109, pp. 181–4.

[10]  See also Ruhe, 'Der *Chevalier errant*', pp. 172–3; Fajen, *Die Lanze*, pp. 225–6 and *passim*.

[11]  Fajen, *Die Lanze*, p. 27; Debae, *La bibliothèque de Marie d'Autriche*, nr. 50, pp. 81–4.

'counter-reformation' use of chivalric elements as a 'strategy of seduction', and speaks of a recuperation of Christian allegory to seduce lay readers with little interest in theological abstractions.[12] Thus the chivalric romance framework is progressively weakened as the story progresses,[13] and the three main sections of the work that mark the knight's spiritual progression, also mark a gradual abandonment of the ostensibly 'chivalric' adventures promised by the book's title.[14] Rather than being a successful quest leading to the acquisition of something like a 'knightly identity', the narrative is largely a parable for the fruitless departure, errance and return of a prodigal son, eventually persuaded to abandon the very knightly identity with which he begins his quest.

The knight starts his quest in the first part with an 'errance' proper, where he is led astray by his governess Folly. The knight is clad in Folly's armour, a parody of the traditional Pauline armour (Part I, Ch. 3), and sets out on his pilgrimage and arrives at a crossroads where he chooses the path of Vice instead of Virtue (I.6), arrives at the Palace of Worldly Felicity (I.7) where he succumbs to numerous temptations until the palace sinks into an abyss and the knight finds himself stuck in the mire (I.13), which finally leads him to cry out against worldly vanity (I.14). As the narration progresses into Part II, the action in the story begins to slacken dramatically in order to make space for the growing need for didactic exposition. The Virtues deliver a primarily verbal, catechetical instruction in the manner of spiritual counsellors, taking the knight through well-ordered successive stages of understanding. So after the knight's rescue through Divine Grace (II.1) and a brief visit to Hell where he meets his fellow revellers from the Palace of Worldly Felicity (II.2), he enters the School of Penance (II.4) where he listens to the accusations of Conscience (II.5), is reminded of God's forgiveness by Memory (II.6), recites the seven penitential psalms in French together with Divine Grace (II.8), listens to Understanding's sermon (II.10) and is finally taken to the Palace of Virtue. In this second part, the knight is turned into a largely passive listener and pupil, as the original framework of the knightly quest is largely forgotten or suspended.

In Part III this tendency to indulge in static doctrinal expositions is made even more prominent. The knightly quest has by now been turned into a catechismal exercise, and most chapters here become mere descriptions of the Virtues. So we have a general eulogy of Virtue (III.2), followed by verbal descriptions of the theological virtues of Faith (III.3), Hope (III.4) and Charity (III.5) and the moral virtues of Prudence, Justice, Fortitude and Temperance (III.7). The knight is then

---

[12]  Oddo, 'Rémanence littéraire', pp. 309 and 316.

[13]  See Ruhe, 'Der *Chevalier errant*', pp. 172–3.

[14]  Evans, *The Wandering Knight*, pp. xxxvi–xlii, points in particular to Saint Bernard's parable, *De Pugna Spirituali*, as a possible source for the tripartite structure. There the motif of the Christian pilgrimage, divided into the three traditional stages of Purgative, Illuminative and Unitive, is fused with the parable of the Prodigal Son. Oddo interprets the tripartition as representing the three penitential stages of contrition, confession and satisfaction; see 'Rémanence littéraire', p. 310.

finally allowed a glimpse of the New Jerusalem (III.8), which is followed by a detailed allegoresis of the City given by Understanding (III.9). The *Voyage* ends with the knight's desire to enter the City, upon which Understanding introduces him to Perseverance, who sets forth his verbal instruction (III.10–11).

Cartheny's *Voyage* reiterates the universal, paradigmatic relevance of the allegory of the Christian pilgrimage, cast into simple didactic prose for a later generation of readers, and thus avoids any direct reference to the highly charged environment of the ongoing Reformation controversy. Yet despite Cartheny's conscious refusal to acknowledge the presence of outward pressures and motives, his work is infiltrated by historical, political and religious pressures in a variety ways. More specifically, his utter silence about the troubled religious and political climate of the Netherlands of the 1550s[15] speaks only too clearly and eloquently about Cartheny's latent affiliation with a Catholic Reformation or Counter-Reformation agenda,[16] and becomes in itself an eloquent polemical statement. The very traditionalism and universalism of Cartheny's allegory, and the refusal to engage with polemics, implies that for the history of the Catholic Church represented by Cartheny, the Reformation is emphatically a non-event.[17] By reiterating Deguileville's paradigm in a radically transformed context, Cartheny affirms the unbroken continuity of the medieval Catholic, monastic tradition in the face of recent religious turmoil.

If the ideals advocated by the *Voyage* are closely related to those presented by the *Vie*, they are nevertheless presented in a distinctively Counter-Reformation form. The work must be seen within a wider scheme of apostolic, missionary attempts to instruct the unlearned, characteristic of the development of the Catholic Church during the Tridentine period.[18] The focus of attention within the monastic orders in the late medieval period had already begun to move away from strictly contemplative ideals towards an active and practical engagement with the laity in the world outside the cloister, a development culminating with the foundation of the Society

---

[15]  On the situation in the Netherlands, see Graham Darby, ed., *The Origins and Development of the Dutch Revolt* (London: Routledge, 2001); on religious issues, Andrew Pettegree, 'Religion and the Revolt', in ibid., pp. 67–83.

[16]  The actual question of an appropriate terminology and its implications has been at the centre of most recent scholarship in the field since Hubert Jedin's *Katholische Reformation oder Gegenreformation? Ein Versuch zur Klärung der Begriffe nebst einer Jubiläumsbetrachtung über das Trienter Konzil* (Luzern: Verlag Josef Stocker, 1946); see e.g. David M. Luebke, ed., *The Counter-Reformation: The Essential Readings* (Oxford: Blackwell, 1999), pp. 1–16.

[17]  Francis M. Higman points out that the publication of traditional, orthodox Catholic books in mid-century France continues unaltered as if to indicate that the Reformation does not exist; Francis M. Higman, 'Le domaine français', in Jean-François Gilmont, ed., *La réforme et le livre: l'Europe de l'imprimé (1517–v. 1570)* (Paris: Les Editions du Cerf, 1990), pp. 105–54.

[18]  For the emergence of such new didactic methods, see H. Outram Evennett, 'Counter-Reformation Spirituality', p. 48 and *passim*, in Luebke, *The Counter-Reformation*, pp. 48–63. See also H. Outram Evennett, 'The Reorientation of the Religious Life', in his *The Spirit of the Counter-Reformation* (Cambridge: Cambridge University Press, 1968), pp. 67–88.

of Jesus.[19] By 1552, estimated date of composition for the *Voyage*, such apostolic efforts embraced by many of the Orders were inevitably doubled by what was at the very least an implicit propagandist subtext and agenda, even when this lay beyond the declared objectives. Such a twofold, apostolic and propagandist agenda fits perfectly within the contemporary Catholic efforts to reclaim print as well as other cultural media and forms of communication that for a long time had served the Reformers' ends alone.[20] The engagement of French Catholic theologians with the vernacular was immense and is often insufficiently stressed: rather than attempting to control the spread of evangelical ideas through censorship, franco-phone Catholics successfully adopted the vernacular to propagate basic doctrinal notions and theological ideas in simple form.[21] Cartheny, a Doctor of Theology writing for the masses, is clearly conscious of such implications, as he specifies in the dedication to his second, revised edition of the work from 1572:[22] '& de rechef le faire imprimer et metre en lumière, pour l'instruction des simples, de ceux prin-cipalement qui se seroient fourvoyez du droit chemin de vertu.'[23]

Such a reference to the loss of the right path is an oblique but clear allusion to the 'errance' of the Christian faithful infatuated with evangelical ideas. The *Voyage* now sees itself as a corrective, as an antidote to the sophistries of Folly – the latter representing of course morally reprehensible behaviour in a wide sense, but more specifically alluding to the recent spread of heretical ideas. Exhorting the knight to remain steadfast in his obedience to the Holy Catholic Church, God's Grace invites the pilgrim to block his ears against the preaching of 'damnables doctrines & propos des heretiques', imagined as the song of sirens, threatening to distract and shipwreck the Christian pilgrim on his journey towards the Heavenly Kingdom (II.3, p. 140v). Explicit mentions of the Reformation, however, are limited to a few isolated passages, such as the mention of Luther and Zwingli as subjects of Folly in the

---

[19] Michael A. Mullet, *The Catholic Reformation* (London: Routledge, 1999), pp. 23–7; Richard L. DeMolen, ed., *Religious Orders of the Catholic Reformation: In Honor of John C. Olin on his Seventy-Fifth Birthday* (New York: Fordham University Press, 1994). On Jesuits in particular, see John W. O'Malley, *The First Jesuits* (Cambridge, MA: Harvard University Press, 1993).

[20] The situation in the French-speaking areas of Europe is somewhat more balanced, as the religious book, even in the early stages of the rupture, had never been evangelical property alone; see Andrew Pettegree, 'The Sixteenth-Century French Religious Book Project', in Andrew Pettegree, Paul Nelles and Philip Conner, eds, *The Sixteenth-Century French Religious Book* (Aldershot: Ashgate, 2001), pp. 1–17. For the use of vernacular educational texts as 'disguised catechisms', see Karin Maag, 'Education and Works of Religious Instruction', in Pettegree *et al.*, eds, *Sixteenth-Century French Religious Book*, pp. 98–109.

[21] Higman, 'Le domaine français'.

[22] On the intensified topical relevance of the second edition in the context of the situation in the Netherlands and the association with the new dedicatee, see Oddo, 'Rémanence littéraire', pp. 311–12.

[23] 'And once more to have it printed and exalted, for the instruction of simple folk, those especially who may have wandered from the straight path of virtue'. Copy consulted: *Le voyage du chevalier errant* (Cambray, 1587), reproducing the 1572 edition.

middle of a lengthy list of heretics (I.5, p. 28r). Elsewhere references to the Reformation are more oblique, such as the mention of 'faulse opinion et mauvaise doctrine'
(I.6, p. 32r), or a condemnation of the disastrous wars resulting from the distortion
of sacred doctrine (I.2, p. 6r).[24]

Cartheny is above all concerned with the reunification of the body politic of
the Church, and polemical denunciation is clearly *not* an appropriate tool to achieve
this. The author dwells at length on the qualities required of the successful Catholic
missionary if he is to avoid merely castigating heretics and thus exacerbating
the schism:

> De ceste mesme vertu doiuent estre ornez & decorez les prelatz, predicateurs &
> docteurs de l'Eglise, pour vaillamment soustenir la foy de l'Eglise, & la defendre
> auec le glaiue de la parolle de Dieu, contre tous heretiques & aduersaires d'icelle
> … Toutesfois ce doiuent ils faire prudentement, de peur qu'il ne s'esleue sedition,
> & plus grand mal en la chrestienneté, & modestement à fin qu'il soit apparent
> qu'ilz desirent le salut des errans & aduersaires, & non pas leur mort &
> condemnation. (III.7, p. 153v)[25]

Strikingly, then, in this doctrinal refashioning of a knightly romance, the military
metaphors of the chivalric quest and crusade hide a pacifist, conciliatory missionary
agenda designed to heal the rift within the Christian world.[26]

One is tempted to draw links with other contemporary manifestations of
Catholic spirituality effecting a similar transposition of the military, chivalric and
crusading rhetoric. The conversion of Ignatius Loyola springs to mind, where his
earlier experience as a knight and courtier as well as his crusading aspirations
provided a set of metaphors later used to articulate the spiritual mission of his
Society of Jesus. Transposed and spiritualised, Ignatius's later career as a knight
of Christ involved service to the Virgin instead of his beloved, mystical pilgrimage
to Jerusalem instead of its physical recovery from infidel hands, and was ultimately
aimed at a peaceful conversion of both heretics and pagans.[27] It has been suggested

---

[24] Other oblique references that systematically avoid identifying the specifically reformed heresy
occur at I.12, p. 59r, III.3, p. 139v.

[25] 'And this same virtue must glorify and exalt the prelates, preachers and doctors of the Church,
so that they may valiantly support the faith of the Church, and defend it with the sword of the
word of God, against all heretics and adversaries of that same Church . . . However they must
do so prudently, for fear of causing resentment and sedition, and still greater evils within
Christendom, and modestly, so that it may be apparent that they desire the salvation of the
wayward and of their enemies, not their death and condemnation'.

[26] See also section II.3.

[27] For a discussion of Ignatius's early career and its impact on later developments, see Philip
Caraman, *Ignatius Loyola* (London: Harper Collins, 1990), pp. 1–32 in particular; see also
O'Malley, *The First Jesuits*, and MacCulloch, *Reformation*, pp. 218–26. On the importance of the
notion of pilgrimage, see John C. Olin, 'The Idea of Pilgrimage in the Experience of Ignatius
Loyola', *Church History* 48:4 (1979), 387–97.

that such imagery may actually derive directly from Deguileville's *Vie*, with which Loyola was familiar through a Castilian translation printed in 1490.[28] Such military/spiritual rhetoric is essential in lending Loyola's masterpiece, the *Spiritual Exercises*, its spirit of battle and perseverance as an ascetic manual.[29] The same spirit of battle also imbues the missionary ideals of the order, symptomatically described in a letter to the order's General in 1563 as a need of 'ever sweetly fighting.'[30] The same militant intensity in confronting one's inner, spiritual enemies in a quest for a closer contact with God is also found in another, later classic of the age, Lorenzo Scupoli's *Combattimento Spirituale*.[31] First published in 1589, it went through thirty Italian editions during the author's lifetime, 250 before 1750. It was first translated into English in 1598 by the Jesuit John Gerrard, printed at a secret press in England while claiming to be produced in Antwerp, and reprinted several times.[32] Again, the only death to be desired in such ascetic literature is that of one's lower self, to be defeated only through spiritual discipline, faith and prayer. Like the *Voyage*, these two spiritual classics shrink away from an open ideological or political confrontation with the forces of the Reformation, and supplant the polemic impetus with a new but distinctively Catholic sense of militant interiority.

## Catechismal Romance

Cartheny's references to the 'simples … fourvoyez du droit chemin' reveals other eminently Catholic, post-tridentine features in the *Voyage*, particularly its concern with religious guidance. Indeed during the second and third parts of the *Voyage* the knight is effectively 'taken through' a succession of meditations, purgations and exercises by a series of spiritual advisors,[33] as would have been the case for anyone

---

[28] Flor Bango de la Campa, 'Deguileville en Espagne: la réception de *El pelegrino de la vida humana*', in Kamath and Nievergelt, *The* Pèlerinage *Allegories* (forthcoming).

[29] John W. O'Malley, 'Was Ignatius Loyola a Church Reformer? How to Look at Early Modern Catholicism', in Luebke, ed., *The Counter-Reformation*, p. 72.

[30] 'e per sempre combatter dolcemente', in a letter from P. Auger, author of the first successful Catholic Catechism in French in 1563, to P. Jacques Lainez; quoted in Jean-Claude Dhôtel, *Les origines du catéchisme moderne: d'après les premiers manuels imprimés en France* (Paris: Aubier, 1967), p. 54.

[31] Lorenzo Scupoli, *The Spiritual Combat*, ed. and trans. Thomas Barns (London: Methuen, 1909); and *Unseen Warfare: Being the Spiritual Combat and Path to Paradise as Edited by Nicodemus of the Holy Mountain and Revised by Theophan the Recluse*, ed. and trans. E. Kadloubovsky and G. E. Palmer, intro. H. A. Hodges (London: Faber and Faber, 1952).

[32] [Lorenzo Scupoli], *The Spiritual Conflict*, trans. anonymous, with Jan van Päschen, *The Spiritual Pilgrimage of Hierusalem*, English Recusant Literature 1558–1640, vol. 8, ed. D. M. Rodgers (Menston: Scolar Press, 1969).

[33] On the increasing importance accorded to spiritual guides and advisors, related to the enhanced role of confession in response to the Reformed threat, see Evennett, 'Counter-Reformation Spirituality', p. 59.

submitting to the ordeal of Ignatius's *Exercises*.[34] Individual chapters in the *Voyage* thus function as sketches of as many stages in a paradigmatic process of conversion, purgation and spiritual enlightenment. The emphasis on the systematic confession and inventory of one's past sins, performed during the first week of Loyola's *Exercises*, is reflected in the knight's own extensive review of his earlier sinful life that triggers his conversion (I.14, II.5), as well as in the *Voyage*'s general insistence on the importance of the sacrament of confession (II.7). The knight's systematic purification from sin lasts seven days (II.9), and echoes the *Exercises*' division into four weekly sequences. The *Voyage*, then, applies the *Exercises*' principles to the devotions of an ordinary layman.[35]

The *cursus* followed by the knight at the School of Penitence and Palace of Virtue in parts II and III of the narrative also functions effectively as a Catechism, instructing him in the basic tenets of the Catholic faith. The section contains all the elements that have been identified as the classic ingredients of every Catechism following Calvin's *Formulaire* of 1541: expositions of liturgy and symbolism, the ten commandments, prayer and the sacraments.[36] So the knight is made to recite the ten commandments (I.12), is taken through the sacrament of confession and performs penitential exercises (II.7), recites the penitential psalms (II.8) and attends mass (II.9). This catechismal dimension is consolidated in the second edition from 1572, which ends with an additional chapter containing a sequence of daily devotions, including the Creed, the Our Father, an exhortation to address prayers to the Virgin and Saints and a further rehearsal of the Ten Commandments. By using the Catechism in such a way, Cartheny is appropriating an eminently Protestant form.[37]

At the same time Cartheny animates his didactic efforts through the use of a lively dialogic form, conspicuously absent from any other contemporary Catechisms, but prominent in Deguileville's model. The choice of a first-person narrative, rather than foreshadowing 'literary' and psychological developments found in the modern novel as is sometimes claimed,[38] must equally be seen in connection with Cartheny's catechismal aims. The narrative 'I' collapses the identities of the knight and the reader and thus strengthens the paradigmatic value of Cartheny's allegory of conversion and purification. This emerges particularly clearly from the embedded

---

[34] For a detailed treatment of the *Spiritual Exercises* see Evennett, 'St. Ignatius and the Spiritual Exercises', in *The Spirit of the Counter-Reformation*, pp. 43–66; and O'Malley, 'The Society of Jesus', in DeMoelen, *Religious Orders of the Catholic Reformation*, pp. 139–64; see also Evennett, 'Counter-Reformation Spirituality', pp. 57–8.

[35] For the spread and influence of the *Exercises* outside the order, see Evennett, 'St. Ignatius and the Spiritual Exercises', p. 44; and ibid., 'Counter-Reformation Spirituality', pp. 55–8.

[36] Dhôtel, *Origines du catéchisme moderne*, p. 60.

[37] For a fuller discussion of the evolution of the Catechism in France, see Dhôtel, *Origines du catéchisme moderne*, pp. 1–81.

[38] Margaret Schlauch, *Antecedents of the English Novel, 1400–1600: From Chaucer to Deloney* (London: Oxford University Press, 1963), pp. 135–7.

catechismal sections designed for recitation, requiring the active participation of the reader who is thus projected into the role of the knight. The entire *Voyage* is angled towards such an integration of the process of reading within the context of a ritualised, sacramental performance, and accordingly Cartheny in his prologue addresses both 'Lecteurs et Auditeurs': he sees his work as equally suitable for silent, private reading and public recitation.[39] Not only does the text contain a large number of such ritualised recitations, but becomes a performative, prayer-like act in itself, as is made clear by the couplet on the title-page: 'Quand purement trois fois leu tu auras, Ce liuret cy, recrée tu seras.' This eminently Catholic blend of the performative and recitative dimension, sees itself as an antidote to the excessively intellectual, probing and argumentative tendency fostered by Protestantism.[40]

By embracing such a ritualised, systematic and even normative conception of the spiritual life, Catholicism equally sees itself as countering Protestantism's excessive drive towards individualism, deemed to be dangerous both on a spiritual and political plane.[41] Yet rather than simply repressing the drive towards interiorisation, possibly fostered by the advent of print,[42] Catholic spirituality produces a different form of interiority, balancing personal introspective spirituality with a sense of corporate belonging and orthodoxy relying on a shared sacramental understanding.[43] This distinctively Catholic interiority is developed on a sacramental basis, and not as in the Protestant tradition as a mere solitary exercise of probing intellectual introspection. So in the *Voyage*, the knight's reading of Scripture is constantly interspersed with moments of prayer and devotion in the company of Grace Divine (II.8, p. 113v). Catholicism develops the ideal of a collectively proffered, spoken Word of prayer as an alternative to the passively absorbed and intellectually dissected Word of the sermon.[44]

Cartheny only refers obliquely and indirectly to the Reformation itself, and

---

[39] This may in turn again be linked to the typically Catholic conception of the catechism, favouring collective recitation in Church or other public settings rather than private reading; see Dhôtel, *Origines du catéchisme moderne*, p. 21.

[40] These ingredients are again most prominent in Jesuit evangelical ideals, where notions of *'pietas'* and *'christianitas'* replace the abstract and argumentative dynamics of much Protestant literature; see O'Malley, 'The Society of Jesus', p. 147.

[41] For the theological and ecclesiological reasons that nourish Catholicism's general reservations about the desirability of solitary reading of printed material in the period, see Dominique Julia, 'Reading and the Counter-Reformation', in Guglielmo Cavallo and Roger Chartier, eds, *A History of Reading in the West*, trans. Lydia G. Cochrane (Cambridge: Polity Press, 1999), pp. 238–68.

[42] This assumption has been increasingly questioned, disputed and nuanced by more recent scholarship, e.g. Jean-François Gilmont, 'L'imprimerie à l'aube du XVI$^{\text{ème}}$ siècle', in *La réforme et le livre*, pp. 19–28.

[43] Evennett, 'Counter-Reformation Spirituality', p. 62.

[44] For a detailed discussion of these two contrasting approaches to the 'Word', as well as reading and language more generally, see Jean-François Gilmont, 'Protestant Reformation and Reading', and Julia, 'Reading and the Counter-Reformation', both in Cavallo and Chartier, eds, *A History of Reading in the West*, pp. 213–37 and 238–68.

conceals his specific criticism of the new evangelical heresy behind the use of more slippery personifications such as Folly. As a consequence the knight's departure from Folly into the arms of Understanding reverberates with echoes of a conversion from the Protestant heresy to Catholic orthodoxy. Yet despite this commitment to Catholic orthodoxy, it is impossible to speak of a neat confessional dichotomy in the *Voyage*. So isolated elements in Understanding's instruction point to an unobtrusive but persistent influence of reformed concerns in Cartheny's thought, particularly issues of election and predestination (e.g. III.1, p. 131r; III.3, p. 142v; III.9, p. 163r), despite his great care to align himself with the Tridentine position.[45] Cartheny even comes close to embracing something like a mitigated form of Lutheran fideism, insisting on the necessity of Faith as precondition for the efficacy of the Sacraments (II.3, p. 83r), although he eventually rejects the argument of *sola fides* (III.3, p. 141r), again along the lines of the Council of Trent.[46] Similarly, his emphasis on the vital importance of Grace is still in keeping with Trent, but often smacks of a Lutheran overtone (e.g. II.2, p. 75v).

Cartheny was certainly no closet Calvinist, but his constructive response to eminently Protestant arguments points beyond a merely oppositional confessional dichotomy, and reveals his intimate acquaintance with Protestant doctrine. In the light of Cartheny's early evangelical sympathies it is nevertheless tempting to speculate about the exact nature of the events that led to his condemnation in 1539.[47] In the early stages of the controversy Luther's call for reform aroused much sympathy within the traditional Church, and precisely within many religious Orders.[48] Cartheny's acquaintance with Luther's ideas thus seems to go back to an early period when it was still hoped that a 'reformation' might be achieved without shattering the unity of the Church, a hope that is also reflected in Cartheny's nonpolemical stance. Cartheny's later associations suggest the persistence of a careful, silent sympathy with some Lutheran ideas: Mary of Hungary, dedicatee of the first edition of the work, despite the obligations imposed by her ultra-Catholic Habsburg lineage, was renowned for cultivating evangelical and particularly Lutheran sympathies that ultimately led to her abdication in 1555.[49] By that time the sharpened climate of religious conflict must have debilitated any remaining hopes for reconciliation, and Cartheny seems to have forsaken his earlier Lutheran sympathies, or rather modified and integrated them into a solidly Catholic allegiance. The pervasive influence of the Prodigal Son parable raises the question: does

---

[45] For the Tridentine position on Predestination, established since 1546, see J. Pohle, 'Predestination', in *The Catholic Encyclopedia*, vol. 12 (New York: Robert Appleton Company, 1911). Online edn (2003) available at: http://www.newadvent.org/cathen/12378a.htm [accessed 12 February 2012].

[46] For a summary of the Tridentine position, see Mullet, *The Catholic Reformation*, pp. 29–68.

[47] See also Dinaux and Leroy, *Archives historiques*, pp. 279–85.

[48] Evennett, 'Counter-Reformation Spirituality', p. 53.

[49] On the subject, see B. J. Spruyt, '"En bruit d'estre bonne luterienne": Mary of Hungary (1505–58) and Religious Reform', *The English Historical Review* 109:431 (1994), 275–307.

Cartheny's first-person narrative of the knight's infatuation with Folly – despite its catechismal purpose, despite its paradigmatic relevance, despite the 'impersonal' position represented by Cartheny himself – not also reverberate with a muffled autobiographical echo of Cartheny's own youthful 'errance'?[50]

## From Catholic to 'catholic'

A translation of Cartheny's *Voyage*, under the title of *The Voyage of the Wandering Knight*, first appeared in 1581. The translation was made by a 'William Goodyear of South-hampton, Merchant' (title page), about whom nothing else is known, and revised and prepared for publication by Robert Norman, an instrument-maker and hydrographer known mostly for his scientific publications.[51] The work must have enjoyed considerable success as it was reprinted a number of times, running to ten further editions in the hundred years following its first appearance.[52] Like many works of 'popular literature' from the period it seems to have been read widely across different social groups,[53] and it has been suggested that both Sidney and Spenser may have known the work.[54] The translation remains surprisingly close to the

---

[50] This seems to be confirmed also by Cartheny's overstated defensiveness against potential accusations of heterodoxy, as in the prologue: 'Oultre plus ie proteste de rien dire ny escrire en ce liure contre la sainte foy catholique, ou les determinations de sainte Eglise. Que si par inaduertance ou ignorance il aduenoit le contraire (que Dieu ne vueille) ie le tiens pour reuoqué, & des maintenant le reuoque, soubzmettant le tout au iugement des plus sçauans, et principalement à la censure de nostre mere l'Eglise.' ('Furthermore I proclaim that I do not intend to say or write anything in this book against the Holy Catholic faith, or the decrees of Holy Church. And if through carelessness or ignorance the contrary should come to pass (God defend us) I hold that to be revoked, yea do revoke it promptly, submitting all to the judgement of the wisest, and especially to the censure of the Church our mother'), *Voyage*, prologue.

[51] See Evans, *The Wandering Knight*, pp. xxvii–xxix.

[52] Further editions date from 1584, 1607, 1609, 1620, 1626, 1650, 1661, 1670 (two editions) and 1687.

[53] On the broad 'inclusiveness' of audiences for popular printed matter, see Tessa Watt, *Cheap Print and Popular Piety, 1550–1640* (Cambridge: Cambridge University Press, 1991), pp. 1–8; Bob Scribner, 'Is a History of Popular Culture Possible?', *History of European Ideas* 10:2 (1989), 175–91.

[54] For Sidney, see Elisabeth Porges Watson, '(Un)bridled Passion: Chivalric Metaphor and Practice in Sidney's *Astrophil and Stella*', *Reinardus* 15:1 (2002), 117–29; for Spenser, see Atkinson, 'The Wandering Knight, the Red Cross Knight, and "Miles Dei"'; for the possibility of further impact see also the Introduction to Robert Parry, *Moderatus*, ed. John Simons (Aldershot: Ashgate, 2002), pp. 13–14; Schlauch, *Antecedents of the English Novel*, pp. 135–7; Evans, *The Wandering Knight*, pp. xlii–xlvii. The argument for a direct and specific influence on Bunyan is now generally rejected since Louis B. Wright's remark in *Middle-Class Culture in Elizabethan England* (Chapel Hill, NC: University of North Carolina Press, 1935), p. 395, in turn going back to Wharey, *A Study of the Sources of Bunyan's Allegories*, pp. 69–77. Instead, a case has been made for the influence of Bunyan onto a late reworking of Goodyear's translation by John Harris (1687), see Evans, *The Wandering Knight*, pp. xxvi–xxvii.

original as will be seen, except for theological and doctrinal issues that are in fact scrupulously aligned with the position of the English Church. This already raises the central, problematic question about the reasons and implications of Goodyear's translation of such an unmistakably Catholic work as the *Voyage*. Advertised on its title page as the work of a Carmelite, imbued with Roman doctrine and theology, the work's Catholicism could not have escaped the notice of its accomplished translator, who, like many other translators in the period,[55] had acquired his linguistic skills through his profession, in this case trade with the continent. The role of merchants in fostering the book trade between England and the continent has rightly been stressed repeatedly, particularly in connection with the circulation and smuggling of forbidden Catholic books printed on the continent for the English market.[56]

It is tempting to speculate further along the mercantile connection. John Bossy has stressed the importance of mercantile routes for the establishment of an international network of Catholic *diaspora*, observing that the practice of smuggling Catholic books into England was so common as to lead to the adoption of the term 'merchant' as a covert periphrasis designating a 'Catholic Priest'.[57] Such a mercantile rhetoric is conspicuous also in contemporary Jesuit documents, where the mission to England is often thought of in terms of a rich 'commerce' of luxurious goods and rare commodities, thus providing an interesting counterpoint to the otherwise military rhetoric of Jesuit missionaries.[58] Moreover, the centre of the early Catholic book-production for the English market was located precisely in the southern Netherlands, geographic areas associated with Cartheny's original, and the trade between Antwerp and the English ports afforded the best possibilities for importing such literature.[59] Goodyear's association with Southampton would seem to corroborate the thesis of some Catholic connection: Hampshire had remained a

---

[55] This was a familiar situation, see H. S. Bennett, *English Books and their Readers 1558–1603: Being a Study in the History of the Book Trade in the Reign of Elizabeth I* (Cambridge: Cambridge University Press, 1965), pp. 101–3. The case of another merchant-translator has been the object of a recent study by Donald Beecher, 'The Legacy of John Frampton: Elizabethan Trader and Translator', *Renaissance Studies* 20:3 (2006), 320–39. See also William H. Sherman, 'Bringing the World to England: The Politics of Translation in the Age of Hakluyt', *Transactions of the Royal Historical Society* 14 (2004), 199–207; Edward Miller, *The Professional Writer in Elizabethan England: A Study of Nondramatic Literature* (Cambridge, MA: Harvard University Press, 1959), 204–6.

[56] On the importance of commercial routes for the circulation of Catholic works in England, see A. C. Southern, *Elizabethan Recusant Prose, 1559–1582: A Historical and Critical Account of the Books of the Catholic Refugees Printed and Published Abroad and at Secret Presses in England Together with an Annotated Bibliography of the Same* (London: Sands, 1950), pp. 33–43; see also John Bossy, 'The Character of Elizabethan Catholicism', *Past & Present* 21 (1962), 39–59, here 47–8; H. S. Bennett, *English Books 1558–1603*, pp. 74–5.

[57] Bossy, 'Elizabethan Catholicism', p. 48.

[58] John Bossy, *The English Catholic Community 1570–1850* (London: Darton, Longman and Todd, 1975); and ibid., 'Postscript' to Evennett, *The Spirit of the Counter-Reformation*, p. 129.

[59] See Southern, *English Recusant Prose*, pp. 30 and 34.

generally conservative county where the Reformation had been making only a halting progress, and with the arrival of the first Catholic Jesuit missions in 1577 and particularly 1580, this attachment to the old Faith was consolidated and developed.[60] Southampton itself remained a divided town, but the religious climate in the southern port, as in many other commercial harbours in England and on the continent, was characterised by a certain permissiveness due to the presence of various foreign congregations, such as the exiled French-speaking Calvinist community that settled in Southampton from about 1567 onwards.[61] Thus Goodyear's knowledge of French may equally well suggest a close contact with the transplanted community of Calvinist merchants. Be that as it may, it is his translation of Cartheny that contains more conclusive evidence about the matter.

The reliability of internal evidence is compromised, however, by the possibility of collective authorship. The respective roles of Goodyear and Robert Norman in giving the *Wandering Knight* its final shape, theologically as well as generally speaking, are not easily separated. Norman's statement in the preface contains no concrete indication as to the extent and nature of his revisions and alterations, but is presented in terms that are closely reminiscent of other contemporary 'revisions' of doctrinally dubious works:

> Having in my hands a notable work entitled *The Voyage of the Wandering Knight*, [I was inspired] to overrun the same according to my superficial skill and slender knowledge, to polish and burnish it, to restore and make it perfect in some such limbs whereon in seemed to halt, that it might with so much the more grace *Proripere in publicum, et in hominum manus involare*, for their larger delight. (*WK*, p. l)

The practice of 'rewriting' doctrinally unacceptable works by means of a theologically inflected translation was by no means an uncommon strategy in the period.[62] Two main types of works were targeted by such strategies of theological appropriation through translation by the English reformers: first, there were the spiritual and devotional classics from the age preceding the schism that were deemed to be timelessly valid, despite their associations with a decadent Roman Church from which they needed rescuing. In Thomas Rogers's translation of Thomas à Kempis's *Imitation of Christ*, for instance, the text is provided with a 'scholarly' apparatus of biblical and other references, and the whole is scrupulously aligned with the theology and doctrine of the Elizabethan Church.[63]

---

[60]  John E. Paul, 'Hampshire Recusants in the Reign of Elizabeth I with Special Reference to Winchester', *Proceedings of the Hampshire Field Club* 21:2 (1959), 61–81.

[61]  Andrew Spicer, *The French-Speaking Reformed Community and their Church in Southampton, 1567–c. 1620* (Stroud: Sutton, 1997), pp. 97–100.

[62]  See Alison Shell, *Catholicism, Controversy, and the English Literary Imagination, 1558–1660* (Cambridge: Cambridge University Press, 1999), pp. 16–17; and Bennett, *English Books 1558–1603*, pp. 132–8.

[63]  The first edition from 1579 or 1580 does not survive; see Bennett, *English Books 1558–1603*, p. 27. For a later reprint see Thomas à Kempis, *Of the Imitation of Christ*, trans. Thomas Rogers

The second category of works subjected to such theological sanitisation is that of the 'new' classics produced by the contemporary Catholic tradition. Some of these, despite their association with the Church of Rome, were nevertheless felt to contain essential Christian truths needing to be rescued from papist error, purified, polished and in fact thoroughly reconstructed within a new religious and political context. Even works by Spanish Jesuits were honoured in such fashion, and were quietly disrobed of any Catholic trappings and dressed up in Protestant garb.[64] This process could equally be applied to English works, and culminates with the rewriting of the Catholic Thomas Person's *First Booke of the Christian Exercise* as a 'purged' Protestant work by Edmund Bunny; here 'translation' no longer describes a linguistic, but a strictly confessional transformation.[65] Something similar may have happened to Cartheny's text, which passed through several hands and thus may have moved through multiple 'layers' of revision before ending up as the surviving English *Wandering Knight*. For the sake of simplicity, in the following discussion I will nevertheless refer to William Goodyear as the author of the translation.

Dorothy Atkinson Evans, in her introduction to the *Wandering Knight*, goes some way towards clarifying the work's confessional affiliation.[66] Her study of the wording of all biblical quotations in the text suggests that the author was not referring to any specific bible translation circulating in the period, but was rather translating Cartheny's French independently. Goodyear occasionally incorporated passages from different biblical translations he was familiar with, but often translates the passages using a hybrid or idiosyncratic wording. On the other hand, the final chapter, which contains a miniature catechism, clearly follows the wording of the *Book of Common Prayer*. Evidence arising from these observations is rather inconclusive and needs to be supplemented by a detailed comparative reading of the translation and its immediate source. The translator must have used a copy of the 1572 edition of the *Voyage*, as is suggested by the inclusion of the final chapter containing a daily set of prayers and devotions, absent from the first edition from 1557. The translation is mostly accurate and precise, often word for word. Entire passages, however, are omitted or reduced, mostly for doctrinal but occasionally for stylistic reasons. On the whole, Goodyear's version is more stringently didactic, and therefore tends to condense descriptive passages originally rich in alluring sensual detail and ornate language, which results in the temptations being less suggestively rendered than in the source (e.g. *Voyage*, pp. 30v, 33r, 34r, 36r, 41r–43r, 46r; cf. WK, pp. 28–31, 32, 37, 39).

---

(1592 – STC 23979) and numerous other reprints; Rogers also translated a number of works by Augustine, subjecting them to the same process of 'purification', e.g. *A Right Christian Treatise, Entituled S. Augustines Praiers: … Purged from Diuers Superstitious Points* (1581 – STC 950) and reprints; or *S. Augustines Manuel … Corrected, Translated, and Adorned, by Thomas Rogers* (1581– STC 938) and reprints. See also Bennett, *English Books 1558–1603*, pp. 132.

[64] See Bennett, *English Books 1558–1603*, pp. 132–8; Mullet, *The Catholic Reformation*, pp. 176–7.

[65] Edmund Bunny, *A Booke of Christian Exercise, Appertaining to Resolution* (1584 – STC 19355).

[66] Evans, *The Wandering Knight*, pp. xxix–xxxiv.

Most noticeably, the structural units of the text itself are not identical with Cartheny's. The tripartition survives unaltered, but the translator omits Cartheny's Chapter II.3, dealing with the nature of justification and the necessity of Penance and Confession, and Chapters II.7, 8 and 9, respectively containing a discussion of Absolution by a Priest, the metrical paraphrase of the seven Penitential Psalms, and a description the knight's preparations to attend Mass after seven days of penance. In the third part a chapter containing a detailed allegorical interpretation of the New Jerusalem (III.9) is equally dropped. All these omissions, except maybe for the Psalms, can be explained with reference to the relatively general, broad theological divergences that distinguish the Protestant from the Catholic Faith. Goodyear however finds himself forced to deal with a number of smaller isolated Catholic elements that are either excised or scrupulously aligned with the views of the Elizabethan Church. So the reference to Luther and Zwingli as disciples of Folly is dropped (*Voyage*, p. 28r), as are several references to the Mass (e.g. pp. 33v, 126v) and Priests (p. 89r) as well as a reference to the practice of wearing a crucifix around one's neck (p. 152r). Among more elaborate passages, Goodyear understandably omits Cartheny's oblique condemnation of the Protestant heresy (p. 59r) and his implicit deconstruction of Protestant martyrdom (p. 154r).

Goodyear's reconfiguration of the text runs still deeper and touches on more subtle doctrinal issues. So Cartheny's apology for Christian representational art, included to qualify the first commandment (p. 54r), is dropped, out of sympathy for the iconoclastic tendencies of Protestantism. All references to 'Penance' are either dropped, or systematically altered to 'Repentance', thus emphasising inward contrition over actual acts of Penance, a much more acceptable notion in Protestant circles (e.g. pp. 10v, 70r, 72r, 89v; cf. *WK*, omissions pp. 10, 56, alterations to 'Repentance' pp. 56, 68).[67] Similarly, the issue of 'Confession' is not eliminated altogether but aligned with a Protestant position that envisages Confession rather as an inward admission of one's sins directly to God, or as a public Confession to the congregation rather than a private Confession to a Priest (*Voyage* 95v; cf. *WK*, p. 73).[68] Also, with the loss of two entire chapters dealing specifically with Confession (II.3 and II.7), the importance of the whole issue is drastically reduced in accordance with the Protestant position.

---

[67] On the irreconcilable differences regarding Penance, particularly after the Council of Trent, see for instance Mullet, *The Catholic Reformation*, pp. 50–1.

[68] On public Penance and Confession in the Elizabethan Church, see for instance Patrick Collinson, *Archbishop Grindal, 1519–1583: The Struggle for a Reformed Church* (London: Jonathan Cape, 1979), p. 197. For the reduced importance of individual Confession in English Protestantism, see Susan Doran and Christopher Durston, *Princes, Pastors and People: The Church and Religion in England, 1500–1700*, 2nd edn (London: Routledge, 2003), pp. 185–6; and MacCulloch, *The Later Reformation in England*, pp. 11–12; see also MacCulloch, *Reformation*, p. 230 and *passim*.

Issues of Grace and Free Will are crucial preoccupations for both authors, and reflect the contemporary debate that was so crucial in confirming the irreconcilability of the Catholic and Protestant positions after the Council of Trent.[69] Both works share an emphasis on Grace rather than Free Will, but the *Wandering Knight* is more radical and blunt in attributing spiritual guidance to divine rather than human agency. There are fewer, milder references to 'Works' than in the *Voyage* (pp. 32v, 136r; cf. *WK*, pp. 30, 88), and when references to Works do occur, they are often qualified by the insistence on 'Faith unfeigned' as a necessary precondition (*Voyage*, p. 143; cf. *WK*, p. 94). Also significant is Goodyear's insistence on the certainty of election as a source of consolation, which replaces the trust in good works and righteous living exhibited by Cartheny (p. 69v; *WK*, p. 56). Goodyear, of a different cast of mind from the Carmelite Cartheny, is obviously out of his depth in the more strictly theological passages of the text, as when he contradicts himself on another contentious point that marks the break between Reformed and Catholic doctrine, concerning the certainty of election:[70] 'And therefore it is requisite for assured salvation that thou believe thou shalt be saved', yet inexplicably 'but to hope so is sufficient' (*WK*, p. 93); where Cartheny has subtle theological argument, integrating and balancing seemingly contradictory arguments (*Voyage*, pp. 142r, 131r, 163r), Goodyear has mere contradiction. As suggested by his mercantile background, Goodyear has little interest in theological subtleties and technicalities that abound in Cartheny, and seems often reluctant to engage with this aspect of Cartheny's text. This preference for simple, practical morality also emerges in Goodyear's dislike of Cartheny's typically Catholic, punctilious and legalistic casuistry, prominent for instance in Cartheny's balancing of Grace and Free Will or his commentary on the Ten Commandments, including an arcane distinction between venial and mortal sin (*Voyage*, p. 58v). This attitude also entails an antipathy for Cartheny's medieval scholastic background and his continuous use of medieval *auctoritates*, reflected for instance in Goodyear's omission of the mention of the *Glossa Ordinaria* (*Voyage*, p. 64v) in a passage otherwise unaltered in its substance.

---

[69] For a detailed and revealing outline of English Calvinist predestinarianism, and its links with Protestant notions of Grace, soteriology, fideism and justification by faith, see Wallace, *Puritans and Predestination*, pp. 3–78 in particular. For the irreconcilability with Catholic doctrine on such matters, see the detailed analysis of the Tridentine position given by Mullet, *The Catholic Reformation*, pp. 42–69.

[70] The Catholic position, impeccably represented by Cartheny (*Voyage*, pp. 131r, 142v, 163r), held that certainty of election was in fact *not* possible and therefore *not* a requirement for salvation, see Council of Trent, (Sess. VI, can. xv): 'S. q. d., hominem renatum et justificatum teneri ex fide ad credendum, se certo esse in numero prædestinatorum, anathema sit' ('if any one shall say that the regenerated and justified man is bound as a matter of faith to believe that he is surely of the number of the predestined, let him be anathema'), J. Pohle, 'Predestination', in *The Catholic Encyclopedia*. For the impact of the Calvinist insistence on the necessity of the justified man's certainty of election in England, see for instance MacCulloch, *The Later Reformation in England*, pp. 62–3, 74–8.

Goodyear, then, while he aligns his text with broadly Protestant doctrine, visibly has little interest in the intricacies of theology, and writes out of a concern with popular, practical-minded moral didacticism. He condenses or excises many specifically theological passages, and instead enhances the pragmatic moral dimension of the work. Yet Goodyear's 'translation' of the fundamental message of the *Voyage* into foreign theological soil ultimately raises as many questions through its similarities as through its differences. These questions of course concern the religious sensibility of William Goodyear – and/or Robert Norman – but touch on deeper, more widely significant issues relating to the relationship between different confessional groups and their ideas in Elizabethan England. What is most striking about the *Wandering Knight*, is that it does not supplement the 'translation' of a Catholic text to foreign theological soil with any sort of polemical gloss. Particularly in the immediate context of this study, emerging from the highly charged climate of the 1560s that shaped Stephen Bateman's work, the comparatively almost 'ecumenical' neutrality of the *Wandering Knight* appears as striking. The *Wandering Knight* of course inherits this from its source, but also reflects the sensibilities of a new generation that had had no direct experience of severe religious clashes, turmoil or persecutions such as those occurring during Edward's and Mary's reigns, and had instead grown up in the comparatively stable and safe religious environment of the Elizabethan Settlement.[71] This relative political stability was reflected in a shift of much of the religious literature away from older controversial and apologetic works towards more strictly devotional or edifying works that focused on consolidating the faith of the simple people.[72] So whereas in established, official circles the anti-Catholic rhetoric persisted, popular religious literature often moved away from such a confrontational mode to embrace issues of individual morality.[73] This reorientation suggests the emergence of a relative degree of mutual solidarity and tolerance at the level of popular religion, making it possible to adapt and translate Catholic devotional works without necessarily striking either a heretical or a polemical note.[74]

---

[71] For this stability, coupled with a growing permissiveness in matters of religious diversity, see Patrick Collinson, 'The Elizabethan Church and the New Religion', in Haigh, ed., *The Reign of Elizabeth I*, p. 175 in particular.

[72] Bennett, *English Books 1558–1603*, pp. 129–30; Watt, *Cheap Print and Popular Piety*, p. 8.

[73] For the persistence of officially endorsed anti-Catholic propaganda and the hope of healing the internal divisions of the Elizabethan Church, see MacCulloch, *The Later Reformation in England*, pp. 38–41, 66–8, 120–6; more generally, see Jesse M. Lander, *Inventing Polemic: Religion, Print, and Literary Culture in Early Modern England* (Cambridge: Cambridge University Press, 2006), pp. 1–109; and Peter White, *Predestination, Policy and Polemic: Conflict and Consensus in the English Church from the Reformation to the Civil War* (Cambridge: Cambridge University Press, 1992), pp. 60–123.

[74] Mullet, *The Catholic Reformation*, pp. 176–7. On the persistence of Catholic sensibility within the mixed heritage of the Elizabethan settlement itself, see MacCulloch, *The Later Reformation in England*, pp. 78ff.

Goodyear avoids the controversial tone altogether. Instead, in a newly added original passage, he voices an appeal to resist and overcome sectarian polemics:

> And though we live in the latter times when many sects and errors do abound, and virtue and truth in many places doth fail, yet let us listen what our Lord and saviour saith: 'Whosoever believeth to the end shall be saved'. (*WK*, p. 92)

The passage denounces the general religious climate that is felt to be divisive as a consequence of the excessive insistence on doctrinal technicalities and matters of ecclesiastical polity – the 'errors and sects' ultimately distracting from the central focus of the word of God on 'virtue and truth'.[75] The *Wandering Knight* thus expresses a desire for a return to a simpler, purer form of religion that is not plagued by ultimately sterile sectarian or confessional divisions threatening to dissolve the fabric of Christian Society. This points to a more widespread longing for an inclusive, unified and 'catholic' form of Christian faith, and the *Wandering Knight* attempts to restore such unity by returning to the most basic, universal Christian allegories of the *miles christianus* and *homo viator*. Without going as far as postulating the emergence of the kind of post-Reformation anticlericalism suggested by Christopher Haigh, it may be said that such a reorientation is symptomatic of popular weariness of the arcane polemical and doctrinal intricacies of the official ecclesiastical discourse.[76]

The previous considerations raise more widely meaningful questions for the study of contemporary religious situation in England. Whilst the Protestant affiliation of the *Wandering Knight* may not be denied, the exact manner in which the text does relate to its environment is more complex and rich in meaning. Like many other manifestations of popular religious thought in England in the period, the *Wandering Knight* calls for a reconsideration of terms such as Puritan, Protestant, Calvinist, Anglican, Catholic and so on, in the light of the reality they aim to describe.[77] The fluidity of theological and doctrinal discourses, particularly as reflected in their popular developments, sits oddly with the rigid terms used to describe them, terms that often presuppose a clear discontinuity between

---

[75] For the endless string of controversies that were endemically threatening the unity and stability of the Elizabethan Church, see White, *Predestination, Policy and Polemic*, pp. 60–123; Alexandra Walsham, *Church Papists: Catholicism, Conformity and Confessional Polemic in Early Modern England* (London: The Royal Historical Society, 1993); Lander, *Inventing Polemic*.

[76] See Christopher Haigh, 'Anticlericalism and the English Reformation', in his *The English Reformation Revised* (Cambridge: Cambridge University Press, 1987), pp. 56–74. For a reassessment, see MacCulloch, *The Later Reformation in England*, pp. 117–18.

[77] The unstable, hybrid nature of popular belief and practice is best captured by Walsham in her *Providence in Early Modern England* and *Church Papists*; see also Judith Maltby, *Prayer Book and People in Elizabethan and Early Stuart England* (Cambridge: Cambridge University Press, 1998), pp. 1–19; and Watt, *Cheap Print and Popular Piety*, pp. 1–8. See also Collinson, 'The Elizabethan Church and the New Religion'; Haigh, ed., *The English Reformation Revised*; Peter Lake and Michael Questier, eds, *Conformity and Orthodoxy in the English Church, c. 1560–1660* (Woodbridge: Boydell, 2000).

different theological positions – a discontinuity that simply did not exist.[78] This hybridity is clearly visible in the *Wandering Knight*, awkwardly suspended between its simplified Calvinist soteriology and its exhortatory mode imposed by the frame of the quest-allegory. And despite Goodyear's conscientious efforts, the doctrinal flavour of the final product cannot be said to be entirely free from a Catholic aftertaste. Goodyear is certainly concerned to align himself with the doctrine of the national Church, but there often emerges a certain sense of puzzlement and uncertainty as to what this doctrine actually *is*, reflected in Goodyear's own theological untidiness. As Alexandra Walsham has poignantly expressed it, 'conformists shade obscurely into a body of "mere conformists", whose disinterest in Reformation logomachy . . . challenges us to reassess our lingering presupposition that early modern society was fractured by the confessional dichotomies implied by contemporary polemic'.[79] The *Wandering Knight* itself, with its interesting negotiations between a Catholic original and its Protestant *translatio*, reveals the presence of a rich intermediate hybrid religious world of popular belief and practice beneath the surface of 'mere conformity'. It is in this intermediate world that the negotiations between different doctrines and ideologies are played out, often resulting in unpredictable, theologically eclectic productions such as the *Wandering Knight* itself.[80]

It is not surprising, then, to find that Goodyear's translation, after having undergone such a careful process of confessional reconfiguration, was in turn subjected to the reverse process. With the appearance of a Welsh translation dated to 1585, clearly based on Goodyear's translation rather than Cartheny's original, the work is again reclaimed by the Catholic faith. Surviving in manuscript alone, the circulation of the Welsh translation clearly points towards a limited circulation among Welsh recusant families. Most strikingly, the new Catholic readership must have thought that Goodyear's text itself contained sufficiently clear Catholic echoes to serve their ends without substantial modification.[81] Cartheny has come full circle, as the *Voyage*'s repeated transformations tell the story of ever more fluid and uncertain confessional barriers.

---

[78] Watt characterises popular piety in the period simply as 'post-Reformation' as opposed to strictly 'Protestant', see *Cheap Print and Popular Piety*, 'Preface'; MacCulloch speaks of 'the spectrum of Tudor religion which makes it so difficult to draw exact confessional boundaries', *The Later Reformation in England*, p. 127. Shell equally refers to the unreliability and fluidity of confessional and denominational labels, *Catholicism, Controversy, and the English Literary Imagination*, p. 15. See also Lake and Questier, *Conformity and Orthodoxy*, pp. ix–xx especially.

[79] Walsham, *Church Papists*, p. 99 and *passim*.

[80] Again according to Walsham, the broad base of contemporary religious belief was largely made up of a blend of half-digested predestinarian doctrine and half-remembered Romanist teaching, see Walsham, *Providence in Early Modern England*, p. 331 and *passim*. For the numerous affinities and interactions between Protestant and Catholic devotional writing, ultimately exposing the triviality of the actual doctrinal divergences, see Shell, *Catholicism, Controversy, and the English Literary Imagination*, pp. 16–17.

[81] On the Welsh translation of the *Wandering Knight*, see above, p. 117, n.5.

## From Pilgrim-Knight to Merchant-Adventurer[82]

Goodyear's reworking effectively transplants Cartheny's *Voyage* to a foreign theological soil, but the process of *translatio* is more than merely doctrinal. Goodyear's translation, with its attention to practical divinity rather than theological speculation, reflects a pragmatic mindset that may be seen as characteristically 'mercantile', albeit not strictly 'middle-class'.[83] Goodyear's style too, less ornate and almost matter-of-fact, points in the same direction. The newly added dedicatory epistle helps to put the mercantile overtones of the text into much sharper perspective. Particularly because of Goodyear's surprising fidelity to his source, the preface is invaluable in providing information as to how the text was actually received and understood.

With his dedication to Sir Francis Drake, 'most venturous and no less worshipful Knight' (*WK*, p. xlix), Robert Norman displaces the text to an entirely different imaginative context that suggests a significant amplification of the work's range of meaning. The dedication may be variously interpreted, and sheds light on both the translation and the contemporary Drake-craze. Given his involvement in acts of piracy against Spanish vessels, Drake's achievements were far from uncontroversial, but his reputation on return from his circumnavigation quickly reached epic proportions, and finds its official consecration in his knighting at the behest of Elizabeth on 4 April 1581, less than two months before the *Wandering Knight's* appearance in print.[84] Goodyear and Norman are clearly following in the wake of the generalised enthusiasm for the hero's return – and incidentally go as far as tacitly and tactfully removing a reference to the evils of piracy from Cartheny's text (cf. *Voyage*, p. 63r).

Yet the choice of the dedicatee is more specifically relevant in the present case, beyond Drake's mere prominence as a popular, national hero. The nature of the relationship binding Goodyear, Norman and Drake is unknown, but unmistakeably points to their shared interests in trade, navigation and exploration. Drake's activities preceding his departure for the circumnavigation in 1577 had centred largely on trade, in the attempt to accumulate sufficient wealth to attract the attention of the

---

[82]  A more exhaustive discussion of the ideas presented in the following section can be found in Marco Nievergelt, 'Francis Drake: Merchant, Knight and Pilgrim', *Renaissance Studies* 23:1 (2009), 53–70.

[83]  On the debate about the terminology, sparked by Wright's *Middle Class Culture in Elizabethan England*, see J. H. Hexter, 'The Myth of the Middle Class in Tudor England', in his *Reappraisals in History* (London: Longmans, 1961), pp. 71–116, and Stevenson, *Praise and Paradox*.

[84]  On Drake's reputation on his return, see for instance David B. Quinn, *Drake's Circumnavigation of the Globe: A Review* (Exeter: University of Exeter Press, 1981); David B. Quinn, *Sir Francis Drake as Seen by his Contemporaries* (Providence, RI: John Carter Brown Library, 1996); Harry Kelsey, *Sir Francis Drake: The Queen's Pirate* (New Haven, CT: Yale University Press, 1998), pp. 207–39; John Hampden, ed., *Francis Drake Privateer: Contemporary Narratives and Documents* (London: Eyre Methuen, 1972), pp. 244–6.

rich and powerful,[85] and the contacts with Goodyear the merchant and Norman the mathematician, hydrographer and instrument-maker point to such a common background. Commercial interests also rank high among the motives generally invoked in connection with his circumnavigation.[86] The emergence of something like class-consciousness within this mercantile milieu also helps to explain much of the gist of the actual dedication. Norman's praise, in fact, rather than concentrating exclusively on Drake's naval prowess as would be obvious for a fellow seaman, sees his dedicatee's achievement as heralding a deeper, more inclusive transformation of an entire section of society to which Norman himself also belongs. His praise of Drake is mixed with a more general castigation of the English nation's self-complacency, undoubtedly alluding to England's reticence in emulating Spain's expansionist efforts, an all too common contemporary complaint that is later echoed by Hakluyt:[87]

> This fault being general, and as general so hateful, in the judgment specially of the wise, might seem so much the more tolerable, if that men placed in preëminence and sitting like hills overlooking the valleys below, with their high calling and stately authority, had agreeable hearts. But some, notwithstanding their state be singular, and indeed such as that they may sit down, take their ease, and say 'Hic terminus esto', do carry so base a mind as that if I should compare them to Aesop's cock preferring a barley corn before a precious pearl, I should not do amiss. (*WK*, p. xlix)

Praising Drake's individual initiative and adventurous undertaking, Norman sees his dedicatee as embodying the virtues of a New Age, no longer relying on the 'given' authority and power determined by right of birth and social rank, but striving instead to acquire such recognition through merit and ability. Drake's voyage, itself shaping our reception of the ensuing allegory of the Knight's quest, becomes a complex symbol for spiritual progress doubled by social climb and self-advancement:

> For what is he, unless he be mortified, that is not naturally of an aspiring mind, imitating herein the ivy, which never ceaseth climbing by degrees, *donec ipsam summitatem attigerit*, till it be come to the very top. (*WK*, p. xlix)

The ascent envisaged by Norman is clearly multivalent, reverberating with echoes of social and economic aspirations, encapsulated in the 'pearl' pursued by Drake

---

[85] Kelsey, *Sir Francis Drake: The Queen's Pirate*, pp. 68–89.

[86] Quinn, *Drake's Circumnavigation of the Globe*, pp. 2–3. For the wider debate, see K. R. Andrews, 'The Aims of Drake's Expedition of 1577–80', *The American Historical Review* 73:3 (February 1968), 724–41.

[87] For such exhortations to reach beyond the 'sluggish security' afforded by the neglect of overseas enterprise, see *Sir Francis Drake: An Exhibition to Commemorate Francis Drake's Voyage around the World, 1577–1580* (London: British Museum Publications, 1977), p. 15. See also Helgerson, 'The Voyages of a Nation', in his *Forms of Nationhood: The Elizabethan Writing of England* (Chicago, IL: University of Chicago Press, 1992), pp. 163ff. For the impact on literary production, in particular translations from other European vernaculars, see Sherman, 'Bringing the World to England'.

himself, both symbol of spiritual reward and metonymy for the rich spoils and treasures accumulated on his travels. Drake becomes for Norman a model of social mobility, embodying the ideals of a merchant class that is constantly aspiring to emulate and appropriate the values of the gentry and nobility in their turn. Symptomatically, the image chosen by Norman is that of the ivy, parasitically climbing along the trunks of larger trees, as if to signify Drake's bold impingement and usurpation of the privileges of the ruling classes.[88]

In this light, the knighthood conferred on Drake by the queen acquires an even deeper relevance. To Norman, the knighting acts as a sort of consecration of his own aspirations, shared among what will constitute the emerging 'middling sort'.[89] The appropriation of chivalric ethos and terminology has long been recognised as part of the strategy of self-definition by this emergent social 'class', as yet lacking its own ideological and conceptual baggage. Drake's knighting, prominently flagged up on the title page of the volume, is the most fitting sign for the future success and recognition of such aspirations, leading to the emergence of the hybrid figures of the 'corteous merchant' and 'gentle craftsman' in late Elizabethan literature, so perceptively described by Laura C. Stevenson.[90] Despite the adoption of chivalric and courtly values, these new Elizabethan heroes remain true to their origins, maintaining an element of humbleness alongside their newly emerging self-confidence, as in Deloney's portrait of Jack of Newbury who tellingly declines the offer of knighthood.[91] Similarly, Norman turns Drake into a sort of 'working-class hero' who remains true to his roots despite his advancement:

> For, although you have had Fortune holding the basin while you washed your hands and cast the best chance of the dice, yet for all that, such is your contentment, you hoist not up the lofty sail of self-love, to swell with the wind of vainglory, as vaunting of any exploit which you have achieved, *Per tot Cyclopea saxa, per mundi scopulos, Scyllam, vastamque Charybdim.* But as you went out, so you are come home: familiar to your friend, courteous with your acquaintance, remembering all, forgetting none, still of one mind, will, and affection, the prosperous event of your dangerous voyage notwithstanding. (*WK*, pp. xlix–l)

Drake's achievement is commended not only as such, but becomes an inspirational model to be imitated, generating something like an emerging 'class-consciousness'.

---

[88] Drake's whole life was in fact substantially shaped by his conscious attempt to emulate and attract the attention of the influential nobles of his times, and his ambitious and reckless behaviour often resulted in attracting their hostility and scorn; see Quinn, *Sir Francis Drake as Seen by his Contemporaries*, pp. 1–5 and *passim*; Kelsey, *Sir Francis Drake: The Queen's Pirate*, pp. 68–89, 217 and *passim*.

[89] In describing such social dynamics, terminology remains ultimately inappropriate and unsatisfactory; I use 'middling sort' in order to avoid anachronistic notions of 'social class', following H. R. French, 'The Search for the "Middle Sort of People" in England, 1600–1800', *The Historical Journal* 43:1 (2000), 277–93.

[90] Stevenson, *Praise and Paradox*.

[91] Ibid., p. 122.

For Norman, Drake provides an inspirational example that becomes 'like a right lodestone [that] drew me, an iron lump', in a striking allegorisation of the mechanics of magnetism, incidentally the subject of one of Norman's own scientific works printed in the same year as the *Wandering Knight*.[92]

The additional implications of a social, even economic nature extracted from the analysis of the preface should not be seen as weakening or even undercutting the spiritual impetus of the central allegory of the Christian pilgrimage, but rather as supplementing it. The 'middling sort' represented by Drake and Norman may not be represented as a merely 'mercantile class', concerned with the exclusive accumulation of wealth;[93] their activity and new social consciousness need to be placed within the framework of a society whose sense of values is still inherently and unavoidably religious, and where something like a modern, agnostic utilitarianism is a complete impossibility. As Norman reiterates at the end of his dedication, the ultimate destination of Drake's journey is beyond 'the straits of death ... the port of peace ... the appointed haven for all Christian navigators' (*WK*, p. li), and is still directly descended from Deguileville's Heavenly City. As Richard Helgerson has pointed out, the rhetoric used to express the contemporary English drive towards exploration suggests a convergence of economic, social, nationalistic, ideological and religious motives, and Helgerson warns about the dangers of reducing the religious dimension to a merely rhetorical strategy glossing over the supposedly more 'real', pragmatic motives for such undertakings.[94]

Such simplifications appear reductive if one turns to such a deceptively simple work as the *Wandering Knight*, which reveals the full complexity of the aspirations of the emergent 'middling sort'. To return to Norman's preface, it exemplifies how the traditional pattern of the medieval knightly quest is here charged with a complex and multivalent significance.[95] The *Voyage of the Wandering Knight* acts at once as an allegory of an individual spiritual pilgrimage, a celebration of Drake's own personal voyage, an image of a collective quest for national identity and a vehicle for the social aspirations of a new social 'class'.[96] Drake's circumnavigation becomes the metaphorical expression of a desire for global conquest and incorporation that participates in equal measure of an older, crusading rhetoric and a newer sense of

---

[92] *The Newe Attractiue: Containyng a Short Discourse of the Magnes or Lodestone* (1581 – STC 18647). For an image of a lodestone and a basic description of its use, see *Sir Francis Drake: An Exhibition*, pp. 43–4.

[93] This conception nevertheless existed in the literature of the period, but was largely associated with a stereotypical stock-character, inherited from the tradition of the medieval moralities. Stevenson, *Praise and Paradox*, pp. 92–106, describes it as the figure of the 'merchant-usurer', and stresses its obsolescence and inappropriateness in describing actual contemporary realities.

[94] Helgerson, *Forms of Nationhood*, p. 167.

[95] For such re-interpretations of medieval knightly quests and journeys, see also Goodman, *Chivalry and Exploration*.

[96] The emerging national consciousness in particular is the central concern of Helgerson's discussion of the contemporary literature of travel and exploration in 'The Voyages of a Nation', in his *Forms of Nationhood*, pp. 149–91.

economic expansion and national identity, while maintaining a keen interest in individual soteriology. The impact of the spiritual dimension on the early modern understanding of travel and expansion is also reflected in the frequent prophetic overtones emerging from contemporary literature of exploration.[97] Such prophetic, even eschatological, overtones suggest a richly significant continuity, pointing backwards to the apocalypticism of the generation of Bale and Foxe, while anticipating notions of a Promised Land of the Elect, so prominent in shaping the ideals of the first Puritan settlers in America.[98]

One of the problems created by the dedication is, however, that by as it were casting Drake in the role of its heroic questing knight, it also puts him in the unlikely shoes of a Prodigal Son. The pattern of the Prodigal Son's return, ingrained in the structure of the quest of the *Wandering Knight*, is not so much reproduced but broken by Drake, who appears as a highly unlikely dedicatee for a narrative of repentance, return and submission. Such a complex, twofold dynamic – ostensibly endorsing the patterns of obedience and submission promoted the Prodigal Son parable, while effectively breaking and exploding them – is seen by Helgerson as a dominant theme running through the literature of an entire generation: 'They were thus forced to argue that their work, rightly understood, warns against the very wantonness it portrays, but such arguments only involved them in a maze of self-contradiction, revealing their dilemma – the dilemma of their generation – without resolving it.'[99]

The case of the *Wandering Knight* may be even more complex than that. In fact, the actual narrative of the work, particularly when it is compared with its source, cannot be said to conform entirely and wholeheartedly to a pattern of return, repentance and submission. Goodyear's lack of interest for the sort of institutional ecclesiastical and doctrinal discourse characteristic of official religion goes some way towards rejecting such established authority along the lines of Drake's heroic individualism. Goodyear in fact moves the path of the wandering knight away from a strictly political and ecclesiastical obedience and conformity in the search for new spaces to pursue a more 'catholic' and wholesome form of personal spirituality. Compared with Cartheny's knight, Goodyear's is remarkably independent and individualistic, avoiding any direct confrontation with any institutional force, even if he moves within the area of a loosely defined conformity. Ultimately, both Drake and Goodyear, albeit with very different degrees of radicalism and in different domains,

---

[97] Helgerson, *Forms of Nationhood*, p. 173. The figure of John Dee equally springs to mind, see Frances A. Yates, *Astraea: The Imperial Theme in the Sixteenth Century* (London: Routledge & Kegan Paul, 1975), pp. 48–50; and Glyn Parry, 'John Dee and the Elizabethan British Empire in its European Context', *Historical Journal* 49:3 (2006), 643–75.

[98] See for instance Szilvia Csabi, 'The Concept of America in the Puritan Mind', *Language and Literature* 10:3 (2001), 195–209; Ira V. Brown, 'Watchers for the Second Coming: The Millenarian Tradition in America', *The Mississippi Valley Historical Review* 39:3 (1952), 441–58.

[99] Richard Helgerson, *The Elizabethan Prodigals* (Berkeley, CA: University of California Press, 1976), p. 5.

direct their respective quests towards the exploration of new spaces and possibilities beyond the reach of established authority.

Conversely, just as Goodyear's Knight is not such an impeccable Prodigal, Drake is far from being an uncompromising individualist and revolutionary. Drake's reputation in the wake of his bold undertaking in fact hides unexpected allegiances to the power he is trying to subvert. So, whilst Drake defies and breaks the pattern of the Prodigal's obedience, he nevertheless ultimately submits to the 'powers that be' on his return from his voyage, just as the archetypal Christian Knight submits to the fatherly advice of God's Grace. By accepting the knighthood conferred by none other than the queen – head of state and Church and representative of an ideally immutable social hierarchy – Drake is reintegrated into the framework of the social fabric he is trying to explode. The knighthood, despite Norman's claims to the contrary, is ultimately a sign of Drake's incorporation into a pre-existent elite, a phenomenon entirely unlike that of Deloney's fictional character of Jack of Newbury, boldly declining the honour of knighthood in his attempt to bolster the pride in the intrinsic values of the 'middling sort'. Drake thus assumes an ambiguous position between defiance and complicity, just as Goodyear's knight who sets out to seek a new, non-institutional form of religious belief that however remains within the broad perimeters of a vaguely defined 'orthodoxy'. In both cases it is the allegory of the knightly quest that becomes the vehicle for such novel, tentative attempts at self-definition. The fragile and often paradoxical nature of the ideological synthesis that underlies the multivalent allegorical quests imagined by Drake, Norman and Goodyear, reveals the tentativeness of this new urge to find appropriate conceptual forms to relate to an emerging modernity. And the *Wandering Knight*, beneath its deceptively simple, even seemingly restorative and antiquated narrative pattern of the knightly quest, constitutes a prime example of such negotiations and attempts to sketch a new, experimental and programmatic trajectory for Elizabethan self-fashioning.

# 6

## *Lewes Lewkenor: The Humanist Quest*[1]

Lewes Lewkenor's *Resolved Gentleman* (1594 – STC 15139) is, like Bateman's *Travayled Pylgrime*, a translation of Olivier de La Marche's *Chevalier délibéré*. Unlike Bateman, Lewkenor acknowledges his direct source, Hernando de Acuña's Spanish version, *El caballero determinado*. Spanish is also the source language of another translation of Lewkenor's, *The Spanish Mandevile of Miracles, or, The Garden of Curious Flowers*, a juvenile work only published at a later date by Ferdinando Walker (1600 – STC 24135). Lewkenor's ties to Spain are also of a different, more intimate nature: he had spent a number of years in the service of the Spanish Crown during the 1580s, and appears to have cultivated his Spanish sympathies thereafter, despite his return to England. In order to shed light on his translation, it is necessary to read Lewkenor's literary production in parallel with his often perplexing biography.[2] The son of the politician Thomas Lewknor (c. 1538–96), Lewes Lewknor (c. 1560–1627) entered the Middle Temple in 1579. The following year, however, he found himself forced to leave the country due to his Catholicism,[3] and sought refuge in the Netherlands. He then earned a captaincy in Spanish service, but his military career appears to have been cut short by a serious arm injury. Severe financial problems ensued, due to the loss of his pension and litigation over his wife's dowry. These difficulties eventually forced Lewkenor to return to England, seeking a safe conduct through his relative Sir Robert Sidney in 1590. On returning to England he reported to Burghley on the English in Spanish service, and is generally accepted as the author of *A Discourse of the Usage of the English Fugitives*,

---

[1]  The findings of the present chapter have been published independently in the form of an article, 'Catholic Loyalism, Service and Careerism: Lewes Lewkenor's Quest for Favour', *Renaissance Studies* 24:4 (2010), 536–58.

[2]  For which see Roderick Clayton, 'Lewknor, Sir Lewes (c.1560–1627)', *DNB*. Available at: http://www.oxforddnb.com/view/article/46411 [accessed 12 February 2012].

[3]  This decision may have been due to the tightening of the legislation against Catholic recusants in the late 1570s and early 1580s. See Wallace T. MacCaffrey, 'Catholic Dissent', in his *Queen Elizabeth and the Making of Policy, 1572–1588* (Princeton, NJ: Princeton University Press, 1982), pp. 119–53; and Arnold Pritchard, *Catholic Loyalism in Elizabethan England* (London: Scolar Press, 1979), pp. 3–10.

*by the Spaniard* (pr. 1595, repr. 1596 – STC 15562–3, reprinted and expanded as *The Estate of English Fugitiues vnder the King of Spaine and his Ministers*, 1595, 1596 – STC 15564–5).[4] Lewkenor's career seems to have finally taken off towards the end of the decade, as he was made a Gentleman pensioner in 1599, and became involved in supervising the reception of foreign diplomats and ambassadors. With the accession of James I in 1603 Lewkenor's efforts were finally rewarded. He was knighted in the same year and soon appointed Master of Ceremonies, thus continuing to supervise arrangements for the reception of foreign dignitaries until his death in 1627.

*The Estate of English Fugitiues* is a good place to begin exploring Lewkenor's early career: it may be seen as a piece of anti-Spanish propaganda, describing in great detail the miseries awaiting ambitious foreigners desiring to enter the service of the king of Spain. The work appears to subscribe to the wide anti-Spanish sentiment in the period,[5] but placed alongside Lewkenor's personal experience, his Catholicism and his political views expressed in his later work, the *Estate* appears in a much more complex light. Based on his own past experience, Lewkenor draws a picture of an expatriate community of English Catholics mixing condemnation with apologetic, insisting repeatedly on the naïvety of a community predominantly composed of young hothead adventurers or 'unexperienced gentlemen' (*Estate*, Av). Addressing both the expatriate community and 'credulous Catholickes at home' (ibid.), he attempts to dissuade them from embracing the perilous course of defection, all the while acknowledging the genuine religious reasons behind such a misguided attempt. Thus Lewkenor at once manages to express empathy for the plight of fellow Catholics, exhorting the queen's leniency towards them, but firmly distances himself from any overtly political act such as defection, treason or seditious plotting. The *Estate* also becomes a manifesto of Catholic loyalism, attempting to disentangle Catholicism from the seditious resistance theory advocated by such works as Robert Parsons's *Conference about the Succession of the Crowne of Ingland* (1594 – STC 19398).[6]

Yet the 'public' nature of Lewkenor's report conceals, among other things, a more intensely personal agenda. The *Estate* is both an urgent personal apology and confession of youthful folly, leading in turn to a declaration of renewed allegiance,

---

[4]   There is one surviving copy of the *Discourse* annotated by Burghley himself, see Albert J. Loomie, *The Spanish Elizabethans: The English Exiles at the Court of Philip II* (London: Burns and Oates, 1963), p. 11.

[5]   See William S. Maltby, *The Black Legend in England: The Development of Anti-Spanish Sentiment, 1558–1660* (Durham, NC: Duke University Press, 1972).

[6]   For Catholic loyalist claims in the period, see Pritchard, *Catholic Loyalism in Elizabethan England*, pp. 37–72 in particular, and Michael C. Questier, 'Elizabeth and the Catholics', in Ethan H. Shagan, ed., *Catholics and the 'Protestant Nation': Religious Politics and Identity in Early Modern England* (Manchester: Manchester University Press, 2005), pp. 69–94. See also Alexandra Gajda, *The Earl of Essex and Late Elizabethan Political Culture* (Oxford: Oxford University Press, 2012), pp. 108–40.

and an expression of his desire to serve Queen Elizabeth (*Estate*, Siiv–Siiir). Such a confession, clearly designed to exonerate Lewkenor himself from accusations of treason,[7] incidentally reveals an interesting affinity with the pattern of the Elizabethan Prodigal Son narratives, clearly echoed also in Lewkenor's description of knightly errance and return in the *Resolved Gentleman*.[8] However, given its status as a public, semi-official declaration, the *Estate* must be seen as a diplomatic piece of political apology rather than a strictly autobiographical confession, and its triumphalist enthusiasm over the providential rise of England, set against the background of the decline of Habsburg Spain (*Estate*, e.g. ¶¶Lr), must be treated with care.

In the *Estate* Lewkenor clearly attempts to dispel rumours and accusations constructed around his earlier exile, and thus writes a largely conformist work. Yet in his other, not overtly political works, Lewkenor exhibits a particular sensitivity and subtlety in matters of both policy and rhetoric, and displays an impressive ability to inscribe a seemingly apolitical discourse with an unsuspected dimension of criticism and dissent. This is the case of his translation of Gaspare Contarini's *De magistratibus et republica venetorum* as *The Commonwealth and Gouernment of Venice* (1599 – STC 5642), as well as the *Resolved Gentleman* itself.[9] Lewkenor's association with the Sidney-Dudley circle is highly significant in this respect. The dedication of both the *Resolved Gentleman* and the *Commonwealth* to Anne, Countess of Warwick, as well as Lewkenor's mention of the many past favours granted by 'your noble deceased Husbande, and his most worthy and euer memorable Brother' in his dedicatory epistle for the *Resolved Gentleman* (A3v), point to a close and lasting relationship. This indeed suggests a political affinity that stretches beyond the merely occasional associations imposed by the vicissitudes of patronage and clientage in the context of the factionalism in the 1590s, and places Lewkenor firmly in the political tradition running through the Dudley, Sidney and Essex circles.[10] The tradition may broadly be characterised as inter-

---

[7]   See Questier, 'Elizabeth and the Catholics', pp. 71–2. For the currency of the stock figure of the 'Spaniolised' Catholic exile as traitor, a figure that to some extent Lewkenor himself helps to popularise through his writing of the *Estate*, see Loomie, *The Spanish Elizabethans*, p. 7 and *passim*.

[8]   See Helgerson, *Elizabethan Prodigals*.

[9]   For an analysis of the political dimension of the Contarini translation see Andrew Hadfield, *Literature, Travel, and Colonial Writing in the English Renaissance, 1545–1625* (Oxford: Clarendon Press, 1998), pp. 47–58.

[10]   While the classic notion of the 'factionalist' Elizabethan court has been recently re-examined and qualified, the 1590s remain a particularly tense period that justifies the use of the term. For details, see the work by Simon Adams, collected and reprinted in his *Leicester and the Court*, particularly 'Faction, Clientage and Party: English Politics, 1550–1603', pp. 13–23; 'Eliza Enthroned? The Court and its Politics', pp. 24–45; 'Favourites and Factions at the Elizabethan Court', pp. 46–67. On the 1590s more generally, see John Guy, ed., *The Reign of Elizabeth I: Court and Culture in the Last Decade* (Cambridge: Cambridge University Press, 1995); and Paul E. J. Hammer, 'The Last Decade: An Ageing Regime', *History Today* 53:5 (May 2003), 53–9.

ventionist and militarist in matters of foreign policy, but also advocated the claims of the aristocracy for a more markedly pluralistic political culture at court that may be seen as foreshadowing Republicanism.[11] These demands for a more markedly humanist culture of political advice and debate are already latent in the *Resolved Gentleman*, and culminate in the Republicanism advocated – still only implicitly and tentatively – in *The Commonwealthe*.[12] Also, the dedicatory sonnets supplied by Spenser, John Harington and Robert Dallington for Lewkenor's works, point to an association with the ever more radical and 'republican' political claims of the Essex circle in the 1590s.[13] Lewkenor's Catholicism, while seemingly at odds with Essex's public role as the military champion of the Protestant cause inherited from Philip Sidney, need not have constituted an obstacle in the light of Essex's political secularism and toleration of Catholics.[14] Rather, Republicanism seems to have been a political ideal that often reached across confessional barriers and thus helped to overcome such divisions.[15]

[11] For the Sidney-Dudley circle as an oppositionist group, harbouring ideals of a mixed government and 'monarchical republic' throughout the late sixteenth and early seventeenth centuries, see Blair Worden, 'Classical Republicanism and the Puritan Revolution', in Hugh Lloyd-Jones, Valerie Pearl and Blair Worden, eds, *History and Imagination: Essays in Honour of H. R. Trevor-Roper* (London: Duckworth, 1981), pp. 182–200, here 185–90; and Blair Worden, *The Sound of Virtue: Philip Sidney's* Arcadia *and Elizabethan Politics* (New Haven, CT: Yale University Press, 1996), pp. 209–52. On the ties between Dudleys and Sidneys more generally, see ibid. pp. 41–57.

[12] On the humanist culture of *vita activa* through virtuous advice, and its links with classical Republicanism in the period, see Markku Peltonen, *Classical Humanism and Republicanism in English Political Thought, 1570–1640* (Cambridge: Cambridge University Press, 1995), pp. 1–53.

[13] On the Republicanism implicit in Essex's pressures for mixed government, deriving from an aristocratic honour tradition expressed through chivalric forms ultimately at odds with Tudor theories of monarchy by divine right, see for instance Paul E. J. Hammer, *The Polarisation of Elizabethan Politics: The Political Career of Robert Devereux, 2nd Earl of Essex, 1585–1597* (Cambridge: Cambridge University Press, 1999), pp. 331–40. On Spenser's links with Lewkenor, see Andrew Hadfield, 'Was Spenser a Republican?', *English* 47 (1998), 169–82, esp. 171–2; on Republicanism and literature in the period more generally, see Andrew Hadfield, *Shakespeare and Republicanism* (Cambridge: Cambridge University Press, 2005), pp. 17–95, and for references to Essex *passim*, e.g. pp. 80, 101, 130–1. Hadfield furthermore identifies the Lewkenor family as clients of Essex, p. 92.

[14] For a reconsideration of Essex's ties to Catholics, see especially the work of Gajda, *The Earl of Essex and Late Elizabethan Political Culture*, pp. 54–6, 68–90, 108–40; see also the passing references in Hammer, *The Polarisation of Elizabethan Politics*, p. 291; and James, 'At the Crossroads of Political Culture: The Essex Revolt of 1601', in his, *Society, Politics and Culture*, pp. 416–66, p. 417 especially.

[15] Donna B. Hamilton, *Anthony Munday and the Catholics, 1560–1633* (Aldershot: Ashgate, 2005), pp. 165–6.

## Chivalry, Dynasty and Empire

*The Resolved Gentleman* itself, Lewkenor's first published work (1594), rather seems to discourage such political readings since the translation is presented as an ostensibly politically neutral humanist effort, undertaken for the love of virtue, chivalry and knowledge. In the translator's own words it is a 'poore Treatise (whose harmlesse innocencie shalbe a sufficient shielde agaynst whatsoeuer calumniation)' that 'finally teacheth nothyng more, then how to lyue vertuously, and dye blessedly' (*RG*, A4v–B1r). By stressing the universal, timeless validity of the message contained in his allegory, Lewkenor thus immediately adopts a defensive attitude, rejecting *a priori* any accusations of specific historico-political topicality. The whole translation is presented as a self-effacing antiquarian undertaking, concerned merely with reproducing de La Marche's allegory supplemented by a detailed historiographical apparatus to facilitate its understanding in its original historical context. So Lewkenor would have his readers believe that the voice of the wandering knight's 'I' is in fact that of de La Marche,[16] or possibly Acuña, or at best that of an Everyman; this ostensibly reduces Lewkenor's own role to that of a 'mere' translator, a selfless intermediary who is faithfully reproducing his source, to the point of punctiliously warning about Acuña's own inaccuracies in translating de La Marche's text (*RG*, A4r–A4v).[17]

The introduction and dedicatory epistle, however, provide some additional hints concerning Lewkenor's more specific intentions, and open the doors to a much more personal reading of the work. The choice of Anne, Countess of Warwick as dedicatee is obviously significant in this case, given the intimacy with the queen that seems to account for the numerous dedications she received in the 1590s,[18] and Lewkenor makes no secret of his motives: 'I owe you many other dueties, as well in

---

[16] As emerges from Age's comment: 'Neither am I ignorant of your native countrie, the marches of Burgundie' (*RG*, 6r).

[17] For the development of a new, humanist approach to 'rhetorical' translation in the late Tudor period, see Massimiliano Morini, *Tudor Translation in Theory and Practice* (Aldershot: Ashgate, 2006), pp. 3–34 in particular. A comparison of Bateman and Lewkenor, for instance, separated by an interval of a mere twenty-five years, only too clearly illustrates the transition from 'medieval' to 'humanist' conceptions of literary translation.

[18] On Anne of Warwick's role within the court, as one of the women of the 'inner sanctum' of Elizabeth's privy chamber, and a frequent dedicatee, see Christopher Haigh, 'The Queen and the Court', in his *Elizabeth I*, 2nd edn (Harlow: Pearson, 2001), pp. 121–4; Natalie Mears, *Queenship and Political Discourse in the Elizabethan Realms* (Cambridge: Cambridge University Press, 2005), pp. 54–7; Katherine Duncan-Jones, *Sir Philip Sidney: Courtier Poet* (London: Hamish Hamilton, 1991), pp. 11–12; see also Simon Adams, 'Dudley, Anne, countess of Warwick (1548/9–1604)', *DNB*, available at: http://www.oxforddnb.com/view/article/69744 [accessed 12 February 2012]. On Elizabeth's Privy Chamber more generally, see Pam Wright, 'A Change in Direction: The Ramifications of a Female Household, 1558–1603', in Starkey, *The English Court: From the Wars of the Roses to the Civil War*, pp. 147–72.

regarde of your many honorable fauours, and continuall redinesse to do me good in Court, since my first commyng to her Maiesties seruice' (*RG*, A3v). The *Resolved Gentleman* may thus be read as a witty exercise in self-advertisement and self-fashioning, designed to establish Lewkenor's own suitability for advancement within the court. Lewkenor in fact takes care to paint the exemplary picture of a 'Resolved Gentleman' under the veil of an allegorical quest, an undertaking only too clearly reminiscent of Spenser's own intention 'to fashion a Gentleman' as it was expressed in his Letter to Raleigh (*LR* 8).[19] Yet Lewkenor goes one step further than Spenser, and rather than employing his skills to produce a theoretical, programmatic portrait of the ideal gentleman under the veil of an allegorical narrative, he casts himself in the leading role of the questing knight.

The whole work, then, 'entreating of a minde vertuously Resolved' (*RG*, A3r), is largely designed to advertise Lewkenor's own suitability as a representative of this new breed of Gentlemen, combining virtue, learning, courtly manners, military experience and political acumen, as is confirmed by one of the dedicatory sonnets praising Lewkenor: 'Him vertue, Armes and Languages adorn' (*RG*, A2r). But since Lewkenor's identity as the questing knight remains largely implicit and latent, this allows him to articulate rather subversive personal and political comments while preserving the translator's unaccountability for any passages deemed offensive. Hiding behind the shifting identity of the knight as 'Acteur', Lewkenor encrypts a subtle yet often scathing criticism of a court he is also trying to impress and flatter. Thus, Lewkenor is in fact also displaying his mastery of the most prized of the courtier's qualities, namely his dexterity and tact in dissimulating political counsel and criticism under the veil of flattery.[20]

Despite all these complexities, the first, most obvious layer of meaning in the *Resolved Gentleman* is that of a simple panegyric.[21] Lewkenor's choice of translating the *Chevalier délibéré*, a Burgundian work via a Spanish intermediary, is clearly meant to establish a link between Burgundian chivalry, Habsburg imperialism and the rise of England as an international political power under Elizabeth. This implies a belief in the continuity of a pan-European chivalric, militaristic and imperial tradition, an idea that dominates the middle section of Lewkenor's allegory. Inserted into the middle of his knight's quest, de La Marche had staged a tournament opposing the emissaries of *Atropos* and his Burgundian patrons, Philip the Good, Charles the Bold and Mary of Burgundy. There the tournament, presented in the ceremonial chivalric fashion so familiar to de La Marche, becomes the narrative framework for

[19]  Spenser, *The Faerie Queene*, ed. Hamilton, pp. 714–18.

[20]  This rhetoric of evasiveness and ambivalence is shared by a number of contemporary figures involved with the court to varying degrees, among them Gascoigne, Lyly, Leicester, Sidney, Essex and Spenser. For a study of their uses of the multivalent and oblique language of courtship to articulate an unstable mixture of encomium, advice and criticism, see Catherine Bates, *The Rhetoric of Courtship in Elizabethan Language and Literature* (Cambridge: Cambridge University Press, 1992).

[21]  See Sutch and Prescott, 'Translation as Transformation'.

what is largely an elegiac lament for the downfall of the Burgundian Valois dynasty and their chivalric culture. Acuña, in his *Caballero determinado* had already subtly rewritten this entire section: for him the decline of Burgundy had become merely a prelude to the flowering of the Habsburg dynasty, finding its highest expression in the court culture of Charles V, *carolus redivivus*.[22] Similarly, Lewkenor has little interest in celebrating the decline of past dynasties: 'yet shal my penne proceede and leaue the wofull storie of this worthy Duke vnto some happier writer' (*RG*, 31r). Unlike Bateman, tacitly and abruptly replacing the Habsburgs with the Tudors, Lewkenor now expands the pageant-like progress to include both the Habsburg as well as the Tudor dynasties. The emphasis here is not so much on the waning grandeur of an extinct dynasty, as on the prophetic anticipation of a further apotheosis in history:

> As for the three ended princes, whose vntimely deaths haue brought thee to such excessiue and immoderate sorow, and these other, with the particularitie of whose combats I haue promised to acquaint thee, they shall leaue behind them such and so noble a succession, that their losse shalbe to the whole worlde restored. But especially the great *English Monarch*, who among the rest of his royal issue, shal leaue one so excellent a daughter & so highly of the heauens blessed, that besides the glorifying of the frozen poles, and the fiery equinoctials with the trophes of her inuincible armes, such shalbe the worldes wonder, and admiration of her vertue, that the greatest kings, princes, and estates of the worlde, shall thinke it the greatest happinesse that may befall them, to be shrowded vnder the faire spreading wings of her Imperious gouernment, some of them falling downe at her sacred feete, and flying into her realme for refuge, as to an vnblemished Azyle and inuiolable sanctuarie. (*RG*, 34r–34v)

The Tudors thus represent the last stage in a sort of chivalric *translatio imperii*, insinuating that the advent of Gloriana also coincides with the definitive demise of the house of Habsburg.[23] This reverberates with the wider mythology of the westward transition of 'imperial' power, so clearly sketched in Lewkenor's roughly contemporary *Estate*, tracing the decline and decadence of the once great Habsburg dynasty as a prelude for the transition of divine favour to the English monarchy (*Estate*, ¶¶Lr). Lewkenor's political as well as personal hopes, after his disillusion with Spain, are thus transferred and literally 'translated' to England, fixed on the Tudor monarchy and the 'new' ideal of a 'Resolved Gentleman' and his role in

---

[22]  For Charles V as a New Charlemagne, see Goodman, *Chivalry and Exploration*, pp. 39 and 152. See also Frances A. Yates, 'Charles V and the Idea of the Empire', in her *Astraea*, pp. 1–28. On imperial aspirations and iconography, later partially transplanted to Elizabeth's England, see Marie Tanner, *The Last Descendant of Aeneas: The Hapsburgs and the Mythic Image of the Emperor* (New Haven, CT: Yale University Press, 1993).

[23]  This is also implied by Elizabeth's usurpation of imperial symbols and attributes originally developed by the Habsburgs, as observed by Tanner, *The Last Descendant of Aeneas*, p. 237. See for instance also Roy Strong's discussion of the 'Imperial Column', in *Gloriana: The Portraits of Queen Elizabeth I* (London: Thames and Hudson, 1987), pp. 104–7; and Yates, *Astraea*, pp. 29–87.

shaping England's imperial future. The rise of England as an international power is thus inextricably linked with Lewkenor's humanist ideal of the Gentleman, making *translatio imperii* conditional on a successful *translatio studii*.

By situating the advent of the Tudors in an open-ended future, Lewkenor, like Acuña, radically revises de La Marche's pattern of history. Rather than being a lament for an extinct dynasty, the whole passage becomes a triumphalist celebration of a dynasty yet to emerge, projected into 'that fortunate and golden age, wherein the branches of these deceased Princes shal liue, especially that excellent and matchlesse Empresse of the Ocean' (RG, 45v). By thus turning Elizabeth's reign into an 'inuiolable sanctuarie' (RG, 34v) in a prophetic future, seemingly divorced from the present framework of Atropos's tournament, the Tudor Dynasty is being conceptually removed from the direct threat of mortality and extinction. Beyond the reach of Fortune and Atropos, Elizabeth is turned into the exemplary Monarch, who 'shal both in rules of gouernment, and vertue of gouerning, serue to all Christian Princes as an excellent Paterne and example, preseruing her Subiectes in a quiet estate, full of reposefull blessednesse' (RG, 43v). Furthermore, in an expansion of such divine blessings to the entire body politic:

> she, I say, shall by her princely care, and prudent foresight, maynteine her Subiectes in this calme securitie of vntroubled peace; so shal they againe, with so quiet and unmurmuring a course of faythfull obedience, loue and honour her, that she, if euer any Prince, shalbe blessed in her Subiectes, and they, yf euer any Subiectes, blessed in their Prince. (RG, 43v–44r)

The picture painted by Lewkenor thus seems, at first sight, to be a straightforward, uncomplicated panegyric of *Eliza triumphans* and an Elizabethan Golden Age.

Yet the allegory of the *Resolved Gentleman* is far from being a straightforward panegyric as is often assumed: the work's triumphalism is systematically and cleverly undercut to expose the tensions, dangers and anxieties glossed over by the Eliza-bethan courtly mythology.[24] In order to appreciate the full complexity and seri-ousness of Lewkenor's thought, layer after layer of the allegory needs to be peeled back, digging ever deeper into the contradictions, discontinuities and deceptions lurking underneath its surface. Despite its appearance in print, the *Resolved Gentleman* is at least in part addressed to a restricted circle sharing both its

---

[24] Much recent work has questioned and qualified the iconic mythology constructed around the queen. Contemporary sources in fact suggest that the idealised image was also resisted, crit-icised and deconstructed, and that panegyric often becomes a vehicle for advice, criticism or dissent. See for instance Susan Doran and Thomas S. Freedman, eds, *The Myth of Elizabeth* (Basingstoke: Palgrave, 2003), who characterise the technique as a 'Trojan Horse', pp. 1–23; Julia M. Walker, ed., *Dissing Elizabeth: Negative Representations of Gloriana* (Durham, NC: Duke University Press, 1998); Louis A. Montrose, 'Idols of the Queen: Policy, Gender, and the Picturing of Elizabeth I', *Representations* 68 (1999), 108–61. These recent studies supplement and qualify the classic studies of the 'cult' of Elizabeth by Yates, *Astraea*; and Roy Strong, *The Cult of Elizabeth: Elizabethan Portraiture and Pageantry* (London: Thames and Hudson, 1977); and ibid., *Gloriana*.

translator's political ideas, the resulting 'vocabulary' of politically charged metaphors, and the ability to decrypt otherwise obscure autobiographical references, equally rich in political overtones. So first, in the context of the interventionist militarism of the Essex circle, Lewkenor's praise of untroubled peace and stability can hardly be taken at face value. As in other contemporary literary works tied to Essex's cause, such as the work of Sidney, Lyly or Spenser, such praise is often meant to implicitly highlight the false security afforded by peace, and is thus a covert endorsement of an activist and interventionist ideal.[25] Second, there is the problem of the Tudor claims to semi-divine royal status and immutability. Before moving on to prophesying the advent of Elizabeth the poem in fact already presents Henry VIII as an ostensibly invincible, immortal ruler who seeks to triumph over Death itself: 'what now remayneth for him, hauing by admirable Vertues and inuincible Armes, drawen the worldes loue vnto him, but aspiring to immortalitie to conquer death, and to make himselfe Lorde of this Forest' (*RG*, 40r).[26] Henry VIII's determination of 'aspiring to immortalitie to conquer death', cannot but sit awkwardly with his defeat in the lists a few pages later. And how does this passage affect the status of Elizabeth, at the head of a supposedly stable and untroubled realm, herself represented as unaffected by change and decay and thus beyond the reach of mortality?[27] More generally, the picture of Elizabeth as a triumphant, divinely favoured Monarch beyond mutability in the midst of an allegory largely obsessed with the problem of mortality and transience, cannot leave its attentive readers indifferent.

As Lewkenor makes clear at the end of his work, the whole undertaking is not so much a panegyric as a *memento mori*: 'For in fine, all worldly pompe, Beautie, magnificence, and what els soeuer the world hath goodly or admirable, turneth to rottennesse and corruption: and Death, enemie to nature, equalleth sceptres with mattocks, and kings with beggers' (*RG*, 53r). Whilst any direct implication of Elizabeth's mortality is carefully avoided by projecting her reign into a fictional, prophetic and open-ended future, beyond the reach of Atropos and his champions, the advent of mortality can be suspended but not avoided.[28] Moreover, by adopting

---

[25] See Helen Hackett, *Virgin Mother, Maiden Queen: Elizabeth I and the Cult of the Virgin Mary* (Basingstoke: Macmillan, 1995), pp. 168–74.

[26] Such claims to immortality and semi-divine status are rooted in the Tudor dynasty's systematic exploitation of the medieval conception of sacral kingship and its iconography, for which see King, *Tudor Royal Iconography*; and Sydney Anglo, *Images of Tudor Kingship* (London: Seaby, 1992), pp. 1–39 in particular; McCoy, *Alterations of State*, pp. 1–22.

[27] On Elizabeth and the claims to immutability, see Hackett, *Virgin Mother*, pp. 176–80. Among the many works discussing the problematic significance and development of the 'cult' of the ageless, immortal queen, see for instance Susan Doran, 'Virginity, Divinity and Power: The Portraits of Queen Elizabeth I', in Doran and Freeman, *The Myth of Elizabeth*, pp. 171–99; King, 'Queen Elizabeth I: Representations of the Virgin Queen'.

[28] A similar dynamic is at work in Lewkenor's *Commonwealth*, where the juxtaposition of the English Monarchy and the Venetian Republic, seemingly celebratory, in fact underscores the instability of a political order entirely dependent on the survival of the person of the queen. See Hadfield, *Literature, Travel, and Colonial Writing in the English Renaissance*, pp. 50–1.

the chivalric form of the tournament, Lewkenor is exploiting and subverting one of the principal instruments of royal panegyric and propaganda, namely the Accession Day Tilts, the most remarkable of the regime's public appearances and performances.[29] The tiltyard is no longer the stage for a celebration of the annually reaffirmed absolute and immutable authority of the queen and her dynasty, but now becomes the site for the sorry performance of a *memento mori*. In the light of Lewkenor's ties to the Essex circle such a subversive use of the established tradition of the Accession Day Tilts also calls to mind Essex's own manipulation of chivalric tropes to articulate dissent, during the Accession Day Tilts and elsewhere.[30] Further, by situating the narrative of the queen's supposed triumph over death and fortune in a fictional, prophetically foretold future, Lewkenor is in some ways making it conditional on the queen's own handling of the political problems of her reign, in particular those related to the succession. It appears, then, that beneath the surface of a seemingly uncomplicated triumphalist pageant, Lewkenor in fact questions and deconstructs the cult of Elizabeth and its wider political rhetoric.[31]

### 'trauailing farre from my natiue home & countrie'

The autobiographical references in Lewkenor's allegory further disrupt the picture of an idealised Elizabethan Golden age. Indeed, some of the compliments paid to the queen herself acquire a rather dubious status when put into perspective by Lewkenor's own background. Lewkenor's references to the early reign as a 'Realme diuided in faction, differing in religion' and the prophecy of the queen's subsequent 'swete breathing gale of her well tempered *Mildnesse*' (RG, 44r) acquire an altogether different edge when viewed against Lewkenor's own choice of exile.[32] Also, one is certainly

---

[29] Young, *Tudor and Jacobean Tournaments*, pp. 74–5.

[30] See McCoy, *The Rites of Knighthood*, pp. 79–102; Paul E. J. Hammer, 'Patronage at Court, Faction and the Earl of Essex', in Guy, *The Reign of Elizabeth I*, pp. 65–86, and *The Polarisation of Elizabethan Politics*, pp. 199–216 in particular. More specifically on Essex's use of chivalric symbolism in the Accession Day Tilts to advance his interventionist ideal, see Young, *Tudor and Jacobean Tournaments*, pp. 165–84. More generally, on the use of chivalric tropes to promote visions of empire, see Brian C. Lockey, *Law and Empire in English Renaissance Literature* (Cambridge: Cambridge University Press, 2006), pp. 17–36; Goodman, *Chivalry and Exploration*, pp. 149ff; Linton, *The Romance of the New World*.

[31] For such dissenting appropriation of 'classic' Tudor royal iconography, see Montrose, 'Idols of the Queen'. I find particularly useful Montrose's suggestion that the cult of Elizabeth is neither an example of mere flattery, nor a pseudo-religious cult, but 'a core component of Elizabethan statecraft' (p. 133), a 'language' adopted and spoken by both establishment and dissenters, where 'fashioning and manipulation were reciprocal', as he already argued in his 'The Elizabethan Subject and the Spenserean Text', in Patricia Parker and David Quint, eds, *Literary Theory/Renaissance Texts* (Baltimore, MD: Johns Hopkins University Press, 1986), pp. 303–40, here 318.

[32] Lewkenor's exile during the 1580s in fact coincides with a period of tightening legislation against Catholic recusants; see above, p. 142, n. 3.

invited to question the exact nature of this 'Mildnesse' when a mere page later Lewkenor invokes 'the name of great ELIZABETH, written in the blood of those that resist, and the pardoned lyues of those that yeelde' (RG, 44v). Is Lewkenor referring obliquely to his own forced exile? Or to the queen's mercy in allowing him back to England, and to court, as he will do a year later by writing the Estate? Or is Lewkenor in fact playing with his own mixed experience of exile and return, expressing both bitterness and gratitude?

From the very first paragraph, Lewkenor cleverly exploits the material provided by his source to make it reverberate with his own experience:

> IN the declining season both of the yeere and of my age, trauailing farre from my natiue home & countrie, solitarie & sorowfull all alone, my thoughtfulnes did of a sodayne waken & reuiue my slumbring memorie, by renewing vnto her the time and historie of my passed youth. (RG, 1r)

Lewkenor subtly elaborates the theme of knightly wandering and exile to touch on aspects that are clearly absent from his source, such as the mention of foreign travel, and the distinctive function of Memory in the passage. 'Youth', in the latently autobiographical context, may be taken to refer to Lewkenor's early years, preceding his exile. The idea is elaborated in the paragraph immediately following the opening section:

> First, quoth [Memory], Whosoeuer is forgetfull, or carelesse of himselfe and his estate, flyeth not the pitch of true honor, neyther shall at any tyme see hymselfe beautified with the glorious bryghtnesse of her perfection: in which miserable lethargie yf he perseuere, then is his case most lamentable, and vtterly desperate, as not onely depriued of this worldes honor, but also of that euerlasting glorie and eternall health, to which, blessed myndes with the winges of a vertuous industrie do aspire. (RG, 1r–1v)

The formulation is richly suggestive, and again differs subtly but significantly from both Acuña and de La Marche. 'Lethargie' may be conveniently applied to Lewkenor's time in Spain and suggests a change of mind, a return to his home country that is cast as an 'awakening', a redemption or even a conversion.[33] The language interestingly mixes secular and religious values, 'worldes honor' as well as 'euerlasting glorie and eternall health' in a manner highly characteristic of the official Tudor discourse and its conflation of political obedience and religious orthodoxy. This conflation is particularly relevant in the light of Lewkenor's exile and service for the king of Spain, which by contemporary standards would have been perceived as a twofold betrayal, and his return to England is therefore imagined as a double 'awakening', both political and religious:

> Herewith my thoughtfulnesse ending, I awaked, as it were out of a drowsie traunce or dreame, thanking her in the highest degree for these her carefull admonitions,

---

[33] Philip Sidney and other members of his circle similarly use the language of sleep and oblivion in their poetry to allude to the snares of Catholicism, see Worden, The Sound of Virtue, pp. 61–2.

> and withal tolde her, that for mine owne part, I was redy to performe as much as
> to a true resolved Gentleman did appertaine: and therewithall, presently without
> delay put on my armour, and lyke a Knight aduenturous, passed foorth onward
> on my way. (*RG*, 3r)

This initial recognition of 'Lethargy' provides the motivation for the ensuing quest,
which may therefore also be read as a covert personal plea for pardon, acceptance
and permission to return to one's country, as well as a declaration of allegiance and
submission.

Yet Lewkenor's knight sets out on a taxing, ultimately abortive quest, like de La
Marche's fraught with difficulties and setbacks:

> I came into a very greene and florishing Medowe, the name whereof was Worldly
> pleasure: The outwarde shew whereof presented vnto my senses such pleasure
> and delyght, that rauished with contentment, forgetfull of my iourney and
> vndertaken enterprise, I euen determined to remayne there. (*RG*, 3r)

The deceptive *locus amoenus* suggests that the quest may have been misguided from
the start, and raises the question of what exactly is being alluded to: is it Lewkenor's
experience on returning to England, or the experience of arriving in Spain, or even
a brief allusion to his early experiences in England, preceding his exile? What is
apparent from Lewkenor's use of the Garden of Delights *topos*, is that he, unlike
his source, is referring to the allurements of a distinctively courtly environment. In
the garden he encounters Ill Diet, 'maynteyned with ryches, norished in delices, and
hyghly esteemed in the court of Princes' (*RG*, 3v). Ill Diet's attack also becomes an
unmistakable allegory for the temptations of courtly ease and delight: 'mightie
blowes of banquettes, bathings, quaffings, watchings, wantonnesse, and such lyke:
wherein Time, the treasure of life is consumed' (*RG*, 4r). This suggests a rather
different form of 'Lethargie', no longer associated with Catholic faith but rather
with the life of ease and idleness lived by the courtier,[34] and Lewkenor's knight thus
simply appears to have replaced one form of Lethargy with another, rather than
having made any significant progress on his quest.

Rescued by *Reliquia Juventutis*, the knight pursues his voyage 'amide this
vncertaine way' (*RG*, 4v) until he meets the Hermit Understanding, administering
what is mostly religious instruction. While the Hermit is inherited from Lewkenor's
source, his markedly ascetic, almost monastic tone, strikes a peculiar note in a post-
Reformation allegory seemingly promoting humanist ideals of *vita activa*. The
Hermit's statement that 'I haue retired my selfe vnto this place, to the ende, that by
Gods grace and goodnesse, I might leaue the wyde way of the worlde, that leadeth
to euerlasting perdition' (*RG*, 5v), puts an additional strain on the knight's deter-

---

[34] For such representations of courtly idleness in the literature of the period, interpreted as
resulting from the debilitating influence of Elizabeth's 'feminine', hesitant and insufficiently firm,
or 'virtuous' (Lat. *virtus*) court, see Louis A. Montrose, 'Spenser and the Elizabethan Political
Imaginary', *ELH* 69:4 (2002), 907–46, here 932ff in particular.

mination to pursue his clearly secular quest. After the knight's departure from the hermit, Age presides over the next stage of his instruction. The bulk of Age's advice consists of an extended warning against the evils of life at court, and also constitutes Lewkenor's most extensive and significant addition to his source, running to about six pages of dense prose: 'But aboue all I admonish you, that you keepe your selfe sequestred and free from the courtes of great Princes' (*RG*, 13r). Age goes on to point out the 'ficklenesse of that subiected life', where 'repaire many gallant floorishing youths, pursuing *Loue* and *Honor*, with sumptuous attire, high lookes, proude wordes, and disdainefull thoughts: but in the ende, foyled and ouerthrowen with *Ouer-riotous expence*, reape nothing in their fall and pouertie' (ibid.).

Age's denunciation of the evils of life at court includes details that clearly suggest Lewkenor's firsthand experience of such flattery and backbiting. The portrait he paints of the virtuous, educated and experienced courtier, desirous to serve his sovereign but excluded by the machinations of the flatterers and hypocrites, is too clearly reminiscent of his own situation to be merely coincidental:

> But many there are of my acquaintance, who hauing ouergon, and spent the poasting yeeres of vnmistrustfull youth, either in the vniuersities at home, or in trauayles, or the warres abrode, and by long and paynefull diligence obteined such vertues and qualities as to the seruice of their Prince & Countrey are fitting, do come at length to make shew of themselues, in this most fayre and magnificent market of the worlde, the Court, flattering themselues with great hope of rewarde, honor, and aduancement: and that the rather, because they see there ietting vp and downe, a number of vnprofitable peacockes, that haue no worthy thing els in the worlde to vaunt on, then onely the colour of their plumes. But great is herein their error, and as rare their preferment, as the sight of a blacke Swanne. (*RG*, 13r–13v)

Again, through the intermediary of Age's advice, Lewkenor is here putting himself forward as the ideal embodiment of the 'Resolued Gentleman', excluded from service to his queen by the jealousy of peacock-like dandies flocking to court. The inconclusive, frustrating journey of his knightly Everyman begins to appear more and more like the virtuous courtier's unsteady path towards a preferment that is continuously deferred. The obstacles on this quest are no longer the traditional psychomachic enemies encountered on the path to virtue, but are the strictly courtly enemies of slander, backbiting and hypocrisy:

> For though he misse the almost ineuitable danger of factions and partialities, wherin many haue made shipwracke of their estate, in being by the one sharpely persecuted, & by the other but weakely defended: yet such is the number of malitious parasites, that waite vpon the fortune of great Lords; such the multitude of flatterers, deceiuers, supplanters, vnderminers, espialles, and such like vermine, that attende vpon their court and table, all couering their villanous pretences, vnder the maske of vertue, fidelitie, and officious duetie. (*RG*, 14r)

Lewkenor paints a still darker picture of the court, where all the traditional qualities of the virtuous counsellor and 'Resolued Gentleman', as exposed in

Castiglione's *Cortegiano*,[35] and pursued in the Sidney and Essex circles, are not merely ignored but actively maligned:[36]

> If he speake, talke, or write; yea, or but studie matter of estate, he lookes into the state, and is dangerous: if he do neither, he is argued to be ignorant, and of no experience. If he haue trauailed strange Countries, seene the courtes of foreine Princes, liued in their Pallaces, or serued in their warres, thereby the better to learne and obserue their maner, custome, discipline, and language, suspition shall attende vpon all his actions, the offer of his seruice suspected, and his shew of zealous fidelitie misconstrued. (RG, 14v)

Again the autobiographical dimension of the passage is striking, reflecting on Lewkenor's experience of exile, described and defended in much the same terms in the more openly personal *Estate*. There, all accusations of seditious dissent are explicitly rejected, and his juvenile travels justified by appealing to a 'humanist' interest in languages, the wars and fashions of foreign places (*Estate*, Siiv).

As the quest advances, the autobiographical dimension of meaning is progressively amplified, until what started as a merely personal complaint is transformed into a much wider political argument. Lewkenor in fact uses his knight's misadventures as a springboard to launch into a skilfully dissimulated criticism of the Elizabethan court during the 'nasty nineties'. He insists specifically on the problems caused by the factionalism resulting from the contraction of Royal favour within the court. Through the use of the familiar solar imagery he also alludes to the resulting limited accessibility of the Royal Person herself, a particularly problematic issue given the unique conditions regulating the politics within the Elizabethan court:[37]

> as the ioyes [of courtly life] are exceeding cheerefull & gladsome, to those that are beautified with the rayes and sunshine of their princes fauour, so great must needes be the griefe and discomfort to those, whose vertues and industries are depressed, and they for lacke of due fauour and encouragement, made vnable to do their Prince and Country seruice; especially, hauing wholly dedicated thereunto them selues, and the fruictes of their experience. (RG, 15v)

The implication of the passage is not only that virtuous counsellors are scorned and alienated from the court, but that as a result of the factionalist politics the queen herself has become deaf to the 'sound of virtue'. By obliquely reminding the queen of

---

[35] Baldassarre Castiglione, *The Book of the Courtier*, trans. Sir Thomas Hoby, ed. Virginia Cox (London: J. M. Dent, 1994).

[36] On such humanist ideals within the Essex circle, and the importance of foreign travel in particular, see Gajda, *The Earl of Essex and Late Elizabethan Political Culture*, pp. 87–9. On the origins within the Sidney circle, see Worden, *The Sound of Virtue*, pp. 23–37.

[37] The problem of access to the monarch is often seen as causing the wider political crisis of the realm in the period. See Haigh, 'The Queen and the Court', in *Elizabeth I*, pp. 106–31. On the political significance of access to the sovereign, see Wright, 'A Change in Direction', p. 159 and *passim*.

the crucial importance of virtuous counsel as an antidote to the fickleness of Fortune, Lewkenor clearly revives a Sidneyan discourse.[38] Yet Lewkenor equally draws from a distinctively Catholic tradition of 'evil counsellor' literature, concerned to emphasise the need for a virtuous and therefore wider, more balanced and diverse culture of political advice, designed to consolidate the realm and defend it against the blows of Fortune and the self-interest of favourites.[39] Lewkenor's sharp criticism of the court here begins to modulate into something like disillusion, which coincides with a wider loss of faith in the temporal and political dimension of human existence altogether:

> Besides we see, that the great and all-ruling King of the vniuersal pallace of this faire world, doth not, in the distribution of his temporall rewardes and punishments, always respect the good or yll desertes of him, whom he honoreth with the one, or afflicteth with the other. (RG, 15r)

The final advice of Age's lengthy exposition is correspondingly pessimistic, recommending the pursuit of an ascetic and contemplative quest rather than a secular one: 'If you will follow my counsell, leaue off the Court to men of great happinesse, and bende your minde wholly to the obteining of that celestial honor and preferment, which neuer faileth them that doe vnfeinedly secke it' (RG, 15r–15v). This stands out as a highly unusual piece of advice in a work that up to this point seems clearly designed as a sort of handbook for aspiring young courtiers. Rather than a paradigmatic model for the quest of a 'Resolued Gentleman', this reads like an attempt to dissuade that same gentleman from his resolution to find preferment at court. Age thus prompts the knight to 'take your iorney towards the barren desert of Olde Age' (RG, 16r), as if condemning the ambitious young courtier to a 'Sidneyan', premature and forced retirement from the active life.

The knight however soon grows 'vtterly forgetful of al those good aduices lately deliuered me by Age, in so much, that I entred into a wrong path, called, Deceit' (RG, 16v). There he finds 'the most sense-pleasing and delightfull place', where 'stoode a gorgious & stately royal pallace, whose exterior pompous and delectable shewe, made me verily perswade myselfe, that neuer death, or any of his champions, could be able to approch vnto a place so beautifull and delitious' (RG, 17v). Tellingly, the Palace is presented as an idealised, alluring courtly space that reconfigures the iconography of the heavenly City to devise 'such a Paradice, so voyde of griefe, and so repleate with all sortes of pleasures, as this *seemed* to be' [my italics] (RG, 18r). Further,

---

[38] On Virtue as a remedy against Fortune, see Worden, *The Sound of Virtue*, p. 33, and Barry Taylor, *Vagrant Writing: Social and Semiotic Disorders in the English Renaissance* (Hemel Hampstead: Harvester Wheatsheaf, 1991), Chapter 5, 'Mortality and the Utility of Courtship: Castiglione's *Book of the Courtier*', pp. 151–64.

[39] See Questier, 'Elizabeth and the Catholics'; Adams, 'Favourites and Factions at the Elizabethan Court'. For the 'republican', or rather 'mixed' political implications of such a Catholic tradition of counsel, see Hadfield, *Shakespeare and Republicanism*, pp. 34–5.

> The walles seemed to be of cleere refined siluer, the windowes of bright transparent christal, the pinacles of pure wel burnisht golde, that glistered like the Sun-beames, and the couerings and roofes of radiant Amber, whose goodly fayrenesse and splendor was such, that with amazement it dazeled the beholders eyes. (*RG*, 17v)

Despite the clear warnings about the deceptive nature of this mock-celestial city – which is after all situated on the Path of Deceit – the 'Resolved Gentleman' succumbs to its charms. Dissatisfied with Age's merely ascetic programme implying a *contemptus mundi* incompatible with his choice of the active life, the knight enters the Palace, a transparent mirror for the Elizabethan court, and thus becomes embroiled in its political machinations.

The courtly game of love played by the 'noble company of Gentlemen and Ladyes' (*RG*, 18r) residing in the Palace becomes a clear allusion to the game of political courtship characteristic of the Elizabethan court. Actively encouraged by the queen herself, and best played by Leicester and Essex, the practice developed into an elaborate 'game' that was much more than a decadent and anachronistic revival of medieval patterns of 'courtly love'. The 'game' became a very serious and powerful political tool, consciously and systematically exploited by both the queen and her powerful courtiers as a means to negotiate political tensions and personal aspirations.[40] Lewkenor's connections with the Sidney-Dudley circle inevitably make him particularly receptive to the suitability of the 'language' of chivalry to articulate his political ideas.[41]

Followig Sidney's lead, Lewkenor at once plays the game of political courtship, casting himself as the Petrarchan lover, but also states his unwillingness to maintain the fiction, abandoning his suit to return to the ascetic quest recommended by Age. Again Lewkenor mixes compliment and criticism: 'And there I tooke my farewell of *Loue*, and withall of her, for whose sake (while I was *Loues* enthralled subiect) the paynes and tormentes I endured, seemed to be but pleasures and comfortes' (*RG*, 19r). While the beloved's ethereal, semi-divine perfection is reaffirmed and commended by being placed beyond the reach of the suitor, ultimately this game of inaccessibility is proven sterile, and can engender nothing else but a silence that is at once commendatory and bitterly critical: 'she is one, whom Nature hath more

---

[40] The literature on the subject is enormous. On the political function of gender patterns, particularly the adaptation of Petrarchism, see Philippa Berry, *Of Chastity and Power: Elizabethan Literature and the Unmarried Queen* (London: Routledge, 1989), pp. 61–82, 111–65; Susan Frye, *Elizabeth I: The Competition for Representation* (Oxford: Oxford University Press, 1993), pp. 108–11 and *passim*; Bates, *The Rhetoric of Courtship*. For a reassessment of Elizabethan 'politics of intimacy', based on personal rather than institutional ties, see Mears, *Queenship and Political Discourse*, pp. 33–103 in particular; and Anne N. McLaren, *Political Culture in the Reign of Elizabeth I: Queen and Commonwealth, 1558–1585* (Cambridge: Cambridge University Press, 1999). On the political use of distinctively chivalric patterns and symbolism, see for instance Davis, *Chivalry and Romance*, pp. 73–98; Young, *Tudor and Jacobean Tournaments*, particularly pp. 123–84; McCoy, *The Rites of Knighthood*.

[41] McCoy, *The Rites of Knighthood*, pp. 28–78 in particular.

richly beautified with grace, comlinesse, and perfection, then my worthlesse and vneloquent penne can any way expresse' (ibid.). Lewkenor's use of the inexpressibility *topos* to evoke the boundless virtues of Gloriana elsewhere in the allegory, is again both highly flattering and ambiguous within the 'politicisation of speech and silence' that dominates Elizabethan literature:[42]

> so vnable is my feeble speeche to aspire vnto the heigth of their worthynesse, that forbearing to speake of things so farre aboue my reach, I know no better way then to couer them vnder the vaile of silence, leauing the large campe of her prayses, to the excellent writers of that age wherein shee shall floorish. (*RG*, 45r)

And one of the 'excellent writers' of that future age evoked by Lewkenor is Spenser:

> the following ages among millions of other noble workes penned in her praise, shall as much admire the writer, but farre more the subiect of the fairie Queene, as euer former ages did *Homer* and his *Achilles*, or *Virgill* and his *Aeneas*. (*RG*, 45r)

And yet it can hardly have escaped Lewkenor that Spenser mobilises the same inexpressibility *topos* precisely to complain about the dearth of patronage.[43] Lewkenor, the frustrated courtier-poet barred from the privilege of providing his counsel, trades in the 'voice' of his learned advice for utter silence, just like Spenser's Colin Clout was to do the following year.[44]

Lewkenor's use of the inexpressibility *topos* thus in reality encodes a bitter complaint about the stiffness, sterility and arbitrariness of court politics. The queen's incapacity to handle criticism, counsel and advice is seen to generate a climate that is strictly antithetical to political debate, and is barren ground for the humanist culture of political counsel as articulated for instance in Castiglione's *Cortegiano* and Guazzo's *Civile Conversation*.[45] This echoes contemporary complaints about the scarcity of patronage,[46] and confirms suggestions of the growing alienation of a

---

[42]  The expression is McLaren's, taken from her *Political Culture in the Reign of Elizabeth I*, p. 156.

[43]  For Spenser's use of the inexpressibility *topos* in relation to Elizabeth, see e.g. *FQ* III Proem. On Spenser's ideals, ambitions and self-advertisement, see Richard Helgerson, 'The New Poet Presents Himself: Spenser and the Idea of a Literary Career', *PMLA* 93:5 (1978), 893–911; Derek B. Alwes, '"Who knows not Colin Clout?": Spenser's Self-Advertisement in the *Faerie Queene, Book VI*', *Modern Philology* 88 (1990), 26–42; Judith H. Anderson, Donald Cheney and David A. Richardson, eds, *Spenser's Life and the Subject of Biography* (Amherst, MA: University of Massachusetts Press, 1996), especially Jean R. Brink, '"All his minde on honour fixed": The Preferment of Edmund Spenser', pp. 45–64, and F. J. Levy, 'Spenser and Court Humanism', pp. 65–80.

[44]  See Ch. 7, pp. 181–7. See also Alwes, '"Who knows not Colin Clout?"'; Brink, '"All his minde on honour fixed": The Preferment of Edmund Spenser'.

[45]  Both works circulated widely in England, both in the original and in translation. For modern critical editions, see Hoby, *The Book of the Courtier*, and George Pettie, trans., *The Civile Conversation of M. Steeven Guazzo*, ed. Edward Sullivan (London: Constable & Co., 1925).

[46]  See Alistair Fox, 'The Complaint of Poetry for the Death of Liberality: The Decline of Literary Patronage in the 1590s', in Guy, ed., *The Reign of Elizabeth I*, pp. 229–57.

younger generation of politically ambitious courtiers to the advantage of an ever narrower group of ageing counsellors with a clearly marked political orientation.[47] More specifically, this again points towards the Essex circle, cultivating a humanist ideal of virtuous counsel, and comprising from about 1593 a group of talented and ambitious younger men, many of them Catholic, moving on the outer fringes of the court and responding with increasing bitterness to their exclusion.[48] The group comprised, among others, the Spaniard Antonio Perez, an exile who just like Lewkenor construed his exile as an ongoing 'pilgrimage' following his disillusion with Philip II's Spain.[49] Given the similarities of their past experience in Spain, as well as their ideological affinities such as their interest in classical Republicanism, it is tempting to conjecture the two engaged in heated conversations along with other protégés of Essex.[50] Also, these elements point forward to Lewkenor's translation of Contarini, which as Andrew Hadfield has shown develops such arguments in favour of a more inclusive and pluralistic form of government. There Lewkenor again uses an ostensibly neutral 'translation' to obliquely deconstruct the myth of the Elizabethan Golden Age, this time by celebrating the Glorious Venetian Republic.[51]

## The 'Desert of Olde Age'

The *Resolved Gentleman* also highlights a number of additional political problems related to the contraction of royal favour, namely the dangers incurred by a political system directly dependent on personal rule. This is achieved by cleverly exploiting de La Marche's obsession with Old Age and Death, which is used to make a much more precise, topical and political point. Within the tense and anxious climate of

---

[47] See for instance Hammer, *The Polarisation of Elizabethan Politics*, pp. 389–404. On the political role and importance of counsellors beyond the restricted circle of Elizabeth's Privy Council, see Mears, *Queenship and Political Discourse*, pp. 73–103. More specifically on the court and the council, see Linda Levy Peck, 'Peers, Patronage and the Politics of History'; and on the resulting factionalism, Hammer, 'Patronage at Court, Faction and the Earl of Essex', both in Guy, ed., *The Reign of Elizabeth I*, respectively pp. 87–108 and 65–86.

[48] Hammer, *The Polarisation of Elizabethan Politics*, pp. 290–1.

[49] This is reflected in the title of his *A Treatise Paraenetical, that Is to Say, an Exhortation: By a Pilgrim Spaniard Beaten by Time, and Persecuted by Fortune* (1598 – STC 19838), on which see also Gustav Ungerer, *A Spaniard in Elizabethan England: The Correspondence of Antonio Perez's Exile*, vol. 1 (London: Tamesis Books, 1976), p. 322.

[50] Perez was also the author of *Pedaços de Historia ô Relaçiones*, where war against Philip is defended as being fought in the interest of the people of Spain; the work was further discussed by Essex's secretary Henry Wotton, making use of politically dangerous doctrines of limited monarchy, which equally fits with Lewkenor's Republican tendencies. See Hammer, *The Polarisation of Elizabethan Politics*, p. 338. For Wotton's discussion, see Ungerer, *A Spaniard in Elizabethan England*, vol. 2, pp. 280–321.

[51] See Hadfield, *Literature, Travel, and Colonial Writing in the English Renaissance*, pp. 47–58, and his references to Essex in *Shakespeare and Republicanism*.

the 1590s, the obsession with Age and decay cannot avoid echoing the problem of the advancing age of the queen and the associated question of the dynastic succession.[52] Again Lewkenor's ties to the circle of Essex, who himself aspired to playing a crucial role in handling the issue, gives further relevance to such a reading.[53] The issue was certainly felt to be particularly burning in 1594, with the publication of R. Doleman's – really Robert Parsons's – *A Conference about the Succession of the Crowne of Ingland* (1594 – STC 19398), looking to Essex, albeit tongue-in-cheek, to settle the matter.[54]

As a direct result of his frustrated attempt to develop an amorous relationship at the Palace of Love, Lewkenor makes his knight advance into the 'desert of old Age', chillingly described in an extended passage (*RG*, 19r–19v). This of course alludes at once to Lewkenor's failure to secure patronage as well as the metaphorical sterility generated by the impossibility of political debate, but also points to the literal sterility of the Virgin Queen, unmarried and without direct heirs.[55] Suggestively, 'Infirmitie is there enthronized as princesse, and regent of the whole territorie' (*RG*, 19v), insinuating that far from being beyond the reach of mutability and Death, the queen is the very image of infirmity. Further,

> I espied sundry people both men and women, that did busie them selues in the practise of strange and cosening sleightes: some to hide and dissemble their yeeres, filled vp the wrinkled furrowes of their face with payntinges, some died their heades and beards with waters of their owne mingling, some pulled quite out the gray heares that appeared in them, thinking so to rid them selues of those hatefull messengers of decaying life. (*RG*, 20v)

Again this develops de La Marche's picture of old age and decay, but Lewkenor tweaks the allegory to produce a more precise, chilling commentary on the queen's well-known efforts to dissimulate the ravages of age in the interest of maintaining the cult of the ageless Virgin Queen, reflected also in the 'mask of youth' period of royal portraiture.[56] The queen's and the state's claims to immutability are effectively

---

[52] On the ubiquity of the theme of Age in the literature from the period, see for instance Frye, *Elizabeth I: The Competition for Representation*, pp. 98–104, Berry, *Of Chastity and Power*, pp. 134–65, Marie Axton, *The Queen's Two Bodies: Drama and the Elizabethan Succession* (London: Royal Historical Society, 1977), pp. 88–115.

[53] See Hammer, *The Polarisation of Elizabethan Politics*, p. 139.

[54] Peter Holmes, 'The Authorship and Early Reception of *A Conference About the Succession of the Crowne of Ingland*', *Historical Journal* 23 (1980), 415–29.

[55] Such a negative use of the virginity motif to signify sterility is also exploited by Spenser in his portrait of Belphoebe, as has been observed for instance by Mary Villeponteaux, 'Semper Eadem: Belphoebe's Denial of Desire', in Claude J. Summers and Ted-Larry Pebworth, eds, *Renaissance Discourses of Desire* (Columbia, MO: University of Missouri Press, 1993), pp. 29–45; and Frye, *Elizabeth I: The Competition for Representation*, pp. 114–20 and *passim*.

[56] See for instance King, 'Queen Elizabeth I: Representations of the Virgin Queen'; Frye, *Elizabeth I: The Competition for Representation*, pp. 101–4; Hammer, 'The Last Decade'.

and literally 'unmasked' to reveal an already advanced stage of decay, and playing on the familiar analogy of the queen's personal body and the body politic,[57] Elizabeth is now revealed as a kind of Duessa, 'a filthy foule old woman' hiding behind her 'forged beauty'.[58]

Accordingly, during the meditation on the 'Vniuersal Sepulcher of mankind' (RG, 24v) that follows, Lewkenor puts a special emphasis on women, noble women in particular – a clear invitation to apply such universal wisdom to the specific case of Elizabeth:

> I saw there, of Queenes and Princesses, Ladyes and Gentlewomen, of high degree, such a number, that it passed imagination: of which, though some had bin glorified with regall diademes, some shined with admirable beautie, some adorned with infinite wysedome and incomparable vertue, yet had no one of them all bin able to defende her selfe against the *Neuermissing Dart of Liues enemie* ... Retyred Virgins, new professed Nunnes, and aged Abbesses, vertuous Matrones, and wanton Curtizanes, all had there yeelded vp their lyues to *Deaths* commandement. (RG, 25v–26r)

During this extended middle section of the allegory, describing the tournament of Atropos against the rulers of the Houses of Valois, Habsburg and Tudor, Lewkenor is less concerned with mortality as such, like de La Marche, but rather highlights the strictly political consequences of mortality. This emerges from his comments on the death of Charles the Bold: 'Yet such was the hurt of these vnfortunate encounters, that not only the Duke, but his whole house, estate, & countrey, was thereby greatly weakoned' (RG, 30r). More suggestively still, the description of Mary of Burgundy's encounter with Atropos may be seen as a prefiguration of Elizabeth's fate. Like her, Mary is the last of the dynasty, 'onely daughter and heire to Charles D. of burgundy' (RG, 32r), as Lewkenor takes care to point out in a marginal gloss. The prophecy of the future rise of the Tudor dynasty, being framed by Atropos's tournament, is thus undercut even before it is voiced by the herald. Accordingly, the knight's reaction is not one of triumphal celebration, but of bewildered anxiety: the herald departs, 'leauing mee in a strange confusion, betweene sorow of that which was past, & wonder of that which was to come' (RG, 45v). Once more the knight withdraws and seeks the counsel and advice of the Hermit Understanding, as if to invite the reader himself to ponder on the meaning of the unsettling chivalric spectacle.

---

[57] Axton, *The Queen's Two Bodies*. The analogy, and its usefulness for attacking the political stance of the Queen and the ageing council is explored by Hannah Betts, '"The Image of this Queene so quaynt": The Pornographic Blazon 1588–1603', in Walker, ed., *Dissing Elizabeth*, pp. 154–84, here p. 169.

[58] *FQ* I ii 36.1 and I ii 40.8. For the 'unmasking' of Duessa, again using the same motifs, see *FQ* I viii 46. For a similarly oblique criticism of Elizabeth in the *Faerie Queene* itself, see Andrew Hadfield, 'Duessa's Trial and Elizabeth's Error: Judging Elizabeth in Spenser's *Faerie Queene*', in Doran, *The Myth of Elizabeth*, pp. 56–76.

The figure of the Hermit indeed dominates the final section of Lewkenor's work and presides over the apotheosis of his quest. This final stage of the knight's journey is perceived as a sort of deliverance from the preceding errance, and finally gives the quest a clear objective. Yet, surprisingly, this objective is situated in a hermitage, clearly outside the courtly world that has provided the context for the knight's preceding wandering. The abortive, secular quest for preferment gives way to a radically different kind of journey oriented towards clearly contemplative aspirations. The Hermitage becomes the new vanishing point of the allegory, displacing the Palace of Love, a false, deceptive 'paradice so voyde of griefe' (RG, 18r) – a reorientation gesturing towards the transcendentalising apotheosis in a monastic setting found in Deguileville's paradigm, here reconfigured as withdrawal to a solitary hermitage. The world of the Hermit constitutes an antithesis to the world of courtly flattery, factionalism and dissimulation, and the Hermit himself is tellingly presented as 'a counsayler voyde of all fraude' (RG, 46r). Lewkenor's Hermit is also rich in more precise echoes within its late Elizabethan context. The figure of the Hermit had long played a crucial role in Elizabethan chivalric spectacles, often used to denote the decision to retire from active involvement with the court. Sir Henry Lee had adopted the persona during the 1590s Accession Day Tilts to signify his retirement from his role as the queen's champion.[59]

Yet the figure of the Hermit was most consistently and successfully used within the Sidney circle, as a means to signify a rustication and retirement that is not entirely voluntary but rather suggested the failure of a fruitful political dialogue between the sovereign and her political elite. Sidney himself, the Shepherd Knight, conceived his whole career as suspended between the ideal of the public, active role of political counsellor, and the frustration of this ideal expressed by his premature retirement to a private Arcadian world.[60] Particularly interesting is Sidney's adoption of the role of 'Desert Knight', at once 'deserving' and 'barren', just like the errant knight persona adopted by Lewkenor in the Resolved Gentleman.[61] The figure of the hermit/knight-errant was to be revived once more by Essex, in 1595 and 1600, again to allude to the problem of exclusion from royal favour.[62]

For Lewkenor, then, inheriting such Sidneyan ethos along with its imaginative motifs and patterns, the meaning of the knight's retirement is amplified and complicated. While there is a sense that the knight truly finds a meaningful refuge in contemplation, this resolution cannot avoid being at odds with the humanist ideal that motivates the writing of the Resolved Gentleman in the first place. The ideal of virtue and public service is frustrated, and the contemplative solution, while it is embraced with heartfelt conviction, nevertheless appears like a last resort

---

[59]  Young, Tudor and Jacobean Tournaments, pp. 163–4.
[60]  On Sidney's ideal of virtuous counsel as public service, inherited by Lewkenor, as well as the frustration of his hopes, see Worden, The Sound of Virtue, pp. 23–37 and 58–78 in particular.
[61]  On Sidney as Shepherd, Hermit and Desert Knight, see Young, Tudor and Jacobean Tournaments, pp. 152–64.
[62]  On Essex, see Young, Tudor and Jacobean Tournaments, pp. 165–84.

resulting from the impossibility of putting the ideal of virtuous service into practice. So Lewkenor, like Sidney before him and Spenser after him, in fact abandons the quest rather than completing it, replacing it with a quest of a different kind moving away from the court towards Arcadia, Mount Acidale, or seclusion in a hermitage.[63] The use of the figure of the Hermit to signify the failure of the humanist ideal of counsel furthermore points back to Castiglione, himself using the figures of the monk and hermit to represent an older, medieval ideal of *vita contemplativa* which needs to be superseded by the new, hybrid ideal of the courtier embracing both learning and calculated worldliness.[64] Lewkenor returns to this distinctively medieval ideal in order to signify the failure of humanist values within the Elizabethan court. Lewkenor's wandering, his attempt to redeem himself from an earlier exile, ends in yet another form of exile and 'Lethargie', this time pointing beyond the vicissitudes of the court, beyond political struggles and beyond *vita activa* altogether.

Lewkenor's knight does not merely retire from the world of the court to the world of contemplation, but in doing so he returns to an inevitably pre-humanist and more importantly pre-Reformation ideal, which implies a potential relapse to older confessional and related political allegiances.[65] Lewkenor's hermitage clearly smacks of unregenerate Catholicism, and so his knight is armed by the Hermit with a dagger 'of a pure, vigorous, and true catholique *Faith*' (*RG*, 48r), is ambiguously pointed to 'repaire vnto some godly Father & reuerend Priest of *Christ his Church*' (49v), invited to fortify himself with 'the contemplative meditation of [the] holy crosse and bitter passion' (50v), and practice the 'adoration of his sacred name' (50v). In Lewkenor's case in particular, as a former 'Spaniolised Catholic', the evocation of such possibilities constitutes a daring criticism and warning to the regime.

By evoking the possibility of a relapse into a state that is not merely at odds with the Ciceronian ideal of the *vita activa*, but also potentially seditious, Lewkenor insists on the need for the sovereign to enlarge the range of royal favour. If religiously motivated sedition and political opposition in the manner of Robert Parsons and William Allen is to be avoided, Catholic loyalism needs to be not only acknowledged but rewarded with royal favour and political responsibility. Thus, if one is willing to construe Lewkenor's use of the motif of the rustic hermitage as an allusion to the numerous provincial recusant households, he is lobbying in particular for a more active political involvement of the Catholic

---

[63]  On Spenser, see David Lee Miller, 'Abandoning the Quest', *ELH* 46:2 (1979), 173–92. For a more nuanced reading, see Alwes, '"Who knows not Colin Clout?"'.

[64]  See Hoby, *The Book of the Courtier*, ed. Cox, p. 272.

[65]  While Lewkenor's religious allegiance in the 1590s is ambiguous, he certainly reconverted to Catholicism at some point in James's reign, as shown by his letters printed in Albert J. Loomie, *Spain and the Jacobean Catholics*, vol. 2 (London: Catholic Record Society, 1978), pp. 104–6. Lewkenor's son Thomas eventually joined the Jesuit order, while Lewkenor himself hardly seems to have shed his Spanish sympathies on his return to England. See also *DNB* entry.

gentry and aristocracy. In doing so, he inscribes himself in a long tradition of distinctively Catholic, loyalist insistence on the queen's need for counsel and advice.[66] The aim is that of achieving a solid, balanced and pluralistic authority that relies on a representative body of political advisors that includes Catholics rather than making them politically irrelevant. At the same time, Lewkenor also refuses to construct the identity of his errant knight solely within the framework of the political and historical reality of the Elizabethan court, and returns to a pattern of identity-formation that acknowledges the superior claims of a transcendentalising discourse of silent, solitary contemplation.

[66]  See above, p. 156, n. 39.

# 7

# *Edmund Spenser: The Poetic Quest*

In the introduction to the *Critical Companion to Spenser Studies*, Bart van Es provides an illuminating assessment of the major trends in Spenser studies from the previous twenty years.[1] Among the most fertile trends he identifies, two in particular strike me as highly relevant in the present context, since they help to frame the observations offered in the present chapter and in this book as a whole. First, the recent past has brought to the surface a new form of interest in Spenser's life and career, in terms that have shifted radically from the earlier 'biographical' criticism to embrace more fluid and tentative formulations of what we may call the 'self' and its construction. Resulting from an encounter or a friction between multiple and conflicting discourses and personae, Spenser's identity as inscribed in his writings appears as always shifting, fluctuating and uncertain, in search of a stability that constantly eludes it.[2] Second, recent years have also seen a resurgence of interest in Spenser's relationship to his sources, where the interrogation has moved away from the conveniently stable idea of 'source-study' that characterised criticism of the *Variorum* era, to develop a more complex manner of envisaging the dialogic interaction between Spenser and his literary sources and models. Spenser's sources are no longer mere quarries for narrative matter, but have claimed for themselves a more fully intertextual, participative role in their engagement with

---

[1]  Bart Van Es, 'Introduction', in Van Es, ed., *A Critical Companion to Spenser Studies* (Basingstoke: Palgrave, 2006), pp. 14–17.

[2]  See the articles in Anderson, Cheney and Richardson, eds, *Spenser's Life*; see also e.g. Richard Rambuss, *Spenser's Secret Career* (Cambridge: Cambridge University Press, 1993); Patrick Cheney, *Spenser's Famous Flight: A Renaissance Idea of a Literary Career* (Toronto: University of Toronto Press, 1993); and the useful overview proposed again by Patrick Cheney, 'Life', in Van Es, ed., *Companion*, pp. 18–41; A. C. Spearing, 'The Poetic Subject from Chaucer to Spenser', in David G. Allen and Robert A. White, eds, *Subjects on the World's Stage: Essays on British Literature of the Middle Ages and the Renaissance* (Newark, DE: University of Delaware Press; London: Associated University Presses, 1995), pp. 13–37.

the host-text, and collectively provide not an inert 'background', but rather a dynamic 'forcefield' within which Spenser's own poetry unfolds.[3]

Both the biographical and the bibliographical approaches to Spenser have thus been forced to relinquish the comfortable assumption that 'identity' may designate any single or stable reality – both in terms of strictly poetic identity, or in terms of a more broadly conceived self. Identity now appears as an unstable construct, irreducibly transitory and fictionalised and inevitably mediated by textuality, where an author's specifically poetic identity, as rooted in his literary genealogy and his poetic craft, is no longer separable from, but inextricably implicated in, the production of a broader, inclusive self that erodes the strict boundaries of bibliography to dissolve it in the biographical – and vice-versa. As a consequence, intertexts and contexts appear as part of a single, fluid continuum of discourses, providing Spenser with a range of fictions that nourish his necessarily provisional articulations of identity and selfhood as refracted through his writing. Speaking of this 'Spenserian "I"', Richard McCabe observes that 'autobiography is the condition it never quite attains, auto-fabrication the condition it never quite escapes'.[4]

Within such a framework the weight and importance of individual 'texts' considered as sources in isolation tend to wane, prompting instead an examination of Spenser's problematic yet productive relationship with powerful intertexts or *groups* of texts, understood as complex, fluid and often already multi-vocal *discourses*. Yet this tendency to examine strands of Spenser's literary and cultural ancestry in terms of inevitably restrictive notions of language, canonicity and periodisation has conversely also obscured the traces of literary traditions that fall as it were between chairs. As the

---

[3]  See especially the overview provided by Anne Lake Prescott, 'Sources', in Van Es, ed., *Companion*, pp. 98–115, and the relevant sections in McCabe, ed., *The Oxford Handbook of Edmund Spenser* , pp. 485–636. See also Prescott, 'Spenser (Re)Reading Du Bellay: Chronology and Literary Response', in Anderson *et al.*, *Spenser's Life*, pp. 131–45; Patrick Cheney, 'Afterword' in the same volume, pp. 172–77, which develops the idea of Spenser's construction of identity through a dialogic relationship with his sources, intertexts and contexts. Judith H. Anderson, 'Chaucer's and Spenser's Reflexive Narrators', in her *Reading the Allegorical Intertext: Chaucer, Spenser, Shakespeare, Milton* (New York: Fordham University Press, 2008), pp. 27–41, examines the Spenserean construction of the narrator through intertextual negotiations with Chaucer's work, and touches on the problematic issue of the narrator's relation to the poet's deeper 'self', esp. pp. 32–4, 38, 41. This notion of a self constructed within an expanding web of intertextual references clearly grows out of a number of 'deconstructive' readings of Spenser, which are however 'reconstructed' to provide the raw material for a conditional, shifting and obliquely signified but nevertheless palpable 'self' that is not merely characterised by loss and deferment of identity. See for instance Jonathan Goldberg, *Endless Worke: Spenser and the Structures of Discourse* (Baltimore, MD: Johns Hopkins University Press, 1981); Balachandra Rajan, *The Form of the Unfinished: English Poetics from Spenser to Pound* (Princeton, NJ: Princeton University Press, 1985), pp. 44–84; David Lee Miller, *The Poem's Two Bodies: The Poetics of the 1590* Faerie Queene (Princeton, NJ: Princeton University Press, 1988). For a critique of such deconstructive understandings of intertextuality, see Anderson, *Reading the Allegorical Intertext*, pp. 3–5.

[4]  Richard McCabe, 'Introduction', in McCabe, ed., *Edmund Spenser: Shorter Poems* (London: Penguin, 1999), p. xvii.

previous chapters have suggested, one of those largely invisible underground tributaries of Spenser's imagination is the tradition of the quest-allegory inherited from Deguileville. The presence of this tradition is largely implicit, to be sure, due to its lack of association with what we – or Spenser – would think of as illustrious authorial figures, or even due to its recessive position in the shadow of the more explicitly visible quest narratives of the Italians. Also, the study of the influence of allegorical quest narratives on Spenser suffers, like the tradition as a whole, from its ubiquitous but diffuse presence in the European literary landscape of the fifteenth and sixteenth centuries – in turn going back to Deguileville's frustratingly 'unerring choice of the most familiar and most popular themes of his time'.[5] Then how is it possible to differentiate between direct influence in the manner of more or less complex forms of intertextuality, and a mere recourse on Spenser's part to such ubiquitous *topoi*, sanctified by an older and wider tradition and thus promoted to the status of at least virtual 'archetypes' by the cultural environment in which Spenser lived and wrote?[6]

The powerful continuity that ties together the allegories I have explored in the previous chapters invites us to think of these texts not so much individually, as isolated sources, but rather as a family of interconnected texts and ideas that generate something like the '"magnetic field" ... of recollection' like the one Anne Lake Prescott invokes to visualise Spenser's major intertexts.[7] It is undoubtedly possible to point to specific, concrete points of contact between an individual source within that 'magnetic field' and Spenser's works, and evidence for such borrowings will be reviewed below. I would however also suggest that Spenser's debt to that tradition is cumulative, collective and hence runs deeper – even if it also runs, Bregog-like, deeply underground and remains largely unacknowledged, and therefore somewhat paradoxically appears as diffuse and elusive. If this difficulty of identifying and locating influence persists, it also opens the doors for a more challenging discussion of the relationship between the cumulative tradition of the quest-allegory, its individual texts, and the wider imaginative storehouse of the sixteenth-century literature, culture and mentality – three terms that cannot be satisfactorily isolated from one another.[8] Ultimately, this nebulous but all the more intense relationship is what allows us to speak not merely about a *family* of texts or about a *genre*, but rather about a more fluid but also more intensely vibrant *tradition*,[9] whose ties to the wider cultural framework where these motifs become ubiquitous and nearly archetypal finally guarantee the survival of the tradition itself. It seems after all fitting that if intertextual

[5]   Norman, *Metamorphoses*, p. 186. See also Ch. 1, p. 32.

[6]   The problem was noted long ago by the editors of the *Variorum* Spenser, when discussing the possibility of the influence of Deguileville and Hawes upon Spenser, see *The Works of Edmund Spenser, a Variorum Edition*, vol. 1, ed. E. Greenlaw, C. G. Osgood, F. M. Padelford *et al.* (Baltimore, MD: Johns Hopkins University Press, 1932), pp. 414–18.

[7]   Prescott, 'Sources', p. 98.

[8]   This insight already informs the terms of Tuve's seminal discussion in her *Allegorical Imagery*, especially pp. 31–55.

[9]   See above, Introduction, p. 16.

negotiations are truly 'interfluvial', the bounds and banks of all of those tributaries converging to produce the Spenserean voice would be continuously broken and blurred, until they dissolve into what may be a boundless 'Ocean [where] all riuers spring, / and tribute backe repay as to their King' (FQ VI Proem 7. 4–5).

## Sources

Numerous suggestions have been advanced in the past concerning Spenser's knowledge of and debt to a number of texts belonging to the 'tradition' of the allegorical quest that was outlined in the preceding chapters. Leaving aside broader theoretical reflections for the moment, it is to such firmer ground that I wish to turn, before enlarging the terms of my discussion to address what I see as Spenser's deeper indebtedness to the tradition as a whole.

The earliest suggestions concerning an influence of the allegorical quest tradition on Spenser go back to the *Variorum* era,[10] with entries by Padelford, and an independent journal article by the same critic. Padelford identifies in particular Deguileville's *Vie* as 'one of the moral allegories with which the poet could hardly have failed to be acquainted'.[11] Recent work on the circulation of the *Vie* in various printed versions in French during the sixteenth century makes a direct connection seem more likely still: it appears that at least ten different editions containing different French versions of *Vie* were produced between 1485 and 1520.[12] Padelford identifies a number of structural parallels between the *Vie* and Book 1 of the *Faerie Queene*, and further suggests that Book 2, Canto xii, and episodes in Book 5 equally seem to be elaborating elements from Deguileville – an interesting observation since it suggests that Deguileville was for Spenser more than a merely occasional source of ideas for Book 1 alone.[13] Nellish provides a reading of Guyon's navigation in

---

[10]  Greenlaw *et al.*, eds, *Variorum*, vol. 1, p. 414. I omit here references to James Blanton Wharey, *A Study of the Sources of Bunyan's Allegories*, who provides a list of works that display structural and thematic similarities with Bunyan. For a brief discussion of Bunyan, see the 'coda' to the present study.

[11]  Padelford, 'Spenser and *The Pilgrimage of the Life of Man*', p. 211.

[12]  The most complete list is given by Houghton, 'Deguileville in England', amounting to eight printings of the prose version of *Vie*[1], and two printings of verse *Vie*[2] between 1485 and 1520, pp. 68–72, 91–3.

[13]  Padelford thus suggests, to my mind convincingly, that Guyon's navigation is heavily influenced by Deguileville's depiction of the Sea of the World, and that Deguileville's *Envie*, *Trahison* and *Detraction* (*Vie*[1] 8231ff) may have shaped Spenser's portrait of Envy and Detraction in *FQ* V xii 31–43. Less compelling, I find, is the suggestion that Deguileville's *Sapience* (*Vie*[1] 2879ff) may have influenced Spenser's representation of Sapience in *HHB*. Both Padelford and Nellish, in the following note, refer to Lydgate's version, a translation of the second redaction. The details on which they concentrate are present, with few differences, in both *Vie*[1] and *Vie*[2], and Spenser's liberty in reconfiguring and adapting these elements does not allow for an identification of which version Spenser may have been familiar with.

Book 2 that emphasises the debt to Christian moral allegory, including Deguileville,[14] and although once more the influence of Deguileville appears 'diluted' by the nearly universal currency of many motifs linked to the idea of the Christian life as 'navigation', Deguileville appears as a particularly likely place for Spenser to turn to: not only does the relevant passage of the *Vie* contain a high number of the motifs that Spenser develops during the navigation, but it is the only poem that uses the notion of quest as its main thematic and structural vehicle, and recurs to allegorical navigation to illustrate and recapitulate the dangers of the quest immediately before its conclusion. Later Cullen concurs that in general terms Deguileville 'would seem to provide prototypical language of Spenser's work'.[15]

The next direct source that is often invoked is Hawes, beginning with Zander's doctoral thesis in 1905, which enumerates a great number of parallels between Hawes's *Pastime* and the whole of Spenser's *Faerie Queene*.[16] Many parallels are highly general, and the editors of the *Variorum* later state, precisely, that in his relationship to Hawes, Spenser's 'verbal coincidences are not striking enough to be of any significance . . . Yet . . . it is only reasonable to suppose that [*The Pastime of Pleasure*] formed a part of that rich storehouse of character, episode, plot, description upon which he drew, sometimes consciously, and sometimes unconsciously, for the fabrication of his poem'.[17] C. S. Lewis, perceptive as ever, points out an affinity in character between Hawes's and Spenser's allegories, emphasising Hawes's allegorisation of the erotic interest in his poetry, a useful and conveniently moral complement to Spenser's debt to the Italians, problematic in the context of the ambivalent attitude to chivalric romances in the later sixteenth century.[18] Cullen also discusses Hawes, arguing for a joint influence of both the *Pastime* and the *Example of Vertu*,[19] but it is Carol Kaske who provides the most accurate and perceptive assessment of Hawes's impact on Spenser, mostly through a discussion of parallels in the structure of imagery between Book 1 and the *Example of Vertu*: 'Spenser exploitatively imitated the second half of this work in his [*sic*] genre and purpose, in some themes, characters, and episodes, and in the whole outline of the quest'.[20]

Bateman has equally been invoked and discussed on several occasions, beginning with Koller, who points to similarities in the elaboration of faculty psychology in Book 2 of the *Faerie Queene* and the *Travayled Pylgrime*, and identifies a number of parallels in the two works, but does not venture as far as suggesting that Bateman's

---

[14] B. Nellish, 'The Allegory of Guyon's Voyage: An Interpretation', *ELH* 30:2 (1963), 89–106, here 99–100.

[15] Cullen, *Infernal Triad*, p. 6.

[16] Zander, *Stephen Hawes' 'Passetyme of pleasure'*.

[17] Greenlaw et al., eds, *Variorum*, vol. 1, pp. 414–18, here 418.

[18] C. S. Lewis, *Studies in Medieval and Renaissance Literature*, ed. Walter Hooper (Cambridge: Cambridge University Press, 1966), p. 131; Lewis, *Allegory of Love*, p. 279–87.

[19] Cullen, *Infernal Triad*, pp. 7–13.

[20] Kaske, 'How Spenser Really Used Stephen Hawes', here p. 122.

poem may be a 'source' for Spenser.[21] Prescott, on the other hand, sees Bateman's allegory as a powerful subtext for Book 1, and points out borrowings, verbal parallels as well as thematic and structural analogies. Her discussion is exemplary in pushing further the theoretical subtlety of our understanding of intertextual relations, and in the process manages to tell us something new about both Bateman and Spenser as well as demonstrating beyond any reasonable doubt the existence of a direct link.[22]

A further text invoked by Prescott as a likely source for Spenser is Cartheny's *Wandering Knight*, particularly concerning its impact on Spenser's House of Pride and House of Holiness in Book 1.[23] Cartheny's influence on Book 1 had already been discussed in great detail by Dorothy Evans in her edition of the *Wandering Knight*, where she provides an introductory discussion of numerous parallels in the two works, as well as numerous notes throughout the text to identify further similarities. Here too the cumulative weight of the evidence seems overwhelming, as a brief comparative reading of the two authors' description of the knights' visions of the Holy City will confirm (*FQ* I x 46ff; *WK* III.8–9, pp. 108–12). The question of Cartigny's influence on Spenser is also the subject of a longer independent article by Evans, which has remained sadly overlooked apart from a handful of references, and the parallels noted therein should be able to lay any doubts to rest.[24] Cullen equally discusses the analogies in detail, and argues that the work is 'not merely an analogue but a major source for the Legend of Holiness.'[25]

Unlike his predecessors, Lewkenor has not so far been suggested as a 'source' for the *Faerie Queene*, also because his allegory was printed only in 1594. However, his connection with Spenser would be worth re-examining, if only because the two poets mention each other by name, Spenser in the dedicatory sonnet to Lewkenor's Contarini translation, and Lewkenor in the middle of his own chivalric allegory, paying a compliment to Spenser as the model of his ostensibly eulogistic project. It was suggested in the previous chapter that Lewkenor's work is in fact far from simply eulogistic, and recent developments in Spenser studies make the same point. As I have tried to suggest above, a number of shared ideas and cultural contacts seem to support the argument of some form of contact between Spenser and Lewkenor, and it is entirely possible that Spenser may have been aware of the *Resolved Gentleman* when he was preparing his second instalment of the *Faerie Queen* for publication. The two poems share a number of motifs of course, but more striking to me seems the common tone or mood, as well as a general thematic concern: both poets use quest narratives to express their weariness or even potential bitterness about patronage, refracting wider political discontent, with conspicuous recourse to images of departure, exile and alienation.

---

[21]  Kathrine Koller, '*The Travayled Pylgrime* by Stephen Batman and Book Two of the *Faerie Queene*'.

[22]  Prescott, 'Spenser's Chivalric Restoration'.

[23]  Prescott, 'Spenser's Chivalric Restoration', pp. 182 and 187.

[24]  Atkinson, '*The Wandering Knight*, the Red Cross Knight, and "Miles Dei"'.

[25]  Cullen, *Infernal Triad*, pp. 13–16, here 16.

### 'mirrours more then one'

If Spenser is indeed indebted to several quest-allegories as opposed to a single one, then he must have been confronting a multiplicity of quests that in itself already provided bewildering departures from what was identified as Deguileville's 'paradigmatic', even monologic quest. Adapted to serve the needs of an increasingly wider and more diverse range of lay and even secular ideals, and exploited to articulate ever more localised and private forms of self-representation, the tradition in its later developments at once perpetuates and explodes its original paradigm. This produces the multiple quest allegories studied in the preceding chapters, in a process closely reminiscent of the 'inescapable' multiplication of private quests and adventures typical of the genre of romance,[26] disrupting the teleological linearity found in strictly spiritual allegory where the tradition ultimately has its roots. And yet Spenser, in his uniquely syncretistic and totalising fashion, attempts to engage and 'overgo' his predecessors by devising a quest that both embraces and transcends their cumulative efforts, thereby attempting also to overcome the limitations of their chosen form.

Spenser responds to the bewildering multiplication of diverging quest-allegories by dividing his own quest-pattern into parallel books, virtues and heroes. This allows him to expand the range of the allegory to include the ever greater and more complex range of virtues, skills and qualities required of the 'gentleman' he proposes to 'fashion', while avoiding the disintegration of the very quest-structure under the weight of such an enlarged conceptual range. Surely Spenser was too attentive a reader to overlook the inconsistency of Hawes's rather blunt collapsing of the paths towards worldly honour and heavenly doctrine, Bateman's profound doubts about the viability of his apocalyptic vision, Goodyear's refusal to engage with weighty confessional issues and historical pressures, or Lewkenor's decision to 'abandon' or redirect his quest. Also, Spenser cannot have been unaware of the central problem plaguing all of his predecessors' quests, namely the difficulty of synthesising and integrating the paths of worldly, moral and spiritual progress – or, if you will, Courtesy, Temperance and Holiness. By choosing to 'outsource' specific quests to different heroes with their corresponding virtue Spenser thus seems to acknowledge, crucially, that the ideal he is presenting is too large and ambitious to be carried on the shoulders of a single hero, and goes on to develop a quest-narrative that is not so much individual, but collective and intersubjective.[27]

This notion of a shared, multiple quest contains very interesting suggestions concerning the evolution of a sense of 'self' that may no longer be unified and single

---

[26] See especially Patricia Parker, *Inescapable Romance: Studies in the Poetics of a Mode* (Princeton, NJ: Princeton University Press, 1979), pp. 54–113.
[27] Developing familiar ideas proposed, among others, by A. C. Hamilton, *The Structure of Allegory in the* Faerie Queene (Oxford: Clarendon Press, 1961), especially pp. 89–123.

but rather fractured and plural like the books and heroes that construct it. Crucially, Spenser's aim is not necessarily that of representing this particular 'self' *within* the poem, as had been the case with all his predecessors in the tradition; rather, that self is the result of the integrated sum of its different parts – or books and virtues with their respective heroes – in the mind of the reader, which is ultimately 'fashioned' through the process of reading.[28] Thus, by refusing to provide a single model for the quest of his ideal gentleman, Spenser avoids falling into the trap of devising a predetermined, static blueprint of aristocratic identity destined to go to pieces once it is held up against the contingencies and vicissitudes of historical reality. Conversely, though, by providing a quest that is open, oblique and divided among multiple heroes, he concedes, as it were, that the integration of the ideal gentleman's identity is ultimately beyond the scope of the poem as such, and needs to find its fulfilment in the world beyond the allegorical fiction. Divided up amongst different books, different virtues and different knights, the identity of Spenser's ideal hero appears as irreducibly fragmented, and in this light the poem's 'incomplete' state appears as an inevitable consequence.[29]

The composite identity fashioned by these multiple books is therefore necessarily intersubjective, defined and negotiated in terms of social relations of the different titular heroes – and within those social relations gendered, and specifically amorous relationships play an unprecedented role if compared with the earlier works in the tradition.[30] After two initial books on Holiness and Temperance largely focused on individual heroes who learn to *resist* the world perceived as a sequence of temptations – in a manner that remains fundamentally analogous to Deguileville's pilgrim despite the obvious and numerous differences – the middle books of Chastity and Friendship focus instead on the need to become actively and constructively *involved* with the world, and of achieving an integration of private and public, individual and social identities.[31] Of course, some predecessors in the tradition had integrated amorous elements into their allegories, but none apart from Hawes had made love and especially *marriage* an integral part of their heroes' quest.

---

[28]  Hamilton, *The Structure of Allegory*, p. 89.

[29]  This paragraph develops ideas proposed by A. C. Hamilton, 'Closure in Spenser's *The Faerie Queene*', in H. B. de Groot and Alexander Leggatt, eds, *Craft and Tradition: Essays in Honour of William Blissett* (Calgary: University of Calgary Press, 1990), pp. 13–32.

[30]  For a study of the middle books from this perspective, albeit postulating a greater degree of unity and coherence for the poem than the one I emphasise here, see James W. Broaddus, *Spenser's Allegory of Love: Social Vision in Books III, IV, and V of The Faerie Queene* (London: Associated University Presses, 1995); for a darker reading of the possibilities of mediating between genders in Books 3 and 4, see Lauren Silberman, *Transforming Desire: Erotic Knowledge in Books III and IV of* The Faerie Queene (Berkeley, CA: University of California Press, 1995). See also the classic study by Thomas P. Roche, *The Kindly Flame: A Study of the Third and Fourth Books of Spenser's Faerie Queene* (Princeton, NJ: Princeton University Press, 1964).

[31]  Reed Way Dasenbrock, 'Escaping the Squire's Double Bind in Books III and IV of *The Faerie Queene*', *Studies in English Literature 1500–1900* 26 (1986), 25–45.

One may dismiss this new emphasis on *eros* simply by referring to the greater affinity of Spenser's poem with romance in the strict sense, a genre that is to some extent defined precisely by its very interest in gendered relationships and love. Yet there are more complex and profound reasons. First, in the light of the multiple and incomplete identities brought into play by the poem, love appears as the only means of transcending fragmentation: it is the only manner of achieving closure and assuaging anxiety about the isolation of the self and loss of identity in an otherwise bewilderingly chaotic cosmos.[32] Second, Spenser writes in a Protestant context that embraces the ideal of the active life, and more specifically celebrates and promotes the ideal of chaste marriage.[33] Third, Spenser's entire oeuvre unfolds in a cultural environment where the political imaginary is almost inevitably articulated in the terms of amorous, gendered metaphors,[34] and the allegory of the *Faerie Queene* as it were reproduces the mechanisms of this condition, so that the identity of the questing 'self' is necessarily defined in terms of its relationship to the female monarch, Gloriana. So, whereas the *aim* of the *Faerie Queene* is that of fashioning a gentleman, its *subject*, 'the matter of my song' (*FQ* III iv 3.8), is 'the most excellent and glorious person of our soueraine the Queene' (*LR* 33–4), around whose central and immutable self – *semper eadem* – the whole garland of virtues and the corresponding sequence of books is organised. This is clearly reminiscent of what happens in both Hawes's and Bateman's quests, where ultimately it is precisely the identity of the monarch that is asked to provide the framework for the construction of the hero's identity.

Spenser's poem does encounter, however, a major obstacle in its pursuit of the ideal of married love as a key stage in identity formation, both individual and collective. The ideal is quite simply very difficult to reconcile with the historical and political reality of the Elizabethan reign, where the dedicatee and central subject of the poem, the queen, is herself unmarried, and thus excluded from the cycle of generation and reproduction that Spenser's allegory is emphatically obsessed with.[35] This situation is shadowed in the poem's supreme but unattainable apotheosis, the marriage of Arthur and Gloriana. Crucially, this marriage that could function as

---

[32]  For a study of the poem's drive towards such a kind of integration, in Jungian terms, see Benjamin G. Lockerd, *The Sacred Marriage: Psychic Integration in* The Faerie Queene (Lewiston, PA: Bucknell University Press, 1987).

[33]  Among many discussions of the topic, see e.g. Lisa M. Klein, '"Let us love, dear love, lyke as we ought": Protestant Marriage and the Revision of Petrarchan Loving in Spenser's *Amoretti*', *SpS* 10 (1992), 109–38. King, *Spenser's Poetry*, pp. 148–82.

[34]  E.g. Louis A. Montrose, 'Spenser and the Elizabethan Political Imaginary'. See also Ch. 6, p. 157, n. 40.

[35]  This interest in the positive dimension of human sexuality, understood as a manifestation of the 'generative' process, most conspicuously crystallises in the Garden of Adonis, (*FQ* III vi 30–50). See e.g. Ronald A. Horton, 'The Argument of Spenser's Garden of Adonis', in Kenneth R. Bartlett, Konrad Eisenbichler and Janice Liedl, eds, *Love and Death in the Renaissance* (Ottawa: Dovehouse Editions, 1991), pp. 61–72.

*the* undisputable mark of epic closure in the poem,[36] or even as the moment of supreme cosmic integration,[37] is continuously deferred, and is ultimately only evoked obliquely through a dream that promises to be prophetic, but fails to be so (*FQ* I ix 13–15) – a dream that incidentally can be seen as deconstructing Deguileville's dream vision via the intertextual evocation of a rather different dream in Chaucer's 'Tale of Sir Thopas'.[38]

This powerful focus on the conspicuously absent, frustrated marriage of Arthur and Gloriana has a number of troublesome consequences for the possibilities of achieving an integrated 'private' self, both inside and outside the poem. The vacuum left at the heart of the poem by the absent presence of Gloriana calls for surrogate figures such as Britomart to fill that space and actualise the otherwise interrupted narrative of dynastic prophecy. And yet Britomart too is merely *betrothed* to Arthegall in the poem (*FQ* IV vi 41), and the couple never actually marry within the poem as we have it. Furthermore, if Britomart's quest is meant to pick up the dynastic thread of the narrative left vacant by Elizabeth/Gloriana, enabling the advent of the Tudors as spelled out in Merlin's vision, that same vision ends on a note of precarious open-endedness: 'But yet the end is not. There *Merlin* stayd, / As ouercomen of the spirites powre, / Or other ghastly spectacle dismayd, / That secretly he saw, yet note discoure' (*FQ* III iii 50.1–4). Finally, neither Britomart's quest nor any of the labyrinthine, multiple and repeatedly frustrated quests of the ancillary characters that crowd Books 3 to 5 actually culminate in marriage, and none of these minor quests can assuage the anxiety generated by the failure of dynastic marriage writ large, and the dispersal, even explosion of the identity of the Monarch into 'mirrours more then one' (*FQ* III Proem 5.6). Spenser is merely allowed to speculate obliquely on such a dynastic, cosmic marriage in the form of the utopian fantasy of the marriage of the Thames and Medway (*FQ* IV xi), and even and the marriage of Florimell and Marinell is celebrated only obliquely, as a mythical consummation rather than a human wedding (*FQ* V iii).

As for an Elizabethan such as Spenser the wider web of social relations is felt to be arranged around the 'central' position of the queen, shadowed to some extent in the conceptually central position of Gloriana in the *Faerie Queene*, the failure or denial of the epic-dynastic marriage of Gloriana-Elizabeth creates a void not only in the poem but also at the very centre of the social fabric, and entails a destabili-

---

[36] E.g. Miller, *The Poem's Two Bodies*, pp. 138–42. See also Andrew Fichter, *Poets Historical: Dynastic Epic in the Renaissance* (New Haven, CT: Yale University Press, 1982), pp. 15–16, 190–8, who is more optimistic than Miller, and despite Spenser's deferral of marriage within the poem, stresses the poet's faith in national history to eventually achieve such 'epic closure'.

[37] Leonard Barkan, *Nature's Work of Art: The Human Body as Image of the World* (New Haven, CT: Yale University Press, 1975), pp. 273–5.

[38] For a subtle discussion of the problematic, even parodic overtones of Spenser's use of 'Sir Thopas', against earlier arguments about Spenser's serious reworking of the tale, see especially Judith H. Anderson, '"Pricking on the plaine": Spenser's Intertextual Beginnings and Endings', in her *Reading the Allegorical Intertext*, pp. 54–60.

sation of the balance of the body politic.[39] Unable to count on the centripetal, 'epic' energy provided by the politically, socially and dynastically stabilising experience of a royal marriage, the possibility of attaining an analogous integration of the individual self into the wider body politic appears as impossible – as much for the fictional characters existing in the poem, as for the very real albeit imagined Gentleman-reader outside it.

## History and Apocalypse

It is a critical commonplace that Spenser's allegory begins to unravel in the 'Ariostan' middle books under pressure from the bewildering multiplication of characters and interlaced romance quests;[40] however, such a lack of narrative and amorous closure within the poem ultimately springs from the increasingly radical discrepancies between Spenser's poetic vision and the pressures of history during the 1590s.[41] This is particularly noticeable in the 1596 *Faerie Queene*,[42] which starts by dismantling the hermaphroditic apotheosis of Amoret and Scudamor in 1590. In its refusal or inability to attain closure Spenser's *Faerie Queene* follows, despite all its striking differences, in the footsteps of earlier works in the allegorical quest tradition, characterised by their suspended, frustrated or interrupted quests that are ultimately unable to heal the rift between politics, history and contingency on the one hand, and eschatology and spiritual vision on the other.

Spenser and his questing knights first begin to toy with the future promise of marriage, writ large, in Book 1 (*FQ* I xii 17–42). It is also here that we find Spenser at his most ingenious in revising the allegories of Hawes – and yet we also find him sowing the seeds of the same paradoxes and contradictions that will eventually undermine his own allegory. Like Hawes in the *Example of Vertu*, Spenser concludes his hero's quest with a union that is both literal and eschatological. On the one hand, the marriage, in agreement with the Protestant ideal of the married life so dear to Spenser, clearly asks to be read as a literal, earthly consummation, and as such is subject to time, death and change (e.g. *FQ* I xii 37.1–2); on the other, in the light of the echoes of the marriage of the Lamb to the Church in the Book of Revelation

[39]  Joanne Craig, 'Mirrours More Then One: Marriage and the Body Politic in *The Faerie Queene*', *Cahiers Elisabéthains* 45 (1994), 1–12.

[40]  E.g. Graham Hough, *A Preface to* The Faerie Queene (London: Duckworth, 1962), pp. 167–90; Parker, *Inescapabale Romance*, esp. pp. 91–7.

[41]  Michael O'Connell, *Mirror and Veil: The Historical Dimension of Spenser's* Faerie Queene (Chapel Hill, NC: University of North Carolina Press, 1977), pp. 155–60, 185–9; David Lee Miller, 'Spenser's Vocation, Spenser's Career', *ELH* 50:2 (1983), 197–231, especially 215–25; Richard Helgerson, *Self-Crowned Laureates: Spenser, Jonson, Milton, and the Literary System* (Berkeley, CA: University of California Press, 1983), pp. 82–100.

[42]  Richard Helgerson, 'Tasso on Spenser: The Politics of Chivalric Romance', *Yearbook of English Studies* 21 (1991), 153–67; Theresa Krier, 'The Faerie Queene (1596)', in Van Es, ed., *Companion*, pp. 188–209, especially pp. 202–6.

19 (esp. *FQ* I xii 22), Redcrosse's marriage to Una comes to signify supreme apoc-alyptic deliverance through the definitive triumph of the 'True Church', and thus marks a moment of final closure, a permanent move beyond human history into a state of 'ease and euerlasting rest' (*FQ* I xii 17.9).

Spenser cleverly opts for betrothal, which allows him to avoid the internal contra-dictions that had undermined Hawes's marriage of 'Vertu' and 'Cleanness' in the *Example* (*EV* 1689–968).[43] The postponement of the eschatological marriage turns Redcrosse's individual quest and betrothal into a *prefiguration* of a larger, cosmic and truly eschatological process, thus tying individual agency in history to wider apocalyptic scenario without collapsing the two. Redcrosse's quest, the battle with the Dragon and betrothal to Una, thus function as the microcosmic prototype of a wider, future fulfilment in history, expected to unpack to the full the prophecy of the Book of Revelation.[44] Spenser specifically highlights this historical dimension of the apocalyptic promise by reminding us that Redcrosse is in fact a Saint George figure, 'sprong out from English race' (*FQ* I x 60.1). This, on the back of the prophetic tradition he inherits from Bateman, Bale and Foxe, together with the heightened apocalyptic fervour in post-Armada England,[45] turns the future marriage of Una and Redcrosse into a figure for the final triumph of a specifically 'English' Protestant power over the forces of the antichristian papacy.[46] Clearly, the vision of Book 1 is not just simply a 'historical allegory' of England's recent religious history, despite the possibilities for identifying Una with Elizabeth as borne out for instance in Dixon's marginal annotations from 1597.[47] Such an identification is of course invited, but is clearly made conditional on England's willingness to play a leading role in the eschatological conflict with Antichrist.[48]

In Book 1 Spenser's gaze thus at once opens up onto this prophetically antic-ipated future, and simultaneously recoils from the static vision of the Heavenly City to plunge its protagonist and reader back into the world of action and history, aware that even though the *eschaton* may be imminent, the battle is ongoing.[49] Redcrosse

[43] See also Kaske, 'How Spenser Really Used Stephen Hawes', pp. 131–2.

[44] David Norbrook, *Poetry and Politics in the English Renaissance*, 2nd edn (Oxford: Oxford University Press, 2002), pp. 108–9.

[45] Capp, 'The Political Dimension', pp. 98–9; Bauckham, *Tudor Apocalypse*, pp. 162–84.

[46] Florence Sandler, '*The Faerie Queene*: An Elizabethan Apocalypse', in Patrides and Wittreich, eds, *The Apocalypse in English Renaissance Thought and Literature*, pp. 148–74, especially 156–67; King, *Spenser's Poetry*, pp. 71–5.

[47] John Dixon, *The First Commentary on the Faerie Queene: Being an Analysis of the Annotations in Lord Bessborough's Copy of the First Edition of the* Faerie Queene, ed. Graham Hough (London, 1964), discussed in O'Connell, *Mirror and Veil*, pp. 60–5.

[48] Michael O'Connell, 'Allegory, Historical', and Joseph Wittreich, 'Apocalypse', both in Hamilton, ed., *Spenser Encyclopedia*, respectively pp. 23–4 and 46–8; and O'Connell, *Mirror and Veil*, pp. 67–8.

[49] John Watkins, '"And yet the end was not": Apocalyptic Deferral and Spenser's Literary Afterlife', in Patrick Cheney and Lauren Silberman, eds, *Worldmaking Spenser: Explorations in the Early Modern Age* (Lexington, KY: University Press of Kentucky, 2000), pp. 156–73, here 157–8.

is indeed torn during his visit to the abode of Contemplation (*FQ* I x), and on the one hand, expresses his desire to withdraw into contemplation of timeless universal realities and 'not . . . then turne againe / Backe to the world, whose ioyes so fruitlesse are, / But let me heare for aie in peace remaine' (*FQ* I x 63.1–3); on the other hand however, he is conscious that 'Of ease or rest I may not yet deuize; / For by the faith, which I to armes haue plight, / I bownden am streight after this emprize, / . . . / Backe to retourne to that great Faery Queene' (*FQ* I xii 18.2–6). Redcrosse however does not so much reject as postpone his quest for contemplation, vowing to 'shortly back returne vnto this place, / To walke this way in Pilgrims poore estate' (*FQ* I x 64.3–4) – and the specific mention of the condition of 'pilgrimage' here is certainly not accidental: it designates, precisely, the state of contemplative existence that sends us back to Deguileville, a state that Redcrosse cannot however embrace because of 'the faith, which [he] to armes [has] plight' (*FQ* I xii 18.3). Spenser does not so much ignore or overwrite Deguileville, but rather acknowledges the status of his 'pilgrimage' as the ultimate, highest and final stage in man's journey of life. For Spenser, building his allegory on the foundations of all the later rewritings of Deguileville that attempt to balance such a desire for eschatological deliverance with a positive interest in the active life, this leap into transcendence is both anticipated and resisted, postponed in the interest of an active involvement in history that is perceived as necessary for the very advent of that Heavenly City.

So Spenser's allegory is primarily concerned with the active quest that *precedes* and enables such contemplative withdrawal. Redcrosse's vision of 'the new *Hierusalem*, that God has built / for those to dwell in, that are chosen his' (*FQ* I x 57.2–3) thus functions as a mere anticipation of a truly spiritual pilgrimage, which Redcrosse will be allowed to embark on only once he has completed a more 'terrestrial' cycle of existence appropriately presented in terms of georgic labour (*FQ* I x 66). Only then will Redcrosse be allowed to 'seek this path . . . / Which after all to heauen shall thee send; / Then peaceably thy painefull pilgrimage / To yonder same *Hierusalem* doe bend' (*FQ* I x 61.1–4), and thus fulfil the promise of his marriage to the Heavenly City imagined as a 'bride' in Revelation 21:2. So Spenser does not so much draw up an opposition between the active and the contemplative life, but rather represents them as complementary, successive stages along a continuum. This 'drafting' of a path leading first through *Cleopolis* in order to attain *Hierusalem* (*FQ* I x 58–59) is a *tour de force* in Spenser's rewriting of the quest-allegory tradition to balance the claims of time and eternity.[50] The active life, crucially, is not endowed with inherent value *per se*, but gains its importance precisely from the fact that active service of Gloriana itself participates in the unpacking of the apocalyptic scenario that can bring about the advent of the New Jerusalem.[51] As in Bateman, England is not the Heavenly Kingdom – just like

---

[50] Florence Sandler is thus exactly right in observing that 'Spenser is at pains to have Contemplation himself affirm for the benefit of the Red Cross Knight the value of nationhood', 'The *Faerie Queene*: An Elizabethan Apocalypse', p. 156.

[51] Norbrook, *Poetry and Politics*, 106–9.

*Cleopolis* is not *Hierusalem*; rather than collapsing the two, Spenser establishes a typological relationship, thus stressing the importance of the human effort in bringing about a final apotheosis of history.

Redcrosse's return to Fairyland is accordingly suffused with echoes of a renewed eschatological battle: 'to retourne to that great Faery Queene, / And her so serue six yeares in warlike wize, / Gainst that proud Paynim king, that works her teene' (*FQ* I xii 18.6–8), reminding us that the final battle remains to be fought.[52] In the light of the contemporary belief that deliverance from the oppression of Antichrist could be actively aided and brought about by human action in the world,[53] active service in Fairyland – shadowing the need for military intervention in Spenser's own historical England and Empire[54] – becomes a necessary step in bringing about the apotheosis of history and the advent of the New Jerusalem glimpsed in Book 1. Although Fairyland is of course not identical with the historical world of Spenser's England, it stands for the realm of the possible future fulfilments of vision in history where 'later times thinges more vnknowne shall show' (*FQ* II Proem 3.3).

The eschatology invoked by Book 1, then, is merely apparent, since it does not provide a 'conclusive' solution to the problems of history, and functions rather as a proleptic visionary sketch that prepares us for a return to the realm of action in Fairyland, the subject of all subsequent books. Symptomatically, Redcrosse's apparent triumph is in fact immediately undone as the poem moves into the next book, with Archimago breaking his shackles in the manner of the dragon of Rev. 20:1–3, and running loose through the subsequent books. Frustration, deferment and undoing of the initial programmatic victory of Redcrosse may even be said to characterise the whole of the poem after Books 1 and 2, with a multiplicity of agents of Antichrist making Fairyland progressively more unsafe, as resolution seems to recede ever further into the distance. Accordingly, Merlin's famous prophecy about the dynastic rise and triumph of the Tudors in (*FQ* III iii 50 is undercut by his 'dismayd' reaction to the 'ghastly spectacle' of an uncertain future for England.[55] Indeed Fairyland's future remains open-ended, as the anticipated, final battle with the 'Paynim King' announced in Book 1 – like the marriage of Arthur and Gloriana – never materialises in the poem as we have it. What we find instead, most evidently

---

[52] The 'six years' possibly allude to the oppression of the English Church under Mary, and thus signify the state of continued symbolic captivity of the True Church even after Redcrosse's initial triumph; see Norbrook, *Poetry and Politics*, p. 109.

[53] Capp, 'The Political Dimension', pp. 98–9; Bauckham, *Tudor Apocalypse*, pp. 162–84.

[54] See especially Michael Murrin, *The Allegorical Epic: Essays in its Rise and Decline* (Chicago, IL: University of Chicago Press, 1980), pp. 135–41. On the fluctuating status of Fairyland and its relationship to Spenser's 'real' historical world more generally, see Jacqueline T. Miller, 'The Status of Faeryland: Spenser's "Vniust Possession"', *SpS* 5 (1985), 31–44. For an example of recent readings emphasising the overlap of Faeryland with Spenser's Ireland, see for instance Elizabeth Porges Watson, 'Mutabilitie's Debatable Land: Spenser's Ireland and the Frontiers of Faerie', in Julian B. Lethbridge, ed., *Edmund Spenser: New and Renewed Directions* (Madison, WI: Fairleigh Dickinson University Press, 2006), pp. 286–301.

[55] Watkins, '"And yet the end was not"', pp. 159–60.

in Book 5, is a series of multiple, inconclusive struggles against minor avatars of the forces of Antichrist – the Souldan, Geryoneo, Radigund, Grantorto, the Blatant Beast and others, ever more fragmented and difficult to unmask and apprehend as the poem advances into its later stages.[56]

Book 5 constitutes the culmination of this desire for a historical apotheosis and fulfilment of apocalyptic prophecy, and it has often been argued that Book 5 constitutes the only moment of the *Faerie Queene* where it is permissible to speak of a 'historical allegory' in the narrow sense.[57] The demands and pressures of history on the allegory here seem to have reached such an intensity that the poem merely seems to reproduce historical events, rather than 'shadowing' them according to Spenser's more usual practice. Recent readings however complicate the picture.[58] So while the received view on the Belge episode, for instance, sees it as a celebration of English victory in the Netherlands, it has been pointed out that the episode in fact 'presents a whitewashed version of recent events', rewriting history not as it was, but as Spenser would have liked it to be.[59] I also think that Gregory is correct in stressing that the implications of such an idealised rewriting of Leicester's campaign in the Netherlands are by no means celebratory or optimistic. Rather, by devising a sanitised and fictionalised version of events, Spenser is ironically commenting on England's failure to live up to the weighty apocalyptic expectations that had been attached to a campaign led by Leicester but only half-heartedly supported by the queen, thus ultimately ending in failure instead of the anticipated triumph.[60]

Spenser's criticism here clearly also springs from a broader concern about the failure of the queen to implement the more active and interventionist foreign policy promoted by the likes of Leicester, Walsingham and Essex.[61] This fits with Spenser's reservations about reformation through the word alone and his support of more radical intervention in Ireland, as perceived by Mallette; the same critic equally stresses that by choosing to end Book 5 not with the mock-triumphal Belge-episode but with the problematic Irena-episode and the abuses of the Blatant Beast, Spenser deliberately ends the book on a note of uncertainty and inconclusiveness.[62] Whereas on the surface the apocalyptic epilogue of Book 5 appears to enact in historical terms the eschatological resolution glimpsed in Book 1, in reality it performs a

---

[56]   See especially Richard Mallette, 'Book Five of *The Faerie Queene*: An Elizabethan Apocalypse', *SpS* 11 (1990), 129–59, here 142–44.

[57]   O'Connell, *Mirror and Veil*, pp. 13, 147–60.

[58]   See especially Tobias Gregory, 'Shadowing Intervention: On the Politics of *The Faerie Queene* Book 5 Cantos 10–2', *ELH* 67:2 (2000), 365–97, along with the numerous Ireland-focused studies of Book 5.

[59]   Gregory, 'Shadowing Intervention', 370. The idea is already developed by Norbrook, *Poetry and Politics*, pp. 120–2, and O'Connell, *Mirror and Veil*, p. 158: 'we must see in the poem more wish fulfilment than moral prophecy'.

[60]   Norbrook, *Poetry and Politics*, pp. 117–22.

[61]   Gregory, 'Shadowing Intervention', especially 388–90; Norbrook, *Poetry and Politics*, pp. 133–6

[62]   Mallette, 'An Elizabethan Apocalypse', especially 148–53.

further deferral. The implications for our overall understanding of Spenser's allegory are weighty. Spenser is not merely being polemical in a localised, narrow sense, but also articulates a much wider and more radical feeling of frustration: on the one hand he highlights the inconclusiveness of history, marked by England's refusal or inability to embrace what Spenser sees as its natural role in the historico-apocalyptic scenario of the imminent last days; on the other, more seriously, Spenser begins to doubt the very possibility of ever attaining an 'apocalyptic' apotheosis in history.[63]

## Abandoning the Quest?

Spenser's doubts about England's ability to live up to its apocalyptic destiny echo the very similar reservations expressed by Bateman in his *Travayled Pylgrime*. Admittedly, though, Spenser's poem does not merely reflect history passively, and along with its desire to 'fashion' a gentleman it also seeks to direct, guide and exhort the political powers to steer the Ship of State towards the desired haven where individual, national, political and eschatological destinies converge. The optimism of Book 1, however, where the poet claims that 'I see the hauen nigh at hand' (*FQ* I xii 1.1), progressively gives way to darker images of hampered and frustrated progress, even paralysis as the poem advances.[64] Because of the failure of history to bear out his apocalyptic hopes, along with the realisation of his own poem's inability to persuade the 'rugged forhead that with graue foresight / Welds kingdomes causes, and affaires of state' (*FQ* IV Proem 1.1–2) to pursue such a vision and causing instead 'a mighty Peres displeasure' (*FQ* VI xii 41.6),[65] Spenser begins to contemplate alternative forms of consummation. Like the quests of his many heroes,[66] Spenser's own quest is diverted into ever more centrifugal and self-absorbing wanderings 'Far from the hoped hauen of reliefe' (*FQ* III iv 8.3). As Anne Lake Prescott observes in a different context, Spenser's quest

[63]  This, I suggest, also touches on *the* central debate among Spensereans in the last generation, namely the modality and chronology of Spenser's real or supposed loss of 'faith' in the possibility of completing his projected national epic, and its consequences for our understanding of the 'Late Spenser' in the 1590s. For a useful recent contribution recapitulating the key stages in the debate, see Julian B. Lethbridge, 'Spenser's Last Days: Ireland, Career, Mutability, Allegory', in Lethbridge, ed., *Edmund Spenser: New and Renewed Directions*, pp. 302–36.

[64]  See for instance the comments on the 1596 instalment in William A. Oram, 'Spenserian Paralysis', *Studies in English Literature, 1500–1900* 41:1 (2001), 49–70, here 61–5.

[65]  Alluding specifically to Burghley's unfavourable reception, and staking a claim for addressing the queen directly and bypassing her counsellors: 'To such therefore I do not sing at all, / But to that sacred Saint my soueraigne Queene' (*FQ* IV Proem 4.1–2). For the identification with Burghley, see e.g. Arthur F. Marotti, '"Love Is Not Love": Elizabethan Sonnet Sequences and the Social Order', *ELH* 49:2 (1982), 396–428, here 415–16; or Richard McCabe, *Spenser's Monstrous Regiment: Elizabethan Ireland and the Poetics of Difference* (Oxford: Oxford University Press, 2002), pp. 249–50.

[66]  On the analogy between knightly and poetic quests, see e.g. O'Connell, *Mirror and Veil*, pp. 167–9.

becomes oblique and elliptic, 'move[s] more like pre-copernican planets than Pilgrim on his progress'.[67] In later books Spenser is, like his heroes and his poem, 'in stormie surges tost' (*FQ* VI xii 1.5), and begins to succumb to the temptation of pursuing an individual quest that no longer seeks epic or eschatological fulfilment in the form of a political and historical apotheosis. It is perhaps less a case of Spenser abandoning the quest, than of him redefining the terms under which this voyage may still be continued, 'as a ship, that through the Ocean wyde, / Directs her course vnto one certaine cost / ... / Right so it fares with me in this long way, / Whose course is often stayd, yet neuer is astray' (*FQ* VI xii 1).[68]

And yet the 'certaine cost' sought out by Spenser's poetic quest is clearly no longer the English shore, as the account of the frustrating sea-journey in *Colin Clouts Come Home Againe* makes clear. The significance of the navigation across the Irish Sea and the poem as a whole is of course highly complex, and the sea itself becomes a problematic and multivalent *locus*: it acts as a metonymy for the queen's physical realm ('that same was the Regiment / Of a great shepheardesse, that *Cynthia* hight', *CCH* 233–4)[69] and by extension a symbol of her imperial authority ('For land and sea my *Cynthia* doth deserue', 262), a metaphor for frustrated courtly ambition ('Bold men presuming life for gaine to sell, / Dare tempt that gulf', 209–10), and the menacing wilderness of more traditional moral allegory ('Seek waies vnknowne, waies leading down to hell'; 'Floting amid the sea in ieopardie'; 211, 273). By 'layering' these multiple meanings Spenser manages to suggest that the English court, far from being 'like heauen' (306) as it appears to be on arrival (280–9), is in reality merely another embodiment of the Sea of the World of Christian allegory,[70] teeming with demons and monsters that embody the moral threats awaiting the aspiring courtier:[71] 'Thousand wyld beasts with deep mouthes gaping direfull', in a 'wide wildernesse, / Horrible, hideous, roaring with hoarse crie' (202, 198–9).[72]

Colin's crossing of the Irish Sea as it were subverts and deconstructs both Guyon's voyage, and through it Deguileville's navigation across the Sea of the World. Colin's

---

[67]  Prescott, 'Spenser (Re)Reading Du Bellay', p. 131.

[68]  For Spenser's use of the navigation-*topos* along the lines sketched here, see Jerome S. Dees, 'The Ship Conceit in *The Faerie Queene*: "Conspicuous Allusion" and Poetic Structure', *Studies in Philology* 72 (1975), 208–25. On the idea of abandoning the quest, or redefining its modalities in terms of shifting generic allegiances, see David Quint, 'The Boat of Romance and Renaissance Epic', in Kevin Brownlee and Marina Scordilis Brownlee, eds, *Romance: Generic Transformation from Chrétien de Troyes to Cervantes* (Hanover, NH: University Press of New England, 1985), pp. 178–202. On the issue more generally, see especially the work by David Lee Miller, e.g. 'Abandoning the Quest', and 'Spenser's Vocation, Spenser's Career'.

[69]  For all of Spenser's works other than the *Faerie Queene* I refer to McCabe, ed., *Shorter Poems*.

[70]  For a discussion of Christian allegory of navigation, and descriptions of the 'Sea' peopled by monstrous creatures embodying moral threats, including Deguileville, see Nellish, 'The Allegory of Guyon's Voyage', 96–100 especially.

[71]  On Spenser's attitude towards patronage and the court in the 1590s more generally, see F. J. Levy, 'Spenser and Court Humanism', here pp. 76–80.

[72]  For a very similar picture, see also *FQ* II xii 22–4.

voyage appears as a deceptive simulacrum of an eschatological journey, leading to 'a loftie mount . . . / Which did a stately heape of stones vpreare, / That seemd amid the surges for to fleet' (CCH 284–6). And once he arrives at the English court, his description clearly invites the assimilation of England to the Kingdom of heaven:

> Both heauen and heauenly graces do much more
> (Quoth he) abound in that same land, then this.
> For there all happie peace and plenteous store
> Conspire in one to make contented blisse:
>
> . . .
>
> But vaine it is to thinke by paragone
> Of earthly things, to iudge things diuine
>
> . . .
>
> The image of the heauens in shape humane (CCH 308–11; 344–5; 351)

But Colin's eventual decision to return 'home' to his Irish 'barrein soyle' (CCH 656), the 'waste, where I was quite forgot' (CCH 183), clearly undermines, once more, any claim for identifying England with the New Jerusalem. The poem ultimately deconstructs not only Deguileville's navigation, but also the providential under-standing of the Ship of State such as the one found in Hawes,[73] who promoted the convergence of political, religious and prophetic destinies into a single collective 'journey'. To Spenser the Ship of State boarded by Colin rather appears increasingly like a ship of fools: 'it scorned the dangers of the [water]; / Yet was it but a wooden frame and fraile, / Glewed togither with some subtile matter' (CCH 215–17).

Colin's disappointment and return is also rich in implications for Spenser's own changing understanding of the mission of poetry and his accordingly reconfigured poetic 'quest',[74] and bears out a double shift in focus that seems to characterise his later poetry: first, the poet's identity enters his allegory and his *oeuvre* with greater confidence in later years, refracted in numerous and complex ways that gesture towards the 'autobiographical', the intimate, private or even domestic.[75] This signals

---

[73] See Ch. 3, p. 87.

[74] Or, 'the imaginative journey which was the path followed by Spenser's own poetic career', David R. Shore, 'Spenser's *Colin Clouts Come Home Againe*: The Problem of Poetry', *English Studies in Canada* 8:3 (1982), 262–81, here 266.

[75] A particularly lucid reading of the late Spenser in this sense I find to be Louis A. Montrose, 'Spenser's Domestic Domain: Poetry, Property, and the Early Modern Subject', in Margreta de Grazia, Maureen Quilligan and Peter Stallybrass, eds, *Subject and Object in Renaissance Culture* (Cambridge: Cambridge University Press, 1996), pp. 83–130; see also Donald Cheney, 'Spenser's Fortieth Birthday and Related Fictions', *SpS* 4 (1984), 3–32; Miller, 'Spenser's Vocation, Spenser's Career', especially 217–25; Rambuss, *Spenser's Secret Career*, pp. 96–124. For a different view, insisting on Spenser's continued faith in his 'imperial' poetry to shape public, national and political identity, see for instance the work of Patrick Cheney, e.g. 'The Old Poet Presents Himself: *Prothalamion* as a Defense of Spenser's Career', *SpS* 8 (1990), 211–38; and more recently Thomas Herron, *Spenser's Irish Work: Poetry, Plantation, and Colonial Reformation* (Aldershot: Ashgate, 2007), especially pp. 147–83.

a move away from the concern with establishing the collective identity of his programmatic heroes and the 'fashioned gentleman' who is their integrated sum, towards an articulation of a private self, a self that appears however as an inadequate surrogate for a collective identity that is beyond the reach of the poet's stalled, possibly unravelling national epic.[76] Second, and as a consequence of this 'inward' movement, the poetry, and the *Faerie Queene* in particular, moves away from the search for a historico-political apotheosis towards pursuing a more intimate form of consummation, which may take a variety of overlapping forms: pastoral, erotic in the strict sense, neoplatonic or contemplative. Spenser's oblique self-representation and his loss of faith in 'political', imperial poetry thus appears to be feeding on a pattern shared by nearly all earlier quest-allegories, depicting a hero advancing through the stages of aspiration to virtue, desire for active service in the commonwealth, disillusion, and finally retreat into a solitary, contemplative form of transcendental poetic vision.

## Colin, Ireland, Elizabeth

Spenser's return to pastoral is of course one of the more conspicuous features of his late poetry, and it accordingly inflects his own self-perception in terms of a poetic quest. Spenser's late pastorals are marked by a concern with the local, topical and even topographical. The recognisably 'local' dimension of Spenser's pastoral in Book 6 of the *FQ* thus clearly marks a redrawing of the boundaries of the allegorical imagination, and does indeed invite speculation about the fiction's relationship to Spenser's 'real' life – to the extent to which the two are at all separable.[77] Following Book 5, where a more local and narrow form of historical contingency already begins to encroach on the visionary and genuinely 'apocalyptic' potential of allegory, Book 6 is played out in a more confined, intimate space that overlaps with that of Spenser's own Irish landscape. Whether this is in any sense autobiographical, and

---

[76] Andrew Hadfield, 'The *Faerie Queene*, Books IV–VII', in Hadfield, ed., *The Cambridge Companion to Spenser* (Cambridge: Cambridge University Press, 2001), pp. 124–42; Richard McCabe, 'Edmund Spenser, Poet of Exile', *Proceedings of the British Academy* 80 (1993), 73–103; Rajan, *The Form of the Unfinished*, pp. 44–84, esp. 54–5, 57–8 and 72–84.

[77] On the Irishness of Spenser's pastoral, see especially Benjamin P. Myers, 'The Green and the Golden World: Spenser's Rewriting of the Munster Plantation', *ELH* 76:2 (2009), 473–90. More broadly on the subject, see also the relevant sections in Thomas Herron, *Spenser's Irish Work*, esp. pp. 1–81; Richard McCabe, *Spenser's Monstrous Regiment*, esp. pp. 165–76 and 232–51; Andrew Hadfield, *Edmund Spenser's Irish Experience: Wilde Fruit and Salvage Soyl* (Oxford: Clarendon Press, 1997), esp. pp. 146–84; Willy Maley, *Salvaging Spenser: Colonialism, Culture, and Identity* (New York: St Martin's Press, 1997), esp. pp. 48–98. On the issue of the 'apprehensibility' of Spenser's own thought in his works, see especially the essays in *Spenser's Life and the Subject of Biography*, particularly the foreword and afterword by Anderson and Cheney, pp. ix–xiv and 172–8, and Vincent P. Carey and Clare L. Carroll, 'Factions and Fictions: Spenser's Reflections of and on Elizabethan Politics', pp. 31–44, especially pp. 31–2.

in what way, remains of course open to question, but what is undeniable is that Spenser invites his reader to ask a certain number of questions about the identity of the narrator, poet and colonial administrator in terms that earlier parts of the *Faerie Queene* had not prepared us for.

Colin's appearance in Canto x is the culminating moment of this reorientation. His appearance at the centre of the dancing graces follows immediately upon Calidore's decision, in Canto ix, to abandon his quest for the Blatant Beast in favour of a pastoral existence with the lovely Pastorella. Thematically, this desire by the titular hero of Book 6 to withdraw from the quest and 'lead . . . a life so free and fortunate, / From all the tempests of these worldly seas, / Which tosse the rest in daungerous disease' (*FQ* VI ix 19.3–5), raises the question of public duty to Gloriana, highlighted explicitly by the beginning of Canto x:

> WHO now does follow the foule *Blatant Beast*,
> Whilest *Calidore* does follow that faire Mayd,
> Vnmyndfull of his vow and high beheast,
> Which by the Faery Queene was on him layd? (*FQ* VI x 1.1–4)

This clearly sets the scene for Colin's reappearance, whose pastoral epiphany a little later in the canto is similarly presented as being in opposition with his service of the queen:

> Great Gloriana, greatest Maiesty,
> Pardon thy shepheard, mongst so many layes,
> As he hath sung of thee in all his dayes,
> To make one minime of thy poore handmayd (*FQ* VI x 28.3–6)

Colin's love for the 'countrey lasse' (*FQ* VI x 25.8) is thus charged with implications analogous to those of Calidore's love for Pastorella, distracting both knight and poet from their respective quests in honour of Gloriana.

The substitution of the 'countrey lasse' for the queen here also contributes to refocusing poetry as a more private affair. Alluding to Spenser's own, very real marriage to Elizabeth Boyle, the celebration of the queen's 'handmayd', even though it merely lasts the length of 'one minime', has a profoundly destabilising effect on the original purpose of Spenser's national epic. As is suggested by his play on the 'three Elizabeths' in his life elsewhere (*Am* 74), surely Spenser is only too clearly aware of the potential irony of the implicit substitution of one Elizabeth for another at this stage, at the centre of the final 'allegorical core'[78] of the poem as we have it: his ostensible apology for such a substitution only further focalises the readers' attention on the change of direction in his own poetic quest. Colin's vision thus steps in to replace the frustrated hope for dynastic marriage that would have enabled epic closure, and also provides a surrogate for the unconsummated apocalyptic marriage of Redcrosse and Una that was glimpsed in Book I. In both cases, crucially,

---

[78] The expression comes from Lewis, *Allegory of Love*, p. 334.

we are looking at a *private*, personal event that is made to appear as a compensation for a failed *public*, historical apotheosis.[79] Regardless of Spenser's 'true', but ultimately inaccessible feelings towards his wife, his queen, his country and his epic, this is the manner in which he chooses to represent them in his poetry.

Accordingly, marriage takes on a central role in Spenser's later poetry more generally, most notably the *Amoretti* and the *Epithalamion*, where Spenser revises the traditions of Petrarchan love poetry to celebrate his own union with Elizabeth Boyle according to the Protestant ideal of the married life. The two works, published jointly and intended as a sequence, strive to assuage what Richard McCabe has designated as the 'inadequacy of mere betrothal' that haunts Spenser's *oeuvre*.[80] The collection has been described as attempting to carve out an 'edenic' pastoral *locus* as a setting for a private consummation,[81] an experience that is only briefly adumbrated in Colin's shattered vision (*FQ* VI x). Such a vision of private bliss ultimately finds no legitimate place in the world of Spenser's national epic and needs to be relocated to an independent collection of verse. Here the beloved appears as a the ultimate 'haven' or 'harbour' of the poet's now transformed poetic voyage, in an image that once more plays on the poet's metaphorical quest or sea-voyage:[82]

> After long stormes and tempests sad assay,
> . . .
> . . . my silly barke was tossed sore:
> I doe at length descry the happy shore,
> In which I hope ere long for to arryue,
> Fayre soyle it seemes from far and fraught with store
> Of all that deare and daynty is alyue.
> . . .
> All paines are nothing in respect of this,
> All sorrowes short that gaine eternall blisse. (*Am* 63)

Retrospectively, the allegory in the *Amoretti* overwrites Colin's earlier journey to the English court, itself figured as a navigation that parodies an eschatological journey. Playing also on the Petrarchan echoes of the ship imagery,[83] it is now the poet's beloved, not England, who is presented in terms of Deguileville's eschatological homeland, the 'happy shore . . . fayre soyle . . . fraught with store', thus conflating spiritual and erotic apotheosis.[84]

The image also threatens to displace or at least 'divert' the poet's epic journey

---

[79] Montrose, 'Spenser's Domestic Domain', pp. 111–14; McCabe, *Spenser's Monstrous Regiment*, pp. 247–50.

[80] McCabe, *Shorter Poems*, p. 667.

[81] John D. Bernard, 'Spenserian Pastoral and the *Amoretti*', *ELH* 47:3 (1980), 419–32.

[82] See Bernard, 'Spenserian Pastoral and the *Amoretti*', 425.

[83] Jason Lawrence, 'Spenser and Italian Literature', in McCabe, ed., *Oxford Handbook of Edmund Spenser*, pp. 614–15.

[84] See especially Donna Gibbs, *Spenser's Amoretti: A Critical Study* (Aldershot: Scolar Press, 1990), pp. 139–74.

that Book 6 figures so ubiquitously as sea-travel, by redefining the ultimate 'haven' of the poet's quest in terms of the personal devotion to his beloved instead of the political allegiance to his queen. In order to advance his vision of amorous mutuality,[85] Spenser here deconstructs the familiar Petrarchan *topoi* of an unattainable, cruel beloved; but in doing so he equally dismantles the very discourse of courtship that is the foundation of Montrose's 'Elizabethan political imaginary', where those same Petrarchan motifs figure a desire for political 'involvement' with the queen, herself imagined as an inaccessible Petrarchan Lady. If it is true that 'love is not love'[86] for the makers of the English court – like those visited and castigated by Colin (*CCH* 771–894) – then Spenser's rejection of this role as courtly suitor, Colin's return to Ireland, the publication of the marriage collection and the reappearance of Colin in Book 6 to sing the praises of the 'countrey lasse', suggest that in Spenser's later poetry sometimes 'love *is* love'. Only the amorous mutuality found in married love can assuage the lack of a productive relationship of patronage with the English queen and court.

Spenser deliberately highlights his own operation of substitution by presenting his beloved, a new Elizabeth, as 'some mayden Queene' (*Ep* 158). The marriage is celebrated as a *personal* consummation saturated with 'autobiographical' references, and Spenser makes it explicit that he is engaging in a self-indulgent, even solipsistic exercise: 'So I vnto my selfe alone will sing' (*Ep* 17). More importantly, however, this inward turn threatens to displace the focus on a more public, dynastic or prophetic marriage in the earlier poetry.[87] Spenser still looks forward towards a cosmic, apocalyptic consummation shadowed in an 'endlesse matrimony' (*Ep* 217), but that consummation, crucially, is no longer conceived in historico-political terms. Gone is the expectation for a fulfilment of Redcrosse's betrothal to Una on the plane of national history, and instead it is the personal history of Spenser's own marriage to Elizabeth Boyle that is felt to be 'signifying unto us the mistical union that is betwixt Christ and his Churche', as the Book of Common Prayer (1559) has it.[88] Not only has Spenser substituted one Elizabeth for another, but he has found in his own marriage the fulfilment of the promise of both apocalyptic union and 'epic' closure left hanging ever since the end of Book 1.

## 'deepe within the mynd'

This increased focus on more private, 'autobiographical' form of interiority is equally manifest in Spenser's late 'neoplatonic' streak, which again is timidly glimpsed during

---

[85]  See also Klein, '"Let us love, dear love, lyke as we ought"', esp. 112.

[86]  Marotti, '"Love Is Not Love"'.

[87]  Joanne Craig, 'The Queen, Her Handmaid, and Spenser's Career', *English Studies in Canada* 12 (1986), 255–68.

[88]  Available at: http://justus.anglican.org/resources/bcp/1559/Marriage_1559.htm [accessed 12 February 2012].

Colin's vision on Mount Acidale, but must be relocated like his marriage poetry to a different poetic form in order to be more fully explored. The poetic quest here no longer passes through chivalric and military action in Fairyland: 'the lover's experience, no longer a quest, is stripped of all its chivalric glamour'.[89] Spenser combines and reconfigures neoplatonic and Christian notions of love in order to sanctify human *eros*, understood as a pre-figuration of the divine love that both fulfils and ontologically transcends it.[90] Placed within such a neoplatonic cosmos, human *eros* explicitly subsumes and transcends dynastic and political history:

> Yet fairer is that heauen, in which doe raine
> The soueraine *Powres* and mightie *Potentates*,
> Which *in their high protections doe containe*
> *All mortall Princes, and imperiall States;*
> And fayrer yet, whereas the royall Seates
> And heauenly *Dominations* are set,
> From whom all earthly gouernance is fet. [my italics ll. 87–8] (*HHB* 85–91)

The individual human experience of love reverberates with echoes of universal and divine concord, and accordingly neoplatonic *eros*, rightly conceived, is ultimately identical with *agape*.[91] Thus, if in the *Epithalamion* it is Elizabeth Boyle who takes over from Gloriana as 'some mayden Queene' (*Ep* 158), here Gloriana, metonymy of the earlier concern with the political, is doubly displaced by both earthly *Pleasure*, 'crowne[d] . . . Goddesse and . . . Queene' (*HL* 292) and by divine *Sapience*, 'Clad like a Queene in royall robes' (*HHB* 185).

Whether the new Spenserean turn 'deepe within the mynd' (*FQ* VI Proem 5.8) is inherently 'escapist', and in what sense, is largely a matter of definitions – and ultimately matters less than the fact that Spenser seems to be all too aware that his new vision is inherently problematic, fragile and transitory, despite even the exalted Neoplatonic developments of the *Fowre Hymnes*. Spenser knows that by 'fixing' his poetic vision in the human, earthly framework of an idyllic married life in a distinctively Irish topography, he is exposing his vision to the ravages of time, history and contingency. Already Canto x, the very canto of Colin's vision, contains the prophecy of its undoing: Colin's dance is interrupted by Calidore, the representative of the reality of the court that is inevitably bound to catch up with Spenser. More worryingly still, Calidore's own idyll is equally shattered by the arrival of the brigands at the end of the same canto (*FQ* VI x 39–43) – a chillingly accurate prophecy of

---

[89] Terry Comito, 'A Dialectic of Images in Spenser's *Fowre Hymnes*', *Studies in Philology* 74 (1977), 301–21, here 306, speaking of the *HHB*.

[90] In my reading of the *Fowre Hymnes* here I draw particularly on Elizabeth Biemann, *Plato Baptized: Towards the Interpretation of Spenser's Mimetic Fictions* (Toronto: University of Toronto Press, 1988), pp. 153–62. I believe however that Spenser's faith in the neoplatonic vision of both the *Hymnes* and the *Amoretti* and *Epithalamion* is far from unproblematic, as I develop below.

[91] Bieman, *Plato Baptized*, p. 156.

Spenser's later displacement from Kilcolman in 1598 at the hands of the same 'brigands'. With the benefit of hindsight, then, it becomes clear that even the 'personal history' Spenser would like to write in his late poetry, necessarily partakes in a larger, 'national history'. This is particularly true for Spenser the planter and social climber entrenched in Kilcolman, whose fortunes, like it or not, are inextricably tied up with the destiny of the political body he needs must represent. Spenser indeed doubly 'represents' English colonial rule in Ireland, both by being its representative, its agent and administrator, and by himself becoming its symptomatic 'representation', the very picture of its failures. Despite his efforts to dissociate himself from the wider body politic, Spenser paradoxically ends up embodying precisely the destiny of the political entity he is trying to escape.

This awareness of potential failure and frustration is not merely retrospective, but already haunts the *Amoretti* and the *Fowre Hymnes*, where the possibility of an amorous and spiritual apotheosis that promises an escape from the narrow horizons of time-bound earthly existence is glimpsed but never fully grasped. The narrator in the *Amoretti* is constantly torn between two types of love that he only manages to balance fleetingly and inconclusively. Time and again he becomes painfully aware of the impossibility of discerning ennobling *eros* (as bridge to *agape*) from mere concupiscent desire. Sonnet 72 brilliantly articulates the lover's doubts and anxieties about the problematic status of his own idyll:

> Oft when my spirit doth spred her bolder winges,
> In mind to mount vp to purest sky:
> it down is weighd with thoght of earthly things
> and clogd with burden of mortality,
> Where when that souerayne beauty it doth spy,
> resembling heuens glory in her light:
> *drawne with sweet pleasures bayt, it back doth fly,*
> *and vnto heauen forgets her former flight.*
> There my fraile fancy fed with full delight,
> doth bath in blisse and mantleth most at ease:
> *ne thinks of other heauen, but how it might*
> *her harts desire with most contentment please.*
> Hart need not wish none other happinesse,
> but here on earth to haue such heuens blisse. [my italics] (*Am* 72)

Similarly, the *Hymnes* make use of highly sensual imagery in their depiction of the 'Paradize / Of all delight, and ioyous happie rest' (*HL* 281–2), terms that in Spenser's mouth resonate with highly problematic recollections of Redcrosse's foundational 'delight' in the forest of Book 1 (*FQ* I i 10.1). More explicit still, *Amoretti* 76 develops the profound ambivalence of this 'neast of loue, the lodging of delight: / the bowre of blisse, the paradice of pleasure, / the sacred harbour of that heuenly spright' (*Am* 76, 2–4). To any dedicated reader of Spenser the double reminiscence of Spenser's archetypal amorous *loci*, the Bower of Bliss and the Garden of Adonis, is impossible to miss, and creates a profound ambivalence that reactivates the full range of epistemological anxiety that runs through Spenser's entire *oeuvre*. The same sinister echoes of the Bower of Bliss also resonate throughout Book 6, especially on Mount Acidale: I would suggest with Nohrnberg that here too, as in *Amoretti* 76, Spenser does not evoke the Garden without also simultaneously sending us back to the Bower of Bliss.[92] Although the immediate context of Colin's vision on Acidale is undoubtedly positive, it occurs within a wider framework that is inherently problematic: Book 6 as a whole is in fact introduced by words that are dangerously reminiscent of the vocabulary of sensual self-abandon found in the Bower (*FQ* II xii 58–9), and cast a rather more sinister light over the action that follows, including its exalted vision glimpsed at the heart of its 'allegorical core':

> The waies, through which my weary steps I guyde,
> In this *delightfull* land of Faery,
> Are so exceeding spacious and wyde,
> And sprinckled with such *sweet* variety,
> Of all that *pleasant* is to eare or eye,
> That I nigh *rauisht with rare thoughts delight*,
> *My tedious trauell doe forget thereby* [my italics] (*FQ* VI Proem 1.1–7)

Of course, this is not how the stanza ends; the stanza does continue and Spenser *does* continue his poetic quest, but his claim that 'when I gin to feele decay of might, / It strength to me supplies, and chears my dulled spright' (*FQ* VI Proem 1.8–9) I find impossible to take at face value: how can the very charms of repose and sensual delight become for Spenser – of all poets – an incentive to persevere on the quest? Once more the poet here warns us about the charms of sensual self-abandon, but he now expects this to apply to our understanding of his own poetic quest. Clearly, the political instability associated with the conspicuously Irish setting of Book 6 becomes a brilliant figure for Spenser's own anxiety about the status of the new vision he articulates in his later works. It is less a matter of alluding to either a *locus amoenus in bono* or *in malo*, than of suggesting that even as late as Book 6 and 1595–6 it may have been impossible for Spenser himself to discriminate fully between the two.

If we accept that indeed Spenser deliberately presents his own vision, along with Colin's, in such an ambivalent light, this has a number of implications for our understanding of the nuances of Spenser's later, 'domestic' poetry. The numerous expressions of doubt and uncertainty ask us, at the very least, to mitigate our belief in Spenser's faith in the 'alternative' poetic vision that inflects, counterpoints or even replaces his earlier 'epic' vision. The 'inward' turn may be perceived as a relief from public duty at some basic level, but ultimately Spenser, like René d'Anjou, is aware that by formulating an ostensibly private, self-centred vision, he is also indulging in an operation of self-deception and wishful thinking. Spenser is all too clearly aware of this, and begins

---

[92] James Nohrnberg, 'Acidale', in Hamilton, ed., *Spenser Encyclopedia*, pp. 4–6.

to toy with a much more radical *contemptus mundi*, as expressed in the desire to 'Mount vp aloft through heauenly contemplation, / From this darke world' (*HHB* 136–7).[93]

## Mutabilitie

The *Mutabilite Cantos* have long acted as a watershed for Spenserean criticism, polarising views not only about the *Cantos* themselves, but about the entire *Faerie Queene*. The *Cantos*, following the lead of William Blissett,[94] indeed appear as a retrospective commentary on Spenser's allegory, *oeuvre* and life, and accordingly attract a steady flow of critical attention.[95] Readings of the *Cantos* have traditionally tended to fall into one of two 'camps', with critics finding in them either a tone of desperate and bitter resignation, or on the contrary an exalted contemplative apotheosis.[96] Recent readings have tended to become much more nuanced and complex of course, but the cantos remain a pivotal episode for our understanding of Spenser's work and life, and the question of how seriously Spenser took his concluding prayer in the 'unperfite' Canto viii remains central.[97]

If the *Cantos* were indeed written at the very end of Spenser's career, looking back on his life, career and allegory after the destruction of Kilcolman during Tyrone's rebellion in 1598,[98] then their importance as a retrospective meditation on the 'quest' that precedes is crucial. In the course of this chapter, I have suggested that the literary tradition of the quest-allegory provides a number of powerful intertexts for the allegory of the *Faerie Queene*. I have also tried to illustrate how that same literary tradition provides a model for Spenser's self-representation in terms a poetic and personal quest that seeks to balance and integrate temporal, historical and earthly existence on the one hand, and a transcendental vanishing point on the other. In this sense, the *Mutabilitie Cantos* stand as a revealing

---

[93] This pessimistic, 'ascetic' understanding of fallen man's inability to transcend earthly attachment is, sustained also by Spenser's Calvinism, often invoked by readings of the *Hymnes* that see the poems as articulating a radical opposition between earthly and heavenly love. See e.g. discussion in Bieman, *Plato Baptized*, pp. 153–5.

[94] William Blissett, 'Spenser's Mutabilitie', in Millar MacClure and F. W. Watt, eds, *Essays in Literature from the Renaissance to the Victorian Age* (Toronto: University of Toronto Press, 1964), pp. 26–42.

[95] For a recent collection of essays focusing exclusively on the *Cantos*, see Jane Grogan, ed., *Celebrating Mutability: Essays on Edmund Spenser's* Mutabilitie Cantos (Manchester: Manchester University Press, 2010).

[96] For the darker reading of Mutability, arguing for the 'unconvincing' nature of Spenser's concluding prayer, see especially Kenneth Gross, *Spenserian Poetics: Idolatry, Iconoclasm, and Magic* (Ithaca, NJ: Cornell University Press, 1985), pp. 234–52. For a more positive appreciation of Spenser's 'faith' in the final prayer, see for instance, Bieman, *Plato Baptised*, pp. 212–14.

[97] A particularly useful account, including extensive references to earlier scholarship, I find to be Lethbridge's, 'Spenser's Last Days', especially pp. 313–33, which has considerably shaped my own thinking about the *Cantos*. See also Grogan, 'Introduction', *Celebrating Mutability*, p. 10.

[98] Lethbridge's, 'Spenser's Last Days', pp. 318–26.

conclusion to that quest: like the quests of Hawes, Lewkenor and Bateman, Spenser's quest ends not so much with the attainment of the apotheosis that his knightly heroes – and their authors – set out to seek, but rather with a radical refocusing of the quest itself on a transcendental vanishing point, in at least partial contradiction with the initial attempt to direct the quest towards a secular, earthly and historical apotheosis. This, coming after six dense books of adventures in Fairyland, may appear as an abrupt surrogate apotheosis, and a number of critics accordingly perceive the 'ending' provided by the *Cantos* as 'desperate', 'dark . . . and tragic', a 'shrill cry' or an expression of 'lonely and bitter [faith]',[99] because of its shift to an entirely different register alien to Spenser's commitment to promote an ideal of *vita activa*. And a shift there is,[100] and not merely a rhetorical shift, but an ontological leap – and my contention here is that the study of the allegorical quest tradition presented in this book as a whole should predispose us, at the very least, to responding more sympathetically to Spenser's transcendentalising leap at the end of the poem. In fact, in the light of the very structural conditions inherent in the kind of allegory Spenser is writing, this leap is inevitable.

Over thirty years ago Thomas Cain characterised the *Mutabilite Cantos* in a way that powerfully anticipates both my own reading, and the central contention of this book as a whole. I quote the passage at length, in the hope that Cain's rather general commentary will resonate with the more specific details of the readings I have offered in what precedes:

> Underlying the last two stanzas of the *Cantos* is the Augustinian metaphor, central to medieval culture, of Christian man as a pilgrim seeking his heavenly home while journeying through the world's tribulations. The corresponding Renaissance metaphor receives its classical formulation in the ebullient *Oration on Human Dignity* where Pico urges man's potential for emulating the highest angels in honor and intelligence, to the point of assuming a place just beneath God himself. The *Faerie Queene* begins with just such humanist idealism. Its main encomiastic symbol is a British Queen initially hymned as mediatrix between man and God. By naming her first type Una, Spenser implies that Elizabeth unites man's earthly and heavenly roles, and Contemplation explains Gloriana to Redcrosse in exactly these terms. Such idealism is essential to serious encomium. But the books of 1596 make us aware of increasingly urgent tensions in this idealism that undermine encomium and exacerbate separation of the hero from his goal and the real queen from her heavenly image. When great Renaissance attempts at

---

[99] Respectively, Hadfield, *Spenser's Irish Experience*, p. 200; Elizabeth Fowler, 'The Failure of Moral Philosophy in the Work of Edmund Spenser', *Representations* 51 (1995), 47–76, here 70; Gross, *Spenserian Poetics*, p. 237; Thomas Greene, *The Descent from Heaven: A Study in Epic Continuity* (New Haven, CT: Yale University Press, 1963), p. 323, quoted in Gross, *Spenserian Poetics*, p. 237.

[100] Most recently, see for instance Jane Grogan: '[The *Cantos*] allow for – even solicit? – a renewal of moral, social and political values, this time adjusted not to contemporary exigencies of historical paradigms of order or teleology but by the newly conceived eschatological scenario announced by Nature', 'Introduction', *Celebrating Mutabilitie*, p. 8.

synthesis founder, they sometimes fall back on old medieval certainties. . . . But when the *Mutabilitie Cantos*, and, more broadly, the *Faerie Queene*, conclude with the authorial voice speaking as a pilgrim who sees earthly experience in terms of *contemptus mundi* and the heavenly Sabbath as his only true home, the failure that this betokens for the poem as encomium – as a unitive statement made possible by a queen who invites and fulfills idealization – lies in the collapse of the claim that England partakes in Jerusalem, and a concomitant return to the Augustinian sense that the City of This World opposes the City of God.[101]

Much in this account is likely to strike us as problematic: the notion of *contemptus mundi*, a perhaps blunt characterisation of Spenser's initial intentions and subsequent disappointment, even the now possibly untenable notions of a 'Renaissance' and 'Humanism' as Cain evokes them with reference to Pico and of course the very dichotomy of the 'Renaissance' and the 'medieval'. Cain's analysis can and should of course be qualified by later and more nuanced discussions, but none of these persuade me that Cain's basic point should not nevertheless stand. Indeed, I feel that there is in Cain's own judgement greater sense than he may himself have suspected at the time, and this book as a whole may indeed be thought of as fleshing out, with reference to a specific filiation of texts, Cain's 'intuitive' assessment of the importance of the pilgrimage allegory for Spenser's thought.[102]

The most conspicuous form taken by the influence of the quest-allegory tradition on Spenser is the tenacious resistance of an originally transcendentalising pilgrimage narrative to any successful form of 'secularisation'. Neither Spenser nor any of his predecessors in the tradition manage to balance Deguileville's ascetic paradigm with a sustainable positive view of the active life in the historical and secular world. The *Faerie Queene* is framed, bracketed by such transcendentalism at both ends: on the one hand, we have the foundational and programmatic account of Redcrosse's quest and vision of the Holy City in Book 1, and on the other the *Mutabilitie Cantos* in Book 7: both moments gesture towards a specifically Augustinian – or Deguilevillian – notion of pilgrimage. It is striking that despite the whole distance that Spenser's knights have covered from Book 1 to Book 7, and despite the distance covered by the tradition itself from Deguileville to Spenser, the poem should come full circle back to the Deguilevillian notion of an ascetic pilgrimage in the *Mutabilitie Cantos*. By returning to such a notion of pilgrimage leading *out* of the world, Spenser too is at some level taking leave, closing the door on Gloriana's England, on Ireland, the *Faerie Queene* and the world. He is also doing so with a degree of calm composure that in the aftermath of the destruction of Kilcolman and his expulsion from Ireland I find remarkable, and yet highly typical of Spenser at his most dignified and metaphysical.[103]

---

[101] Thomas H. Cain, *Praise in* The Faerie Queene (Lincoln, NE: University of Nebraska Press, 1978), p. 184.

[102] See also the recent references, and call for revaluating the entire tradition in Borris, 'Allegory, Emblem and Symbol', here 451–4.

[103] My own reading here is close to Lethbridge, 'Spenser's Last Days'.

A number of readings discuss the *Cantos* as performing something quite different from the 'withdrawal' or 'leave-taking' I emphasise here: a lot of attention has been paid in particular to the Irish topography of the *Cantos*, and to the use of legal terminology during Mutability's trial, reminiscent in many ways of the controversies over land tenure in Spenser's contemporary Ireland – controversies of which Spenser himself, as Sheriff of Cork and tenant of Kilcolman, had first-hand experience.[104] Both trends would tend to point to rather more localised, even topical meanings, and some readings have accordingly argued that Spenser's concern here is and remains, until the bitter end, the fate of English colonial rule in Ireland. Yet it seems to me that while it is undeniable that Ireland is a powerful presence in the *Cantos*, it does not necessarily follow that the *Cantos* are necessarily and primarily *about* Ireland.

Montrose observed that the *Cantos* are 'Spenser's most remarkable conjunction of the universal and the particular, the cosmic and the personal',[105] but what is the nature of the relationship between those two terms? While I agree with Richard McCabe and others that Book 7 *can* be read, and indeed *was* read by Spenser's immediate posterity as a forward-looking commentary and warning on the fate of the Irish plantation after Spenser's own time, I also think that this is only one side of the coin. Lethbridge develops Montrose's point to argue more specifically that events in Ireland are 'a *source* for, rather than the *subject* of the cantos', and I also agree with Lethbridge's observation that from Spenser's own, personal point of view – insofar as it can be abstracted from a broader 'political' statement at all – '[t]here is no earthly future at all: the next port is heaven'.[106] The two claims are clearly not contradictory, and surely nothing impeded Spenser from realising that even though *he* was coming to the end of the road, the English struggle for colonial rule had not ended and that his successors would have to face the same kind of resistance and rebellion that had driven him from Kilcolman. Spenser's very last words do not only *allow* for such a double reading, but insistently *demand* it: it is a vision of both labour and rest, continued antagonism and final deliverance. Spenser addresses the 'Sabbaoth God', God of battles and earthly struggle, as if to emphasise the ongoing struggle for civility in Ireland; but his prayer to that God is not a prayer for victory, but a prayer for deliverance and peace, the rest of the 'Sabaoths sight' (*FQ* VII viii 2.9).[107]

The concern with Irish matters in reality is only a counterpoint to the main

---

[104] See, variously, Patricia Coughlan, 'The Local Context of Mutabilitie's Plea', *Irish University Review* 26:2 (1996), 320–41; Herron, *Spenser's Irish Work*, pp. 148–63; Judith Owens, 'Professing Ireland in the Woods of Spenser's Mutabilitie', *Explorations in Renaissance Culture* 29:1 (2003), 1–22; Hadfield, *Spenser's Irish Experience*, pp. 185–202; McCabe, *Spenser's Monstrous Regiment*, pp. 253–69. For a discussion of the jurisprudential register in Spenser, see Fowler, 'The Failure of Moral Philosophy'.

[105] Montrose, 'Spenser's Domestic Domain', p. 105.

[106] Lethbridge, 'Spenser's Last Days', pp. 325–6 (emphasis mine); McCabe, *Spenser's Monstrous Regiment*, pp. 253–69, especially 268–9.

[107] For the implications of the two variant spellings, see the notes in the Hamilton edition. For an elaboration of the idea, see for instance McCabe, 'Edmund Spenser, Poet of Exile', pp. 102–3.

melody of Spenser's song, whose subject is rather the cosmic significance of such events. No longer does the poetry attempt to resist, shape or direct the contingencies of historical, political and earthly 'change'; rather, by embracing and accepting the recalcitrance of such contingent, sublunary change to be shaped by human effort, and by accepting the human inability to perceive, understand and implement a providential scheme of being, Spenser paradoxically reaffirms his stoic faith[108] in such providential control – a profession of faith that gains authority not *in spite of*, but precisely *thanks to* the poet's inability to sound the depths of providence. We may choose, of course, to resist such a reading, arguing that it is postulated on an arguably 'perverse' reasoning, and yet I would suggest that this shift is not merely a last-minute conversion, a 'desperate' last resort, but rather a return to first principles of an Edmund Spenser who is a resolutely transcendentalising poet.

## Last Things and First Beginnings

To unpack this claim I would like to develop a final aspect of Spenser's departure from the allegorical quest tradition, a departure that shows Spenser as having internalised the Deguilevillian paradigm, but grafting its implications onto rather different philosophical and poetic discourses. Deguileville's allegory begins and ends with an eschatological vision that in various and complex ways resonates throughout the entire quest-allegory tradition. It is in a way surprising that Spenser, for whom the Heavenly City is such a powerful vanishing point for the entire allegory in Book 1, should chose *not* to employ the city when it comes to articulating his highest apocalyptic vision in Book 7. The City indeed is conspicuously absent as a final eschatological signifier in Spenser's apocalyptic vision on Arlo Hill, where he uses very different imagery. In Book 1 Spenser had clearly envisaged the possibility of building a bridge between the City of Man and the City of God, an idea implicit in the typological relationship between the two cities of *Cleopolis* and *Hierusalem* sketched by the hermit Contemplation: there the superior splendour of the latter does not so much eclipse the former as provide its fulfilment and apotheosis (*FQ* I x 57–61). But neither the poem, nor, more importantly, the historical events that nourish the poem ultimately ever manage to build such a bridge.

---

[108] I choose the expression 'stoic faith' carefully and consciously, to indicate how Spenser's attitude is inflected by a neostoic discourse, supplemented, however, by a specifically protestant act of 'faith', as is argued by Christopher Burlinson, 'Spenser's "Legend of Caonstancie": Book VII and the Ethical Reader', in Grogan, *Celebrating Mutabilitie*, pp. 201–19, e.g. : '[T]here is a difference between the narrator of the *Mutabilitie Cantos* and the Senecan and Montaignian stoic ... [T]he constancy of Spenser's narrator emerges through *faith*, not reason', p. 208. For a more mitigated view along similar lines, emphasising hardship and uncertainty, see also Ayesha Ramachandran, 'Mutabilitie's Lucretian Metaphysics: Scepticism and Cosmic Process in Spenser's *Cantos*', in the same collection, pp. 220–45.

This would hardly have come as a complete surprise to Spenser, whose foundational poetic act was the publication of *Theatre for Voluptuous Worldlings* in 1569, a collection that develops the perceived vanity of a double imperial/papal Rome into a broader meditation on mutability sustained by apocalyptic vision. The collection is foundational in the sense that it establishes a distinctive aesthetic of decline, mutability and ruin through the use, or rather 'deconstruction', of the architectural metaphor of the 'City' and its associated semantic field. As Anne Lake Prescott has observed, '[s]ometime during the 1570s [Spenser] began absorbing both a set of topics (mutability, the translation of empire) or pictures (a wailing female city, a moribund tree) and a complex of words and phrases that helped structure his literary thought, making a grid through which he could often feel or perceive.'[109] The image of the City as a visualisation of frustrated imperial aspirations necessarily disrupts the more traditional, Deguilevillian iconography of the heavenly City as a signifier of eschatological resolution, and pushes Spenser to look for alternative figures. Accordingly, the apotheosis of the *Mutabilitie Cantos*, of a very different nature than the one originally envisaged, takes place in the distinctively rural setting of Arlo Hill, and thus overwrites or displaces the urban, epic and imperial associations triggered by the New Jerusalem. Prescott makes a similar point: 'Architecturally speaking, the *translatio imperii* . . . can go no farther. Rome – like Jerusalem and maybe even Troynovaunt – has died and gone to heaven.'[110] It is certainly not accidental that in the *Cantos*, in the wake of the destruction of Spenser's own private 'citadel' of Kilcolman, architectural metaphor appears as even more ill-suited to carrying the burden of eschatological deliverance – except in its metonymic refraction as those ethereal 'pillours of Eternity' (*FQ* VII viii 2.4) glimpsed in the final prayer. Spenser's final apocalypse is a vision that accepts and delights in change, embracing and submitting to the continuous metamorphosis of form rather than enshrining it in a vision of citizenship or architectural permanence.[111]

Ultimately, the absence of the figure of the City from Spenser's apocalyptic vision in *Mutabilitie* amounts to nothing short of a rejection of the possibility of finding an apotheosis for his allegory *in history*: this rejection is founded on the realisation that a the eschatological-imperial symbolism of the city is only too easily misappropriated to glorify temporal rule: the roman papacy of course provides the foundational example in Spenser's work, but more dangerously the same strategy

---

[109] Prescott, 'Spenser (Re)Reading Du Bellay', p. 137.

[110] Prescott, 'Spenser (Re)Reading Du Bellay', p. 145. For another reading emphasising such 'implicit' eschatological reference to the New Jerusalem in Mutability, see also Sandler, 'The Faerie Queene: An Elizabethan Apocalypse', pp. 168–71.

[111] For the important remark that Spenser accepts Mutabilite's claim to rule the earthly domain, see Bieman, *Plato Baptized*, p. 228. This insight is essential in the development of the reading offered by James Nohrnberg, 'Supplementing Spenser's Supplement, a Masque in Several Scenes: Eight Literary-Critical Meditations on a Renaissance Numen called *Mutabilitie*', in Grogan, ed., *Celebrating Mutabilitie*, pp. 85–136, particularly pp. 102–7.

had been adopted by the 'godly' nation of England in the aftermath of Bale[112] and the Armada. Closer to Spenser's 'home' in Ireland, colonial planter ideology often availed itself of the image of the Heavenly City to promote the ideal vision of a 'domesticated' Ireland as a 'civilised pastoral New Jerusalem'.[113] Yet Spenser's suspicion of crystallisations in history – ecclesiastical, political, imperial, personal – are too deep-seated to ever allow him to fully believe in the possibility of bringing the New Jerusalem to earth, and again the central insight of Bateman's *Travayled Pylgrime* is lurking in the background here. Spenser never quite forgets that the eternal can never inhabit the temporal, but only be momentarily refracted in it. It is this insight, clearly discernible well before we get to the *Mutabilitie Cantos*, which alone remains constant throughout Spenser's life and career, from the *Theatre for Voluptuous Worldlings*, through Redcrosse's deferred marriage, through Spenser's own misgivings about his own erotic idyll, all the way to the prayer for the 'Sabaoths sight' (*FQ* VII viii 2.9) that remains beyond the grasp of the poem. It is also this same insight, sustained by an eminently Protestant distrust of potentially idolatrous 'crystallisations' in history, that indelibly marks Spenser as a profoundly meta-physical, apocalyptic and ultimately transcendentalising poet.

This final return to a transcendent eschatology is both 'typical' – in the sense that it occurs throughout the quest-allegory tradition – and uniquely Spenserean. Spenser's distinctiveness in this sense is that he avoids the bitterness and anxiety so often associated with the 'failure' of the quest in his predecessors, and finds instead a serenity in reaffirming the primacy of transcendence, not unlike the one found in Goodyear who from the start sets out to bypass the topical relevance of his allegory to seek deliverance from the burden of historical contingency. Strikingly, Spenser sacrifices none of the emotional intensity of his disappointment, but manages, as it were, to transcend the very real and intense human emotion triggered by the failures of his personal, political and poetic aspirations, to transmute that bitterness into the calm confidence that pervades the 'vnperfite' ending of the seventh book[114] – an ending 'all the more exact for being incomplete'.[115] This inability to visualize an apocalyptic scenario, then, is not so much the expression of deep-seated meta-physical anxiety, as a number of 'deconstructive' readings maintain, but rather the natural form taken by the calm acceptance of man's inability to anticipate and 'see'

---

[112] On Bale's influence on the belief of establishing a Heavenly Jerusalem 'on earth', see for instance Norbrook, *Poetry and Politics*, p. 34. For a further discussion of 'ruined cities' as emblems of imperial failure in Spenser's early poetry, and their influence on his mitigated belief in the very possibility of empire – Roman as well as English – see also McCabe, *Spenser's Monstrous Regiment*, pp. 25–7.

[113] See especially the numerous evocations of this idea in Herron, *Spenser's Irish Work*, pp. 12, 26, 54–62, 140–3, here quoting p. 54. Herron, however, is more optimistic concerning Spenser's continued faith in the usefulness of this notion for implementing the colonial 'civilising' process.

[114] Again, here my reading is indebted to Lethbridge, 'Spenser's Last Days'.

[115] Richard McCabe, *The Pillars of Eternity: Time and Providence in* The Faerie Queene (Dublin: Irish Academic Press, 1989), p. 224.

fully, face to face the reality of the *eschaton* before its occurrence. Spenser's final prayer is for a 'Saboaths sight', but that sight is a blank slate. It is beyond form, beyond 'doubtful Allegories' prone to misconstruction (cf. *LR* 3) that Spenser situates the most elevated eschatological moment.

It is also significant that this metaphysical leap is articulated in terms of a prayer for a 'Saboaths sight' which suggests an interesting shift from the agency of the written, authored *word* of the poet to a *vision* that is given, offered gratuitously by the deity. The 'happie rest' desired in *An Hymne in Honour of Love* (281) is thus no longer of the poet's, the planter's or the husband's making but becomes a deferred but intensely 'Real' sight that symptomatically is never 'revealed', described or even 'shadowed' in the poem as we have it. The poem does of course provide 'Mirrours more then one' (*FQ* III Proem 5.6), but none of them reflects, like Deguileville's, the ultimate reality of the eschatological *locus*. And whereas this absence may surely be construed as expressing something like 'metaphysical anxiety', I would argue instead that it reinforces and reiterates the intensity of Spenser's encounter with the metaphysical – all the more powerful for being absent, deferred, and only accessible through indirection and prayer. If anything, Spenser the sceptic is a more challenging and more deeply transcendentalising metaphysical thinker than his (seemingly) confident ancestor Deguileville, who avails himself of the traditional, sanctified image of the Heavenly City to represent union with the divine. Spenser replaces the city as eschatological *locus* with the unlocalised emptiness of the 'Sabaoth's sight', which alone can signify the incommensurable nature of the divine.

In the closing lines the arch-image-maker Spenser – with his anxieties about his own art that swings between orphic and vatic vision on the one hand, and the abuses of Archimago and the Blatant beast on the other – ultimately finds a promise of repose through the very sacrifice of his poetic art, forsaking its necessarily conditional and hence ultimately false images. The *Faerie Queene* ends with prayer and not poetry, a plea to hear the voice that is no longer that of the poet or the individual 'self' that has materialised out of the cracks in Spenser's desire for unifying poetic vision, but the voice of God. Spenser's personal history, thanks to its very vicissitudes and frustrations, becomes a lens through which the inverted image of eternity may be projected into the present, to relieve the existential anxiety that deconstructive criticism would like to read back into Spenser's supposedly 'desperate' cry of loneliness at the end of the *Faerie Queene*. I hear none of that bitterness – all the more striking in the aftermath of the increasingly more anxious tone of Spenser's later work – but rather find here, for the first time maybe, serene and genuine reconciliation with the inherent limitations of earthly forms, at a moment in Spenser's 'career' where he must have felt that life itself was slipping away from him.

# Coda: Reflections on the Unfinished Quest

So what is left, at the end of the *Faerie Queene* and at the end of this book, of that supposedly 'modern self' whose emergence is glimpsed and refracted through the complex transformations of the allegorical quest tradition? For all its differences from the allegories that precede it, Spenser's narrative seems to me a good place to stop and look back as well as forward – even if this has nothing to do with Spenser's real or supposed 'literary' merits in 'overgoing' his predecessors. Like its ancestors the allegory of the *Faerie Queene* once more fails for the same reasons, divided between metaphysical longings on the one hand, and more earthly, time-bound aspirations on the other. Spenser's allegory is the last to exploit quest narratives in such a way and to experience their characteristic 'failure', which marks a possible 'end' of the tradition. This however also raises a fundamental question for the history of the early modern subject constructed by quest narratives of this type: to what extent is the constitution of this emerging individual self – despite all its implications in temporal, political, affective and religious affairs of a distinctively *secular* sort – still shaped by a transcendentalising and deeply spiritual understanding of the 'pilgrimage of human life'? I can offer only a tentative answer, anecdotal but I believe symptomatic of wider realities in the period: first, I would suggest that to some extent the very concept of an individual, modern self is constructed in opposition to the notion of a more inclusive, universal and paradigmatic Christian self such as it is articulated by Deguileville. The 'modern self' is therefore necessarily and inextricably implicated in the universalising discourse it attempts to rewrite, counter or displace – and accordingly that discourse reasserts itself with a vengeance at the end of all these allegories. Second, it seems to me that all the quest narratives explored here converge in the admission of the failure of the 'modern self', or at least the realisation of its insufficiency. Or more precisely, I would submit that such an experience of failure, frustration and loss constitutes the core, the essence of that very 'modern self', which thus in turn requires the presence of an at least abstract, latent notion – or maybe a platonic 'memory' – of completeness and deliverance, which can only ever be metaphysical. Ultimately, it seems that the modern self crystallises out of its very failure to become that supposedly fully emancipated 'modern self', and modernity is thus paradoxically characterised by its longing for a putative 'pre-modern', more integrated and metaphysical model of identity.

But why conclude with Spenser? After all the *Faerie Queene* is not the final chapter in the history of the evolution of this 'self-representation' through allegorical quest-narratives – we have Bunyan, further Coleridge's *Rime of the Ancient Mariner*,

Conrad's *Heart of Darkness* or even Kerouac's *On the Road*, to name only a few. The short answer is, of course, that every quest narrative has to stop sooner or later, even if that 'conclusion' is often more of an exhaustion than the apotheosis initially sought – at best a coda, glancing towards new, or old, or simply alternative possibilities. Nevertheless, it seems to me that Spenser's allegory constitutes the endpoint of a long and problematic evolution, and although Bunyan arguably perpetuates the tradition and even breathes new life into it, he does so in a way that radically alters the chemistry of its ingredients.[1] On the formal level the most obvious difference is that in the *Pilgrim's Progress* we no longer find the same attempt to integrate spiritual allegory and knightly romance; Bunyan's Christian is, quite simply, no longer a knight, although he is eventually clad in Pauline Armour and engages in a memorable fight with the Giant Apollyon. As has been pointed out repeatedly, Bunyan's relationship with chivalric romance is inherently problematic and ambivalent, since he both borrows its formal features and *topoi*, but ultimately dismisses the entire genre as harmful, as evidenced by his remarks about his youthful reading habits in his early work: 'Alas, what is the Scripture, give me a Ballad, a Newsbook, *George* on horseback, or *Bevis of Southhampton*.'[2] As Andrew King observes, 'The *Pilgrim's Progress* is an account of the proper moral navigation of romance – ultimately a renunciation of or escape from the form – and each romance element in the text overcome by Christian can be likened to Bunyan's own rejection of his youthful reading.'[3] By appropriating romance in such a way, Bunyan thus writes the romance tradition *out* of the allegory, subsuming it within a pilgrimage narrative that is both similar to and profoundly different from the 'Deguilevillian' tradition.

It is tempting to explain Bunyan's decision to free his pilgrim from any chivalric trappings with reference to the supposedly more general 'decline' of knighthood in the seventeenth century in the aftermath of Quixotic and other satires. Whereas this simplistic narrative has been corrected and nuanced in recent years,[4] it is undeniable that chivalric forms were transformed, often 'classicised' in the early seventeenth century, and that the experience of Civil War may have further contributed to their decline in a number of complex ways.[5] But the shift away from chivalric motifs, both in Bunyan and in the age in which he wrote, seems to me to have deeper, as it were structural reasons to do with the implications of martial imagery

---

[1] The question of Bunyan's familiarity with the tradition would deserve further study. The classic account is Wharey's *A Study of the Sources of Bunyan's Allegories*. For a recent reconsideration of Bunyan's possible debt to a seventeenth century adaptation of the Middle English *Manhode*, see *The Pilgrime*, ed. Walls, pp. 159–63.

[2] John Bunyan, *A Few Sighs from Hell: or, The Groans of a Damned Soul* (London, 1658), p. 157.

[3] Andrew King, 'Sir Bevis of Hampton: Renaissance Influence and Reception', in Jennifer Fellows and Ivana Djordjevic, eds, *Sir Bevis of Hampton in Literary Tradition* (Cambridge: D. S. Brewer, 2008), pp. 176–91, here 191.

[4] Davis, *Chivalry and Romance*.

[5] J. S. A. Adamson, 'Chivalry and Political Culture in Caroline England', in Kevin Sharpe and Peter Lake, eds, *Culture and Politics in Early Stuart England* (Basingstoke: Macmillan, 1994), pp. 161–97.

and knightly allegory. Adamson points out how post-Civil War epic distances itself from Spenser's allegorical practice, perceived by Davenant as a 'continuance of extraordinary dreams'. Not only is chivalry as an imaginative 'language' abandoned, but the function and role of a certain kind of allegorical fiction and imagery within society is totally redefined. Adamson stresses how Davenant's Gondibert 'rejects the prescriptive authority of fictive conceits and didactic allegory as models for political action', and how this is symptomatic of a phenomenon that amounts to nothing less than 'the rejection of that union between the worlds of politics and the imagination'.[6]

Like every broad claim, this is bound to raise a few eyebrows, and yet it seems to describe rather well what happens in Bunyan, who writes the account of a pilgrimage very explicitly directed 'from THIS WORLD to that which is to come', and this from its inception, as advertised on the title page. Of course, this is not to say that in many ways Bunyan's allegory is not a 'political' work, but it is an account of a journey leading emphatically *away* from this world and its political vicissitudes. As in the case of the romance *topoi* appropriated by Bunyan, the entire politics of the *Pilgrim's Progress* are used to signify what lies beyond them, and accordingly have no value in themselves. It could be said of Bunyan, as Envy says of Christian and Faithful to the Judge, 'I heard him once my self affirm, *That Christianity, and the Customs of our Town of* Vanity, *were Diametrically opposite, and could not be reconciled*'.[7] Bunyan in his pilgrimage allegory indeed never contemplates the possibility of integrating his pilgrim within society – let alone of transforming and redeeming society at large, which is doomed from the very first lines of the poem: indeed the dreamer sees Christian 'open the Book, and Read therein; and as he Read, he wept and trembled'. But the 'Book' here does no longer inspire the author to plunge into his own, often puzzling but consciousness-expanding dream, as it does with Deguileville or Chaucer, but it unpacks and lays bare all the answers: 'I am for certain informed, that this our City will be burned with fire from Heaven, in which fearful overthrow [we] shall miserably come to ruine; except . . . some way of escape can be found'.[8]

The formulation of the initial situation is all too telling: the City of Man is doomed, I know for certain; we must depart, flee, fighting is no use – and accordingly Christian leaves everything and everyone behind, wife and children included. By basing his entire poem on such an initial assumption – or, in fact, certitude – Bunyan is writing an eminently 'dualistic' allegory, ultimately very different from the integrative and syncretistic tendencies of Spenserean allegory and the *Hinterland* of earlier quest-allegories. By writing an allegory directed emphatically away from the world, Bunyan as it were short-circuits all the attempts to balance the pilgrim's transcendentalising longings with his hopes for social, historical or political achievements and integration. In this sense it could almost be

---

[6]    Adamson, 'Chivalry and Political Culture', p. 195.

[7]    John Bunyan, *The Pilgrim's Progress from this World to That which is to Come*, ed. James Blanton Wharey, rev. Roger Sharrock (Oxford: Clarendon Press, 1960), p. 93.

[8]    Bunyan, *The Pilgrim's Progress*, pp. 8–9.

said that Bunyan starts where all other quest-allegories leave off, taking as a starting point the impossibility of reconciling the two 'worlds' of spiritual allegory and knightly romance, eschatology and worldly aspiration. Bunyan's allegory is fundamentally different in that it never attempts to heal the rift between the City of God and the City of Man, between a hopelessly corrupt human history and society on the one hand, and the desire for eschatological deliverance on the other.

In its desire to leave history behind Bunyan's allegory seems to come closest to Cartheny's, which also presents us with a knight whose chivalric attributes, together with all his mundane, social or political aspirations need to be left behind. But Cartheny's allegory nevertheless has a very powerful, albeit silent and implicit vision of its desired impact on society: both in its French, Catholic version and its English, 'conformist' translation, the work seeks to restore a universalising, inclusive and paradigmatic allegory of the Christian life beyond confessional dichotomies – and through this it attempts to heal sectarian divisions within society, and ultimately pursues a socially and metaphysically integrative agenda. Bunyan the nonconformist, on the other hand, starts his allegory already with the separation of the elect from the reprobate, and even on the very threshold of heaven's gates condemns Ignorance the Anglican to hell; the pilgrim is *not* an Everyman, and Bunyan writes an emphatically non-paradigmatic, Calvinist and divisive allegory.[9] Bunyan's staunchly predestinarian Calvinism also distinguishes him from Deguileville, even though the latter too writes an allegory very firmly directed away from this world, and dependent on the vital interventions of Grace Dieu rather than the pathetic-yet-endearing efforts of the oh-so-human pilgrim. The workings of Grace Dieu are memorably revealed through her gift of the ABC-Prayer to the pilgrim, which functions rather differently from Bunyan's concept of *sola gratia*, since it invites the pilgrim to participate indirectly in his own salvation by articulating the very prayer that is however given to him. And although prayer plays an important role in Bunyan too as an alternative to combat,[10] ultimately it is not an ABC-prayer to the Virgin that saves him, but a rather different type of document: a Roll conveniently tucked away in the pilgrim's bosom from the very start of his quest, readily available for consultation and lifting of spirits during hard times.[11]

As with the Book found by Christian at the beginning of the allegory, so it is with the Roll: it is as if Christian's election and the reprobation of his neighbours were already written into Bunyan's allegory before he sets pen to paper – and his pilgrimage therefore lacks the tentative, experimental *frisson* of setting out on a quest into the unknown that characterises all earlier quest narratives. The Roll itself lacks the performative and participative dimension of Deguileville's ABC-prayer, and

[9]  Cooper, *The English Romance in Time*, p. 91; Roger Pooley, 'The *Pilgrim's Progress* and the Line of Allegory', in Anne Dunan-Page, ed., *The Cambridge Companion to Bunyan* (Cambridge: Cambridge University Press, 2010), pp. 80–94, here 86.

[10]  E.g. Bunyan, *The Pilgrim's Progress*, p. 63.

[11]  Bunyan, *The Pilgrim's Progress*, pp. 10, 44. Tellingly the lack of such a 'certificate' disqualifies Ignorance the Anglican from entering the Gates of Heaven, p. 163.

requires nothing from Christian apart from his acknowledgment of its promise. As a consequence, there is no real 'adventure' in the allegory, since the 'struggle' of justification has already taken place before, within Christian's 'bosom' – certainly within Bunyan himself on whose experiences the account is partly based – and hence the pilgrim's quest is largely an unpacking of a foregone conclusion. More importantly in the present context, there is no genuine knightly or psychomachic battle because there is no possibility of shaping or influencing predestination – no matter how heroically, determinedly or violently one is willing to fight. As Thomas Luxon expands this idea, '[i]n other words, only Christ has really "been in the battle himself"; all others have been in it by imputation. So only Christ can "tell" the story (ventriloquized through Christian, Paul, and others) and only those newly born in Christ can hear the story as their own.'[12] As a consequence of such a radical espousal of a Calvinist theology of Grace, the pilgrim, even when he fights in full armour, adopts a posture of patient endurance rather than heroic determination, and the very notion of psychomachia – so easily and so naturally carried by the figure of the battling knight – loses much of its attraction.

This is not to say that Bunyan is insensitive to the appeal of the allegory of the psychomachia, and indeed he follows the writing of the *Pilgrim's Progress* with *The Holy War* – but this is precisely my point: the allegories of the pilgrimage *out of this world* and the psychomachia *in this world* are no longer fused, collapsed or balanced, but they become alternative, even contradictory representations of the Christian life from fundamentally different ontological perspectives. In choosing to decouple quest and pilgrimage, Bunyan breaks down the tradition into its basic components that were identified in Chapter 1. Regardless of the vexed question of Bunyan's actual familiarity with individual works in the tradition, this marks the end of a certain manner of conceiving the quest as a balancing act between the eschatological focus of the pilgrimage, and the more experiential, earthly – Spenser would say 'georgic' – toil of battle. The tension between these two motions had ultimately produced the quest-allegory tradition, but also condemned it to inevitable failure: in the face of the sprawling variety and multiplication of personal experience and the endless setbacks of history, the reconstruction of a paradigmatic teleology pointing beyond contingency towards a final resolution appears as impossible. What started as a quest degenerates into mere wandering, producing the kind of anxiety, disillusion and frustration that we find at the end of all quest-allegories, and which eventually prompts a return to an 'older' pilgrimage-model 'out of this world' postulated on a radical *contemptus mundi*. And yet, crucially, this same tension between the earthly and the eschatological is necessary to the very possibility of allegory, or at least the possibility of an allegory as conceived by all quest-narratives discussed in what precedes but not, I suggest, by Bunyan. It is an allegory that is

---

[12]  Thomas H. Luxon, *Literal Figures: Puritan Allegory and the Reformation Crisis in Representation* (Chicago, IL: University of Chicago Press, 1995), p. 198, quoting Bunyan, *The Pilgrim's Progress*, p. 130.

able, for a time at least, to represent a higher Reality by refracting it within an earthly reality while also maintaining a distinction between the two, thus enabling a hermeneutics of experience.

Yet this subtle balance seems to be exploded in Bunyan, who 'preaches the anti-hermeneutics of "experience" available only to those who have been spiritually parted from this world and reborn into the next'.[13] The tensions can no longer be 'contained' in the single allegory of the quest, which is thus stretched beyond its limits and is finally 'exploded' into three separate works that as it were explore these tensions from three very different angles. In his early spiritual autobiography, *Grace Abounding*, Bunyan indeed expresses just such anxiety, produced by his attempt to fit his personal experience within the patterns of biblical narratives and to organise his spiritual experience according to a structured *ordo salutis*.[14] The anxiety persists also in the *Holy War*, which manifests more interesting affinities with the allegorical quest tradition than the *Progress*: in it Bunyan writes an allegory that functions on at least three levels: that of Christian world history, individual spiritual struggle and recent English history – possibly with an added apocalyptic-millenarian dimension.[15]

But far from being a confident and 'closed' system of correspondences, the allegory of the *Holy War* remains – like the *Faerie Queene* and other quest-allegories once they reach their exhaustion – open-ended, unfinished, waiting for personal, political and cosmic history to complete and conclude the narrative. Indeed, Bunyan's confidence in the neat correspondence of the multiple layers of the allegory appears to have been seriously compromised by the disappointments of his early millenarian hopes, and accordingly the system of analogies he works through in the *Holy War* is tentative, fragmentary and ultimately incomplete.[16] And nothing expresses this lack of resolution *in time and history* better than the allegory of battle, signifying as it were an incessant, never-ending struggle that characterises man's existential condition on earth. For Bunyan, battle no longer signifies the psychomachia of Deguileville and the quest-allegory tradition, where knightly combat ultimately evokes the belief in the possibility of contributing to one's salvation through one's own strength – through the 'works' that are such anathema for Calvinism. For Bunyan battle is rather endlessly repeated and renewed, and paradoxically becomes a static, non-directional figure of man's existential condition, caught in a deadlock that finally gets him nowhere. This also conditions Bunyan's rejection of any hermeneutics whatsoever, unlike the earlier quest-allegories that see in the knight's combats an image of their own attempts to 'make sense' of the world. For Bunyan

---

[13] Luxon, *Literal Figures*, p. 32; see also pp. 164–9 and *passim*.

[14] John Bunyan, *Grace Abounding to the Chief of Sinners*, ed. Roger Sharrock (Oxford: Clarendon Press, 1962); Michael Davies, 'Grace Abounding to the Chief of Sinners: John Bunyan and Spiritual Autobiography', in Dunan-Page, ed., *Cambridge Companion to Bunyan*, pp. 67–79.

[15] John Bunyan, *The Holy War: Made by Shaddai upon Diabolus, for the Regaining of the Metropolis of the World, or, The Losing and Taking again of the Town of Mansoul*, ed. Roger Sharrock and James F. Forrest (Oxford: Clarendon Press, 1980), p. xxvi.

[16] Bunyan, *The Holy War*, pp. xxx–xxxvi.

such hermeneutic struggle can only ever signify its inability to signify, since 'the only point of interpretation is to be reminded "again and again" to stop interpreting; the only point of living in this world of temporal-spatial forms is eventually to stop living in it'.[17]

But little of such an immobilistic anxiety is visible in the *Pilgrim's Progress*, a confident account of the human pilgrimage written from the vantage point of a justified Calvinist elect who has already, as it were, reached the final haven before he even sets out. Bunyan's pilgrimage-allegory is thus written from a higher ontological perspective than the *Holy War*: it is a retrospective, or downward gaze that allows him to short-circuit the lack of historical, political and cosmic closure, springing from the certainty of his election no matter what. This allows Bunyan to envisage a completed teleological journey viewed *from the perspective of eternity* – even while it remains impossible for him to discern hermeneutically, in the open-ended *Holy War* for instance, how exactly this journey is going to crystallise out of the apparent chaos of battle, perceived *from the perspective of experience*. But that is ultimately unimportant: from the perspective of an already justified elect, the created world disappears into nothingness despite its opacity and imperviousness to human discernment.

This decoupling of eschatological and experiential perspectives also marks a clearly transformed conceptualisation of the self, according to a more radically 'modern', dualistic and dissociative ontology in its *a priori* admission of a more radically inscrutable relationship between human history, society and individual experience on the one hand, and spiritual and eschatological realities on the other. Again, here Bunyan seems to start where all earlier quest-allegories leave off, taking their sobering lessons and hard-won failures already for granted. The failure to integrate metaphysical and earthly aspirations no longer needs to be experienced and explored; it is already accepted, embraced as the very point of departure of a rather different kind of pilgrimage. Accordingly, Bunyan's self is more fundamentally and radically 'fractured', since that fracture is not a reluctant outcome of an idealistic quest and struggle for integration that eventually fails. Rather, fracture is the point of departure – and explicitly so, since here the self is constructed through the disso-ciation of the 'elect' Christian, whether corporate or strictly individual, from the rest of doomed society as much as through the integration of that self in a transcen-dentalising discourse.

This dissociation of the figures of pilgrimage and psychomachia also has a curiously twofold effect on metaphysical self-understanding: on the one hand, the focus on the idea of a teleological pilgrimage enables the preservation of the confidence in eschatological reunion with the Divine even if the latter cannot be 'attained' through hermeneutic or psychomachic efforts – and accordingly the *Pilgrim's Progress* is an allegory remarkably free from self-doubt not *despite* its rejection of hermeneutics, but precisely *thanks to* this rejection. On the other hand, the fragmentary, open-ended and experiential apprehension of human existence

---

[17] Luxon, *Literal Figures*, p. 164.

signified by the metaphor of battle, is diverted, relegated to and 'contained' by a different allegory altogether in the *Holy War*. However, the very need to dissociate the two allegories springs from a latent fear that the predestinarian security in the *Pilgrim's Progress* may be 'contaminated' by entering the metaphorical battleground of history, becoming embroiled in its contradictions and indirections.

Bunyan still dares to confront this risk in *Grace Abounding* and *The Holy War*, where he explores spiritual struggle in terms of intense, even anguished conflict, both corporate and individual – but without recourse to the pilgrimage-motif as 'controlling structure' of the allegory.[18] Only the *Pilgrim's Progress* uses the pilgrimage-motif in such a way, but conversely writes real conflict effectively out of existence, since its very confidence in election stifles every possibility of contributing to the operation of grace through combat, effort and 'work(s)', both of the moral and hermeneutic variety. This provides an allegorical pilgrimage model that is both extremely close and radically at odds with that of Deguileville: both pilgrimages lead emphatically out of this world, but whereas the *Vie* is a didactic guidebook for Christian pilgrims written with the aim of aiding them by providing a series of moral grids to organise their individual but ultimately analogous experiences of the world, Bunyan rejects the very notion of a pilgrimage *paradigm* as defined in Chapter 1. Indeed in Bunyan only the distant *idea* of pilgrimage persists, since 'there is not one but an infinity of ways, each of which shapes itself to the inclinations of its single traveller'.[19] Hence Bunyan never postulates a truly didactic function for his poem – except in the transposed sense of attracting the reader's attention to allegory's inability to have any impact on human understanding and experience: 'the progress that Bunyan encourages his readers to experience, the "work of Grace" in the heart, is not something "a man may learn by *talk*", even Bunyan's talk'.[20]

Accordingly, Bunyan's allegorical practice in the *Pilgrim's Progress* is also of a radically different nature, and is in need of a reassessment in the light of both earlier practice and later developments. In it, I suggest, we find none of the invitation to the reader to indulge in daring, often dangerous open-ended hermeneutic and epist-emological (self-)explorations found in earlier allegories from Alain de Lille to Spenser. Instead we have an anti-hermeneutics that performs a radical 'othering' of its ultimate vanishing point (and of its 'other' self), which paradoxically ends up producing an allegory that is less exploratory and more neatly explicative, doctrinaire rather than didactic. Bunyan's allegory in the *Pilgrim's Progress* may indeed be situated at the juncture between the prolonged 'medieval' practice of allegory described by Tuve, and modern reconfigurations (a medievalist is always tempted to term these 'misunderstandings') culminating in nineteenth-century notions of a 'mechanical', 'naïve' and flatly 'attributive' allegory.[21] Indeed, Bunyan's anti-

---

[18]  See Introduction, p. 27.

[19]  Stanley Fish, *Self-Consuming Artifacts: The Experience of Seventeenth-Century Literature* (Berkeley, CA: University of California Press, 1972), p. 230, quoted in Luxon, *Literal Figures*, p. 170.

[20]  Luxon, *Literal Figures*, p. 178.

[21]  See for instance the revealing discussion in Hagen, *Allegorical Remembrance*, pp. 130–40.

hermeneutics of allegory, while it is designed to send man back to his own experience of God's Grace apprehended in the heart, ends up disqualifying the reader from being actively implicated in the discovery and exploration of meaning through the experience of 'reading' – reading an allegory, the world and oneself. This conversely necessitates an appeal to a higher instance to 'attribute' meaning to experience, as it were 'retrospectively' from the higher ontological perspective of the justified Calvinist elect as author and sole interpreter of allegory. And thus where Hawes, Spenser, Bateman and Lewkenor boldly reflected on the possibilities and failures of their allegories and their own deeply implicated 'selves' in the face of the open-endedness of history and the fallibility of human understanding, Bunyan – or rather the justified narrative voice behind the *Pilgrim's Progress* – short-circuits all such 'questions', rendering the 'quest' itself irrelevant. The 'self' of Bunyan's pilgrim, viewed through the eyes of the justified elect narrator mobilised by the *Pilgrim's Progress*, is still of course a metaphysical self – but it is no longer properly *constructed* within the allegory; rather, like the Roll, it is 'given' from the start, always and already 'promised', constantly deferred and yet utterly and absolutely present.

Such a self, in the aftermath of the many 'failures' of earlier quest-allegories, appears as totally and absolutely 'other', more radically isolated, self-righteous-yet-self-confined and even possibly 'alienated' since it lacks the courage to genuinely test its metaphysics against experience.[22] If this pilgrim-self achieves stability and integration, it is only because its identity is no longer defined in terms of a conflict and commerce with the world or by making its path through it as a process of *becoming* – but by embarking on a preordained path already traced, leading safely away 'from this world to that which is to come' where its *being* is already given. But the very 'modernity' implied by its self-alienation is again, and still, a function of the self's implication within metaphysics – a metaphysical longing that for all the self's 'othering' is not in fact displaced but rather enhanced – one is tempted to say, in Bunyan's case, 'exacerbated'. This illustrates how even when allegory as a mode is stretched to its breaking point, 'decentered subjectivity' is utterly inconceivable without a latent yet powerful, even overwhelming sense of union with something larger that can only ever be metaphysical. Furthermore, to end with Luxon, this also suggests something much deeper about 'how broadly dependent early modern concepts of identity are upon allegorical schemes of ontology'.[23]

---

[22]   This needs to be tempered, of course, by Bunyan's intense appeal to a sense of 'fellowship' within the Bedford congregation; see e.g. Davies, 'Grace Abounding', esp. pp. 75–8. The Bedford community, however, is in turn defined in terms of separation from and opposition to the larger body of reprobate humankind, and thus reproduces the same model of fracture and isolation on the level of corporate identity formation.

[23]   Luxon, *Literal Figures*, p. x.

# Bibliography

## Primary Works

Alain de Lille. *Anticlaudianus, or, The Good and Perfect Man*, trans. and commentary James Sheridan. Toronto: Pontifical Institute of Mediaeval Studies, 1973.

———. *The Plaint of Nature*, trans. and commentary James Sheridan. Toronto: Pontifical Institute of Medieval Studies, 1980.

Augustine, Saint. *Confessions*, trans. Henry Chadwick. Oxford: Oxford University Press, 1992.

———. *On Christian Teaching*, ed. and trans. R. P. H. Green. Oxford: Oxford University Press, 1997.

———. *The City of God*, ed. G. R. Evans, trans. Henry Bettenson. London: Penguin, 2003.

Bale, John. *The Image of Bothe Churches: After Reulacion of Saynt Iohan the Euangelyst*. Antwerp, 1545 – STC 1296.5

———. *Scriptorium Illustrium Maioris Brytanniae, quam nunc Angliam et Scotiam vocant: catalogus*, 2 vols. Basel, 1557–9.

———. *John Bale's King Johan*, ed. B. B. Adams. San Marino, CA: Huntington Library, 1969.

Baspoole, William. *The Pilgrime*, ed. Kathryn Walls and Marguerite Stobo. Tempe, AZ: Renaissance English Text Society, 2008.

Bateman, Stephen. *A Christall Glasse of Christian Reformation: Wherein the Godly Maye Beholde the Coloured Abuses Vsed in this our Present Tyme*. London, 1569 – STC 1581.

———. *Trauayled Pylgrime: Bringing Newes from all Partes of the Worlde, Such Like Scarce Harde of before. Seene and Allowed According to the Order Appointed*. London, 1569 – STC 1585.

———. *Golden Booke of the Leaden Goddes: Wherein Is Described the Vayne Imaginations of Heathen Pagans, and Counterfaict Christians*. London, 1577 – STC 1583.

———, trans.; Konrad Lykostenes. *The Doome Warning all Men to the Iudgemente: In Maner of a Generall Chronicle, Gathered out of Sundrie Approued Authors by S. Batman*. London, 1581 – STC 1582.

———, trans.; Bartolomaeus Anglicus. *Batman vppon Bartholome: His Booke* De proprietatibus rerum, *Newly Corrected, Enlarged and Amended: With such Additions as Are Requisite, vnto Euery Seuerall Booke: Taken Foorth of the Most Approued Authors, the Like heretofore Not Translated in English. Profitable for all Estates, as well for the Benefite of the Mind as the Bodie*. London, 1582 – STC 1538.

Bernardus Silvestris. *Cosmographia*, trans. and intro. Winthrop Wetherbee. New York: Columbia University Press, 1973.

*The Book Of Common Prayer* (1559). Transcription available online at: http://justus.anglican.org/resources/bcp/1559/BCP_1559.htm [accessed 12 February 2012].

Bonaventure, Saint. *Itinerarium Mentis in Deum*, trans. Ewert Cousins, *The Soul's Journey into God*. New York: Paulist Press, 1978.

*The Booke of the Pylgrymage of Man*. London: R. Faques, 1520 – STC 19918.

*The Book of Vices and Virtue: A Fourteenth Century English Translation of the Somme le roi of Lorens d'Orléans*, ed. W. Nelson Francis, EETS OS 217. London: Oxford University Press, 1942.

Bradford, John. *The Writings of John Bradford*, 2 vols, ed. A. Townsend. Cambridge: Cambridge University Press, 1848–53.

Bunny, Edmund. *A Booke of Christian Exercise, Appertaining to Resolution, by R. P. Perused and Accompanied with a Treatise Tending to Pacification*. London, 1584 – STC 19355.

Bunyan, John. *A Few Sighs from Hell: or, The Groans of a Damned Soul*. London, 1658.

———. *The Pilgrim's Progress from this World to That which is to Come*, ed. James Blanton Wharey, rev. Roger Sharrock. Oxford: Clarendon Press, 1960.

———. *Grace Abounding to the Chief of Sinners*, ed. Roger Sharrock. Oxford: Clarendon Press, 1962.

———. *The Holy War: Made by Shaddai upon Diabolus, for the Regaining of the Metropolis of the World, or, The Losing and Taking again of the Town of Mansoul*, ed. Roger Sharrock and James F. Forrest. Oxford: Clarendon Press, 1980.

Calvin, Jean. *Institutes of the Christian Religion*, ed. John McNeill, trans. Ford Lewis Battles. London: S.C.M. Press, 1961

Caxton, William, trans.; Ramon Llull. *The Book of the Ordre of Chivalry*, ed. A. T. P. Byles, EETS OS 168. London: Oxford University Press, 1926.

Chaucer, Geoffrey. *The Vvorkes of our Ancient and Lerned English Poet, Geffrey Chaucer, Newly Printed*. London, 1602 – STC 5080–1.

———. *The Riverside Chaucer*, ed. Larry Benson, 3rd edn. Oxford: Oxford University Press, 1988.

Crowley, Robert. *The Voyce of the Laste Trumpet Blowen bi the Seue[n]th Angel (as Is Me[n]tioned in the Eleuenth of the Apocalips): Callynge al the Estates of Menne to the Right Path of their Vocation, wherin Are Contayned xii. Lessons to Twelue Seueral Estates of Menne, whych if they Learne and Folowe, al Shal Be Well and Nothynge Amise*. 1549 – STC 6094.

De Acuña, Hernando, trans.; Olivier de la Marche. *El caballero determinado*, ed. Nieves Baranda and Victor Infantes. Toledo: Antonjo Pareja, 2000.

De Cartheny, Jean. *Le voyage du chevalier errant*. Anvers: J. Bellère, 1557. Available online at: http://gallica.bnf.fr/ark:/12148/bpt6k54605b [accessed 12 February 2012].

De Cartheny, Jehan. *Le voyage du chevalier errant*. Cambray, 1587.

De la Marche, Olivier. *Mémoires*, 4 vols, ed. H. Beaune and J. d'Arbaumont. Paris: Société de l'Histoire de France, 1883–8.

———. *Le Chevalier Délibéré. The Illustrations of the Edition of Schiedam Reproduced*, with a preface by F. Lippmann and a reprint of the text. London: Bibliographical Society, 1898.

———. *Le Chevalier Délibéré by Olivier de La Marche, printed at Paris in 1488*. Washington, DC: Library of Congress, 1946.

———. *Le chevalier délibéré (The Resolute Knight)*, Medieval and Renaissance Texts and Studies 199, ed. and trans. Carleton W. Carroll, trans. C. Hawley Wilson. Tempe, AZ: Arizona Centre for Medieval and Renaissance Studies, 1999.

Dixon, John. *The First Commentary on the* Faerie Queene: *Being an Analysis of the Annotations in Lord Bessborough's Copy of the First Edition of the* Faerie Queene, ed. Graham Hough. London, 1964.

Dudley, Edmund. *The Tree of Commonwealth*, ed. D. M. Brodie. Cambridge: Cambridge University Press, 1948.

Elyot, Sir Thomas. *A Critical Edition of Sir Thomas Elyot's* The Boke Named the Governour, ed. Donald W. Rude. New York: Garland, 1992.

Erasmus, Desiderius. *Enchiridion Militis Christiani: An English Version*, ed. Anne M. O'Donnell, EETS OS 282. Oxford: Oxford University Press, 1981.

Foxe, John. *Two Latin Comedies by John Foxe the Martyrologist: Titus et Gesippus; Christus Triumphans*, ed. and trans. John H. Smith. Ithaca: Cornell University Press, 1973.

———. *The Unabridged Acts and Monuments Online* (HRI Online Publications, Sheffield, 2011). Available online at: http://www.johnfoxe.org [accessed 12 February 2012].

Gaguin, Robert. *Roberti Gaguini Epistole et Orationes*, ed. Louis Thuasne. Paris: E. Bouillon, 1903; repr. Geneva: Slatkine, 1977.

Geoffroi de Charny. *The Book of Chivalry of Geoffroi de Charny: Text, Context, and Translation*, ed. Richard W. Kaeuper and Elspeth Kennedy. Philadelphia, PA: University of Pennsylvania Press, 1996.

Goodyear, William, trans.; Jean de Cartigny (Cartheny). *The Wandering Knight*, ed. Dorothy Atkinson Evans. Seattle, WA: University of Washington Press, 1951.

Guillaume de Deguileville. *Le pèlerinage de vie humaine*, ed. J. J. Stürzinger. London: Roxburghe Club, 1893.

———. *Le pèlerinage de l'âme*, ed. J. J. Stürzinger. London: Roxburghe Club, 1895.

———. *Le pèlerinage Jhesucrist*, ed. J. J. Stürzinger. London: Roxburghe Club, 1897.

———. *Le Pelerinaige de Vie Humaine: Reproduced in Facsimile from the Printed Book in the Library of the Earl of Ellesmere with a Bibliographical Note by Alfred W. Pollard*. Manchester: Roxburghe Club, 1912.

———. *The Pilgrimage of Human Life*, ed. and trans. Eugene Clasby. New York: Garland, 1992.

Guillaume de Lorris and Jean de Meun. *Le roman de la rose*, 3 vols, ed. Félix Lecoy. Paris: Champion, 1973–5.

Guiot de Provins. *L'Armeüre du Chevalier*, in John Orr, ed., *Œuvres de Guiot de Provins*. Genève: Slatkine, 1974, pp. 94–113.

Harington, John, trans.; Ludovico Ariosto. *Orlando Furioso*, ed. Graham Hough. London: Centaur Press, 1962.

Hawes, Stephen. *The Pastime of Pleasure*, ed. W. E. Mead, EETS OS 173. London: Oxford University Press, 1928.

———. *The Minor Poems*, ed. Florence W. Gluck and Alice B. Morgan, EETS OS 271. London: Oxford University Press, 1974.

Hoby, Sir Thomas, trans.; Baldassarre Castiglione. *The Book of the Courtier*, ed. Virginia Cox. London: J. M. Dent, 1994.

Hoccleve, Thomas. *'My Compleinte' and Other Poems*, ed. Roger Ellis. Exeter: University of Exeter Press, 2001.

Jean de Courcy. *Le Chemin de vaillance di Jean de Courcy e l'allegoria*, ed. Saverio Panunzio. Bari: Adriatica, 1979.

Langland, William. *The Vision of Piers Plowman: A Critical Edition of the B-text*, ed. A. V. C. Schmidt, 2nd edn. London: Dent, 1995.

Lewkenor, Lewes, trans.; Olivier de la Marche. *The Resolved Gentleman*. London, 1594 – STC 15139.

———. *A Discourse of the Usage of the English Fugitives, by the Spaniard*. London, 1595; repr. 1596 – STC 15562–3.

———. *The Estate of English Fugitiues vnder the King of Spaine and his Ministers: Containing, Besides, a Discourse of the Sayd Kings Manner of Gouernment, and the Iniustice of many Late Dishonorable Practises by him Contriued*. London, 1595; repr. 1596 – STC 15564–5.

———. *The Commonvvealth and Gouernment of Venice*. London, 1599 – STC 5642.

———, trans.; Antonio de Torquemada. *The Spanish Mandevile of Miracles, or, The Garden of Curious Flowers: Wherein Are Handled Sundry Points of Humanity, Philosophy, Diuinity, and Geography, Beautified with many Strange and Pleasant Histories*. London, 1600 – STC 24135.

Luther, Martin. *D. Martin Luthers Werke: Kritische Gesamtausgabe*, 120 vols. Weimar: Hermann Böhlaus Nachfolger, 1883–2009.

Lydgate, John, trans.; Guillaume de Deguileville. *The Pilgrimage of the Life of Man*, 3 vols, ed. F. J. Furnivall and Katharine B. Locock, EETS OS 78, 83 and 92. London: Kegan Paul, Trench, Trübner & Co., 1899–1904.

Macrobius Ambrosius Theodosius. *Commentary on the Dream of Scipio*, trans. William Harris Stahl. New York: Columbia University Press, 1952.

Malory, Sir Thomas. *Le Morte Darthur*, ed. Stephen H. A. Shepherd. New York: Norton, 2004.

Marten, Anthony. *A Second Sound, or, Warning of the Trumpet unto Judgment: Wherein is Proued, that all the Tokens of the Latter Day, Are Not Onelie Come, but Welneere Finished. With an Earnest Exhortation, to Be in Continuall Readinesse*. London, 1589 – STC 17941.

*Mystères et Moralités du Manuscrit 617 de Chantilly*, ed. Gustave Cohen. Paris: Champion, 1920.

Norman, Robert. *The Newe Attractiue: Containyng a Short Discourse of the Magnes or Lodestone, and amongest other his Vertues, of a Newe Discouered Secret and Subtill Propertie, Concerning the Declinyng of the Needle, Touched therewith under the Plaine of the Horizon.* London, 1581 – STC 18647.

*Ordène de Chevalerie/Le Roman des Eles de Raoul de Hodenc*, ed. Keith Busby. Utrecht: John Benjamins, 1983.

Parry, Robert. *Moderatus*, ed. John Simons. Aldershot: Ashgate, 2002.

Parsons, Robert. *A Conference about the Next Succession of the Crowne of Ingland.* 1594 – STC 19398.

*Peregrinatio humani generis.* London: Pynson, 1508 – STC 19917.5.

Perez, Antonio. *A Treatise Paraenetical, that Is to Say, an Exhortation: By a Pilgrim Spaniard Beaten by Time, and Persecuted by Fortune.* London: W. Ponsonby, 1598 – STC 19838.

Perkins, William. 'A Dialogue of the State of a Christian Man', in *A Treatise Tending vnto a Declaration whether a Man Be in the Estate of Damnation or in the Estate of Grace.* London, 1590 – STC 19752.

———. *Of the Combat of the Flesh and Spirit.* 1593 – STC 19758.

Pettie, George, trans.; Stefano Guazzo. *The Civile Conversation of M. Steeven Guazzo*, ed. Edward Sullivan. London: Constable & Co., 1925.

Philippe de Mézières. *Le songe du vieil pèlerin*, ed. George Coopland. Cambridge: Cambridge University Press, 1969.

Prudentius. *Psychomachia*, in *Prudentius*, vol. 1, ed. and trans. H. J. Thomson. London: Heinemann, 1949, pp. 274–343.

*Die Pilgerfahrt zum himmlischen Jerusalem: ein allegorisches Gedicht des Spätmittelalters aus der Heidelberger Bilderhandschrift Cod. Pal. Lat. 1969 'Pèlerinage de vie humaine' des Guillaume de Deguileville*, ed. Rosemarie Bergmann. Wiesbaden: Reichert, 1983.

*The Pilgrimage of the Lyfe of the Manhode*, 2 vols, ed. Avril Henry, EETS OS 288 and 292. Oxford: Oxford University Press, 1985–8.

*The Pilgrimage of the Soul. Vol. 1: A Critical Edition of the Middle English Dream Vision*, ed. Rosemarie Potz McGerr. New York: Garland, 1990.

*The Pylgremage of the Sowle*, pr. by William Caxton. 1483 – STC 6473.

*The Receyt of the Ladie Kateryne*, ed. Gordon Kipling, EETS OS 296. Oxford: Oxford University Press, 1990.

René d'Anjou. *Le mortifiement de vaine plaisance de René d'Anjou: étude du texte et des manuscrits à peintures*, ed. Frédéric Lyna. Paris: Rousseau; Bruxelles: Weckesser, 1926.

———. *Le coeur d'amour épris: reproduction intégrale en fac-similé des miniatures du Codex Vindobonensis 2597 de la Bibliothèque nationale de Vienne*, eds Marie-Thérèse Gousset, Daniel Poirion and Franz Unterkircher. Paris: Philippe Lebaud, 1981.

———. *The Book of the Love-Smitten Heart*, ed. and trans. Stephanie Viereck Gibbs and Kathryn Karczewska. London: Routledge, 2001.

———. *Le livre du cœur d'amour épris*, ed. Florence Bouchet. Paris: Le Livre de Poche, 2003.

Rogers, Thomas, trans.; Augustine, Saint. *A Right Christian Treatise, Entituled S. Augustines Praiers: Published in More Ample Sort than Yet It Hath Bin in the English Tong; Purged from Diuers Superstitious Points.* London, 1581 – STC 950.

———, trans.; Augustine, Saint. *S. Augustines Manuel: Conteining Special, and Piked Meditations, and Godlie Praiers: Drawne out of the Word of God, and Writings of the Holie Fathers, for the Exercise of the Soule. Corrected, Translated, and Adorned, by Thomas Rogers.* London, 1581 – STC 938.

———, trans.; Thomas à Kempis. *Of the Imitation of Christ: Three, Both for Wisedome, and Godlines, Most Excellent Bookes.* London, 1592 – STC 23979.

*St. Patrick's Purgatory: Two Versions of Owayne Miles and The Vision of William of Stranton; Together with the Long Text of the Tractatus de Purgatorio Sancti Patricii*, ed. Robert Easting, EETS OS 298. Oxford: Oxford University Press, 1991.

Scrope, Stephen, trans.; Christine de Pizan. *The Epistle of Othea*, ed. Curt F. Bühler, EETS OS 264. London: Oxford University Press, 1970.

Scupoli, Lorenzo. *The Spiritual Combat*, ed. and trans. Thomas Barns. London: Methuen, 1909.

——. *Unseen Warfare: Being the Spiritual Combat and Path to Paradise as Edited by Nicodemus of the Holy Mountain and Revised by Theophan the Recluse*, ed. and trans. E. Kadloubovsky and G. E. Palmer, intro. H. A. Hodges. London: Faber and Faber, 1952.

——. *The Spiritual Conflict*, trans. anonymous, with Jan van Päschen, *The Spiritual Pilgrimage of Hierusalem*, English Recusant Literature 1558–1640, vol. 8, ed. D. M. Rodgers. Menston: Scolar Press, 1969.

Segar, Sir William. *The Book of Honor and Armes (1590) and Honor Military and Civil (1602)*. Delmar: Scholars' Facsimiles and Reprints, 1975.

Skelton, John. *Magnyfycence*, ed. Paula Neuss. Manchester: Manchester University Press, 1980.

——. *The Complete English Poems*, ed. John Scattergood. Harmondsworth: Penguin, 1983.

Spenser, Edmund. *The Works of Edmund Spenser, a Variorum Edition*, 11 vols, ed. E. Greenlaw, C. G. Osgood, F. M. Padelford *et al.* Baltimore, MD: Johns Hopkins University Press, 1932–57.

——. *The Shorter Poems*, ed. Richard McCabe. London: Penguin, 1999.

——. *The Faerie Queene*, ed. A. C. Hamilton. Harlow: Pearson, 2001.

Tommaso III di Saluzzo (Thomas de Saluces). *Le chevalier errant*, ed. and trans. Daniel Chaubet. Moncalieri: Centro interuniversitario di ricerche per il viaggio in Italia, 2001.

——. *Il Libro del Cavaliere Errante (BnF ms. fr. 12559)*, ed. Marco Piccat and Laura Ramello. Boves: Araba Fenice, 2008.

Thomas Aquinas. *Summa theologica : edito altera romana ad emendatiores editiones impressa et noviter accuratissime recognita*. Roma: Forzani, 1894.

*Treigl Y Marchog Crwydrad*, ed. D. Mark Smith. Caerdydd: Gwasg Prifysgol Cymru, 2002.

*Vindiciae, Contra Tyrannos, or, Concerning the Legitimate Power of a Prince over the People, and of the People over a Prince*, ed. George Garnett. Cambridge: Cambridge University Press, 1994.

Wever, R. *Lusty Juventus*, in *Four Tudor Interludes*, ed. J. A. B. Somerset. London: The Athlone Press, 1974.

## Secondary Works

Adams, Simon. 'A Patriot for Whom? Stanley, York and Elizabeth's Catholics', *History Today* 37:7 (July 1987), 46–50.

——. 'The Patronage of the Crown in Elizabethan Politics: The 1590s in Perspective', in John Guy, ed., *The Reign of Elizabeth I: Court and Culture in the Last Decade*. Cambridge: Cambridge University Press, 1995, pp. 20–45.

——. 'Eliza Enthroned? The Court and its Politics', in Simon Adams, *Leicester and the Court: Essays on Elizabethan Politics*. Manchester: Manchester University Press, 2002, pp. 24–45.

——. 'Faction, Clientage and Party: English Politics, 1550–1603', in Simon Adams, *Leicester and the Court: Essays on Elizabethan Politics*. Manchester: Manchester University Press, 2002, pp. 13–23.

——. 'Favourites and Factions at the Elizabethan Court', in Simon Adams, *Leicester and the Court: Essays on Elizabethan Politics*. Manchester: Manchester University Press, 2002, pp. 46–67.

——. *Leicester and the Court: Essays on Elizabethan Politics*. Manchester: Manchester University Press, 2002.

——. 'The Succession and Foreign Policy', *History Today* 53:5 (May 2003), 42–8.

——. 'Dudley, Anne, countess of Warwick (1548/9–1604)', *DNB*. Available online at: http://www.oxforddnb.com/view/article/69744 [accessed 12 February 2012].

Adamson, J. S. A. 'Chivalry and Political Culture in Caroline England', in Kevin Sharpe and Peter Lake, eds, *Culture and Politics in Early Stuart England*. Basingstoke: Macmillan, 1994, pp. 161–97.

Aers, David. *Community, Gender and Individual Identity: English Writing 1360–1430*. London: Routledge, 1988.

——. '"In Arthurus Day": Community, Virtue, and Individual Identity in *Sir Gawain and the*

*Green Knight*', in David Aers, *Community, Gender and Individual Identity: English Writing 1360–1430*. London: Routledge, 1988, pp. 153–78.

——, ed. *Culture and History, 1350–1600: Essays on English Communities, Identities and Writing*. Hemel Hempstead: Harvester Wheatsheaf, 1992.

——.'A Whisper in the Ear of Early Modernists; or, Reflections on Literary Critics Writing the "History of the Subject"', in David Aers, ed., *Culture and History, 1350–1600: Essays on English Communities, Identities and Writing*. Hemel Hempstead: Harvester Wheatsheaf, 1992, pp. 177–202.

——. 'The Self Mourning: Reflections on *Pearl*', *Speculum* 68:1 (1993), 54–73.

Allen, David G., and Robert A. White, eds. *Subjects on the World's Stage: Essays on British Literature of the Middle Ages and the Renaissance*. Newark, DE: University of Delaware Press; London: Associated University Presses, 1995.

Alwes, Derek B. "'Who knows not Colin Clout?": Spenser's Self-Advertisement in the *Faerie Queene*, Book VI', *Modern Philology* 88 (1990), 26–42.

Anderson, Judith H. 'Chaucer's and Spenser's Reflexive Narrators', in Judith H. Anderson, *Reading the Allegorical Intertext: Chaucer, Spenser, Shakespeare, Milton*. New York: Fordham University Press, 2008, pp. 27–41.

——. '"Pricking on the plaine": Spenser's Intertextual Beginnings and Endings', in Judith H. Anderson, *Reading the Allegorical Intertext: Chaucer, Spenser, Shakespeare, Milton*. New York: Fordham University Press, 2008, pp. 54–60.

——. *Reading the Allegorical Intertext: Chaucer, Spenser, Shakespeare, Milton*. New York: Fordham University Press, 2008.

Anderson, Judith H., Donald Cheney and David A. Richardson, eds. *Spenser's Life and the Subject of Biography*. Amherst, MA: University of Massachusetts Press, 1996.

Andrews, K. R. 'The Aims of Drake's Expedition of 1577–1580', *The American Historical Review* 73:3 (February 1968), 724–41.

Anglo, Sydney, ed. *Chivalry in the Renaissance*. Woodbridge: Boydell, 1990.

——. *Images of Tudor Kingship*. London: Seaby, 1992.

——. *Spectacle, Pageantry, and Early Tudor Policy*, 2nd edn. Oxford: Clarendon Press, 1997.

Archer, Rowena.'Alice Chaucer, Duchess of Suffolk (d. 1475) and her books'. Talk given at the Maison Française d'Oxford on Tuesday 16 January 2007.

Ashe, Laura, Ivana Djordjevic, and Judith Weiss, eds. *The Exploitations of Medieval Romance*. Cambridge: D. S. Brewer, 2010.

Atkinson, David W. 'The English *ars moriendi*: Its Protestant Transformation', *Renaissance and Reformation* 6:1 (1982), 1–10.

Atkinson, Dorothy F.'*The Wandering Knight*, the Red Cross Knight, and "Miles Dei"', *Huntington Library Quarterly* 7:2 (February 1944), 109–34.

Axton, Marie. *The Queen's Two Bodies: Drama and the Elizabethan Succession*. London: Royal Historical Society, 1977.

Backhouse, Janet.'Founders of the Royal Library: Edward IV and Henry VII as Collectors of Illuminated Manuscripts', in Daniel Williams, ed., *England in the Fifteenth Century: Proceedings of the 1986 Harlaxton Symposium*. Woodbridge: Boydell, 1987, pp. 23–41.

——. 'The Royal Library from Edward IV to Henry VII', in Lotte Hellinga and J. B. Trapp, eds, *The Cambridge History of the Book in Britain*, vol. 3. Cambridge: Cambridge University Press, 1999, pp. 267–73.

Backus, Irena D. *Reformation Readings of the Apocalypse: Geneva, Zurich, and Wittenberg*. Oxford: Oxford University Press, 2000.

Badel, Pierre-Yves. *Le* Roman de la Rose *au XIV$^e$ siècle: étude de la réception de l'oeuvre*. Genève: Droz, 1980.

——. 'Le poème allégorique', in Daniel Poirion, ed., *La littérature française aux XIV$^e$ et XV$^e$ siècles*, Grundriss der Romanischen Literaturen des Mittelalters, vol. 8:1. Heidelberg: Carl Winter, 1988, pp. 139–60.

Barber, Richard. *The Knight and Chivalry*. Woodbridge: Boydell, 1970.

———. 'Chivalry, Cistercianism and the Grail', in Carol Dover, ed., *A Companion to the Lancelot-Grail Cycle*. Cambridge: D. S. Brewer, 2003, pp. 3–12.

Barkan, Leonard. *Nature's Work of Art: The Human Body as Image of the World*. New Haven, CT: Yale University Press, 1975.

Bartlett, Kenneth R., Konrad Eisenbichler, and Janice Liedl, eds. *Love and Death in the Renaissance*. Ottawa: Dovehouse Editions, 1991.

Bates, Catherine. *The Rhetoric of Courtship in Elizabethan Language and Literature*. Cambridge: Cambridge University Press, 1992.

Bauckham, Richard. *Tudor Apocalypse: Sixteenth-Century Apocalypticism, Millenarianism and the English Reformation, from John Bale to John Foxe and Thomas Brightman*. Appleford: Sutton Courtenay Press, 1978.

Bedford, Ronald, Lloyd Davis and Philippa Kelly. *Early Modern English Lives: Autobiography and Self-Representation, 1500–1660*. Aldershot: Ashgate, 2007.

Bedos-Rezak, Brigitte Miriam and Dominique Iogna-Prat, eds. *L'individu au Moyen Age: individuation et individualisation avant la modernité*. Paris: Flammarion, 2005.

Beecher, Donald. 'The Legacy of John Frampton: Elizabethan Trader and Translator', *Renaissance Studies* 20:3 (June 2006), 320–39.

Bennett, H. S. *English Books and Readers 1558–1603: Being a Study in the History of the Book Trade in the Reign of Elizabeth I*. Cambridge: Cambridge University Press, 1965.

———. *English Books and Readers 1475–1557: Being a Study in the History of the Book Trade from Caxton to the Incorporation of the Stationers' Company*. Cambridge: Cambridge University Press, 1969.

Bernard, John D. 'Spenserian Pastoral and the *Amoretti*', *ELH* 47:3 (1980), 419–32.

Berry, Philippa. *Of Chastity and Power: Elizabethan Literature and the Unmarried Queen*. London: Routledge, 1989.

Besserman, Lawrence, ed. *Sacred and Secular in Medieval and Early Modern Cultures; New Essays*. Basingstoke: Palgrave, 2006.

Betteridge, Tom. 'From Prophetic to Apocalyptic: John Foxe and the Writing of History', in David Loades, ed., *John Foxe and the English Reformation*. Aldershot: Scolar Press, 2005, pp. 210–32.

Betts, Hannah. '"The Image of this Queene so quaynt": The Pornographic Blazon 1588–1603', in Julia M. Walker, ed., *Dissing Elizabeth: Negative Representations of Gloriana*. Durham, NC: Duke University Press, 1998, pp. 153–84.

Bevington, David. *From Mankind to Marlowe: Growth of Structure in the Popular Drama of Tudor England*. Cambridge, MA: Harvard University Press, 1962.

Bezzola, Reto. *Le sens de l'aventure et de l'amour*. Paris: La Jeune Parque, 1947.

Bieman, Elizabeth. *Plato Baptized: Towards the Interpretation of Spenser's Mimetic Fictions*. Toronto: University of Toronto Press, 1988.

Blanchard, Joël. 'L'effet autobiographique dans la tradition: le *Livre du cuer d'amours espris* de René d'Anjou', in Keith Busby and Erik Kooper, eds, *Courtly Literature: Culture and Context*. Amsterdam: Benjamins, 1990, pp. 11–21.

Blissett, William. 'Spenser's Mutabilitie', in Millar MacClure and F. W. Watt, eds, *Essays in English Literature from the Renaissance to the Victorian Age*. Toronto: University of Toronto Press, 1964, pp. 26–42.

Bloomfield, Morton W. *The Seven Deadly Sins: An Introduction to the History of a Religious Concept, with Special Reference to Medieval English Literature*. East Lansing, MI: Michigan State University Press, 1952; repr. 1967.

Blumenberg, Hans. *The Legitimacy of the Modern Age*, trans. Robert M. Wallace. Cambridge, MA: MIT Press, 1983.

———. *Die Legitimität der Neuzeit*. Frankfurt am Main: Suhrkamp, 1966; repr. 1988.

Blythe, Joan H. 'The Influence of Latin Manuals on Medieval Allegory: Deguileville's Presentation of Wrath', *Romania* 95 (1974), 256–83.

———. 'Deguileville, Guillaume de', in A. C. Hamilton, ed., *The Spenser Encyclopedia*. Toronto: University of Toronto Press, 1990.

Boitani, Piero. '"His desir wol fle withouten wynges": Mary and Love in Fourteenth-Century Poetry', in Joerg O. Fichte, ed., *Chaucer's Frame Tales: The Physical and the Metaphysical*. Cambridge: D. S. Brewer; Tübingen: Günter Narr, 1987, pp. 83–218.

Boitani, Piero, and Anna Torti, eds. *The Body and the Soul in Medieval Literature*. Cambridge: D. S. Brewer, 1999.

Bordone, Renato. 'Une tres noble jouste', in Marco Piccat and Laura Ramello, eds, *Il Libro del Cavaliere Errante (BnF ms. fr. 12559)*. Boves: Araba Fenice, 2008, pp. 5–25.

Borris, Kenneth. 'Allegory, Emblem and Symbol', in Richard McCabe, ed., *The Oxford Handbook of Edmund Spenser*. Oxford: Oxford University Press, 2010, pp. 437–61.

Bossy, John. 'The Character of Elizabethan Catholicism', *Past & Present* 21 (1962), 39–59.

———. *The English Catholic Community 1570–1850*. London: Darton, Longman and Todd, 1975.

Bouchet, Florence. 'Le *Chevalier errant* de Thomas de Saluces: lectures de la description et description de la lecture vers la fin du Moyen Age', *Bien dire et bien aprandre* 11 (1993), 81–104.

———. 'De la lecture à l'écriture, quelques modes de transfert dans le *Chevalier errant* de Thomas de Saluces', *Bien dire et bien aprandre* 13 (1995), 217–35.

———. 'Voyage et quête de soi: le *Livre du Chevalier errant* de Thomas de Saluces', in Alain Labbé, Daniel W. Lacroix and Danielle Quéruel, eds, *Guerres, voyages et quêtes au Moyen Age*, Paris: Champion, 2000, pp. 31–42.

———. 'Postface', in Thomas III de Saluces, *Le chevalier errant*, ed. and trans. Daniel Chaubet. Moncalieri: Centro interuniversitario di ricerche per il viaggio in Italia, 2001, pp. 389–98.

Boureau, Alain. 'Un royal individu', *Critique* 593 (1996), 845–57.

Bowman, Leonard J., ed. *Itinerarium: The Idea of Journey*. Salzburg: Institut für Anglistik und Amerikanistik, Universität Salzburg, 1983.

———. 'Itinerarium: The Shape of the Metaphor', in Leonard J. Bowman, ed., *Itinerarium: The Idea of Journey*. Salzburg: Institut für Anglistik und Amerikanistik, Universität Salzburg, 1983, pp. 3–33.

———. 'What Kind of Journey Is Bonaventure's *Itinerarium*?', in Leonard J. Bowman, ed., *Itinerarium: The Idea of Journey*. Salzburg: Institut für Anglistik und Amerikanistik, Universität Salzburg, 1983, pp. 94–112.

Brewer, Derek. 'The Arming of the Warrior in European Literature and Chaucer', in Edward Vasta and Zacharias P. Thundy, eds, *Chaucerian Problems and Perspectives*. Notre Dame, IN: University of Notre Dame Press, 1979, pp. 221–43.

Brink, Jean R. '"All his minde on honour fixed": The Preferment of Edmund Spenser', in Judith H. Anderson, Donald Cheney and David A. Richardson, eds, *Spenser's Life and the Subject of Biography*. Amherst, MA: University of Massachusetts Press, 1996, pp. 45–64.

Broaddus, James W. *Spenser's Allegory of Love: Social Vision in Books III, IV, and V of The Faerie Queene*. London: Associated University Presses, 1995.

Brook, V. J. K. *A Life of Archbishop Parker*. Oxford: Clarendon Press, 1962.

Brown, Ira V. 'Watchers for the Second Coming: The Millenarian Tradition in America', *The Mississippi Valley Historical Review* 39:3 (1952), 441–58.

Brownlee, Kevin, and Marina Scordilis Brownlee, eds. *Romance: Generic Transformation from Chrétien de Troyes to Cervantes*. Hanover, NH: University Press of New England, 1985.

Burckhardt, Jacob. *The Civilization of the Renaissance in Italy*, trans. S. G. C. Middlemore. London: Phaidon Books, 1965.

Burlinson, Christopher. 'Spenser's "Legend of Constancie": Book VII and the Ethical Reader', in Jane Grogan, ed., *Celebrating Mutabilitie: Essays on Edmund Spenser's Mutabilitie Cantos*. Manchester: Manchester University Press, 2010, pp. 201–19.

Burrow, Colin. 'The Experience of Exclusion: Literature and Politics in the Reigns of Henry VII and Henry VIII', in David Wallace, ed., *The Cambridge History of Medieval English Literature*. Cambridge: Cambridge University Press, 1999, pp. 793–820.

———. '*The Swerve* by Stephen Greenblatt – A Review', *The Guardian*, Review Section, 24 December 2011, p. 9.

Burrow, John. 'Autobiographical Poetry in the Middle Ages: The Case of Thomas Hoccleve', *Proceedings of the British Academy* 68 (1982), 389–412.

———. *The Ages of Man: A Study in Medieval Writing and Thought*. Oxford: Clarendon Press, 1988.

———. *Langland's Fictions*. Oxford: Oxford University Press, 1993.

Bury, Emmanuel, and Francine Mora, eds. *Du roman courtois au roman baroque*. Paris: Les Belles Lettres, 2004.

Busby, Keith, and Erik Kooper, eds. *Courtly Literature: Culture and Context*. Amsterdam: Benjamins, 1990.

Buschinger, Danielle, ed. *La croisade: réalités et fictions (Actes du colloque d'Amiens, 1987)*. Göppingen: Kümmerle Verlag, 1989.

Bynum, Caroline Walker. 'Did the Twelfth Century Discover the Individual?', *Journal of Ecclesiastical History* 31 (1980), 1–17.

———. *Metamorphosis and Identity*. New York: Zone Books, 2001.

Cain, Thomas H. *Praise in* The Faerie Queene. Lincoln, NE: University of Nebraska Press, 1978.

Calin, William. *The French Tradition and the Literature of Medieval England*. Toronto: University of Toronto Press, 1994.

———. 'The French Presence in Medieval Scotland: Le roi René and *King Hart*', *Florilegium* 24 (2007), 11-20.

Cambronne, Patrice. 'Métamorphoses de la Terre Promise: Le Temple de l'Âme dans la *Psychomachia* de Prudence', *Revue des études anciennes* 104:3–4 (2002), 445–74.

Camille, Michael. 'Reading the Printed Image: Illuminations and Woodcuts of the *Pèlerinage de la vie humaine* in the Fifteenth Century', in Sandra Hindman, ed., *Printing the Written Word: The Social History of Books circa 1450–1520*. Ithaca, NY: Cornell University Press, 1991, pp. 259–91.

———. 'The Iconoclast's Desire: Deguileville's Idolatry in France and England', in Jeremy Dimmick, James Simpson, and Nicolette Zeeman, eds, *Images, Idolatry, and Iconoclasm in Late Medieval England*. Oxford: Oxford University Press, 2002, pp. 151–71.

Campbell, Joseph. *The Hero with a Thousand Faces*. Princeton, NJ: Princeton University Press, 1972.

Cantor, Norman F. *The Last Knight: The Twilight of the Middle Ages and the Birth of the Modern Era*. New York: Free Press, 2004.

Capp, Bernard. 'The Political Dimension of Apocalyptic Thought', in C. A. Patrides and Joseph Wittreich, eds, *The Apocalypse in English Renaissance Thought and Literature*. Manchester: Manchester University Press, 1984, pp. 93–124.

Caraman, Philip. *Ignatius Loyola*. London: Harper Collins, 1990.

Carden, Sally Tartline. '*Forment pensifz ou lit me mis*: le songe dans *Le Livre du cuer d'amours espris*', *Lettres Romanes* 49 (1995), 21–36.

Carey, Vincent P., and Clare L. Carroll. 'Factions and Fictions: Spenser's Reflections of and on Elizabethan Politics', in Judith H. Anderson, Donald Cheney and David A. Richardson, eds, *Spenser's Life and the Subject of Biography*. Amherst, MA: University of Massachusetts Press, 1996, pp. 31–44.

Carr, Mary, K. P. Clarke, and Marco Nievergelt, eds. *On Allegory: Some Medieval Aspects and Approaches*. Newcastle on Tyne: Cambridge Scholars Publishing, 2008.

Carroll, Carleton W. 'Transformations d'un texte: les premières éditions du *Chevalier Délibéré*', *Le Moyen Français* 44–45 (1999), 75–85.

———. 'Representations of Death in *Le Chevalier Délibéré*', *Sewanee Mediaeval Studies* 10 (2000), 77–85.

Cavallo, Guglielmo, and Roger Chartier, eds. *A History of Reading in the West*, trans. Lydia G. Cochrane. Cambridge: Polity Press, 1999.

Charlet, Jean-Louis. 'État des études sur la *Psychomachia* de Prudence', *Vita Latina* 167 (2002), 80-7.

Cheney, Donald. 'Spenser's Fortieth Birthday and Related Fictions', *SpS* 4 (1984), 3–32.

Cheney, Patrick. 'The Old Poet Presents Himself: *Prothalamion* as a Defense of Spenser's Career', *SpS* 8 (1990), 211–38.

———. *Spenser's Famous Flight: A Renaissance Idea of a Literary Career*. Toronto: University of Toronto Press, 1993.

———. 'Afterword', in Judith H. Anderson, Donald Cheney, and David A. Richardson, eds, *Spenser's Life and the Subject of Biography*. Amherst, MA: University of Massachusetts Press, 1996, pp. 172–7.

———. 'Life', in Bart Van Es, ed., *A Critical Companion to Spenser Studies*. Basingstoke: Palgrave, 2006, pp. 18–41.

Cheney, Patrick, and Lauren Silberman, eds. *Worldmaking Spenser: Explorations in the Early Modern Age*. Lexington, KY: The University Press of Kentucky, 2000.

Chew, Samuel C. 'Time and Fortune', *ELH* 6:2 (1939), 83–113.

———. *The Pilgrimage of Life*. New Haven, CT: Yale University Press, 1962.

Chrimes, Stanley B. *Henry VII*. New Haven, CT: Yale University Press, 1999.

Clark, Gregory T. et al., eds. *A Tribute to Robert A. Koch: Studies in the Northern Renaissance*. Princeton, NJ: Princeton University Press, 1994

Clark, Robert L. A., and Pamela Sheingorn. 'Were Guillaume de Digulleville's *Pèlerinages* "Plays"? The Case for Arras MS 845 as Performative Anthology', *European Medieval Drama* 12 (2008), 109–47.

Claveria, Carlos. *Le Chevalier Délibéré de Olivier de la Marche y sus versiones españolas del siglo XVI*. Zaragoza: Institución 'Fernando el Católico', 1950.

Clayton, Roderick. 'Lewknor, Sir Lewes (*c*.1560–1627)', *Oxford Dictionary of National Biography*. Available online at: http://www.oxforddnb.com/view/article/46411 [accessed 12 February 2012].

Coldiron, A. E. B. 'Translation's Challenge to Critical Categories: Verses from French in the Early English Renaissance', *The Yale Journal of Criticism* 16:2 (2003), 315–44.

———. 'A Survey of Verse Translations from French Printed between Caxton and Tottel', in Ian Frederick Moulton, ed., *Reading and Literacy in the Middle Ages*. Turnhout: Brepols, 2004, pp. 63–84.

Collinson, Patrick. *Archbishop Grindal, 1519–1583: The Struggle for a Reformed Church*. London: Jonathan Cape, 1979.

———. 'The Elizabethan Church and the New Religion', in Christopher Haigh, ed., *The Reign of Elizabeth I*. Basingstoke: Macmillan, 1984, pp. 169–94.

———. *From Iconoclasm to Iconophobia: The Cultural Impact of the Second English Reformation*. Reading: University of Reading, 1986.

———. 'The Monarchical Republic of Queen Elizabeth I', *Bulletin of the John Rylands Library* 69:2 (1986–7), 394–424.

———. 'Ecclesiastical Vitriol: Religious Satire in the 1590s and the Invention of Puritanism', in John Guy, ed., *The Reign of Elizabeth I: Court and Culture in the Last Decade*. Cambridge: Cambridge University Press, 1995, pp. 150–70.

Comito, Terry. 'A Dialectic of Images in Spenser's *Fowre Hymnes*', *Studies in Philology* 74 (1977), 301–21.

Condon, Margaret. 'Ruling Elites in the Reign of Henry VII', in John Guy, ed., *The Tudor Monarchy*. London: Arnold, 1997, pp. 283–307.

Cooney, Helen, ed. *Nation, Court and Culture: New Essays on Fifteenth-Century English Poetry*. Dublin: Four Courts Press, 2001.

———. 'Skelton's *Bowge of Court* and the Crisis of Allegory in Late-Medieval England', in Helen Cooney, ed., *Nation, Court and Culture: New Essays on Fifteenth-Century English Poetry*. Dublin: Four Courts Press, 2001, pp. 153–67.

Cooper, Helen. *The English Romance in Time: Transforming Motifs from Geoffrey of Monmouth to the Death of Shakespeare*. Oxford: Oxford University Press, 2004.

———. 'Quest and Pilgrimage: "The adventure that God shall send me"', in Helen Cooper, *The English Romance in Time: Transforming Motifs from Geoffrey of Monmouth to the Death of Shakespeare*. Oxford: Oxford University Press, 2004, pp. 45–105.

Cooper, Lisa H. '"Markys ... off the Workman": Heresy, Hagiography, and the Heavens in *The Pilgrimage of the Life of Man*', in Lisa H. Cooper and Andrea Denny-Brown, eds, *Lydgate Matters: Poetry and Material Culture in the Fifteenth Century*. Basingstoke: Macmillan, 2007, pp. 89–111.

Cooper, Tarnya. 'Queen Elizabeth's Public Face', *History Today* 53:5 (May 2003), 38–41.

Copeland, Rita. 'Lydgate, Hawes, and the Science of Rhetoric in the Late Middle Ages', *Modern Language Quarterly* 53:1 (1992), 57–82.

Coste, Didier, and Michel Zéraffa, eds. *Le Récit Amoureux*. Seyssel: Champ Vallon, 1984.

Coughlan, Patricia. 'The Local Context of Mutabilitie's Plea', *Irish University Review* 26:2 (1996), 320–41.

Cousins, Ewert. 'Bonaventure and Dante: The Role of Christ in the Spiritual Journey', in Leonard J. Bowman, ed., *Itinerarium: The Idea of Journey*. Salzburg: Institute für Anglistik und Amerikanistik, Universität Salzburg, 1983, pp. 113–31.

Craig, Joanne. 'The Queen, Her Handmaid, and Spenser's Career', *English Studies in Canada* 12 (1986), 255–68.

———. 'Mirrours More Then One: Marriage and the Body Politic in *The Faerie Queene*', *Cahiers Elisabéthains* 45 (1994), 1–12.

Csabi, Szilvia. 'The Concept of America in the Puritan Mind', *Language and Literature* 10:3 (2001), 195–209.

Cullen, Patrick. *Infernal Triad: The Flesh, the World, and the Devil in Spenser and Milton*. Princeton, NJ: Princeton University Press, 1974.

Cummings, Brian. *The Literary Culture of the Reformation: Grammar and Grace*. Oxford: Oxford University Press, 2002.

Daniélou, Jean. *Bible et liturgie: la théologie biblique des sacrements et des fêtes d'après les Pères de l'Église*. Paris: Editions du Cerf, 1951.

Darby, Graham, ed. *The Origins and Development of the Dutch Revolt*. London: Routledge, 2001.

Dasenbrock, Reed Way. 'Escaping the Squire's Double Bind in Books III and IV of *The Faerie Queene*', *Studies in English Literature 1500–1900* 26 (1986), 25–45.

Davies, Michael. '*Grace Abounding to the Chief of Sinners*: John Bunyan and Spiritual Autobiography', in Anne Dunan-Page, ed., *The Cambridge Companion to Bunyan*. Cambridge: Cambridge University Press, 2010, pp. 67–79.

Davis, Alex. *Chivalry and Romance in the English Renaissance*. Cambridge: D. S. Brewer, 2003.

Davis, David. '"The vayle of Eternall Memorie": Contesting Representations of Queen Elizabeth in English Woodcuts', *Word and Image* 27:1 (2011), 65–76.

Debae, Marguerite. *La Librairie de Marguerite d'Autriche*. Brussels: Bibliothèque royale Albert I$^{er}$, 1987.

——— . *La bibliothèque de Marie d'Autriche. Essai de reconstitution d'après l'inventaire de 1523–1524*. Louvain: Peeters, 1995.

Dees, Jerome S. 'The Ship Conceit in *The Faerie Queene*: "Conspicuous Allusion" and Poetic Structure', *Studies in Philology* 72 (1975), 208–25.

Delacotte, Abbé Joseph. *Guillaume de Deguileville; Trois romans-poèmes du XIV$^{ème}$ siècle*. Paris: Desclée de Brouwer, 1932.

DeMolen, Richard L., ed. *Religious Orders of the Catholic Reformation: In Honor of John C. Olin on his Seventy-Fifth Birthday*. New York: Fordham University Press, 1994.

de Grazia, Margreta, Maureen Quilligan, and Peter Stallybrass, eds. *Subject and Object in Renaissance Culture*. Cambridge: Cambridge University Press, 1996.

de Groot, H. B., and Alexander Leggatt, eds. *Craft and Tradition: Essays in Honour of William Blissett*. Calgary: University of Calgary Press, 1990.

de la Marche, A. Lecoy. *Le Roi René: sa vie, son administration, ses travaux artistiques et littéraires. D'après les documents inédits des archives de France et d'Italie*, 2 vols. Paris: Firmin-Didot, 1875.

de la Rue, Abbé. *Essais historiques sur les bardes, les jongleurs et les trouvères normands et anglo-normands*. Caen: F. Poisson, 1834.

de Mérindol, Christian. *Le Roi René (1409–1480): décoration de ses chapelles et demeures*. Paris: Editions de la Réunion des musées nationaux, 1981.

de Weerdt, Denise. 'Bibliothèque Royale D'Albert Iᵉʳ', *Archives et Bibliothèques de Belgique* 52 (1981), 59–122.

Dhôtel, Jean-Claude. *Les origines du catéchisme moderne: d'après les premiers manuels imprimés en France*. Paris: Aubier, 1967.

Dimmick, Jeremy, James Simpson, and Nicolette Zeeman, eds. *Images, Idolatry, and Iconoclasm in Late Medieval England*. Oxford: Oxford University Press, 2002.

Dinaux, Arthur, and Aimé Leroy. *Archives historiques et littéraires du Nord de la France et du midi de la Belgique*, vol. 4. Valenciennes, 1834.

Dogaer, Georges, and Marguerite Debae. *La librairie de Philippe le Bon*. Brussels: Bibliothèque Albert Iᵉʳ, 1967.

Dollimore, Jonathan. *Radical Tragedy: Religion, Ideology, and Power in the Drama of Shakespeare and his Contemporaries*, 2nd edn. Hemel Hempstead: Harvester Wheatsheaf, 1989.

Doran, Susan. 'Why Did Elizabeth Not Marry?', in Julia M. Walker, ed., *Dissing Elizabeth: Negative Representations of Gloriana*. Durham, NC: Duke University Press, 1998, pp. 30–59.

———. 'Elizabeth I: Gender, Power and Politics', *History Today* 53:5 (May 2003), 29–35.

———. 'Virginity, Divinity and Power: The Portraits of Queen Elizabeth I', in Susan Doran and Thomas S. Freeman, eds, *The Myth of Elizabeth*. Basingstoke: Palgrave, 2003, pp. 171–99.

Doran, Susan, and Christopher Durston. *Princes, Pastors and People: The Church and Religion in England, 1500–1700*, 2nd edn. London: Routledge, 2003.

Doran, Susan, and Thomas S. Freeman, eds. *The Myth of Elizabeth*. Basingstoke: Palgrave, 2003.

Doutrepont, Georges. *La littérature française à la cour des ducs de Bourgogne: Philippe le Hardi, Jean sans Peur, Philippe le Bon, Charles le Téméraire*. Paris: Champion, 1909.

Dover, Carol, ed. *A Companion to the Lancelot-Grail Cycle*. Cambridge: D. S. Brewer, 2003.

Dubuc, B. Doris. 'Le *Chemin de vaillance*: mise à point sur la date de composition et la vie de l'auteur', in Peter Rolfe Monks and D. D. R. Owen, eds, *Medieval Codicology, Iconography, Literature and Translation: Studies for Keith Val Sinclair*. Leiden: Brill, 1994, pp. 276–83.

Duby, Georges. 'Dans la France du Nord-Ouest au XIIᵉ siècle: les "jeunes" dans la société aristo-cratique', *Annales. Économies, Sociétés, Civilisations* 19 (1964), 835–46.

———. *La société chevaleresque. Hommes et structures du Moyen Age 1*. Paris: Flammarion, 1988.

Duffy, Eamon. *The Stripping of the Altars: Traditional Religion in England 1400–1580*. New Haven, CT: Yale University Press, 1992.

Dunan-Page, Anne, ed. *The Cambridge Companion to Bunyan*. Cambridge: Cambridge University Press, 2010.

Duncan-Jones, Katherine. *Sir Philip Sidney: Courtier Poet*. London: Hamish Hamilton, 1991.

Duval, Frédéric. 'La mise en prose du *Pèlerinage de l'âme* de Guillaume de Digulleville par Jean Galopes', *Romania* 128 (2010), 394–427.

———. 'La traduction latine du *Pèlerinage de l'âme* de Guillaume de Digulleville par Jean Galopes (1427)', forthcoming.

Dyas, Dee. *Pilgrimage in Medieval English Literature, 700–1500*. Cambridge: D. S. Brewer, 2001.

Ebin, Lois. *Illuminator, Makar, Vates: Visions of Poetry in the Fifteenth Century*. Lincoln, NE: University of Nebraska Press, 1988.

Edwards, A. S. G. 'Poet and Printer in Sixteenth-Century England: Stephen Hawes and Wynkyn de Worde', *Gutenberg Jahrbuch* (1980), 82–8.

———. *Stephen Hawes*. Boston, MA: Twayne Publishers, 1983.

Elton, G. R. *The Tudor Revolution in Government: Administrative Changes in the Reign of Henry VIII*. Cambridge: Cambridge University Press, 1953.

Emerson, Catherine. *Olivier de La Marche and the Rhetoric of 15th-Century Historiography*. Woodbridge: Boydell, 2004.

Emison, Patricia. 'Dürer's Rider', *Renaissance Studies* 19:4 (2005), 511–22.

Emmerson, Richard K. 'A "Large Order of the Whole": Intertextuality and Interpictoriality in the *Hours of Isabella Stuart*', *Studies in Iconography* 28 (2007), 51–110.

Evans, Michael. 'An Illustrated Fragment of Peraldus's *Summa* of Vice: Harleian MS 3244', *Journal of the Warburg and Courtauld Institutes* 45 (1982), 14–68.

Evennett, H. Outram. *The Spirit of the Counter-Reformation*. Cambridge: Cambridge University Press, 1968.

——. 'St. Ignatius and the Spiritual Exercises', in H. Outram Evennett, *The Spirit of the Counter-Reformation*. Cambridge: Cambridge University Press, 1968, pp. 43–66.

——. 'Counter-Reformation Spirituality', in David M. Luebke, ed., *The Counter-Reformation: The Essential Readings*. Oxford: Blackwell, 1999, pp. 47–63.

Fajen, Robert. *Die Lanze und die Feder: Untersuchungen zum* Livre du Chevalier Errant *von Thomas III., Markgraf von Saluzzo*. Wiesbaden: Reichert, 2003.

Faral, Edmond. 'Guillaume de Digulleville, Jean Galloppes et Pierre Virgin', in *Études Romanes dédiées à Mario Roques par ses amis, collègues et élèves de France*. Paris: E. Droz, 1946, pp. 89–102.

——. *Guillaume de Deguileville, moine de Châalis*. Histoire Littéraire de la France 39. Paris: Imprimerie Nationale, 1952.

Felch, Susan. 'Shaping the Reader in the *Acts and Monuments*', in David Loades, ed., *John Foxe and the English Reformation*. Aldershot: Scolar Press, 2005, pp. 52–65.

Fellows, Jennifer, and Ivana Djordjevic, eds. Sir Bevis of Hampton *in Literary Tradition*. Cambridge: D. S. Brewer, 2008.

Ferguson, Arthur B. *The Indian Summer of English Chivalry: Studies in the Decline and Transformation of Chivalric Idealism*. Durham, NC: Duke University Press, 1960.

——. *The Chivalric Tradition in Renaissance England*. Washington, DC: Folger Shakespeare Library, 1986.

Fichter, Andrew. *Poets Historical: Dynastic Epic in the Renaissance*. New Haven, CT: Yale University Press, 1982.

Fish, Stanley. *Self-Consuming Artifacts: The Experience of Seventeenth-Century Literature*. Berkeley, CA: University of California Press, 1972.

Firth, Katharine R. *The Apocalyptic Tradition in Britain, 1530–1645*. Oxford: Oxford University Press, 1979.

Fleming, John V. 'The Moral Reputation of the *Roman de la Rose* before 1400', *Romance Philology* 18 (1965), 430–5.

Fletcher, Angus. *Allegory: The Theory of a Symbolic Mode*. Ithaca, NY: Cornell University Press, 1964.

Flori, Jean. *L'essor de la chevalerie, XIᵉ–XIIᵉ siècles*. Genève: Droz, 1986.

——. *La chevalerie*. Paris: Gisserot, 1998.

Fowler, Alastair. *Kinds of Literature: An Introduction to the Theory of Genres and Modes*. Cambridge, MA: Harvard University Press, 1982.

Fowler, Elizabeth. 'The Failure of Moral Philosophy in the Work of Edmund Spenser', *Representations* 51 (1995), 47–76.

Fox, Alistair. 'Stephen Hawes and the Political Allegory of *The Comfort of Lovers*', *English Literary Renaissance* 17 (1987), 3–21.

——. *Politics and Literature in the Reigns of Henry VII and Henry VIII*. Oxford: Blackwell, 1989.

——. 'The Complaint of Poetry for the Death of Liberality: The Decline of Literary Patronage in the 1590s', in John Guy, ed., *The Reign of Elizabeth I: Court and Culture in the Last Decade*. Cambridge: Cambridge University Press, 1995, pp. 229–57.

French, H. R. 'The Search for the "Middle Sort of People" in England, 1600–1800', *The Historical Journal* 43:1 (2000), 277–93.

Frye, Susan. *Elizabeth I: The Competition for Representation*. Oxford: Oxford University Press, 1993.

Gajda, Alexandra. *The Earl of Essex and Late Elizabethan Political Culture*. Oxford: Oxford University Press, 2012.

Gardiner, F. C. *The Pilgrimage of Desire: A Study of Theme and Genre in Medieval Literature.* Leiden: Brill, 1971.

Gewande, Herbert Werner. *Guillaume de Deguileville: Eine Studie zum 'Pèlerinage de Vie Humaine'.* PhD thesis. Göttingen: Studentenwerk, 1927.

Gibbs, Donna. *Spenser's Amoretti: A Critical Study.* Aldershot: Scolar Press, 1990.

Gilman, Ernest B. *Iconoclasm and Poetry in the English Reformation: Down Went Dagon.* Chicago, IL: University of Chicago Press, 1986.

Gilmont, Jean-François, ed. *La réforme et le livre: l'Europe de l'imprimé (1517–v. 1570).* Paris: Les Editions du Cerf, 1990.

———. 'L'imprimerie à l'aube du XVI$^{\text{ème}}$ siècle,' in Jean-François Gilmont, ed., *La réforme et le livre: l'Europe de l'imprimé (1517–v. 1570).* Paris: Les Editions du Cerf, 1990, pp. 19–28.

———. 'Protestant Reformation and Reading,' in Guglielmo Cavallo and Roger Chartier, eds, *A History of Reading in the West,* trans. Lydia G. Cochrane. Cambridge: Polity Press, 1999, pp. 213–37.

Gilson, Etienne. *La théologie mystique de saint Bernard.* Paris: Vrin, 1934.

———. *La philosophie au Moyen Age,* 2 vols, 2nd edn. Paris: Payot, 1947.

———. '*Regio dissimilitudinis* de Platon à saint Bernard de Clairvaux,' *Medieval Studies* 9 (1947), 108–30.

Goldberg, Jonathan. *Endlesse Worke: Spenser and the Structures of Discourse.* Baltimore, MD: Johns Hopkins University Press, 1981.

Gombrich, E. H. 'The Evidence of Images,' in Charles S. Singleton, ed., *Interpretation: Theory and Practice.* Baltimore, MD: Johns Hopkins University Press, 1969, pp. 98–102.

Goodman, Jennifer R. *Chivalry and Exploration, 1298–1630.* Woodbridge: Boydell, 1998.

Gousset, Marie-Thérèse, Daniel Poirion, and Franz Unterkircher, eds. *Le coeur d'amour épris: reproduction intégrale en fac-similé des miniatures du Codex Vindobonensis 2597 de la Bibliothèque nationale de Vienne.* Paris: Philippe Lebaud, 1981.

Green, Richard Firth. 'Lydgate and Deguileville Once More,' *Notes and Queries* 25 (1978), 105–6.

Greene, Thomas. *The Descent from Heaven: A Study in Epic Continuity.* New Haven, CT: Yale University Press, 1963.

Greenblatt, Stephen. *Renaissance Self-Fashioning: From More to Shakespeare.* Chicago, IL: University of Chicago Press, 1980.

———. *Hamlet in Purgatory.* Princeton, NJ: Princeton University Press, 2001.

———. *The Swerve: How the World Became Modern.* New York and London: W. W. Norton, 2011.

Gregory, Tobias. 'Shadowing Intervention: On the Politics of *The Faerie Queene* Book 5 Cantos 10–12,' *ELH* 67:2 (2000), 365–97.

Griffiths, Jane. *John Skelton and Poetic Authority: Defining the Liberty to Speak.* Oxford: Oxford University Press, 2006.

———. 'The Object of Allegory: Truth and Prophecy in Stephen Hawes' *Conforte of Lovers*,' in Mary Carr, Kenneth P. Clarke and Marco Nievergelt, eds, *On Allegory: Some Medieval Aspects and Approaches.* Newcastle upon Tyne: Cambridge Scholars Publishing, 2008, pp. 133–55.

Grogan, Jane, ed. *Celebrating Mutabilitie: Essays on Edmund Spenser's Mutabilitie Cantos.* Manchester: Manchester University Press, 2010.

Gross, Kenneth. *Spenserian Poetics: Idolatry, Iconoclasm, and Magic.* Ithaca, NY: Cornell University Press, 1985.

Gunn, S. J. 'Chivalry and the Politics of the Early Tudor Court,' in Sydney Anglo, ed., *Chivalry in the Renaissance.* Woodbridge: Boydell, 1990, pp. 107–28.

———. *Early Tudor Government, 1485–1558.* Basingstoke: Macmillan, 1995.

Gurevich, Aaron. *The Origins of European Individualism,* trans. Katharine Judelson. Oxford: Blackwell, 1995.

Guy, John. *Tudor England.* Oxford: Oxford University Press, 1988.

———, ed. *The Reign of Elizabeth I: Court and Culture in the Last Decade.* Cambridge: Cambridge University Press, 1995.

———, ed. *The Tudor Monarchy*. London: Arnold, 1997.

Hackett, Helen. *Virgin Mother, Maiden Queen: Elizabeth I and the Cult of the Virgin Mary*. Basingstoke: Macmillan, 1995.

Hadfield, Andrew. *Literature, Politics and National Identity: Reformation to Renaissance*. Cambridge: Cambridge University Press, 1994.

———. *Edmund Spenser's Irish Experience: Wilde Fruit and Salvage Soyl*. Oxford: Clarendon Press, 1997.

———. *Literature, Travel, and Colonial Writing in the English Renaissance, 1545–1625*. Oxford: Clarendon Press, 1998.

———. 'Was Spenser a Republican?', *English* 47 (1998), 169–82.

———, ed. *The Cambridge Companion to Spenser*. Cambridge: Cambridge University Press, 2001.

———. 'The Faerie Queene, Books IV–VII', in Andrew Hadfield, ed., *The Cambridge Companion to Spenser*. Cambridge: Cambridge University Press, 2001, pp. 124–42.

———. 'Duessa's Trial and Elizabeth's Error: Judging Elizabeth in Spenser's *Faerie Queene*', in Susan Doran and Thomas S. Freeman, eds, *The Myth of Elizabeth*. Basingstoke: Palgrave, 2003, pp. 56–76.

———. *Shakespeare and Republicanism*. Cambridge: Cambridge University Press, 2005.

Hagen, Susan K. *Allegorical Remembrance: A Study of* The Pilgrimage of the Life of Man *as a Medieval Treatise on Seeing and Remembering*. Athens, GA: University of Georgia Press, 1990.

Haidu, Peter. *The Subject Medieval/Modern: Text and Governance in the Middle Ages*. Stanford, CA: Stanford University Press, 2004.

Haigh, Christopher, ed. *The Reign of Elizabeth I*. Basingstoke: Macmillan, 1984.

———, ed. *The English Reformation Revised*. Cambridge: Cambridge University Press, 1987.

———. 'Anticlericalism and the English Reformation', in Christopher Haigh, ed., *The English Reformation Revised*. Cambridge: Cambridge University Press, 1987, pp. 56–74.

———. *English Reformations: Religion, Politics, and Society under the Tudors*. Oxford: Clarendon Press, 1993.

———. *Elizabeth I*, 2nd edn. Harlow: Pearson, 2001.

Haller, William. *Foxe's Book of Martyrs and the Elect Nation*. London: Jonathan Cape, 1963.

Hamilton, A. C. 'Closure in Spenser's *The Faerie Queene*', in H. B. de Groot and Alexander Leggatt, eds, *Craft and Tradition: Essays in Honour of William Blissett*. Calgary: University of Calgary Press, 1990, pp. 13–32.

———, ed. *Essential Articles for the Study of Edmund Spenser*. Hamden: Archon Books, 1972.

———, ed. *The Spenser Encyclopedia*. Toronto: University of Toronto Press, 1990.

———. *The Structure of Allegory in the* Faerie Queene. Oxford: Clarendon Press, 1961.

Hamilton, Donna B. *Anthony Munday and the Catholics, 1560–1633*. Aldershot: Ashgate, 2005.

Hammer, Paul E. J. 'Patronage at Court, Faction and the Earl of Essex', in John Guy, ed., *The Reign of Elizabeth I: Court and Culture in the Last Decade*. Cambridge: Cambridge University Press, 1995, pp. 65–86.

———. *The Polarisation of Elizabethan Politics: The Political Career of Robert Devereux, 2nd Earl of Essex, 1585–1597*. Cambridge: Cambridge University Press, 1999.

———. 'The Last Decade: An Ageing Regime', *History Today* 53:5 (May 2003), 53–9.

Hampden, John, ed. *Francis Drake Privateer: Contemporary Narratives and Documents*. London: Eyre Methuen, 1972.

Hanna, Ralph III. 'The Sources and the Art of Prudentius' *Psychomachia*', *Classical Philology* 72:2 (1977), 108–15.

Hardman, Phillipa, ed. *The Matter of Identity in Medieval Romance*. Cambridge: D. S. Brewer, 2002.

Heal, Felicity. 'Appropriating History: Catholic and Protestant Polemics and the National Past', *Huntington Library Quarterly* 68:1/2 (2005), 109–34.

Heitmann, Klaus. 'Die Spanischen Uebersetzer von Olivier de la Marches *Chevalier Délibéré*: Hernando de Acuña und Jeronimo de Urrea', in Karl-Hermann Körner and Klaus Rühl, eds, *Studia Iberica: Festschrift für Hans Flasche*. Bern: Franke, 1973, pp. 229–46.

Helgerson, Richard. *The Elizabethan Prodigals*. Berkeley, CA: University of California Press, 1976.
———. 'The New Poet Presents Himself: Spenser and the Idea of a Literary Career', *PMLA* 93:5 (1978), 893–911.
———. *Self-Crowned Laureates: Spenser, Jonson, Milton, and the Literary System*. Berkeley, CA: University of California Press, 1983.
———. 'Tasso on Spenser: The Politics of Chivalric Romance', *Yearbook of English Studies* 21 (1991), 153–67.
———. *Forms of Nationhood: The Elizabethan Writing of England*. Chicago, IL: University of Chicago Press, 1992.
Hellinga, Lotte, and J. B. Trapp, eds. *The Cambridge History of the Book in Britain*, vol. 3. Cambridge: Cambridge University Press, 1999.
Henry, Avril. 'The Pilgrimage of the Lyfe of the Manhode: The Large Design, with Special Reference to Books 2–4', *Neuphilologische Mitteilungen* 87 (1986), 229–36.
———. 'The Structure of Book 1 of *The Pilgrimage of the Lyfe of the Manhode*', *Neuphilologische Mitteilungen* 87 (1986), 128–41.
Herron, Thomas. *Spenser's Irish Work: Poetry, Plantation, and Colonial Reformation*. Aldershot: Ashgate, 2007.
Hexter, J. H. 'The Myth of the Middle Class in Tudor England', in J. H. Hexter, *Reappraisals in History*. London: Longmans, 1961, pp. 71–116.
———. *Reappraisals in History*. London: Longmans, 1961.
Higman, Francis M. 'Le domaine français, 1520–1562', in Jean-François Gilmont, ed., *La réforme et le livre: l'Europe de l'imprimé (1517–v. 1570)*. Paris: Les Editions du Cerf, 1990, pp. 105–54.
Hindman, Sandra, ed. *Printing the Written Word: The Social History of Books circa 1450–1520*. Ithaca, NY: Cornell University Press, 1991.
Holloway, Julia Bolton. *The Pilgrim and the Book: A Study of Dante, Langland and Chaucer*. New York: Peter Lang, 1987.
Holmes, Peter. 'The Authorship and Early Reception of *A Conference about the Next Succession to the Crown of England*', *Historical Journal* 23 (1980), 415–29.
Honig, Edwin. *Dark Conceit: The Making of Allegory*. London: Faber and Faber, 1959.
Hopkins, Andrea. *The Sinful Knights: A Study of Middle English Penitential Romance*. Oxford: Clarendon Press, 1990.
Horton, Ronald A. 'The Argument of Spenser's Garden of Adonis', in Kenneth R. Bartlett, Konrad Eisenbichler and Janice Liedl, eds, *Love and Death in the Renaissance*. Ottawa: Dovehouse Editions, 1991, pp. 61–72.
Hough, Graham. *A Preface to* The Faerie Queene. London: Duckworth, 1962.
Huot, Sylvia. *The Romance of the Rose and its Medieval Readers: Interpretation, Reception and Manuscript Transmission*. Cambridge: Cambridge University Press, 1993.
Huizinga, Johan. *The Waning of the Middle Ages: A Study of the Forms of Life, Thought, and Art in France and the Netherlands in the Fourteenth and Fifteenth Centuries*, trans. F. Hopman. London: Penguin, 1955.
Hunt, Tony. 'The Emergence of the Knight in France and England 1000–1200', *Forum for Modern Language Studies* 17:2 (1981), 93–114.
Hutton, Ronald. 'The Local Impact of the Tudor Reformations', in Christopher Haigh, ed., *The English Reformation Revised*. Cambridge: Cambridge University Press, 1987, pp. 114–38.
Iorga, N. *Thomas III, marquis de Saluces: étude historique et littéraire; avec une introduction sur la politique de ses prédécesseurs et un appendice de textes*. Saint-Denis: Bouillant, 1893.
Jackson, Ken, and Arthur F. Marotti. 'The Turn to Religion in Early Modern Studies', *Criticism* 46 (2004), 167–90.
Jambeck, Karen K. 'The Library of Alice Chaucer, Duchess of Suffolk', *Profane Arts* 6:2 (1998), 106–35.
James, Heather. *Shakespeare's Troy: Drama, Politics, and the Translation of Empire*. Cambridge: Cambridge University Press, 1997.

James, Mervyn. 'At the Crossroads of Political Culture: The Essex Revolt of 1601', in Mervyn James, *Society, Politics and Culture: Studies in Early Modern England*. Cambridge: Cambridge University Press, 1986, pp. 416–66.

——. 'English Politics and the Concept of Honour 1485–1642', in Mervyn James, *Society, Politics and Culture: Studies in Early Modern England*. Cambridge: Cambridge University Press, 1986, pp. 308–415.

——. *Society, Politics and Culture: Studies in Early Modern England*. Cambridge: Cambridge University Press, 1986.

Jedin, Hubert. *Katholische Reformation oder Gegenreformation? Ein Versuch zur Klärung der Begriffe nebst einer Jubiläumsbetrachtung über das Trienter Konzil*. Luzern: Verlag Josef Stocker, 1946.

Jones, Norman L. 'Matthew Parker, John Bale, and the Magdeburg Centuriators', *Sixteenth-Century Journal* 12:3 (1981), 35–49.

Julia, Dominique. 'Reading and the Counter-Reformation', in Guglielmo Cavallo and Roger Chartier, eds, *A History of Reading in the West*, trans. Lydia G. Cochrane. Cambridge: Polity Press, 1999, pp. 238–68.

Kablitz, Andreas, and Ursula Peters, eds, *Mittelalterliche Textualität als Retextualisierung: Das 'Pèlerinage'-Corpus des Guillaume de Deguileville im europäischen Mittelalter*. Heidelberg: Winter Verlag, forthcoming 2012.

Kaeuper, Richard W. *Chivalry and Violence in Medieval Europe*. Oxford: Oxford University Press, 2001.

Kamath, Stephanie Viereck Gibbs. *Authorship and First-Person Allegory in Late Medieval England and France*. Cambridge: D. S. Brewer, 2012.

Kamath, Stephanie Viereck Gibbs, and Marco Nievergelt, eds, *The Pèlerinage Allegories of Guillaume de Deguileville: Authority, Tradition, and Influence*. Forthcoming.

Kane, George. *Chaucer and Langland: Historical and Textual Approaches*. London: The Athlone Press, 1989.

Kanno, Masahiko *et al.*, eds. *Medieval Heritage: Essays in Honour of Tadahiro Ikegami*. Tokyo: Yushodo Press, 1997.

Kaske, Carol V. 'How Spenser Really Used Stephen Hawes in the Legend of Holiness', in George M. Logan and Gordon Teskey, eds, *Unfolded Tales: Essays on Renaissance Romance*. Ithaca, NY: Cornell University Press, 1989, pp. 119–36.

Katzenellenbogen, Adolf. *Allegories of the Virtues and Vices in Medieval Art from Early Christian Times to the Thirteenth Century*, trans. Alan J. P. Crick. London: Warburg, 1939.

Kay, Sarah. *The Place of Thought: The Complexity of One in Late Medieval French Didactic Poetry*. Philadelphia, PA: University of Pennsylvania Press, 2007.

Kearney, James. 'Enshrining Idolatry in *The Faerie Queene*', *English Literary Renaissance* 32 (2002), 3–30.

Keen, Maurice. 'Huizinga, Kilgour and the Decline of Chivalry', *Medievalia et Humanistica* 8 (1977), 1–20.

——. *Chivalry*. New Haven, CT: Yale University Press, 1984.

Keenan, Joseph M. 'The Cistercian Pilgrimage to Jerusalem in Guillaume de Deguilville's *Pèlerinage de la Vie Humaine*', in John R. Sommerfeldt, ed., *Studies in Medieval Cistercian History II*. Kalamazoo, MI: Cistercian Publications, 1976, pp. 166–85.

Kelsey, Harry. *Sir Francis Drake: The Queen's Pirate*. New Haven, CT: Yale University Press, 1998.

Kendall, R. T. *Calvin and English Calvinism to 1649*. Oxford: Oxford University Press, 1979.

Kilgour, Raymond Lincoln. *The Decline of Chivalry as Shown in the French Literature of the Late Middle Ages*. Cambridge, MA: Harvard University Press, 1937.

King, Andrew. The Faerie Queene *and Middle English Romance: The Matter of Just Memory*. Oxford: Clarendon Press, 2000.

——. 'Sir Bevis of Hampton: Renaissance Influence and Reception', in Jennifer Fellows and Ivana Djordjevic, eds, *Sir Bevis of Hampton in Literary Tradition*. Cambridge: D. S. Brewer, 2008, pp. 176–91.

King, John N. 'Allegorical Pattern in Stephen Hawes's *The Pastime of Pleasure*', *Studies in the Literary Imagination* 11:1 (1978), 57–67.

———. *English Reformation Literature: The Tudor Origins of the Protestant Tradition.* Princeton, NJ: Princeton University Press, 1982.

———. *Tudor Royal Iconography: Literature and Art in an Age of Religious Crisis.* Princeton, NJ: Princeton University Press, 1989.

———. 'Queen Elizabeth I: Representations of the Virgin Queen', *Renaissance Quarterly* 43:1 (Spring 1990), 30–74.

———. *Spenser's Poetry and the Reformation Tradition.* Princeton, NJ: Princeton University Press, 1990.

Kipling, Gordon. *The Triumph of Honour: Burgundian Origins of the Elizabethan Renaissance.* The Hague: Leiden University Press, 1977.

———. 'Henry VII and the Origins of Tudor Patronage', in Guy Fitch Lytle and Stephen Orgel, eds, *Patronage in the Renaissance.* Princeton, NJ: Princeton University Press, 1981, pp. 117–64.

Klein, Lisa M. '"Let us love, dear love, lyke as we ought": Protestant Marriage and the Revision of Petrarchan Loving in Spenser's *Amoretti*', *SpS* 10 (1992), 109–38.

Koelbing, Arthur. *Zur Charakteristik John Skelton's.* Stuttgart: Strecker und Schröder, 1904.

Kohl, Stephan. 'More than Virtues and Vices: Self-Analysis in Hoccleve's "Autobiographies"', *Fifteenth-Century Studies* 14 (1988), 115–27.

Koller, Kathrine. 'The *Travayled Pylgrime* by Stephen Bateman and Book Two of *The Faerie Queene*', *Modern Language Quarterly* 3 (1942), 535–41.

Kolve, V. A. *Chaucer and the Imagery of Narrative: The First Five Canterbury Tales.* Stanford, CA: Stanford University Press, 1984.

Körner, Karl-Hermann, and Klaus Rühl, eds. *Studia Iberica: Festschrift für Hans Flasche.* Bern: Franke, 1973.

Kremer, Manfred. 'Der Landzerstörer als *miles christianus?* Überlegungen zum Verhältnis des *Gusman von Alfarche* zu *Deß Irrenden Ritters Raiß*', *Simpliciana* 11 (1989), 99–113.

Krier, Theresa. 'The Faerie Queene (1596)', in Bart Van Es, ed., *A Critical Companion to Spenser Studies.* Basingstoke: Palgrave, 2006, pp. 188–209.

Kuntz, Paul G. 'Augustine: From *Homo Erro* to *Homo Viator*', in Leonard J. Bowman, ed., *Itinerarium: The Idea of Journey.* Salzburg: Institut für Anglistik und Amerikanistik, Universität Salzburg, 1983, pp. 34–53.

Labbé, Alain, Daniel W. Lacroix and Danielle Quéruel, eds. *Guerres, voyages et quêtes au Moyen Age: mélanges offerts à Jean-Claude Faucon.* Paris: Champion, 2000.

Ladner, Gerhart B. '*Homo Viator*: Mediaeval Ideas on Alienation and Order', *Speculum* 42:2 (1967), 233–59.

Lake, Peter. *Anglicans and Puritans? Presbyterianism and English Conformist Thought from Whitgift to Hooker.* London: Unwin Hyman, 1988.

Lake, Peter, and Michael Questier, eds. *Conformity and Orthodoxy in the English Church, c. 1560–1660.* Woodbridge: Boydell, 2000.

Lander, Jesse M. *Inventing Polemic: Religion, Print, and Literary Culture in Early Modern England.* Cambridge: Cambridge University Press, 2006.

Langlois, Charles-Victor. 'Pèlerinages par Guillaume de Deguileville', in Charles-Victor Langlois, *La vie spirituelle: enseignements méditations et controverses; d'après des écrits en français à l'usage des laïcs.* La vie en France au Moyen Age 4. Paris: Hachette, 1928, pp. 199–268.

Lawrence, Jason. 'Spenser and Italian Literature', in Richard McCabe, ed., *The Oxford Handbook of Edmund Spenser.* Oxford: Oxford University Press, 2010, pp. 602–19.

Le Briz-Orgeur, Stéphanie. 'La réécriture du *Pèlerinage de vie humaine* dans la *Moralité de Bien Avisé et Mal Avisé*', in Fabienne Pomel and Fréderic Duval, eds, *Guillaume de Digulleville: les pèlerinages allégoriques.* Rennes: Presses Universitaires de Rennes, 2008, pp. 365–92.

Legaré, Anne-Marie. 'La réception du *Pèlerinage de Vie humaine* de Guillaume de Digulleville dans le milieu angevin d'après les sources et les manuscrits conservés', in Sophie Cassagnes-

Brouquet, Amaury Chanou, Daniel Pichot and Lionel Rousselot, eds, *Religion et mentalités au Moyen Age: mélanges en l'honneur d'Hervé Martin*. Rennes: Presses Universitaires de Rennes, 2003, pp. 543–52.

———. *Le 'Pelerinage de Vie humaine' en prose de la Reine Charlotte de Savoie*. Ramsen: Heribert Tenschert, 2004.

Lemmi, C. W. 'The Influence of Boccaccio on Hawes's *Pastime of Pleasure*', *Review of English Studies* 5:18 (1929), 195–8.

Lerer, Seth. 'The Rhetoric of Fame: Stephen Hawes's Aureate Diction', *SpS* 5 (1984), 169–84.

Lethbridge, Julian B., ed. *Edmund Spenser: New and Renewed Directions*. Madison, WS: Fairleigh Dickinson University Press, 2006.

———. 'Spenser's Last Days: Ireland, Career, Mutability, Allegory', in Julian B. Lethbridge, ed., *Edmund Spenser: New and Renewed Directions*. Madison, WS: Fairleigh Dickinson University Press, 2006, pp. 302–36.

Levy, F. J. 'Spenser and Court Humanism', in Judith H. Anderson, Donald Cheney, and David A. Richardson, eds, *Spenser's Life and the Subject of Biography*. Amherst, MA: University of Massachusetts Press, 1996, pp. 65–80.

Lewalski, Barbara K. *Protestant Poetics and the Seventeenth-Century Religious Lyric*. Princeton, NJ: Princeton University Press, 1979.

Lewis, C. S. *The Allegory of Love: A Study in Medieval Tradition*. Oxford: Clarendon Press, 1936.

———. *Studies in Medieval and Renaissance Literature*, ed. Walter Hooper. Cambridge: Cambridge University Press, 1966.

Linton, Joan Pong. *The Romance of the New World: Gender and the Literary Formations of English Colonialism*. Cambridge: Cambridge University Press, 1998.

Loades, David, ed. *John Foxe and the English Reformation*. Aldershot: Scolar Press, 2005.

Lockerd, Benjamin G. *The Sacred Marriage: Psychic Integration in* The Faerie Queene. Lewisburg, PA: Bucknell University Press, 1987.

Lockey, Brian C. *Law and Empire in English Renaissance Literature*. Cambridge: Cambridge University Press, 2006.

Lofthouse, Marion. '*Le Pèlerinage de vie humaine* by Guillaume de Deguileville with Special Reference to the French MS 2 of the John Rylands Library', *Bulletin of the John Rylands Library* 19 (1935), 170–215.

Logan, George M., and Gordon Teskey, eds. *Unfolded Tales: Essays on Renaissance Romance*. Ithaca, NY: Cornell University Press, 1989.

Loomie, Albert J. *The Spanish Elizabethans: The English Exiles at the Court of Philip II*. London: Burns and Oates, 1963.

———. *Spain and the Jacobean Catholics*, 2 vols. London: Catholic Record Society, 1973–8.

Luebke, David M., ed. *The Counter-Reformation: The Essential Readings*. Oxford: Blackwell, 1999.

Luxon, Thomas H. *Literal Figures: Puritan Allegory and the Reformation Crisis in Representation*. Chicago, IL: University of Chicago Press, 1995.

Lynch, Kathryn L. *Chaucer's Philosophical Visions*. Cambridge: D. S. Brewer, 2000.

———. 'Dating Chaucer', *Chaucer Review* 42:1 (2007), 1–22.

Lytle, Guy Fitch, and Stephen Orgel, eds. *Patronage in the Renaissance*. Princeton, NJ: Princeton University Press, 1981.

Maag, Karin. 'Education and Works of Religious Instruction', in Andrew Pettegree, Paul Nelles and Philip Conner, eds, *The Sixteenth-Century French Religious Book*. Aldershot: Ashgate, 2001, pp. 96–109.

McCabe, Richard. *The Pillars of Eternity: Time and Providence in* The Faerie Queene. Dublin: Irish Academic Press, 1989.

———. 'Edmund Spenser, Poet of Exile', *Proceedings of the British Academy* 80 (1993), 73–103.

———. *Spenser's Monstrous Regiment: Elizabethan Ireland and the Poetics of Difference*. Oxford: Oxford University Press, 2002.

———, ed. *The Oxford Handbook of Edmund Spenser*. Oxford: Oxford University Press, 2010.

MacCaffrey, Isabel. *Spenser's Allegory: The Anatomy of Imagination*. Princeton, NJ: Princeton University Press, 1976.

MacCaffrey, Wallace T. *Queen Elizabeth and the Making of Policy, 1572–1588*. Princeton, NJ: Princeton University Press, 1981.

MacClure, Millar, and F. W. Watt, eds. *Essays in English Literature from the Renaissance to the Victorian Age*. Toronto: University of Toronto Press, 1964.

McCoy, Richard C. *The Rites of Knighthood: The Literature and Politics of Elizabethan Chivalry*. Berkeley, CA: University of California Press, 1989.

———. *Alterations of State: Sacred Kingship in the English Reformation*. New York: Columbia University Press, 2002.

MacCulloch, Diarmaid. *The Reign of Henry VIII: Politics, Policy and Piety*. Basingstoke: Macmillan, 1995.

———. *Tudor Church Militant: Edward VI and the Protestant Reformation*. London: Allen Lane, 1999.

———. *The Later Reformation in England, 1547–1603*, 2nd edn. Basingstoke: Palgrave, 2001.

———. *Reformation: Europe's House Divided, 1490–1700*. London: Allen Lane, 2003.

Macfarlane, Alan. *The Origins of English Individualism: The Family, Property and Social Transition*. New York: Cambridge University Press, 1978.

McLaren, Anne N. *Political Culture in the Reign of Elizabeth I: Queen and Commonwealth, 1558–1585*. Cambridge: Cambridge University Press, 1999.

McLoughlin, Kate. 'Magdalene College MS Pepys 2498 and Stephen Batman's Reading Practices', *Transactions of the Cambridge Bibliographical Society* 10:4 (1994), 525–34.

McMullan, Gordon, and David Matthews, eds. *Reading the Medieval in Early Modern England*. Cambridge: Cambridge University Press, 2007.

Maley, Willy. *Salvaging Spenser: Colonialism, Culture, and Identity*. New York: St Martin's Press, 1997.

Mallette, Richard. 'Book Five of *The Faerie Queene*: An Elizabethan Apocalypse', *SpS* 11 (1990), 129–59.

Maltby, Judith. *Prayer Book and People in Elizabethan and Early Stuart England*. Cambridge: Cambridge University Press, 1998.

Maltby, William S. *The Black Legend in England: The Development of Anti-Spanish Sentiment, 1558–1660*. Durham, NC: Duke University Press, 1971.

Marotti, Arthur F. '"Love Is Not Love": Elizabethan Sonnet Sequences and the Social Order', *ELH* 49:2 (1982), 396–428.

Matarasso, Pauline. *The Redemption of Chivalry: A Study of the* Queste del Saint Graal. Genève: Droz, 1979.

Maupeu, Philippe. *Pèlerins de vie humaine: autobiographie et allégorie narrative, de Guillaume de Deguileville à Octovien de Saint-Gelais*. Paris: Champion, 2009.

Mears, Natalie. *Queenship and Political Discourse in the Elizabethan Realms*. Cambridge: Cambridge University Press, 2005.

Ménage, René. 'Le voyage délibéré du chevalier de la Marche', in Huguette Taviani, ed., *Voyage, quête, pèlerinage dans la littérature et la civilisation médiévales*. Aix-en-Provence: CUER-MA, 1976, pp. 209–19.

Meyer, Ann R. *Medieval Allegory and the Building of the New Jerusalem*. Cambridge: D. S. Brewer, 2003.

Meyer-Lee, Robert J. *Poets and Power from Chaucer to Wyatt*. Cambridge: Cambridge University Press, 2007.

Miller, David Lee. 'Abandoning the Quest', *ELH* 46:2 (1979), 173–92.

———. 'Spenser's Vocation, Spenser's Career', *ELH* 50:2 (1983), 197–231.

———. *The Poem's Two Bodies: The Poetics of the 1590* Faerie Queene. Princeton, NJ: Princeton University Press, 1988.

Miller, Edward. *The Professional Writer in Elizabethan England: A Study of Nondramatic Literature*. Cambridge, MA: Harvard University Press, 1959.

Miller, Jacqueline T. 'The Status of Faeryland: Spenser's "Vniust Possession"', *SpS* 5 (1985), 31–44.

Minnis, Alastair J. *Medieval Theory of Authorship: Scholastic Literary Attitudes in the Later Middle Ages*. London: Scolar Press, 1984.

———. *Magister Amoris: The* Roman de la Rose *and Vernacular Hermeneutics*. Oxford: Oxford University Press, 2001.

Monks, Peter Rolfe, and D. D. R. Owen, eds. *Medieval Codicology, Iconography, Literature and Translation: Studies for Keith Val Sinclair*. Leiden: Brill, 1994.

Montrose, Louis A. 'The Elizabethan Subject and the Spenserian Text', in Patricia Parker and David Quint, eds, *Literary Theory/Renaissance Texts*. Baltimore, MD: Johns Hopkins University Press, 1986, pp. 303–40.

———. 'Spenser's Domestic Domain: Poetry, Property, and the Early Modern Subject', in Margreta de Grazia, Maureen Quilligan and Peter Stallybrass, eds, *Subject and Object in Renaissance Culture*. Cambridge: Cambridge University Press, 1996, pp. 83–130.

———. 'Idols of the Queen: Policy, Gender, and the Picturing of Elizabeth I', *Representations* 68 (1999), 108–61.

———. 'Spenser and the Elizabethan Political Imaginary', *ELH* 69:4 (2002), 907–46.

Morini, Massimiliano. *Tudor Translation in Theory and Practice*. Aldershot: Ashgate, 2006.

Moulton, Ian Frederick, ed. *Reading and Literacy in the Middle Ages*. Turnhout: Brepols, 2004.

Mullet, Michael A. *The Catholic Reformation*. London: Routledge, 1999.

Murrin, Michael. *The Allegorical Epic: Essays in its Rise and Decline*. Chicago, IL: University of Chicago Press, 1980.

Myers, Benjamin P. 'The Green and the Golden World: Spenser's Rewriting of the Munster Plantation', *ELH* 76:2 (2009), 473–90.

Nelles, Paul. 'Three Audiences for Religious Books in Sixteenth-Century France', in Andrew Pettegree, Paul Nelles and Philip Conner, eds, *The Sixteenth-Century French Religious Book*. Aldershot: Ashgate, 2001, pp. 256–85.

Nellish, B. 'The Allegory of Guyon's Voyage: An Interpretation', *ELH* 30:2 (1963), 89–106.

Nievergelt, Marco. 'Francis Drake: Merchant, Knight and Pilgrim', *Renaissance Studies* 23:1 (2009), 53–70.

———. 'Catholic Loyalism, Service and Careerism: Lewes Lewkenor's Quest for Favour', *Renaissance Studies* 24:4 (2010), 536–58.

———. 'The Chivalric Imagination in Elizabethan England', *Literature Compass* 8:5 (2011), 266–79.

———. 'Paradigm, Intertext, or Residual Allegory: Guillaume Deguileville and the *Gawain-Poet*', *Medium Ævum* 80:1 (2011), 18–40.

———. 'The Quest for Chivalry in the Waning Middle Ages: The Wanderings of René d'Anjou and Olivier de la Marche', *Fifteenth-Century Studies* 36 (2011), 137–67.

Nohrnberg, James. 'Acidale', in A. C. Hamilton, ed., *The Spenser Encyclopedia*. Toronto: University of Toronto Press, 1990, 4–6.

———. 'Supplementing Spenser's Supplement, a Masque in Several Scenes: Eight Literary-Critical Meditations on a Renaissance Numen called *Mutabilitie*', in Jane Grogan, ed., *Celebrating Mutabilitie: Essays on Edmund Spenser's* Mutabilitie Cantos. Manchester: Manchester University Press, 2010, pp. 85–136.

Nolan, Edward Peter. *Now Through a Glass Darkly: Specular Images of Being and Knowing from Virgil to Chaucer*. Ann Arbor, MI: University of Michigan Press, 1990.

Norbrook, David. *Poetry and Politics in the English Renaissance*, 2nd edn. Oxford: Oxford University Press, 2002.

Norman, Joanne S. *Metamorphoses of an Allegory: The Iconography of the Psychomachia in Medieval Art*. New York: Peter Lang, 1988.

O'Connell, Michael. *Mirror and Veil: The Historical Dimension of Spenser's* Faerie Queene. Chapel Hill, NC: University of North Carolina Press, 1977.

————. 'Allegory, Historical', in A. C. Hamilton, ed., *The Spenser Encyclopedia*. Toronto: University of Toronto Press, 1990, 23–4.

Oddo, Nancy. 'Rémanence littéraire et propagande catholique: les pieux enjeux du *Voyage du Chevalier errant* de Jean de Cartheny (1557)', in Emmanuel Bury and Francine Mora, eds, *Du roman courtois au roman baroque*. Paris: Les Belles Lettres, 2004, pp. 309–21.

Olin, John C. 'The Idea of Pilgrimage in the Experience of Ignatius Loyola', *Church History* 48:4 (1979), 387–97.

O'Malley, John W. *The First Jesuits*. Cambridge, MA: Harvard University Press, 1993.

————. 'The Society of Jesus', in Richard L. DeMolen, ed., *Religious Orders of the Catholic Reformation: In Honor of John C. Olin on his Seventy-Fifth Birthday*. New York: Fordham University Press, 1994, pp. 139–64.

————. 'Was Ignatius Loyola a Church Reformer? How to Look at Early Modern Catholicism', in David M. Luebke, ed., *The Counter-Reformation: The Essential Readings*. Oxford: Blackwell, 1999, pp. 66–82.

Omont, Henri. 'Les manuscrits français des rois d'Angleterre au château de Richmond', in *Etudes romanes dédiées à Gaston Paris*. Paris: E. Bouillon, 1891, pp. 1–13.

Ong, Walter J. *The Presence of the Word: Some Prolegomena for Cultural and Religious History*. Minneapolis, MN: University of Minnesota Press, 1981.

Oram, William A. 'Spenserian Paralysis', *Studies in English Literature, 1500–1900* 41:1 (2001), 49–70.

O'Sullivan, Sinéad. *Early Medieval Glosses on Prudentius' Psychomachia: The Weitz Tradition*. Leiden: Brill, 2004.

Owens, Judith. 'Professing Ireland in the Woods of Spenser's Mutabilitie', *Explorations in Renaissance Culture* 29:1 (2003), 1–22.

Padelford, Frederick Morgan. 'Spenser and *The Pilgrimage of the Life of Man*', *Studies in Philology* 28:2 (1931), 211–18.

Page, R. I. *Matthew Parker and his Books: Sandars Lectures in Bibliography Delivered on 14, 16, and 18 May 1990 at the University of Cambridge*. Kalamazoo, MI: Medieval Institute Publications, 1993.

Panofsky, Erwin. *The Life and Art of Albrecht Dürer*, 4th edn. Princeton, NJ: Princeton University Press, 1955.

Parker, Patricia. *Inescapable Romance: Studies in the Poetics of a Mode*. Princeton, NJ: Princeton University Press, 1979.

Parker, Patricia, and David Quint, eds. *Literary Theory/Renaissance Texts*. Baltimore, MD: Johns Hopkins University Press, 1986.

Parkes, M. B. 'Stephen Batman's Manuscripts', in Masahiko Kanno *et al.*, eds, *Medieval Heritage: Essays in Honour of Tadahiro Ikegami*. Tokyo: Yushodo Press, 1997, pp. 125–56.

Parry, Glyn. 'John Dee and the Elizabethan British Empire in its European Context', *Historical Journal* 49:3 (2006), 643–75.

Patch, Howard Rollin. *The Goddess Fortuna in Mediaeval Literature*. London: Cass, 1967.

Patrides, C. A., and Joseph Wittreich, eds. *The Apocalypse in English Renaissance Thought and Literature*. Manchester: Manchester University Press, 1984.

Patterson, Lee. 'On the Margin: Postmodernism, Ironic History, and Medieval Studies', *Speculum* 65:1 (1990), 87–108.

————. *Acts of Recognition: Essays on Medieval Culture*. Notre Dame, IN: University of Notre Dame Press, 2010.

————. '"What is Me?": Hoccleve and the Trials of the Urban Self', in Lee Patterson, *Acts of Recognition: Essays on Medieval Culture*. Notre Dame, IN: University of Notre Dame Press, 2010, pp. 84–109.

Paul, John E. 'Hampshire Recusants in the Time of Elizabeth I with Special Reference to Winchester', *Proceedings of the Hampshire Field Club* 21:2 (1959), 61–81.

Paviot, Jacques. 'Le *chevalier délibéré* d'Olivier de la Marche dans la littérature morale (XVᵉ–XVIᵉ s.)', in *Publications du Centre Européen d'Etudes Bourguignonnes* 43 (2003), 161–70.

Paxson, James J. *The Poetics of Personification*. Cambridge: Cambridge University Press, 1994.

Pearsall, Derek. *The Life of Geoffrey Chaucer: A Critical Biography*. Oxford: Blackwell, 1994.

Peck, Linda Levy. 'Peers, Patronage and the Politics of History', in John Guy, ed., *The Reign of Elizabeth I: Court and Culture in the Last Decade*. Cambridge: Cambridge University Press, 1995, pp. 87–108.

Peltonen, Markku. *Classical Humanism and Republicanism in English Political Thought, 1570–1640*. Cambridge: Cambridge University Press, 1995.

Pérez-Jean, Brigitte and Patricia Eichek-Lojkine, eds. *L'allégorie de l'Antiquité à la Renaissance*. Paris: Champion, 2004.

Peters, Ursula. 'Das *Pèlerinage* - Corpus im europäischen Mittelalter: Retextualisierungsprozessen im Spiegel der Prologe', *Zeitschrift für deutsches Altertum und deutsche Literatur* 139:2 (2010), 160–190.

Pettegree, Andrew. 'Religion and the Revolt', in Graham Darby, ed., *The Origins and Development of the Dutch Revolt*. London: Routledge, 2001, pp. 67–83.

——. 'The Sixteenth-Century French Religious Book Project', in Andrew Pettegree, Paul Nelles and Philip Conner, eds, *The Sixteenth-Century French Religious Book*. Aldershot: Ashgate, 2001, pp. 1–17.

Pettegree, Andrew, Paul Nelles and Philip Conner, eds. *The Sixteenth-Century French Religious Book*. Aldershot: Ashgate, 2001.

Phillips, Helen. 'Chaucer's French Translations', *Nottingham Medieval Studies* 37 (1993), 65–82.

——. 'Chaucer and Deguileville: The *ABC* in Context', *Medium Ævum* 62 (1993), 1–19.

Piaget, Arthur. 'Le *Chemin de Vaillance* de Jean de Courcy et l'hiatus final des polysyllabes aux XIV^e et XV^e siècles', *Romania* 27 (1898), 582–607.

Piccat, Marco. 'Tommaso III, marchese errante: l'autobiografia cavalleresca di un Saluzzo', in Marco Piccat and Laura Ramello, eds, *Il Libro del Cavaliere Errante (BnF ms. fr. 12559)*. Boves: Araba Fenice, 2008, pp. 5–25.

Pichaske, David R. *The Movement of the Canterbury Tales: Chaucer's Literary Pilgrimage*. Norwood, PA: Norwood Editions, 1977.

Picot, Emile, and Henri Stein, eds. *Recueil de pièces historiques imprimées sous le règne de Louis XI reproduites en fac-similé avec des commentaires historiques et bibliographiques*. Paris: Société des Bibliophiles François, 1923.

Pincombe, Mike. *Elizabethan Humanism: Literature and Learning in the Later Sixteenth Century*. Harlow: Longman, 2001.

——, ed. *Travels and Translation in the Sixteenth Century: Selected Papers from the Second International Conference of the Tudor Symposium (2000)*. Aldershot: Ashgate, 2004.

Pincombe, Mike, and Cathy Shrank, eds, *The Oxford Handbook of Tudor Literature, 1485–1603*. Oxford: Oxford University Press, 2009.

Poirion, Daniel. 'L'allégorie dans le *Livre du cuer d'amours espris* de René d'Anjou', *Travaux de linguistique et de littérature* 9:2 (1971), 51–64.

——. 'Le miroir magique', in Marie-Thérèse Gousset, Daniel Poirion, and Franz Unterkircher, eds, *Le coeur d'amour épris: reproduction intégrale en fac-similé des miniatures du Codex Vindobonensis 2597 de la Bibliothèque nationale de Vienne*. Paris: Philippe Lebaud, 1981, pp. 13–80.

——, ed. *La littérature française aux XIV^e et XV^e siècles*, Grundriss der Romanischen Literaturen des Mittelalters, vol. 8:1. Heidelberg: Carl Winter, 1988.

——. 'Les tombeaux allégoriques et la poétique de l'inscription dans *Le Livre du cuer d'amour espris* de René d'Anjou', *Comptes rendus des séances de l'Académie des Inscriptions et Belles-Lettres* (1990), 321–34.

Pohle, J. 'Predestination', in *The Catholic Encyclopedia*, vol. 12. New York: Robert Appleton Company, 1911. Available online at: http://www.newadvent.org/cathen/12378a.htm [accessed 12 February 2012].

Pollard, Alfred W. *Le Pelerinaige de Vie Humaine: Reproduced in Facsimile from the Printed Book in the Library of the Earl of Ellesmere with a Bibliographical Note by Alfred W. Pollard*. Manchester: Roxburghe Club, 1912.

Pollet, Maurice. *John Skelton: Poet of Tudor England*, trans. John Warrington. London: J. M. Dent & Sons, 1971.

Pomel, Fabienne. *Les voies de l'au-delà et l'essor de l'allégorie au Moyen Age*. Paris: Champion, 2001.

———. 'Enjeux d'un travail de réécriture: les incipits du *Pèlerinage de vie humaine* de Guillaume de Digulleville et leurs remaniements ultérieurs', *Le Moyen Age* 109 (2003), 457–71.

———, ed. *Miroirs et jeux de miroirs dans la littérature médiévale*. Rennes: Presses Universitaires de Rennes, 2003.

Pomel, Fabienne, and Fréderic Duval, eds. *Guillaume de Digulleville: les pèlerinages allégoriques*. Rennes: Presses Universitaires de Rennes, 2008.

Pooley, Roger. 'The *Pilgrim's Progress* and the Line of Allegory', in Anne Dunan-Page, ed., *The Cambridge Companion to Bunyan*. Cambridge: Cambridge University Press, 2010, pp. 80–94.

Powell, Susan. 'Lady Margaret Beaufort and her Books', *The Library*, 6th series, 20:3 (1998), 197–240.

Prescott, Anne Lake. 'Spenser's Chivalric Restoration: From Bateman's *Travayled Pylgrime* to the Redcrosse Knight', *Studies in Philology* 86:2 (1989), 166–97.

———. 'Spenser (Re)Reading Du Bellay: Chronology and Literary Response', in Judith H. Anderson, Donald Cheney and David A. Richardson, eds, *Spenser's Life and the Subject of Biography*. Amherst, MA: University of Massachusetts Press, 1996, pp. 131–45.

———. 'Sources', in Bart Van Es, ed., *A Critical Companion to Spenser Studies*. Basingstoke: Palgrave, 2006, pp. 98–115.

Prévost, M., and Roman D'Amat. *Dictionnaire de biographie française*, vol. 7. Paris: Letouzey et Ané, 1956.

Pritchard, Arnold. *Catholic Loyalism in Elizabethan England*. London: Scolar Press, 1979.

Questier, Michael C. *Conversion, Politics and Religion in England, 1580–1625*. Cambridge: Cambridge University Press, 1996.

———. 'Elizabeth and the Catholics', in Ethan H. Shagan, ed., *Catholics and the 'Protestant Nation': Religious Politics and Identity in Early Modern England*. Manchester: Manchester University Press, 2005, pp. 69–94.

Quilligan, Maureen. *The Language of Allegory: Defining the Genre*. Ithaca, NY: Cornell University Press, 1979.

Quinn, David B. *Drake's Circumnavigation of the Globe: A Review*. Exeter: University of Exeter Press, 1981.

———. *Sir Francis Drake as Seen by his Contemporaries*. Providence, RI: John Carter Brown Library, 1996.

Quint, David. 'The Boat of Romance and Renaissance Epic', in Kevin Brownlee and Marina Scordilis Brownlee, eds, *Romance: Generic Transformation from Chrétien de Troyes to Cervantes*. Hanover, NH: University Press of New England, 1985, pp. 178–202.

Rajan, Balachandra. *The Form of the Unfinished: English Poetics from Spenser to Pound*. Princeton, NJ: Princeton University Press, 1985.

Ramachandran, Ayesha. 'Mutabilitie's Lucretian Metaphysics: Scepticism and Cosmic Process in Spenser's *Cantos*', in Jane Grogan, ed., *Celebrating Mutabilitie: Essays on Edmund Spenser's Mutabilitie Cantos*. Manchester: Manchester University Press, 2010, pp. 220–45.

Rambuss, Richard. *Spenser's Secret Career*. Cambridge: Cambridge University Press, 1993.

Reeves, Marjorie. *The Influence of Prophecy in the Later Middle Ages: A Study in Joachimism*. Oxford: Clarendon Press, 1969.

———. 'The Development of Apocalyptic Thought: Medieval Attitudes', in C. A. Patrides and Joseph Wittreich, eds, *The Apocalypse in English Renaissance Thought and Literature*. Manchester: Manchester University Press, 1984, pp. 40–73.

Rinne, Susanne. 'René d'Anjou and his *Livre du cuer d'amours espris*: The Roles of Author, Narrator, and Protagonist', *Fifteenth-Century Studies* 12 (1987), 145–60.

Robertson, D. W. *A Preface to Chaucer: Studies in Medieval Perspectives*. Princeton, NJ: Princeton University Press, 1962.

Robinson, Benedict Scott. "'Darke Speech": Matthew Parker and the Reforming of History', *Sixteenth-Century Journal* 29:4 (1998), 1061–83.

Roche, Thomas P. *The Kindly Flame: A Study of the Third and Fourth Books of Spenser's* Faerie Queene. Princeton, NJ: Princeton University Press, 1964.

Rosenwein, Barbara H. 'Y avait-il un "moi" au haut Moyen Age?', *Revue historique* 633 (2005), 31–52.

Rossky, William. 'Imagination in the English Renaissance: Psychology and Poetic', *Studies in the Renaissance* 5 (1958), 49–73.

Ruhe, Ernstpeter. 'Der *Chevalier errant* auf enzyklopädischer Fahrt', in Friedrich Wolfzettel, ed., *Artusrittertum im späten Mittelalter: Ethos und Ideologie*. Giessen: Schmitz, 1984, pp. 159–76.

Saenger, Paul H. 'Silent Reading: Its Impact on Late Medieval Script and Society', *Viator* 13 (1982), 367–414.

Salzman, Paul. *English Prose Fiction 1558–1700: A Critical History*. Oxford: Clarendon Press, 1985.

Sandler, Florence. '*The Faerie Queene*: An Elizabethan Apocalypse', in C. A. Patrides and Joseph Wittreich, eds, *The Apocalypse in English Renaissance Thought and Literature*. Manchester: Manchester University Press, 1984, pp. 148–74.

Sargent-Baur, Barbara N., ed. *Journeys Toward God: Pilgrimage and Crusade*. Kalamazoo, MI: Medieval Institute Publications, 1992.

Scheper, George L. 'Reformation Attitudes toward Allegory and the Song of Songs', *PMLA* 89:3 (1974), 551–62.

Schlauch, Margaret. *Antecedents of the English Novel, 1400–1600: From Chaucer to Deloney*. London: Oxford University Press, 1963.

Schmitt, Jean-Claude. 'La découverte de l'individu: une fiction historiographique?', in Jean-Claude Schmitt, *Le corps, les rites, les rêves, le temps: essais d'anthropologie médiévale*. Paris: Gallimard, 2001, pp. 241–62.

Scott-Warren, Jason. *Sir John Harington and the Book as Gift*. Oxford: Oxford University Press, 2001.

———. 'Harington's Gossip', in Susan Doran and Thomas S. Freeman, eds, *The Myth of Elizabeth*. Basingstoke: Palgrave, 2003, pp. 221–41.

Scribner, Bob. 'Is a History of Popular Culture Possible?', *History of European Ideas* 10:2 (1989), 175–91.

Shagan, Ethan H., ed. *Catholics and the 'Protestant Nation': Religious Politics and Identity in Early Modern England*. Manchester: Manchester University Press, 2005.

Sharpe, Kevin, and Peter Lake, eds. *Culture and Politics in Early Stuart England*. Basingstoke: Macmillan, 1994.

Shell, Alison. *Catholicism, Controversy, and the English Literary Imagination, 1558–1660*. Cambridge: Cambridge University Press, 1999.

Sherman, William H. 'Bringing the World to England: The Politics of Translation in the Age of Hakluyt', *Transactions of the Royal Historical Society* 14 (2004), 199–207.

Shore, David R. 'Spenser's *Colin Clouts Come Home Againe*: The Problem of Poetry', *English Studies in Canada* 8:3 (1982), 262–81.

Silberman, Lauren. *Transforming Desire: Erotic Knowledge in Books III and IV of* The Faerie Queene. Berkeley, CA: University of California Press, 1995.

Simpson, James. *Reform and Cultural Revolution*. Oxford: Oxford University Press, 2002.

———. 'Diachronic History and the Shortcomings of Medieval Studies', in Gordon McMullan and David Matthews, eds, *Reading the Medieval in Early Modern England*. Cambridge: Cambridge University Press, 2007, pp. 17–30.

Singleton, Charles S., ed. *Interpretation: Theory and Practice*. Baltimore, MD: Johns Hopkins University Press, 1969.

*Sir Francis Drake: An Exhibition to Commemorate Francis Drake's Voyage around the World, 1577–1580*. London: British Museum Publications, 1977.

Small, Graeme. *George Chastelain and the Shaping of Valois Burgundy: Political and Historical Culture at Court in the Fifteenth Century*. London: The Royal Historical Society, 1997.

Smith, D. Mark. 'Y Marchog Crwydrad a'r Alegori yn yr Oesoedd Canol', *Dwned* 6 (Hydref 2000), 129–42.

———. 'Cyfieithu'r Marchog Crwydrad: Testun Llenyddol/Crefyddol', *Llên Cymru* 24 (Gorffennaf 2001), 61–78.

———. 'English and Welsh Texts of *The Voyage of the Wandering Knight*', transcription of talk presented at the sixth Lomers Annual Conference at the University of London, 17 June 2005.

Sommerfeldt, John R., ed. *Studies in Medieval Cistercian History II*. Kalamazoo, MI: Cistercian Publications, 1976.

Sommerville, Charles John. *The Secularisation of Early Modern England: From Religious Culture to Religious Faith*. Oxford: Oxford University Press, 1992.

Southern, A. C. *Elizabethan Recusant Prose, 1559–1582: A Historical and Critical Account of the Books of the Catholic Refugees Printed and Published Abroad and at Secret Presses in England Together with an Annotated Bibliography of the Same*. London: Sands, 1950.

Spearing, A. C. *Medieval Dream Poetry*. Cambridge: Cambridge University Press, 1976.

———. *Readings in Medieval Poetry*. Cambridge: Cambridge University Press, 1987.

———. 'The Poetic Subject from Chaucer to Spenser', in David G. Allen and Robert A. White, eds, *Subjects on the World's Stage: Essays on British Literature of the Middle Ages and the Renaissance*. Newark, DE: University of Delaware Press; London: Associated University Presses, 1995, pp. 13–37.

Spica, Anne-Elisabeth. 'L'emblématique de dévotion, une héritière indirecte des *Pèlerinages* spirituels allégoriques de Guillaume de Diguleville', in Fabienne Pomel and Fréderic Duval, eds, *Guillaume de Digulleville: les pèlerinages allégoriques*. Rennes: Presses Universitaires de Rennes, 2008, pp. 53–80.

Spicer, Andrew. *The French-Speaking Reformed Community and their Church in Southampton, 1567–c. 1620*. Stroud: Sutton, 1997.

Spruyt, B. J. '"En bruit d'estre bonne luterienne": Mary of Hungary (1505–58) and Religious Reform', *The English Historical Review* 109:431 (1994), 275–307.

Starkey, David, ed. *The English Court: From the Wars of the Roses to the Civil War*. London: Longman, 1987.

———. 'Intimacy and Innovation: The Rise of the Privy Chamber, 1485–1547', in David Starkey, ed., *The English Court: From the Wars of the Roses to the Civil War*. London: Longman, 1987, pp. 71–118.

———. 'Representation through Intimacy: A Study of the Symbolism of Monarchy and Court Office in Early Modern England', in John Guy, ed., *The Tudor Monarchy*. London: Arnold, 1997, pp. 42–78.

Stein, Henri. *Olivier de la Marche: historien, poète et diplomate bourguignon*. Bruxelles: F. Hayez; Paris: A. Picard, 1888.

Stevenson, Laura Caroline. *Praise and Paradox: Merchants and Craftsmen in Elizabethan Popular Literature*. Cambridge: Cambridge University Press, 1984.

Strauss, Gerald. *Luther's House of Learning: Indoctrination of the Young in the German Reformation*. Baltimore, MD: Johns Hopkins University Press, 1978.

Strong, Roy. *The Cult of Elizabeth: Elizabethan Portraiture and Pageantry*. London: Thames and Hudson, 1977.

———. *Gloriana: The Portraits of Queen Elizabeth I*. London: Thames and Hudson, 1987.

Stroud, Michael. 'Chivalric Terminology in Late Medieval Literature', *Journal of the History of Ideas* 37:2 (1976), 323–34.

Strubel, Armand. *'Grant senefiance a': allégorie et littérature au Moyen Age*. Paris: Champion, 2002.

———. 'Le *Livre du cuer d'amours espris*, un "tombeau" de l'allégorie', in Brigitte Pérez-Jean and Patricia Eichek-Lojkine, eds, *L'allégorie de l'Antiquité à la Renaissance*. Paris: Champion, 2004, pp. 401–14.

Summers, Claude J., and Ted-Larry Pebworth, eds. *Renaissance Discourses of Desire*. Columbia, MO: University of Missouri Press, 1993.

Summit, Jennifer. 'Monuments and Ruins: Spenser and the Problem of the English Library', *ELH* 70:1 (2003), 1–34.

Sumption, Jonathan. *Pilgrimage: An Image of Mediaeval Religion*. London: Faber and Faber, 1975.

Sutch, Susie Speakman. 'La réception du *Chevalier délibéré* d'Olivier de la Marche aux XV$^e$ et XVI$^e$ siècles', *Le Moyen Français* 57–8 (2006), 335–50.

Sutch, Susie Speakman, and Anne Lake Prescott. 'Translation as Transformation: Olivier de La Marche's *Le Chevalier délibéré* and its Hapsburg and Elizabethan Permutations', *Comparative Literature Studies* 25 (1988), 281–317.

Sutton, Anne, and Livia Visser-Fuchs. *Richard III's Books: Ideals and Reality in the Life and Library of a Medieval Prince*. Stroud: Sutton, 1997.

Tanis, James R., and Jennifer A. Thompson, eds. *Leaves of Gold: Manuscript Illumination from Philadelphia Collections*. Philadelphia, PA: Philadelphia Museum of Art, 2001.

Tanner, Marie. *The Last Descendant of Aeneas: The Hapsburgs and the Mythic Image of the Emperor*. New Haven, CT: Yale University Press, 1993.

Taviani, Huguette, ed. *Voyage, quête, pèlerinage dans la littérature et la civilisation médiévales*. Aix-en-Provence: CUER-MA, 1976.

Taylor, Barry. *Vagrant Writing: Social and Semiotic Disorders in the English Renaissance*. Hemel Hampstead: Harvester Wheatsheaf, 1991.

Taylor, Charles. *Sources of the Self: The Making of Modern Identity*. Cambridge: Cambridge University Press, 1989.

Tenenti, Alberto. *La vie et la mort à travers l'art du XV$^{ème}$ siècle*. Paris: Armand Colin, 1952.

Thompson, Benjamin, ed. *The Reign of Henry VII: Proceedings of the 1993 Harlaxton Symposium*, Harlaxton Medieval Studies V. Stamford: Paul Watkins, 1995.

Thurley, Simon. *The Royal Palaces of Tudor England: Architecture and Court Life, 1460–1547*. New Haven, CT: Yale University Press, 1993.

Trachsler, Richard. *Disjointures – conjointures : étude sur l'interférence des matières narratives dans la littérature française du Moyen Age*. Tübingen: Francke, 2000.

Tucker, George Hugo. *Homo Viator: Itineraries of Exile, Displacement and Writing in Renaissance Europe*. Geneva: Droz, 2003.

Tuve, Rosemond. 'Guillaume's Pilgrim and the *Hous of Fame*', *Modern Language Notes* 45:8 (1930), 518–22.

———. *Allegorical Imagery: Some Mediaeval Books and their Posterity*. Princeton, NJ: Princeton University Press, 1966.

Tyndale, William. *Obedience of a Christian Man; facsimile of the 1528 Edition*. London: Scolar Press, 1970.

Tyson, Diana B. 'Olivier de la Marche: l'homme dans l'oeuvre', *Neophilologus* 86:4 (2002), 507–23.

Ungerer, Gustav. *A Spaniard in Elizabethan England: The Correspondence of Antonio Perez's Exile*, 2 vols. London: Tamesis Books, 1974–6.

van den Boogert, Bob. *Maria van Hongarije: Koningin tussen Keizers en Kunstenaars, 1505–1558*. Zwolle: Waanders, 1993.

Van Dyke, Carolynn. *The Fiction of Truth: Structures of Meaning in Narrative and Dramatic Allegory*. Ithaca, NY: Cornell University Press, 1985.

Van Es, Bart, ed. *A Critical Companion to Spenser Studies*. Basingstoke: Palgrave, 2006.

———. 'Introduction', in Bart Van Es, ed., *A Critical Companion to Spenser Studies*. Basingstoke: Palgrave, 2006, pp. 14–17.

van Gemert, Guilliaume. *Die Werke des Aegidius Albertinus (1560–1620): ein Beitrag zur Erforschung des deutschsprachigen Schrifttums der katholischen Reformbewegung in Bayern um 1600 und seiner Quellen*. Amsterdam: Holland University Press, 1979.

van Oort, Johannes. *Jerusalem and Babylon: A Study into Augustine's City of God and the Sources of his Doctrine of the Two Cities*. Leiden: Brill, 1991.

Van Si, Nguyen. 'Les symboles de l'itinéraire dans l' *Itinerarium mentis in Deum* de Bonaventure', *Antonianum* 68:2–3 (1993), 327–47.

Vasta, Edward, and Zacharias P. Thundy, eds. *Chaucerian Problems and Perspectives*. Notre Dame, IN: University of Notre Dame Press, 1979.

Vaughan, Richard. *Valois Burgundy*. London: Allen Lane, 1975.

Venckeleer, Theo. 'Olivier de la Marche: chroniqueur et/ou rhétoriqueur?', *Le Moyen Français* 34 (1994), 217–27.

Veysseyre, Géraldine. 'Lecture linéaire ou consultation ponctuelle? Structuration du texte et apparats dans les manuscrits des *Pèlerinages*', in Fabienne Pomel and Fréderic Duval, eds, *Guillaume de Digulleville: les pèlerinages allégoriques*. Rennes: Presses Universitaires de Rennes, 2008, pp. 315–30.

Villeponteaux, Mary. '*Semper Eadem*: Belphoebe's Denial of Desire', in Claude J. Summers and Ted-Larry Pebworth, eds, *Renaissance Discourses of Desire*. Columbia, MO: University of Missouri Press, 1993, pp. 29–45.

Wakelin, Daniel. 'Stephen Hawes and Courtly Education', in Mike Pincombe and Cathy Shrank, eds, *The Oxford Handbook of Tudor Literature, 1485–1603*. Oxford: Oxford University Press, 2009, pp. 53–68.

Walker, Greg. *John Skelton and the politics of the 1520s*. Cambridge: Cambridge University Press, 1988.

———. *Writing under Tyranny: English Literature and the Henrician Reformation*. Oxford: Oxford University Press, 2005.

Walker, Julia M., ed. *Dissing Elizabeth: Negative Representations of Gloriana*. Durham, NC: Duke University Press, 1998.

Wallace, David, ed. *The Cambridge History of Medieval English Literature*. Cambridge: Cambridge University Press, 1999.

Wallace, Dewey D. Jr. *Puritans and Predestination: Grace in English Protestant Theology, 1525–1695*. Chapel Hill, NC: University of North Carolina Press, 1982.

Wallen, Burr. 'Burgundian Gloire vs. Vaine Gloire: Patterns of Neochivalric Psychomachia', in Gregory T. Clark *et al.*, eds, *A Tribute to Robert A. Koch: Studies in the Northern Renaissance*. Princeton, NJ: Princeton University Press, 1994, pp. 147–75.

Waller, Gary. *English Poetry of the Sixteenth Century*, 2nd edn. London: Longman, 1993.

Walls, Kathryn. 'Did Lydgate Translate the *Pèlerinage de Vie Humaine*?', *Notes and Queries* 24 (1977), 103–5.

Walsham, Alexandra. *Church Papists: Catholicism, Conformity and Confessional Polemic in Early Modern England*. London: The Royal Historical Society, 1993.

———. *Providence in Early Modern England*. Oxford: Oxford University Press, 1999.

———. '"Domme Preachers"? Post-Reformation English Catholicism and the Culture of Print', *Past & Present* 168 (2000), 72–123.

———. 'Translating Trent? English Catholicism and the Counter Reformation', *Historical Research* 78:201 (2005), 288–310.

Walton, Thomas. 'Les poèmes d'Amé de Montgesoie', *Medium Ævum* 2:1 (1933), 1–33.

Wang, Andreas. *Der 'Miles Christianus' im 16. und 17. Jahrhundert und seine Mittelalterliche Tradition: ein Beitrag zum Verhältnis von sprachlicher und graphischer Bildlichkeit*. Bern: Peter Lang, 1975.

Ward, H. L. D. *Catalogue of Romances in the Department of Manuscripts in the British Museum*, 3 vols. London: British Museum, 1961–2.

Watkins, John. '"And yet the end was not": Apocalyptic Deferral and Spenser's Literary Afterlife', in Patrick Cheney and Lauren Silberman, eds, *Worldmaking Spenser: Explorations in the Early Modern Age*. Lexington, KY: The University Press of Kentucky, 2000, pp. 156–73.

Watson, Elisabeth Porges. '(Un)bridled Passion: Chivalric Metaphor and Practice in Sidney's *Astrophil and Stella*', *Reinardus* 15:1 (2002), 117–29.

———. 'Mutabilitie's Debateable Land: Spenser's Ireland and the Frontiers of Faerie', in Julian

B. Lethbridge, ed., *Edmund Spenser: New and Renewed Directions*. Madison, WI: Fairleigh Dickinson University Press, 2006, pp. 286–301.

Watt, Tessa. *Cheap Print and Popular Piety, 1550–1640*. Cambridge: Cambridge University Press, 1991.

Watts, John L. "'A Newe Ffundacion of is Crowne": Monarchy in the Age of Henry VII', in Benjamin Thompson, ed., *The Reign of Henry VII: Proceedings of the 1993 Harlaxton Symposium*, Harlaxton Medieval Studies V. Stamford: Paul Watkins, 1995, pp. 31–53.

Webb, Diana. *Pilgrimage in Medieval England*. London: Hambledon and London, 2000.

———. *Medieval European Pilgrimage, c. 700–c. 1500*. Basingstoke: Palgrave, 2002.

Weintraub, Karl Joachim. *The Value of the Individual: Self and Circumstance in Autobiography*. Chicago, IL: University of Chicago Press, 1978.

Weiss, Judith. 'The Exploitation of Ideas of Pilgrimage and Sainthood in *Gui de Warewic*', in Laura Ashe, Ivana Djordjevic and Judith Weiss, eds, *The Exploitations of Medieval Romance*. Cambridge: D. S. Brewer, 2010, pp. 43–56.

Wenzel, Siegfried. 'The Pilgrimage of Life as a Late Medieval Genre', *Medieval Studies* 35 (1973), 370–88.

Wessels, Gabriel, ed. *Bibliotheca Carmelitana: notis criticis et dissertationibus illustrata*. Rome: In aedibus Collegii S. Alberti, 1927.

Wharey, James Blanton. *A Study of the Sources of Bunyan's Allegories, with Special Reference to Deguileville's Pilgrimage of Man*. Baltimore, MD: J. H. Furst, 1904.

White, Peter. *Predestination, Policy and Polemic: Conflict and Consensus in the English Church from the Reformation to the Civil War*. Cambridge: Cambridge University Press, 1992.

Whitehead, Christiania. *Castles of the Mind: A Study of Medieval Architectural Allegory*. Cardiff: University of Wales Press, 2003.

Whitman, Jon. *Allegory: The Dynamics of an Ancient and Medieval Technique*. Oxford: Clarendon Press, 1987.

———. 'The Body and the Struggle for the Soul of Romance: *La Queste del Saint Graal*', in Piero Boitani and Anna Torti, eds, *The Body and the Soul in Medieval Literature*. Cambridge: D. S. Brewer, 1999, pp. 31–61.

Williams, Daniel, ed. *England in the Fifteenth Century: Proceedings of the 1986 Harlaxton Symposium*. Woodbridge: Boydell, 1987.

Williams, Deanne. *The French Fetish from Chaucer to Shakespeare*. Cambridge: Cambridge University Press, 2004.

Wimsatt, James I. *Allegory and Mirror: Tradition and Structure in Middle English Literature*. New York: Pegasus, 1970.

Wittreich, Joseph. 'Apocalypse', in A. C. Hamilton, ed., *The Spenser Encyclopedia*. Toronto: University of Toronto Press, 1990, pp. 46–8.

Wolfe, Jessica. *Humanism, Machinery, and Renaissance Literature*. Cambridge: Cambridge University Press, 2004.

Wölfflin, Heinrich. *The Art of Albrecht Dürer*, trans. Alastair and Heide Grieve. London: Phaidon, 1971.

Wolfzettel, Friedrich, ed. *Artusrittertum im späten Mittelalter: Ethos und Ideologie*. Giessen: Schmitz, 1984.

Womersley, David. 'Sir Henry Savile's Translation of Tacitus and the Political Interpretation of Elizabethan Texts', *Review of English Studies* 42:167 (1991), 313–42.

Worden, Blair. 'Classical Republicanism and the Puritan Revolution', in Hugh Lloyd-Jones, Valerie Pearl, and Blair Worden, eds, *History and Imagination: Essays in Honour of H. R. Trevor-Roper*. London: Duckworth, 1981, pp. 182–200.

———. *The Sound of Virtue: Philip Sidney's* Arcadia *and Elizabethan Politics*. New Haven, CT: Yale University Press, 1996.

Wright, Louis B. *Middle-Class Culture in Elizabethan England*. Chapel Hill, NC: University of North Carolina Press, 1935.

Wright, Pam. 'A Change in Direction: The Ramifications of a Female Household, 1558–1603', in David Starkey, ed., *The English Court: From the Wars of the Roses to the Civil War*. London: Longman, 1987, pp. 147–72.

Wright, Steven. 'Deguileville's *Pèlerinage de Vie Humaine* as "Contrepartie Edifiante" of the *Roman de la Rose*', *Philological Quarterly* 68:4 (1989), 399–422.

Yates, Frances A. *Astraea: The Imperial Theme in the Sixteenth Century*. London: Routledge & Kegan Paul, 1975.

Young, Alan. *Tudor and Jacobean Tournaments*. London: George Philip, 1987.

Zander, Friedrich. *Stephen Hawes' 'Passetyme of pleasure' verglichen mit Edmund Spenser's 'Faerie Queene' unter Berücksichtigung der allegorischen Dichtung in England. Ein Beitrag zur Quellenfrage der Faerie Queene*. Rostock: Hinstorffs Buchdruckerei, 1905.

Zim, Rivkah. 'Batman , Stephan (c.1542–1584)', *Oxford Dictionary of National Biography*. Available online at: http://www.oxforddnb.com/view/article/1704 [accessed 12 February 2012].

Zimerman, H. 'Inventar des gesamten Besitzes der Erzherzogin Margarethe, Tochter Keisers Maximilian, an Kunstgegenständen und Büchern', in 'Urkunden und Regesten aus dem K. und K. Haus-, Hof- und Staats- Archiv in Wien', *Jahrbuch der kunsthistorischen Sammlungen des allerhöchsten Kaiserhauses* 3:2 (1885), XCIII–CXXIII.

Zink, Michel. 'La tristesse du coeur dans *Le Livre du cuer d'amour espris* de René d'Anjou', in Didier Coste and Michel Zéraffa, eds, *Le Récit Amoureux*. Seyssel: Champ Vallon, 1984, pp. 22–38.

——. *La subjectivité littéraire: autour du siècle de Saint Louis*. Paris: Presses Universitaires de France, 1985.

## Unpublished Theses

Brockhurst, E. J. 'The Life and Works of Stephen Batman, 15??–1584', MA dissertation, University of London, 1947.

Camille, Michael. 'The Illustrated Manuscripts of Guillaume Deguileville's Pèlerinages, 1330–1426', PhD thesis, Cambridge University, 1985.

Dubuc, B. Doris. 'Étude critique et édition partielle du *Chemin de vaillance* de Jean de Courcy d'après le manuscrit BM Royal 14 E. II', PhD thesis, University of Connecticut, 1981.

Houghton, Josephine E. 'The Works of Guillaume Deguileville in Late Medieval England: Transmission, Reception and Context with Special Reference to *Piers Plowman*', PhD thesis, University of Birmingham, 2007.

Ward, Marvin James. 'A Critical Edition of Thomas III, Marquis of Saluzzo's *Le Livre du Chevalier Errant*', PhD Thesis, University of North Carolina at Chapel Hill, 1984.

# Index

Note: all primary works are listed under author names, if known. Exceptions are cross referenced.